Carbon Democracy

POLITICAL POWER IN THE AGE OF OIL

Timothy Mitchell

VERSO

London • New York

First published by Verso 2011
© Timothy Mitchell 2011

1 3 5 7 9 10 8 6 4 2

Verso
UK: 6 Meard Street, London W1F 0EG
US: 20 Jay Street, Suite 1010, Brooklyn, NY 11201
www.versobooks.com

Verso is the imprint of New Left Books

ISBN-13: 978-1-84467-745-0

British Library Cataloguing in Publication Data
A catalogue record for this book is available from the British Library

Library of Congress Cataloging-in-Publication Data
A catalog record for this book is available from the Library of Congress

Typeset in Minion Pro by Hewer UK Ltd, Edinburgh
Printed in the US by Maple Vail

To Adie and JJ

Contents

Acknowledgements   ix

Introduction   1

1 Machines of Democracy   12

2 The Prize from Fairyland   43

3 Consent of the Governed   66

4 Mechanisms of Goodwill   86

5 Fuel Economy   109

6 Sabotage   144

7 The Crisis That Never Happened   173

8 McJihad   200

   Conclusion: No More Counting On Oil   231

Bibliography   255

Index   271

Acknowledgements

I have benefited from the comments and criticisms of participants in numerous seminars and lectures where parts of this work were presented, and from more extended discussions with Andrew Barry, Michel Callon, Geoff Eley, Mahmood Mamdani and Robert Vitalis. A number of former students shared with me their work on related topics, and in several cases contributed their assistance to my own research; these include Katayoun Shafiee, Munir Fakher Eldin, Canay Özden, Fırat Bozçalı, Ryan Weber and Sam Rubin.

Certain sections of the book draw on material I have published elsewhere. Parts of Chapter 1 first appeared as 'Carbon Democracy', *Economy and Society* 38: 3, 2009: 399–432; parts of Chapter 7 were published in 'The Resources of Economics: Making the 1973 Oil Crisis', *Journal of Cultural Economy* 3: 2, 2010: 189–204; and an earlier version of Chapter 8 was published as 'McJihad: Islam in the US Global Order', *Social Text* 20: 4, 2002: 1–18.

Three people made a special contribution to the writing of the book. Adrian and Justine Mitchell provided a critical ear and every kind of encouragement to finish; Lila Abu-Lughod shared her irreplaceable wisdom, insight, patience and care. I cannot thank them enough.

Introduction

Fossil fuels helped create both the possibility of modern democracy and its limits. To understand the limits, this book begins by exploring what made the emergence of a certain kind of democratic politics possible, the kind I call carbon democracy. Before turning to the past, however, let me explain some of the contemporary limits I have in mind.

In the wake of the US invasion of Iraq in 2003, one of those limits was widely discussed. A distinctive feature of the Middle East, it has often been said, is its lack of democracy. For many who write about the region, this lack has something to do with oil. Countries that depend upon petroleum resources for a large part of their earnings from exports tend to be less democratic. The wave of uprisings that spread across the Arab world in 2011 appeared to confirm this relationship between large oil earnings and the difficulty of mounting claims to a more democratic and egalitarian life. By and large, the less oil a country produced, and the faster its production was declining, the more readily the struggles for democracy unfolded. Tunisia and Egypt, where the uprisings began, and Yemen, Bahrain and Syria, where they quickly spread, were among the region's smallest oil producers, and in all of them the production of oil was declining. Of the eight large producers in the Middle East, only in Libya, the smallest producer among them (and where production had also suffered a recent decline), did a similar political struggle gain momentum, although the conflict in the Libyan case was the quickest to collapse into violence and foreign intervention.[1]

Most of those who write about the question of the 'oil curse', as the problem is sometimes called, have little to say about the nature of oil and how it is produced, distributed and used. They discuss not the oil but the oil money – the income that accrues after the petroleum is converted into government revenue and private wealth. The reasons they offer for the anti-democratic properties

---

1 In 2010, oil production for the first five countries ranged from 668,000 barrels per day (Egypt) to 44,000 bpd (Bahrain). The eight large producers (Algeria, Iran, Iraq, Kuwait, Libya, Saudi Arabia, and the United Arab Emirates, plus Qatar), produced from 10.51 million bpd (Saudi Arabia) to 1.79 million bpd (Libya); Qatar produced only 1.43 million bpd of oil, but had the largest production per capita, and in addition was the region's second-largest producer of natural gas. Oman (869,000 bpd, mild political protests in spring 2011) fell neatly between the two groups. The five countries of the region with minimal or zero oil production include four whose political dynamic is interconnected through the Palestine conflict more than oil politics (Israel/Palestine, Jordan and Lebanon) and one dependent on a different mineral export, the booming phosphate industry (Morocco). Figures are for crude oil and other liquids, from www.eia.gov.

of petroleum focus on this surplus revenue: it gives governments the resources to repress dissent, buy political support, or relieve pressures for a more equal sharing of prosperity, with public handouts and price subsidies. The explanations have nothing to do with the ways in which oil is extracted, processed, shipped and consumed, the powers of oil as a concentrated source of energy, or the apparatus that turns this fuel into forms of affluence and power. They treat the oil curse as an affliction only of the governments that depend on its income, not of the processes by which a wider world obtains the energy that drives its material and technical life.[2]

Ignoring the apparatus of oil production reflects an underlying conception of democracy. This is the conception shared by an American expert on democracy sent to southern Iraq, nine months after the US invasion of 2003, to discuss 'capacity building' with the members of a provincial council: 'Welcome to your new democracy', he said, as he began displaying PowerPoint slides of the administrative structure the Americans had designed. 'I have met you before. I have met you in Cambodia. I have met you in Russia. I have met you in Nigeria.' At which point, we are told, two members of the council walked out.[3] For an expert on democracy, democratic politics is fundamentally the same everywhere. It consists of a set of procedures and political forms that are to be reproduced in every successful instance of democratisation, in one variant or another, as though democracy occurs only as a carbon copy of itself. Democracy is based on a model, an original idea, that can be copied from one place to the next. If it fails, as it seems to in many oil states, the reason must be that some part of the model is missing or malfunctioning.

An idea is something that is somehow the same in different places – that can be repeated from one context to another, freeing itself from local histories, circumstances, and material arrangements, becoming abstract, a concept. An expert in democracy has to make democracy into an abstraction, something that moves easily from place to place, so that he can carry it in his suitcase, or his PowerPoint presentation, from Russia to Cambodia, from Nigeria to Iraq, showing people how it works.

Once one has made democracy into something that moves around the world as an idea, in order to move with it, one is committed to a particular

---

2   An important exception to this tendency to ignore the materiality of oil in discussions of the rentier state is Fernando Coronil, *The Magical State: Nature, Money and Modernity in Venezuela*, Chicago: University of Chicago Press, 1997, where the problem is connected to a wider erasure of nature in understanding the formation of wealth. See also Michael Watts's discussion of the 'oil complex' and the 'governable spaces' it builds, drawing on pre-oil political structures, in 'Resource Curse? Governmentality, Oil and Power in the Niger Delta, Nigeria', *Geopolitics* 9, 2004: 50–80; and Robert Vitalis's examination of the labour regime and image-making that organised the production of oil in Saudi Arabia, in *America's Kingdom: Mythmaking on the Saudi Oil Frontier*, 2nd edn, London: Verso, 2009.

3   Rory Stewart, *Occupational Hazards: My Time Governing in Iraq*, London: Picador, 2006: 280.

way of explaining how the idea works, how people become democratic. If democracy is an idea, then countries become democratic by the idea getting into people's heads. The problem of democracy becomes a question of how to manufacture a new model of the citizen, one whose mind is committed to the idea of democracy.

A central theme in discussions of the contemporary Middle East in the United States has been the question of how to manufacture new kinds of citizen. In debates about the war in Iraq, economic reform, the future of Palestine, political Islam, obstacles to democratisation, the spread of anti-Americanism, and the 2011 uprisings, one finds a recurrent interest in the question of how to produce a new kind of political agent. How can one create subjects of power who are adequately equipped to impose limits on authority? How does one form a citizenry that refuses to authorise authoritarianism? What kinds of education, enlightenment, training or experience are required to engender forms of economy based on agents who act according to their rational self-interest rather than corruption or cronyism? What produces forms of politics based on mutual trust and respect for opponents rather than suspicion and repression? In short, these debates ask, how can people learn to recognise themselves and respond as subjects of new forms of power? What forms of power, conversely, can engineer the liberal or democratic political subject?

There has been plenty of criticism of the way these questions have been posed and answered, especially in the debates about democratisation, often faulting them for ignoring the so-called 'larger forces' at work. American writings on the problem of democracy in the Middle East typically have little to say about capitalist globalisation and the work being done to turn people into the docile workers and willing consumers required to solve economic crises in the West; about the forces of empire for whom democratisation schemes are a minor, diplomatic part of wider efforts to shore up a weakening hegemony; and about the tools of violence and repression that occupying powers and military regimes deploy. Such criticisms, however, overlook what is interesting in these debates: the notion that democracy is an engineering project, concerned with the manufacture of new political subjects and with subjecting people to new ways of being governed.

Take a recent example of research on democratisation in the Middle East, the Arab Barometer project. The project carried out opinion surveys in five Arab countries, in order to measure the presence of individual attitudes and orientations that might be conducive to the establishment of democracy. These orientations include 'political tolerance, respect for diversity, civic engagement, and interpersonal trust'.[4] The project was funded, initially, by the Middle East

---

4 Mark Tessler and Amaney Jamal, 'Political Attitude Research in the Arab World: Emerging Opportunities', *PS: Political Science and Politics* 39: 3, 2006: 433–7.

Partnership Initiative of the US Department of State and governed by a board that includes scholars from each of the countries whose political culture the project seeks to measure and record. The Arab Barometer project forms part of a wider initiative called the Global Barometer, which carries out similar research in Africa, Latin America and other regions. The Arab version, along with a number of similar surveys of the region, has published results of opinion surveys that claimed to put in question many of the prevailing assumptions in official circles in the United States about political attitudes in the Arab world.

Whatever the usefulness of showing us some of the limits of official discourse, the project seems at first sight to suffer from a weakness that affects much of the research on questions of democratisation and civil society. It appears to be looking for what one might call 'democracy without democratization'.[5] The premise of the project is that 'successful democratization requires a citizenry that values democracy and possesses the elements of a democratic political culture'.[6] Yet there is no reliable evidence, as far as I am aware, that the presence of a civic culture – attitudes of trust, tolerance, mutual respect and other liberal virtues – facilitates the emergence of democracy. There is, in fact, no shortage of historical evidence to suggest the opposite. One can find repeated examples in the history of democratic struggles in the West of tolerant, educated, liberal political classes who were opponents of democratisation, fighting to prevent the extension of effective political rights to those who did not own property, to religious and racial minorities, to women, and to colonial subjects. In many cases, the civic virtues that dominant political classes possessed provided the grounds on which to oppose democratisation. Their own civility and reasonableness, they often claimed, qualified them to act as spokespersons for the interests of those who were not yet ready to speak for themselves. Once democratic rights have been achieved, their exercise may encourage the development of virtuous civic attitudes, at least among members of the expanded political class – virtues whose inculcation and practice become a mode through which people subject themselves to democratic authority. Democratisation, on the other hand, has often been a battle against those attitudes. It has required a more intransigent set of engagements and practices.[7]

This book is concerned with those more intransigent engagements, and with the ways in which carbon energy helped manufacture forms of agency capable of effective intransigence.

I began writing the book because I wanted a better understanding of the relations between democracy and oil. Initially, like everyone else, I thought of oil as

---

5   Ghassan Salamé, ed., *Democracy Without Democrats*, London: I. B. Tauris, 1994.

6   Tessler and Jamal, 'Political Attitude Research'.

7   See Bruno Latour, *Politics of Nature: How to Bring the Sciences into Democracy*, Cambridge, MA: Harvard University Press, 2004; and Lisa Disch 'Representation as "Spokespersonship": Bruno Latour's Political Theory', *Parallax* 14: 3, 2008: 88–100.

one thing and democracy as another, and wanted to make better sense of why one seemed to be bad for the other. But after following the way the oil industry was built in the Middle East, as I traced the ways in which people had explored for oil, built pipelines and terminals, transformed the petroleum into forms of heat energy and transportation, converted the income from those processes into profits, and sought ways to circulate and govern those flows of money, it became increasingly clear that carbon energy and modern democratic politics were tied intricately together. Rather than a study of democracy and oil, it became a book about democracy *as* oil – as a form of politics whose mechanisms on multiple levels involve the processes of producing and using carbon energy.

When studies of oil and democracy confine their attention to the problem of oil money – the income from oil and its corrupting powers – rather than starting with the process through which oil is produced and distributed, they are unconsciously imitating the way energy networks were first built. In 1914, when Royal Dutch/Shell began producing oil in Venezuela, the country's dictator, General Gómez, asked the company to build its refinery offshore, on the Dutch island of Curaçao. He wanted the money from oil, but did not want the large concentration of workers and accompanying labour demands that a refinery would bring.[8] A decade later, when the company now known as BP began building an oil industry in Iraq, it planned a pipeline to carry the oil across neighbouring countries to the Mediterranean, from where most of the oil would be shipped to refineries in Europe, stretching out the thin line of oil production over an even greater distance. When a nationalist government later requested that BP build a modern refinery in Iraq, the company vigorously opposed the demand. In other words, if oil appears to affect the producer states largely after its transformation into flows of money, that appearance reflects the building of pipelines, the placing of refineries, the negotiation of royalties, and other arrangements that from the start, in their effort to evade the demands of an organised labour force, were concerned with questions of carbon democracy. The transformation of oil into large and unaccountable government incomes is not a cause of the problem of democracy and oil, but the outcome of particular ways of engineering political relations out of flows of energy.

Failing to follow the production and circulation of oil itself, accounts of the oil curse diagnose it as a malady located within only one set of nodes of the networks through which oil flows and is converted into energy, profits and political power – in the decision-making organs of the individual producer states. This diagnosis involves isolating the symptoms found in producer states that are not found in non-oil states. But what if democracies are not carbon copies, but carbon-based? What if they are tied in specific ways to the history of

---

8   Coronil, *Magical State*: 107.

carbon fuels? Can we follow the carbon itself, the oil, so as to connect the problem afflicting oil-producing states to other limits of carbon democracy?

The leading industrialised countries are also oil states. Without the energy they derive from oil their current forms of political and economic life would not exist. Their citizens have developed ways of eating, travelling, housing themselves and consuming other goods and services that require very large amounts of energy from oil and other fossil fuels. These ways of life are not sustainable, and they now face the twin crises that will end them.

First, new discoveries of oil are unable to keep pace with the exhaustion of existing supplies. Although estimating reserves of fossil fuels is a politico-technical process involving rival methods of calculation, it appears that we are about to enter an era of declining supplies.[9] The earth's stores of fossil fuels will not be exhausted. As coal and oil become more scarce and the difficulty in extracting them increases, the cost and the expenditure of energy their extraction requires will bring the era of fossil fuels to an end, with consequences that we cannot know.[10] The earth's stock of this 'capital bequeathed to mankind by other living beings', as Jean-Paul Sartre once described it, will be consumed in a remarkably short period.[11] In the case of oil, the fossil fuel that was the easiest to extract but has now become the most difficult to increase in supply, more than half the total consumed in the 150 years between the 1860s, when the modern petroleum industry began, and 2010 was burned in the three decades after 1980.[12] From the perspective of human history, the era of fossil fuels now appears as a brief interlude.

The second crisis is that, in using up these sources of energy, humankind has been 'unwittingly conducting a vast geophysical experiment', as the US President's Science Advisory Committee warned almost half a century ago, in 1965. By burning within a few generations the fossil fuels that had accumulated in the earth over the previous 500 million years, humanity was injecting carbon dioxide into the atmosphere that by the year 2000 was expected to increase the concentration of atmospheric CO_2 by 25 per cent. 'This may be sufficient to produce measurable and perhaps marked changes in climate', the 1965 report had warned, adding that

---

9   See Conclusion.

10   Vaclav Smil, *Energy in Nature and Society: General Energetics of Complex Systems*, Cambridge, MA: MIT Press, 2008: 204. On the increasing quantity of energy required to produce fossil energy as supplies become more difficult to extract, a problem known as declining EROI (energy return on energy invested), see ibid.: 275–80.

11   Jean-Paul Sartre, *Critique of Dialectical Reason*, vol. 1, *Theory of Practical Ensembles*, London: Verso, 1977: 154.

12   Until recently it was assumed that coal reserves would long outlast oil, with plentiful supplies for hundreds of years. Recent studies suggest that estimates of coal reserves are even less reliable than those for oil, that production in the US – the country with the largest reserves – has already peaked and begun to decline, and that global production may peak as early as 2025. Werner Zittel and Jörg Schindler, 'Coal: Resources and Future Production', EWG Paper no. 1/01, 10 July 2007, available at www.energywatchgroup.org.

these changes could be 'deleterious from the point of view of human beings'.[13] The experiment proceeded more rapidly than expected. Levels of carbon dioxide in the atmosphere have now increased by 40 per cent since the start of the industrial age, with half that increase happening since the late 1970s. The consequent changes in the earth's climate threaten to become not just deleterious from the human point of view, but catastrophic on a planetary scale.[14] A larger limit that oil represents for democracy is that the political machinery that emerged to govern the age of fossil fuels, partly as a product of those forms of energy, may be incapable of addressing the events that will end it.[15]

Following the carbon does not mean replacing the idealist schemes of the democracy experts with a materialist account, or tracing political outcomes back to the forms of energy that determine them – as though the powers of carbon were transmitted unchanged from the oil well or coalface to the hands of those who control the state. The carbon itself must be transformed, beginning with the work done by those who bring it out of the ground. The transformations involve establishing connections and building alliances – connections and alliances that do not respect any divide between material and ideal, economic and political, natural and social, human and nonhuman, or violence and representation. The connections make it possible to translate one form of power into another. Understanding the interconnections between using fossil fuels and making democratic claims requires tracing how these connections are built, the vulnerabilities and opportunities they create, and the narrow points of passage where control is particularly effective.[16]

---

13   R. Revelle, W. Broecker, H. Craig, C. D. Keeling and J. Smagorinsky, 'Atmospheric Carbon Dioxide', in *Restoring the Quality of Our Environment: Report of the Environmental Pollution Panel*, Washington: White House, President's Science Advisory Committee, November 1965: 126–7.

14   Intergovernmental Panel on Climate Change, *Fourth Assessment Report*, 2007, available at www.ipcc.ch. Research by James Hansen and his colleagues on paleoclimate data suggests that feedback loops in the melting of ice can cause a rapid acceleration in the loss of ice cover, forcing much more extreme climate change with potentially cataclysmic consequences. These findings make even the dire warnings from the IPCC look absurdly optimistic. James Hansen, Makiko Sato, Pushker Kharecha, Gary Russell, David W. Lea and Mark Siddall, 'Climate Change and Trace Gases', *Philosophical Transactions of the Royal Society A*, vol. 365, 2007: 1,925–54.

15   Elmer Altvater offers a lucid account of these twin threats, and goes on to suggest that they represent the end of a period of 'congruence' between the logics of capitalism and the physical properties of fossil energy ('The Social and Natural Environment of Fossil Capitalism,' *Socialist Register* 43, 2007: 37–59). In the chapters that follow I offer a different account of those properties – the transportability of oil, for example, is very different from that of coal – which is difficult to fit with the idea of capitalism as a historical process with a set of unchanging 'logics'.

16   Gavin Bridge directs attention away from the exclusive focus on producer states and the resource curse, to look at the diverse network of firms involved in oil, from production, refining and distribution, to those now involved in the capture and storage of carbon and the trading of carbon credits, each of which may be governed by a different political regime. 'Global Production Networks and the Extractive Sector: Governing Resource-Based Development', *Journal of Economic Geography* 8, 2008: 389–419. On the sociology of translation, and 'obligatory passage points', see Michel Callon, 'Some Elements of a Sociology of Translation: Domestication of the Scallops and the Fishermen of St Brieuc Bay', in John Law, ed., *Power, Action and Belief: A New Sociology of Knowledge?*, London: Routledge, 1986.

Political possibilities were opened up or narrowed down by different ways of organising the flow and concentration of energy, and these possibilities were enhanced or limited by arrangements of people, finance, expertise and violence that were assembled in relationship to the distribution and control of energy.

Like energy from fossil fuels, democratic politics is a recent phenomenon. The development of the two kinds of power has been interwoven from the start. This book traces the way they were co-assembled, starting in Chapter 1 with coal and the rise of mass politics in Europe and America in the late nineteenth and early twentieth centuries. It has long been understood that the rise of coal, made possible by the use of steam power to access seams of carbon deep underground, allowed the development of large-scale manufacturing and the modern city, and that out of mines, factories and modern urban life emerged the forces that struggled for democracy. But these forces have usually been thought of, one-sidedly, as 'social movements'. Gathering in workplaces, labour unions, and political clubs, it is said, people forged a political consciousness with which they fought for more egalitarian and democratic collective lives. The account is one-sided because it leaves out the equipment with which this political agency was assembled, and ignores the technical vulnerability to which oligarchic forms of rule were now exposed. As Chapter 1 shows, the socio-technical worlds built with the vast new energy from coal were vulnerable in a particular way, and it was the movement of concentrated stores of carbon energy that provided the means for assembling effective democratic claims.

Keeping in mind this new understanding of the relations between energy flows and the emergence of democracy, I turn in Chapter 2 to examine the beginnings of the oil industry in the Middle East. The standard history tells a story of heroic pioneers discovering oil in remote and difficult locations and of far-sighted statesmen on the eve of the First World War acting to secure this strategic prize. Having learned from the history of coal and democracy that the politics of energy involves acquiring the power to interrupt the flow of energy as much as securing its supply, I propose a different account. I explore how oil companies collaborated to delay the emergence of an oil industry in the Middle East, and politicians saw the control of oil overseas as a means of weakening democratic forces at home. From its beginnings, the history of Middle Eastern oil forms part of the making and unmaking of democratic politics.

The struggle against democracy helped trigger the First World War, out of which emerged the League of Nations and a new machinery to control the oil regions of the Middle East – the system of League of Nations Mandates. These events are usually described as a battle between the idealism of President Woodrow Wilson's 'Fourteen Points', championing the democratic principle of self-determination, and the self-interest of the European powers that took control of the main oil regions of the Middle East, in particular Iraq. Chapter

3 provides a different history, in which a wartime battle for a more demo-cratic control of imperialism and the acquisition of raw materials, fought by the European left, was translated into an undemocratic machinery for produc-ing 'the consent of the governed'. The most important site for producing this 'consent' to imperial rule was Iraq. In Chapter 4 I examine how political forces in Iraq and other parts of the Middle East responded, and the way in which control over the oil reserves of Iraq was forged. The subsequent construction of an oil industry in Iraq and neighbouring countries opened up new possibilities for organising democratic political claims. At the same time, the distribution and scale of the new energy flows made the advancing of those claims increas-ingly difficult.

The term 'democracy' can have two kinds of meaning. It can refer to ways of making effective claims for a more just and egalitarian common world. Or it can refer to a mode of governing populations that employs popular consent as a means of limiting claims for greater equality and justice by dividing up the common world. Such limits are formed by acknowledging certain areas as matters of public concern subject to popular decision while establishing other fields to be administered under alternative methods of control. For example, governmental practice can demarcate a private sphere governed by rules of property, a natural world governed by laws of nature, or markets governed by principles of economics. Democratic struggles become a battle over the distri-bution of issues, attempting to establish as matters of public concern questions that others claim as private (such as the level of wages paid by employers), as belonging to nature (such as the exhaustion of natural resources or the compo-sition of gases in the atmosphere), or as ruled by laws of the market (such as financial speculation). In the mid-twentieth century, this 'logic of distribution' began to designate a large new field of government whose rules set limits to alternative political claims: the field that became known as 'the economy'.[17]

Chapter 5 traces the making of the economy as a new object of politics in the mid-twentieth century (most accounts mistakenly locate the emergence of the economy one or two centuries earlier). It also examines how the production of rapidly increasing quantities of low-cost carbon energy, in the form of oil, contributed to this new mode of political calculation and democratic rule. In contrast to the forms of material calculation characteristic of government in the age of coal, the new calculations made possible by the abundance of oil allowed ways of administering collective life based on the novel principle of unlimited economic growth. The management of economic growth provided new kinds of reason and modes of regulation to govern carbon democracy.

---

17 Cf. Jacques Rancière, *Hatred of Democracy*, London: Verso, 2006, which discusses democratic struggles as a battle against a logic of distribution that designates some matters as public and others as private.

While the making of the economy provided ways of ordering material life at the level of the nation-state, it was unable to manage the forces that many people considered responsible for the crisis of democracy in the interwar period: the flows of private international capital whose speculative movement had caused the collapse of European financial and political systems. Here, too, oil appeared to provide an answer, underwriting the creation, after the Second World War, of a new method of controlling international capital. Alongside the making of the national economy, Chapter 5 traces the building of international financial mechanisms that were intended to curb the threat of speculation by private international banks – a threat to democratic politics that was to re-emerge on a new scale later in the twentieth century. Since the new machinery of control operated partly by governing flows of oil, and the Middle East was becoming the main source of the world's oil, organising the region under imperial control again became important for the possibility of democracy as a mode of government in the West. Postwar attempts to place Middle Eastern oil under a form of US-run 'international trusteeship' were blocked by the oil companies, to be replaced with the simpler framework of the 'Cold War'. The logic of distribution that designated certain areas as inappropriate arenas for advancing democratic claims incorporated the Middle East as just such an area.

My account of carbon democracy began by tracing a rather simple relationship between the vulnerabilities created by a dependence on coal and the ability to make effective egalitarian demands. By this point in the book, however, it has taken on multiple dimensions, reflecting the switch from coal to the increasing use of oil, the much more extended networks for producing and distributing energy, the new forms of collective life that abundant fossil fuels made possible, and the rapidly expanding circulations of goods and finance that were dependent upon the production of oil.

In Chapter 6 I return to Iraq and the wider Middle East, examining how domestic political struggles in the 1950s and 1960s were transformed into struggles with the oil companies over the control of oil. The history of the rise of OPEC is well known, along with the role of nationalist forces in driving the effort by the oil-producing states to assert control, first over the rate at which the production of oil by foreign companies was taxed, and then over the ownership and operation of those companies. From the perspective of carbon democracy, however, we need to emphasise new aspects of this story. The chapter traces the battle over oil at the level of refineries, pipelines and shipping routes, and of their sabotage; it explores how the purchase of high-tech weaponry by the oil states, beginning with Iran, could provide a uniquely tailored mechanism for recycling oil revenues, and how new doctrines of 'security' were packaged with arms sales; and it connects the question of oil in the Middle East to new methods of managing democratic political demands in the West. These developments led to the crisis of 1973–74, explored in Chapter 7. Misleadingly called simply an 'oil crisis', the pivotal events of this period involved a transformation in modes of governing international finance, national economies and flows of energy, placing the weakened carbon democracy of the West into a new relationship with the oil states of the Middle East. The shift in US relations with oil-producing states also allowed political forces on the right, opposed to the management of 'the economy' as a democratic mode of governing collective life, to reintroduce and expand the laws of 'the market' as an alternative technology of rule, providing a more effective means of placing parts of the common world beyond the reach of democratic contestation.

Over the three decades that followed, from the 1979 Islamic Revolution in Iran to the Arab uprisings in the spring of 2011, two themes came to dominate discussions of oil and democracy in relation to the Middle East. One was the rise of Islamist political movements that appeared to many to present an obstacle to building more democratic forms of politics. The other was the growing level of military violence in which the oil states were involved – in particular the series of wars in the Gulf, culminating in the US invasion of Iraq in 2003. A popular study of this period described its dynamic as a conflict between the globalising powers of capital and the narrow forces of tribal and religious identity, or 'Jihad vs. McWorld'. Chapter 8 offers a different way of thinking about the relations between oil, so-called globalisation, and the powers of political Islam, using the concept of 'McJihad'.

In the concluding chapter, I return to some of the contemporary limits to carbon democracy: the ending of the era of abundant, low-cost carbon energy, as the difficulty of replacing depleted oil fields with new discoveries deepens, and as new discoveries become increasingly expensive and energy-intensive to exploit; and the accelerating threat of climate collapse, as existing forms of democratic government appear incapable of taking the precautions needed to protect the long-term future of the planet. I show how the technical uncertainty around these questions allows a certain form of reasoning – that of economic calculation – to occupy the space of democratic debate, and argue that the socio-technical understanding of carbon democracy pursued in this book offers a better way to overcome this obstacle to our shaping of collective futures.

CHAPTER 1

Machines of Democracy

Understanding the question of oil and democracy starts with the question of democracy and coal. Modern mass politics was made possible by the development of ways of living that used energy on a new scale. The exploitation of coal provided a thermodynamic force whose supply in the nineteenth century began to increase exponentially. Democracy is sometimes described as a consequence of this change, emerging as the rapid growth of industrial life destroyed older forms of authority and power. The ability to make democratic political claims, however, was not just a by-product of the rise of coal. People forged successful political demands by acquiring a power of action from within the new energy system. They assembled themselves into a political machine using its processes of operation. This assembling of political power was later weakened by the transition from a collective life powered with coal to a social and technical world increasingly built upon oil.

BURIED SUNSHINE

Until 200 years ago, the energy needed to sustain human existence came almost entirely from renewable sources, which obtain their force from the sun. Solar energy was converted into grain and other crops to provide fuel for humans, into grasslands to raise animals for labour and further human fuel, into woodlands to provide firewood, and into the wind energy and water power used to drive transportation and machinery. For most of the world, the capture of solar radiation in replenishable forms continued to supply the main source of energy until perhaps the mid-twentieth century (thanks to the success of China and India in maintaining viable forms of rural life, only in 2008 did the world's urban population begin to outnumber those living in villages). From around 1800, however, these organic supplies were steadily replaced with highly concentrated stores of buried solar energy, the deposits of carbon laid down 150 to 350 million years ago, when peat bog forests and marine organisms decayed in a watery, oxygen-deficient environment that interrupted the normal process for returning carbon to the atmosphere as carbon dioxide. Instead the decomposed biomass was compressed into the relatively rare but extraordinarily potent accumulations of coal and oil.[1]

---

1   E. A. Wrigley, 'Two Kinds of Capitalism, Two Kinds of Growth', in *Poverty, Progress, and Population*, Cambridge, UK: CUP, 2004: 68–86. Coal replaced wood and other biomass materials

Humans had exploited coal since ancient times, but only on a limited scale. The limit was set by the energy required to produce the fuel – a limit that approaches again today, as oil companies attempt to exploit the world's most inaccessible reserves of oil. Mines tended to fill with ground water, which in deeper pits was pumped out using teams of animals. At a certain depth, keeping the workings dry consumed more energy than could be obtained from mining them. In Britain, where the shortage of timber increased the value of coal and a dense network of waterways was developed to lower the cost of its transportation, Newcomen's atmospheric-pressure steam engine overcame this limit. Introduced in 1712, the engine used coal from the mine to produce steam that drove a vacuum pump and enabled miners to extend the workings deep underground using less energy than the energy they produced.[2] The engine was inefficient, converting less than 1 per cent of the energy it burned into useful motion and consuming large amounts of the mined coal. Since waste coal was now abundant at the mines, however, there was little need to improve the pump's efficiency. Not until 1775 did Boulton and Watt introduce and patent a more efficient design with a separate condenser, which was adopted initially where coal was scarce, especially in iron smelting and in the copper and tin mines of Cornwall. The patent may have delayed further improvements, but its expiry in 1800 enabled Cornish mining engineers to develop more efficient high-pressure engines, allowing steam power to replace animal and water power more widely, both in manufacturing and transportation.[3]

The transition to an energy system based on the combination of coal and steam power required a third component – the iron used for building the pumps and other mining machinery. Previously dependent on the high process heat of charcoal, iron production had been limited by the considerable areas of woodland required to run even a small smelter. By the end of the eighteenth century iron smelters had mastered the difficult process of smelting with coke, with

---

as the main source of the world's commercial energy as early as the 1880s, but until well into the twentieth century the bulk of this fossil energy was consumed by just a handful of countries. Bruce Podobnik, *Global Energy Shifts: Fostering Sustainability in a Turbulent Age*, Philadelphia: Temple University Press, 2006: 5.

2   Rolf Peter Sieferle, *The Subterranean Forest: Energy Systems and the Industrial Revolution*, Cambridge, UK: White Horse Press, 2001: 78–89; and 'Why Did Industrialization Start in Europe (and not in China)?' in Rolf Peter Sieferle and Helga Breuninger, eds, *Agriculture, Population and Economic Development in China and Europe*, Stuttgart: Breuninger-Stiftung, 2003. See also Smil, *Energy in Nature and Society*.

3   Alessandro Nuvolari and Bart Verspagen, 'Technical Choice, Innovation and British Steam Engineering, 1800–1850', *Economic History Review* 62, 2009: 685–710; Alessandro Nuvolari, Bart Verspagen and Nick von Tunzelmann, 'The Early Diffusion of the Steam Engine in Britain, 1700–1800: A Reappraisal', *Cliometrica*, 5 March 2011, 1–31; Alessandro Nuvolari, 'Collective Invention During the British Industrial Revolution: The Case of the Cornish Pumping Engine', *Cambridge Journal of Economics* 28, 2004: 347–63.

the aid of steam-driven bellows, allowing the production of iron to keep pace with the increased supply of coal. The Cornish high-pressure engines were then combined with iron and coal to build steam railways, whose initial function was the carrying of coal. The abundant supplies of energy could now be moved in bulk from the coal pit to the nearest waterway or industrial plant, facilitating the switch from water-driven to steam-powered manufacturing.

Freed from the limits of the muscular power of animals and the speed of regeneration of woodlands, the supply of energy began to grow at an exponential rather than a linear rate. Human societies had known previous episodes of exponential growth, where each year's increase is greater than the previous one, fuelled by a sudden technical advance or the rapid colonisation of new territories. However, the nineteenth-century increase was different. Technical breakthroughs and, as we will see, the control of large additional areas of the earth's surface were combined with the opening up of a third dimension: the subterranean stores of carbon. Whereas previous bursts of accelerating growth might have lasted a generation or two, the new ability to access and rapidly deplete the world's stores of fossil fuel allowed such exponential growth to continue for over 200 years, into the early twenty-first century.[4] The amount of energy produced was extraordinary. Britain's coal reserves, today virtually exhausted, produced a quantity of energy equivalent to the cumulative oil production of Saudi Arabia, allowing the motive power used in British industry to expand by about 50 per cent every decade, from an estimated 170,000 horsepower in 1800, almost all water-driven, to about 2.2 million horsepower in 1870 and 10.5 million in 1907. This growth in turn was dwarfed by later increases, including the use of fossil fuels to generate electrical power. The 10.5 million horsepower of 1870 included a capacity for generating electricity of 1.56 million horsepower. That sector alone grew to about 22 million horsepower (15,000 megawatts) by 1950, and about 100 million horsepower (70,000 megawatts) by 1977.[5]

The constantly accelerating supply of energy altered human relations in space and time in ways that were to enable new forms of mass politics. Since the solar radiation that powered pre-industrial life was a much weaker form of energy, converting it for human use required a sizeable terrain. The need for energy encouraged relatively dispersed forms of human settlement – along

---

4   Sieferle, 'Why Did Industrialization Start?': 17–18.

5   John W. Kanefsky, 'Motive Power in British Industry and the Accuracy of the 1870 Factory Return', *Economic History Review* 32: 3, August 1979: 374. After 1973 the rate of increase began to slow, reaching 85,000 MW by 2009 (statistics at www.decc.gov.uk). Ultimate cumulative British coal production, now slowed to a trickle from a handful of remaining mines, is projected to be about 29 Gt (billions of metric tons). David Rutledge, 'Estimating Long-Term World Coal Production with Logit and Probit Transforms', *International Journal of Coal Geology* 85: 1, 2011: 23–33. At a nominal energy value of 27 GJ per ton, this is equivalent to the cumulative oil production of Saudi Arabia from 1936 to 2008, estimated at 128 Gb (billions of barrels), with a nominal energy value of 6.1 GJ per barrel of oil (equivalent).

rivers, close to pastureland, and within reach of large reserves of land set aside as woods to provide fuel. The timescale of energy production was dependent on the rate of photosynthesis in crops, the lifespan of animals, and the time taken to replenish grazing lands and stands of timber.[6] In contrast, fossil fuels are forms of energy in which great quantities of space and time, as it were, have been compressed into a concentrated form. One way of envisioning this compression is to consider that a single litre of petrol used today needed about twenty-five metric tons of ancient marine life as precursor material, or that organic matter equivalent to all of the plant and animal life produced over the entire earth for four hundred years was required to produce the fossil fuels we burn today in a single year.[7] Coal and oil made available stores of energy equivalent to decades of organic growth and acres of biomass in compact, transportable solids and liquids.

This transformation released populations from dependence on the large areas of land previously required for primary energy production. Regions that had relied on timber to provide fuel for cooking, heating and industrial processes were now freed from the limits set by the size and proximity of woodlands. In Great Britain, substitution of wood by coal created a quantity of energy that would have required forests many times the size of existing wooded areas if energy had still depended on solar radiation. By the 1820s, coal freed, as it were, an area of woodland equivalent to the total surface area of the country. By the 1840s, coal was providing energy that in timber would have required forests covering twice the country's area, double that area by the 1860s, and double again by the 1890s. Thanks to this new social-energetic metabolism, a majority of the population could now be concentrated together without immediate access to agricultural land, in towns whose size was no longer limited by energy supply.[8]

DEMOCRACY AND COLONY

The change from the use of wood and other renewable energy sources to the use of coal underlies the 'great divergence' between the development of northern and central Europe after 1800 and the development of China, India, the Ottoman Empire and other regions that until then had enjoyed comparable

---

6   Wrigley, 'Two Kinds of Capitalism': 75.

7   Jeffrey S. Dukes, 'Burning Buried Sunshine: Human Consumption of Ancient Solar Energy', *Climatic Change* 61: 1–2, November 2003: 33–41 (figures from 1997); Helmut Haberl, 'The Global Socioeconomic Energetic Metabolism as a Sustainability Problem', *Energy* 31: 1, 2006: 87–99.

8   Sieferle, *Subterranean Forest*; Kenneth Pomeranz, *The Great Divergence: China, Europe, and the Making of the Modern World Economy*, Princeton: Princeton University Press, 2000; Haberl, 'Global Socioeconomic Energetic Metabolism'.

standards of living. Other parts of the world faced similar pressures to overcome shortages of land or develop new sources of energy, and China had large reserves of coal. But its coalfields faced different technical obstacles to their development and were not linked to the main centres of population by navigable waterways. These regions pursued other solutions, which did not happen to trigger the switch to an energy system capable of expanding exponentially.[9]

Although other world regions continued initially on different paths, the transition to a new energy regime was never an event confined only to Europe. From its beginnings, the switch in one part of the world to modes of life that consumed energy at a geometric rate of growth required changes in ways of living in many other places. Coal made available thermal and mechanical energy in unprecedented quantity and concentration, but this energy was of no benefit unless there were ways to put it to work. Its use in manufacturing required a large increase in the supply of industrial raw materials. Many of these, such as cotton, still depended on dispersed, organic (including human) energy for their production. So, at the same time as the opening of subterranean stores reduced the amount of land required to supply process energy, ever larger areas of surface territory were needed to produce the materials to which this increasing quantity of energy was applied. As growing human labour forces worked on the production of industrial goods, and no longer grew the food required to provide their own energy, further territory and populations outside the industrialising regions had to be organised to supply these workforces with energy, especially concentrated food energy in forms such as sugar.

We think of industrialisation (and the democracy that followed) as an urban phenomenon based on fossil fuels, but it depended on an agrarian – and colonial – transformation based on organic forms of energy. By freeing areas previously reserved as woodland for the supply of fuel, allowing more land for grazing and cultivation, the use of coal in northern Europe contributed to the creation of additional farmland. However, the development of fossil energy required a means of making much greater areas of land available for solar-based production, along with large amounts of human labour, in areas of the world beyond Europe.

The commodities Europe needed as industrial raw materials could not be obtained simply through relations of trade, for two reasons. First, agrarian populations typically preferred to use their land and labour to produce materials largely for their own needs, making only a small surplus available for export. Europe now required methods that would compel people to devote an exceptionally large proportion of solar-based production to supplying its

---

9   Pomeranz, *Great Divergence*; Wrigley, 'Two Kinds of Capitalism'; Terje Tvedt, 'Why England and Not China and India? Water Systems and the History of the Industrial Revolution', *Journal of Global History* 5: 1, 2010: 29–50.

fossil-fuel-driven needs. Second, when one world region developed a new process that gave it a technological advantage, other regions typically adopted the innovation as soon as possible.[10] The coal-based energy system was both more difficult to emulate and more dependent on not being imitated. It was difficult to emulate because large reserves of coal and iron ore were concentrated in few places, and the exponential increase in energy that coal supplied gave Europe very rapidly a considerable head start over other regions; and it depended on not being imitated because the large overseas regions that Europe now required for solar-energy-based products like cotton and sugar would turn their organic energy systems to their own needs if they were able to introduce fossil-fuel-based manufacturing of their own.

Unable to rely on relations of trade, Europe needed alternative ways of obtaining materials from overseas, using methods that prevented those farming the land from controlling what they grew and impeded local efforts to industrialise. In acquiring lands for sugar and cotton production in the New World, Europeans had relied on the total dispossession of the local population and the importing of slave or indentured workforces. In places where the agrarian population could not be removed en masse – India and Egypt were the main examples – Europeans and their local allies pioneered a method of localised dispossession known as private land ownership. This replaced older ways of claiming shares of agricultural revenue with a regime where one claimant, now designated the 'landowner', determined the crops to be grown and asserted exclusive control of the product. These colonial arrangements secured the extensive, solar-based production used to supply agricultural goods in quantities that allowed the development of intensive, coal-based mass production in the towns and cities of Europe.

The relationship between coal, industrialisation and colonisation provides a first set of connections between fossil fuels and democracy. Forms of representative central government had developed in parts of Europe and its settler colonies in the eighteenth and nineteenth centuries. The advocates of representative government had seen it not as a first step towards democracy but as an oligarchic alternative to it, in which the power of government was reserved to those whose ownership of property (the control of land, but also of women, servants and slaves) gave them power over the point of passage for the revenues on which government depended, and qualified them to be concerned with public matters. In most of these countries, property qualifications and registration procedures restricted the electorate to no more than 30 to 40 per cent of adult males, or less than one-fifth of the adult population. In many cases, moreover, the rise of a centralised fiscal-military state in which representation justified the exercise of power coincided with the weakening of other, dispersed forms of participation

---

10   Pomeranz, *Great Divergence*.

and self-government that were sometimes more accountable to their constituents, such as the elected corporate bodies in England that governed universities, towns, companies and societies.[11] By the 1870s, a wave of upheavals in Europe and the Near East – including the unification of Italy and of Germany, the creation of the Third Republic in France, constitutional settlements or liberal revolutions in countries from Spain and Greece to Serbia and Austria-Hungary, and liberal reforms in the Russian and Ottoman Empires – had created varieties of representative government. While continuing to exclude most people from a role in public life, these constitutional arrangements provided in many cases a legal order under which labour unions and popular political parties could emerge. Across the industrialising regions of northern and western Europe in particular, in protest against the exclusion of the majority from public life and against the great inequalities in well-being that industrialisation had brought, mass political movements and organised political parties began to emerge and to create a new form of politics.[12]

The period of transformation that followed, from the 1870s to the First World War, has been called both the age of democratisation and the age of empire.[13] The mobilisation of new, democratising political forces depended upon the concentration of population in cities and in manufacturing, associated with the forms of collective life made possible by organising the flow of unprecedented quantities of non-renewable stores of carbon. At the same time, utilising fossil fuels whose supply increased by as much as 50 per cent each decade required the rapidly expanding control of colonised territories. Those territories were connected to the same assembly of energy flows based on coal and steam power, but were connected in ways that could not easily be used to manufacture effective political claims. To understand why the rise of coal produced democracy at some sites and colonial domination at others, we must look more closely at the way the flow of fossil energy could be employed to organise successful collective demands.

CONTROLLING CARBON CHANNELS

When most energy was derived from widely dispersed renewable sources, a significant part of the population was involved in the work of generating and

---

11   Jacques Rancière, *Hatred of Democracy*, London and New York: Verso, 2009; Bernard Manin, 'The Metamorphoses of Representative Government', *Economy and Society* 23: 2, 1994: 133–71; and Mark Knights, *Representation and Misrepresentation in Later Stuart Britain: Partisanship and Political Culture*, Oxford: OUP, 2006. The changes in voting restrictions in the British case are explained in Neal Blewett, 'The Franchise in the United Kingdom 1885–1918', *Past and Present* 32, December 1965.

12   Geoff Eley, *Forging Democracy: The History of the Left in Europe 1850–2000*, Oxford: OUP, 2002, stresses the pan-European constitutional transformation of the 1860s as a basis for the subsequent role of the left in creating democracy.

13   Eric Hobsbawm, *The Age of Empire, 1875–1914*, New York: Vintage, 1989: 88.

transporting energy, in small amounts. With the large-scale use of fossil fuels, and especially following the advent of electricity in the 1880s, a large majority of people in industrialised countries became consumers of energy generated by others, and most work involved the handling or supervision of processes that were driven by energy from elsewhere. A much smaller part of the population now handled the production and distribution of energy, and they handled it in huge quantities.

The concentration of energy supplies in large amounts at specific sites led to the creation of an apparatus of energy supply with which the democratic politics of the late nineteenth and early twentieth centuries would be built. Large stores of high-quality coal were discovered and developed in relatively few areas: in central and northern England and south Wales, along the belt running from northern France through Belgium to the Ruhr Valley and Upper Silesia, and in the Appalachian coal belt in North America. Most of the world's industrial regions were assembled above or adjacent to these supplies of coal.[14] The creation of the new energy system, as we saw, resulted not just from the quantity of coal produced but from the mutually reinforcing interactions between coal, steam technology, and iron and steel. The introduction of iron rails, produced in blast furnaces fired by coal using steam-driven bellows, and of iron bridges, allowed the rapid development of railway lines. By the end of the nineteenth century, industrialised regions had built water and rail networks that moved concentrated carbon stores from the underground coalface to the surface, to railways, to ports, to cities and to sites of manufacturing and electrical power generation.

Great volumes of energy now flowed along narrow, purpose-built channels. Specialised bodies of workers were concentrated at the end-points and main junctions of these conduits, operating the cutting equipment, lifting machinery, switches, locomotives and other devices that allowed stores of energy to move along them. Their position and concentration gave them opportunities, at certain moments, to forge a new kind of political power.

The power derived not just from the organisations they formed, the ideas they began to share or the political alliances they built, but from the extraordinary quantities of carbon energy that could be used to assemble political agency, by employing the ability to slow, disrupt or cut off its supply.

Coal miners played a leading role in contesting work regimes and the private powers of employers in the labour activism and political mobilisation of the 1880s and onward. Between 1881 and 1905, coal miners in the United

---

14   Sidney Pollard, *Peaceful Conquest: The Industrialization of Europe, 1760–1970*, Oxford: OUP, 1981: 120–1. European capital also developed coal resources further afield, both in British colonies – Natal and the Transvaal, parts of Queensland and New South Wales, and West Bengal – and in the Donets Basin in Russia.

States went on strike at a rate of about three times the average for workers in all major industries, and at double the rate of the next-highest industry, tobacco manufacturing. Coal-mining strikes also lasted much longer than strikes in other industries.[15] With the same pattern found in Europe, waves of industrial action swept across the world's coal-mining regions in the later nineteenth and early twentieth centuries, and again after the First World War.[16]

The militancy of the miners can be attributed in part to the fact that moving carbon stores from the coal seam to the surface created unusually autonomous places and methods of work. The old argument that mining communities enjoyed a special isolation compared with other industrial workers, making their militancy 'a kind of colonial revolt against far-removed authority', misrepresents this autonomy.[17] In his classic study of 1925, *The Miner's Freedom*, Carter Goodrich had argued that autonomy was a product not of the geographical isolation of coal-mining regions from political authority but of 'the very geography of the working places inside a mine'.[18] In the traditional room-and-pillar method, a pair of miners worked a section of the coal seam, leaving pillars or walls of coal in place between their own chamber and adjacent chambers to support the roof. They usually made their own decisions about where to cut and how much rock to leave in place to prevent cave-ins. Before the widespread mechanisation of mining, 'the miner's freedom from supervision is at the opposite extreme from the carefully ordered and regimented work of the modern machine-feeder'.[19] The militancy that formed in these workplaces was typically an effort to defend

---

15   The strike rates per 1,000 employees for coal mining and for all industries, respectively, were 134 and 72 (1881–86); 241 and 73.3 (1887–99); 215 and 66.4 (1894–1900); and 208 and 86.9 (1901–05). P. K. Edwards, *Strikes in the United States, 1881–1974*, New York: St Martin's Press, 1981: 106.

16   Podobnik, *Global Energy Shifts*.

17   Clark Kerr and Abraham Siegel, 'The Interindustry Propensity to Strike: An International Comparison', in Arthur Kornhauser, Robert Dubin and Arthur M. Ross, eds, *Industrial Conflict*, New York: McGraw-Hill, 1934: 192. More recent accounts stress the diversity of mining communities and the complexity of their political engagements with other groups, with mine owners and with state authorities. Roy A. Church, Quentin Outram and David N. Smith, 'The Militancy of British Miners, 1893–1986: Interdisciplinary Problems and Perspectives', *Journal of Interdisciplinary History* 22: 1, 1991: 49–66; Royden Harrison, ed., *Independent Collier: The Coal Miner as Archetypal Proletarian Reconsidered*, New York: St Martin's Press, 1978; Roger Fagge, *Power, Culture, and Conflict in the Coalfields: West Virginia and South Wales, 1900–1922*, Manchester: Manchester University Press, 1996; John H. M. Laslett, *Colliers Across the Sea: A Comparative Study of Class Formation in Scotland and the American Midwest, 1830–1924*, Champaign, IL: University of Illinois Press, 2000.

18   Carter Goodrich, *The Miner's Freedom: A Study of the Working Life in a Changing Industry*, Boston: Marshall Jones Co., 1925: 19.

19   Goodrich, *Miner's Freedom*: 14; Podobnik, *Global Energy Shifts*: 82–5. On the relative autonomy of coal miners and its loss under mechanisation, see also Keith Dix, *What's a Coal Miner to Do? The Mechanization of Coal Mining*, Pittsburgh: University of Pittsburgh Press, 1988; and Chris Tilly and Charles Tilly, *Work Under Capitalism*, Boulder, CO: Westview Press, 1998: 43–51.

this autonomy against the threats of mechanisation, or against the pressure to accept more dangerous work practices, longer working hours or lower rates of pay.

The rise of mass democracy is often attributed to the emergence of new forms of political consciousness. The autonomy enjoyed by coal miners lends itself to this kind of explanation. There is no need, however, to detour into questions of a shared culture or collective consciousness to understand the new forms of agency that miners helped assemble. The detour would be misleading, for it would imply that there was some shortage in earlier periods or other places of people demanding a less precarious life.[20]

What was missing was not consciousness, not a repertoire of demands, but an effective way of forcing the powerful to listen to those demands. The flow and concentration of energy made it possible to connect the demands of miners to those of others, and to give their arguments a technical force that could not easily be ignored. Strikes became effective, not because of mining's isolation, but on the contrary because of the flows of carbon that connected chambers beneath the ground to every factory, office, home or means of transportation that depended on steam or electric power.

Strikes were also common among coal workers outside Europe and North America. The workers of the Zonguldak coalfield on the Black Sea coast of Turkey organised repeated strike actions, and a strike in April 1882 by the coal heavers at Port Said, the world's largest coaling station, is recorded as the first collective action by an emergent Egyptian workers' movement. However, without the linkages that connected coal to large centres of industrial production within the country, these actions could not have paralysed local energy systems and gained the political force they enjoyed in northern Europe and the United States.[21]

SABOTAGE

The power of the miner-led strikes appeared unprecedented. In Germany, a wave of coal-mining strikes in 1889 shocked the new kaiser, Wilhelm II, into abandoning Bismarck's hard-line social policy and supporting a programme

---

20   Staying just with England, E. P. Thompson's classic *The Making of the English Working Class*, New York: Pantheon Books, 1964, is evidence enough. On the precariousness of life, see Karl Polanyi, *The Great Transformation: The Political and Economic Origins of Our Time*, New York: Farrar & Rhinehart, 1944; and Judith Butler, *Precarious Life: The Powers of Mourning and Violence*, New York: Verso, 2004.

21   Donald Quataert, *Miners and the State in the Ottoman Empire: The Zonguldak Coalfield, 1822–1920*, New York: Berghahn Books, 2006; Joel Beinin and Zachary Lockman, *Workers on the Nile: Nationalism, Communism, Islam, and the Egyptian Working Class, 1882–1954*, Princeton: Princeton University Press, 1987: 23, 27–31.

of labour reforms.[22] The kaiser convened an international conference in March 1890 that called for international standards to govern labour in coal mining, together with limits on the employment of women and children. By a 'curious and significant coincidence', as the *New York Times* reported, on the same day that the conference opened in Berlin, 'by far the biggest strike in the history of organized labor' was launched by the coal miners of England and Wales. The number of men, women and children on strike reached 'the bewildering figure of 260,000'. With the great manufacturing enterprises of the north of England about to run out of coal, a correspondent reported 'the possibilities of a gigantic and ruinous labor conflict open before us'.[23]

The strike was not the only method of disrupting the flow of energy and the critical functions it supplied. In 1889, striking dockworkers in Glasgow were forced back to work after their employers hired groups of strike-breakers. The dockers decided to work as slowly and clumsily as the unskilled men brought in to replace them. After three days they won their demand for increased wages.[24] The newly formed National Union of Dock Labourers publicised the success of this method of disruption, and it was emulated in France and formally adopted there by railwaymen, miners and other workers as a means of fighting for the right to unionise and for improvements in working conditions. In 1909 Émile Pouget published the book that popularised the method's name, *Le Sabotage*.[25] Within a year the new word 'sabotage' had been adopted in English, initially to describe an industrial action by French railwaymen, but then to refer to the slow-down, the work-to-rule and other means of interrupting the normal functioning of a critical process.[26]

Foot-dragging and other forms of worker protest were nothing new. But the term 'sabotage' reflected the discovery that a relatively minor malfunction, mistiming or interruption, introduced at the right place and moment, could

---

22   Kathleen Canning, *Languages of Labor and Gender: Female Factory Work in Germany, 1850–1914*, Ithaca, NY: Cornell University Press, 1996: 130–3; G. V. Rimlinger, 'Labour and the State on the Continent, 1800–1939', The Cambridge Economic History of Europe, vol. 8, *The Industrial Economies: The Development of Economic and Social Policies*, ed. Peter Mathias and Sidney Pollard, Cambridge, UK: CUP, 1989: 576–8.

23   'Labor's Cause in Europe: The Kaiser's Conference and the English Strike', *New York Times*, 16 March 1890: 1.

24   Geoff Brown, *Sabotage: A Study in Industrial Conflict*, Nottingham: Bertrand Russell Peace Foundation for Spokesman Books, 1977.

25   Émile Pouget, *Le Sabotage*, Paris: M. Rivière, 1911 [1909], English translation, *Sabotage*, transl. Arturo M. Giovannitti, Chicago: C. H. Kerr & Co., 1913.

26   The Oxford English Dictionary records the first use of the term in English, in 1910, in an article in the *Church Times* deploring 'the sabotage of the French railway strikers'. During the First World War the word was used in military operations to refer to the disabling or destruction of enemy resources, giving it the connotation of deliberate violence. But in 1921 Thorstein Veblen described its common meaning as 'any manœuvre of slowing-down, inefficiency, bungling, obstruction', or what the Industrial Workers of the World called 'conscientious withdrawal of efficiency'. Thorstein Veblen, *The Engineers and the Price System*, New York: B. W. Huebsch, 1921: 1.

now have widespread effects. 'With two pennies-worth of a certain substance, used in the right way', explained the leader of the French railwaymen's union in 1895, 'we can make a locomotive unable to work.'[27] A coal-fired steam locomotive could deliver three megawatts of power (about 4,000 horsepower), or thirty times the motive power of the first reciprocating steam engines of a century or so earlier.[28] The new effectiveness of sabotage derived from this vast concentration of kinetic energy in a mechanism that a single operator could disable.

By the turn of the twentieth century, the vulnerability of these mechanisms and the concentrated flows of energy on which they depended had given workers a greatly increased political power. Large coal strikes could trigger wider mobilisations, as happened with the violent strike that followed the 1906 Courrières colliery disaster in north-eastern France, which helped provoke a general strike that paralysed Paris.[29] The most common pattern, however, was for strikes to spread through the interconnected industries of coal mining, railways, docking and shipping.[30] In Britain, the miners, railwaymen and transport workers organised three great national strikes in 1911–12, formalising their relationship in the Triple Alliance created on the eve of the First World War.[31] The coordination of strikes, slow-downs and other forms of sabotage enabled the construction, at certain moments, of a new political instrument: the general strike. 'A new force has arisen in trades unionism', warned Winston Churchill, who as home secretary in Britain confronted this novel threat. 'Shipping, coal, railways, dockers etc. etc. are all uniting and breaking out at once. The general strike "policy" is a factor which must be dealt with.'[32]

A generation earlier, in 1873, Friedrich Engels had rejected the idea of using a general strike as a political instrument, likening it to ineffectual plans for the 'holy month' – a nationwide suspension of work that the Chartist movement had advocated in England in the 1840s. The idea reflected an anarchist belief in locally based, spontaneous rebellion, Engels argued, whereas in practice workers lacked the resources and organisation to make a general strike effective. Were they to acquire such resources and powers of organisation, he said, they

27   Quoted in Pouget, *Le Sabotage*, available at raforum.apinc.org.

28   Smil, *Energy in Nature and Society*: 228–30.

29   In one of world's worst pit disasters, a gas explosion destroyed the Courrières mine on 10 March 1906, leaving 1,100 dead. Robert G. Neville, 'The Courrières Colliery Disaster, 1906', *Journal of Contemporary History* 13: 1, January 1978: 33–52.

30   Beverly J. Silver, *Forces of Labor: Workers' Movements and Globalization Since 1870*, Cambridge, UK: CUP, 2003: 98, shows that strikes were concentrated in these industries rather than in manufacturing.

31   John H. M. Laslett, 'State Policy Towards Labour and Labour Organizations, 1830–1939: Anglo-American Union Movements', *Cambridge Economic History of Europe*, vol. 8: 522.

32   Randolph S. Churchill, *Winston S. Churchill: Young Statesman 1901–1914*, London: Heinemann, 1967: 365.

would already be powerful enough to overthrow the state, so the general strike would be an unnecessary detour.[33]

Thirty years later the general strike still appeared to many on the European left as an anarchist tactic that should not take the place of organised political action. The Belgian general strike of 1902, led by the coal miners in an effort to win universal suffrage, reopened the debate about the tactics of social democracy in Europe – although even supporters like Rosa Luxemburg argued that the efficacy of the general strike in Belgium's case rested on the geographical concentration of the country's industry and could not be replicated in larger countries.[34] Three years later, she changed her mind. After witnessing the wave of strikes that paralysed Russia in the 1905 Revolution, she argued in *The Mass Strike* that workers could now organise a social revolution without a unified political movement, because isolated economic struggles were somehow connected into a single political force. This force, she wrote, 'flows now like a broad billow over the whole kingdom, and now divides into a gigantic network of narrow streams'.[35] Luxemburg's language tried to capture the dispersed yet interconnected power that workers had somehow acquired. But her fluvial metaphor missed the fact that it was not streams and tides that brought workers together into a novel political force but railways, rivers and canals and the concentrated stocks of energy they carried.

During the First World War, US and British coalfields and railways were placed under the direction of government administrators, and coal and rail workers were in some cases exempted from conscription and integrated into the war effort industrially. The number of strikes was reduced, but the critical role of these energy

---

33   Friedrich Engels, 'The Bakunists at Work', in Karl Marx and Friedrich Engels, *Revolution in Spain*, London: Lawrence & Wishart, 1939, first published in *Der Volksstaat*, 31 October, and 2 and 5 November 1873; see also Adrian Shubert, *The Road to Revolution in Spain: The Coal Miners of Asturias 1860–1934*, Urbana: University of Illinois Press, 1987. The rejection of the general strike was part of Marx and Engels's battle with the anarchists, led by Bakunin – a fight that led to the breakup of the First International. The anarchists advocated locally based, widespread rebellion, epitomised by the general strike. Marx and Engels argued for the steady organisation of the working class in order to win the political reforms that would enable them to conquer the power of the state at the national level. In their view the role of trade unions, beyond gaining economic improvements within the workplace, was to promote the political education of the working class so that they would act increasingly in their own collective interests. See Paul Thomas, *Karl Marx and the Anarchists*, London: Routledge & Kegan Paul, 1980: 249–340.

34   Ernest Mahaim and Harald Westergaard, 'The General Strike in Belgium, April 1902', *Economic Journal* 12: 47, 1902; Janet L. Polasky, 'A Revolution for Socialist Reforms: The Belgian General Strike for Universal Suffrage', *Journal of Contemporary History* 27, 1992, 449–66; Carl E. Schorske, *German Social Democracy, 1905–1917: The Development of the Great Schism*, Cambridge, MA: Harvard University Press, 1983: 28–58.

35   Rosa Luxemburg, *The Mass Strike, the Political Party, and the Trade Unions*, (a translation of *Massenstreik, Partei und Gewerkschaften* 1906), Detroit: Marxist Educational Society, 1925: 44. Georges Sorel offered another contemporary reflection on the new power of the general strike in *Reflections on Violence*, transl. Thomas Ernest Hulme, New York: B. W. Huebsch, 1914 [1908].

networks became more visible. In Germany, compulsory works councils were set up in major industries, and in France the government banned strikes in industries related to the war and took a direct role in setting wages and working conditions.[36] The war's duration and destructiveness, to which the energy from coal contributed, undermined political orders everywhere, in many cases bringing the new populist forces to power. In central and eastern Europe these forces overthrew the old order; in western and northern Europe and the US they were accommodated within it. From the West Virginia coal strikes of 1919 to the German general strike of 1920 and the British general strike of 1926, the coordination of industrial action by mine workers, dockers and railwaymen reaffirmed their new power to shut down energy nodes. The dispersed energy systems of solar radiation had never allowed groups of workers to assemble a political capability of this sort.

The power of the general strike put large industrial employers on the defensive. In 1918, the Rockefeller Foundation in New York issued a report explaining the vulnerability:

> If the recent past has revealed the frightful consequences of industrial strife, do not present developments all over the world afford indications of possibilities infinitely worse? Syndicalism aims at the destruction by force of existing organization, and the transfer of industrial capital from present possessors to syndicates or revolutionary trades unions. This it seeks to accomplish by the 'general strike.' What might not happen, in America or in England, if upon a few days' or a few weeks' notice, the coal mines were suddenly to shut down, and the railways to stop running! . . . Here is power which, once exercised, would paralyze the . . . nation more effectively than any blockade in time of war.[37]

The Rockefeller family had commissioned the report following the Ludlow Massacre of 1914. The killing of striking coalminers by the Colorado National Guard – armed with machine guns and brought in to defeat the attempt by the United Mine Workers to unionise a Rockefeller-owned mine in the Great Coalfield War of 1913–14 – had caused a national political crisis that threatened the 'present possessors' of large industrial capital.[38] The Rockefellers hired

---

36 David Corbin, *Life, Work, and Rebellion in the Coal Fields: The Southern West Virginia Miners, 1880–1922*, Champaign, IL: University of Illinois Press, 1981; Thomas E. Reifer, 'Labor, Race and Empire: Transport Workers and Transnational Empires of Trade, Production, and Finance', in Gilbert G. Gonzalez, Raul A. Fernandez, Vivian Price, David Smith, and Linda Trinh Võ, eds, *Labor Versus Empire: Race, Gender, and Migration*, London: Routledge, 2004: 17–36; Rimlinger, 'Labour and the State': 582, 587.

37 William Lyon Mackenzie King, *Industry and Humanity: A Study in The Principles Underlying Industrial Reconstruction*, Boston: Houghton Mifflin, 1918: 494–5.

38 Thomas G. Andrews, *Killing for Coal: America's Deadliest Labor War*, Cambridge, MA: Harvard University Press, 2008; Ron Chernow, *Titan: The Life of John D. Rockefeller, Sr.*, New York: Random House, 1998: 571–90.

William Lyon Mackenzie King, who had helped resolve more than forty coal, railway, shipping and other strikes as minister of labour in Canada, to devise a less violent method of defeating the mine workers. The Rockefeller Plan, widely copied in the interwar period, created company unions that allowed workers to negotiate over pay and working conditions while preventing them from joining independent unions.[39]

Large American firms portrayed the new company unions and other forms of worker representation as 'industrial democracy', and compared them to the 'self-government' that the United States championed in the Middle East and other regions in the same period.[40] The firms compared the difference between the old industrial relations and the new to 'the difference between a feudalistic state – the government of which, however enlightened, contains nothing of the consent of the governed – and a democracy', explaining that, 'if people have a voice in the making of the regulations which affect them, they are more able to understand and accept law'.[41]

Labour movements in the US and other countries fought against the paternalism of welfare industrialism, and later managed to have company-controlled unions made illegal; but industrialists continued to promote corporate benevolence and welfare as a method of weakening union power. They supported broader welfare measures where they promised to weaken organised labour. After working as an industrial relations consultant to Rockefeller and other firms, Mackenzie King returned to politics in Canada, where he served as prime minister for twenty-two years, opposed attempts to introduce New Deal–style protections for workers, and became the architect of the country's welfare state.[42] As workers in industrialised regions fought for a more egalitarian life, the democracy they began to achieve was always liable to slip from providing a means of making effective egalitarian claims to offering a means of regulating populations through the provision of their welfare.

Between the 1880s and the interwar decades, workers in the industrialised countries of Europe and North America used their new powers over energy flows to acquire or extend the right to vote and, more importantly, the right to form labour unions, to create political organisations, and to take collective action including strikes. In most cases, these changes enabled mass-based parties to win power for the first time. Workers also acquired the right to an eight-hour

---

39   Jonathan Rees, *Representation and Rebellion: The Rockefeller Plan at the Colorado Fuel and Iron Company, 1914–1942*, Boulder, CO: University Press of Colorado, 2010.

40   A comparison I will explore further in Chapter 3, where I examine Britain's adoption of the policy of 'self-determination' as a mode of governing the oil regions of the Arab world.

41   Cited in Lizabeth Cohen, *Making a New Deal: Industrial Workers in Chicago, 1919–1939*, Cambridge, UK: CUP, 1990: 171–2.

42   'William Lyon Mackenzie King', *Dictionary of Canadian Biography Online*, at www.biographi.ca.

day and to social insurance programmes, including provisions against industrial accidents, sickness and unemployment, as well as to public pensions in retirement.[43] The emergent women's movements fought against the exclusion of women from public political life, sometimes with the support of socialist parties, and gradually forced the granting of voting rights to women. Large industrialists often came to support limited versions of these reforms, since improving workers' well-being would increase their stamina and discipline and reduce industrial protest, while welfare measures that strengthened domestic hierarchies could reinforce the maternal roles that women had begun to escape during wartime mobilisation.[44] Labour organisations sometimes opposed proposals for social insurance as partial measures that would undermine their efforts to achieve a more effective change in the ownership of wealth. Where more radical change was threatened, as in interwar Germany and Austria, industrialists supported the destruction of the parliamentary system.

Despite such limits and setbacks, working people in the industrialised West acquired a power that would have seemed impossible before the late nineteenth century. The rise of large industry had exposed populations to extraordinary forms of social insecurity, physical risk, overwork and destitution. But the concentration and movement of coal required to drive those industrial processes had created a vulnerability. Workers were gradually connected together not so much by the weak ties of a class culture, collective ideology or political organisation, but by the increasing and highly concentrated quantities of carbon energy they mined, loaded, carried, stoked and put to work. The coordinated acts of interrupting, slowing down or diverting its movement created a decisive political machinery, a new form of collective capability built out of coalmines, railways, power stations, and their operators. More than a mere social movement, this socio-technical agency was put to work for a series of democratic claims whose gradual implementation radically reduced the precariousness of life in industrial societies.

THE BATTLE FOR COAL

After the Second World War, the leading industrialised countries began to reorganise the relations between labour forces and energy flows. In the United States, the change began in response to a strike by oil workers. In September 1945, workers at a Standard Oil refinery in Michigan organised a strike that spread to Texas and California and became the first nation-wide oil strike, closing down

---

43   Despite the vast increase in the production of wealth in the nineteenth century, measures of human welfare even in industrialised countries did not begin to improve until the twentieth century. John Coatsworth, 'Welfare', *American Historical Review* 101: 1, 1996.

44   Susan Pedersen, 'The Failure of Feminism in the Making of the British Welfare State', *Radical History Review* 43, 1989: 86–110.

a majority of the country's refineries. *Time* described the oil workers' union as 'the world's . . . most recalcitrant labor union'. It was the oil companies, however, that rejected government arbitration. In response, the government used the War Powers Act to place the refineries under military control. Strikes spread to coal mining, electrical power, iron and steel, railroads, and automobile manufacture, producing the most concentrated period of industrial conflict in American history. To end the oil strike, the government forced the Standard Oil companies and other large refiners to concede the right of national unions to represent a collective workforce, while limiting their role to bargaining over remuneration and working conditions.[45] The settlement provided a new model of labour relations, which replaced the company unions pioneered by Rockefeller in coal mining and the oil industry, and was also adopted in automobile manufacturing and other large industries. The concession defeated more far-reaching postwar proposals for industrial democracy, in which workers would play a role in managing an enterprise and earn shares in its profits. Instead, government and industry promoted the new science of industrial management, which focused on methods of increasing 'productivity'. Improvements in pay and terms of employment would in future depend on workers' accepting speedups, closer supervision, the elimination of jobs, and increased physical exhaustion, rather than any more radical redistribution of shares of the nation's wealth.[46]

The American model of industrial relations was exported to postwar Europe, along with a decisive switch in sources of energy. In France, Germany and Britain, the 'battle for coal' of the late 1940s shaped postwar politics, as coal miners led campaigns not just for improved pay and working conditions but for more extensive changes to the way prosperity and well-being were distributed. Following the nationalisation of the French coal industry in 1944, the Communist-led union movement turned coal mining into a showcase of increased productivity, in exchange not only for improved wages but for a direct role in the management of industry. Three years later, however, after rapid inflation caused real wages to collapse, coal miners joined a series of strikes demanding that the government increase pay levels or extend food rations.[47] Rather

---

45   'The Last Traffic Jam', *Time*, 15 December 1947; Myron L. Hoch, 'The Oil Strike of 1945', *Southern Economic Journal* 15, 1948: 117–33.

46   Anthony Carew, *Labour Under the Marshall Plan: The Politics of Productivity and the Marketing of Management Science*, Detroit: Wayne State University Press, 1987; Victoria de Grazia, *Irresistible Empire: America's Advance through Twentieth-Century Europe*, Cambridge, MA: Harvard University Press, 2005: 336–75.

47   Darryl Holter, *The Battle For Coal: Miners and the Politics of Nationalization in France, 1940–1950*, DeKalb: Northern Illinois University Press, 1992; Adam Steinhouse, *Worker's Participation in Post-Liberation France*, Lanham: Lexington Books, 2001. Gabrielle Hecht, *The Radiance of France: Nuclear Power and National Identity after World War II*, Cambridge, MA: MIT Press, 1998, explores the subsequent battles among labour unions to shape a postwar political role for workers through their place in the production of a new form of energy – nuclear power.

than yield to these claims, France and other European governments turned to the United States. Keen to promote their new corporate management model abroad (and to have Washington subsidise their exports), American industrialists used a fear of the popularity of Communist parties in Western Europe to win support for postwar aid to Europe. 'The Communists are rendering us a great service', commented the future French prime minister Pierre Mendès-France. 'Because we have a "Communist danger" the Americans are making a tremendous effort to help us. We must keep up this indispensable Communist scare.'[48] The European Recovery Program (ERP), popularly known as the Marshall Plan, sought to engineer a political order in Europe built on a new relationship between organised labour and large industrial enterprises, similar to the order America was pioneering at home.

There were three elements to the American-funded reorganisation of the power of labour. First, the Marshall Plan promoted US-style industrial management. The Labour Division of the ERP became a laboratory for developing and testing the new American methods of managing manpower and machines. The doctrine of productivity justified increased supervision of labour, and paying wages that failed to keep pace with rising prices. 'The only answer to Britain's difficulties', the American ambassador to London reported to the secretary of state, George Marshall, 'is to work harder and, I fear, for less.' Studies showed, however, that most of the difference between American and European productivity could be explained not by Americans working harder but by America's abundant supplies of coal and oil, which allowed its industry to use between two and three times as much electrical power per worker.[49]

Second, the recovery programme as a whole was made conditional on the acceptance by European governments of plans for economic integration, which began with the integration of Western Europe's coal industry. The European Coal and Steel Community, established as a first step towards the political union of Europe, reduced competition in the coal industry and supported the mechanisation of production, with funds provided to alleviate the effects of the resulting pit closures and unemployment. The United States helped finance the programme, which reduced the ability of coal miners to carry out effective strikes by rapidly reducing their numbers and facilitating the supply of coal across national borders.

The third element was the most extensive. The US funded initiatives to convert Europe's energy system from one based largely on coal to one increasingly dependent on oil. An important goal of the conversion to oil was to permanently weaken the coal miners, whose ability to interrupt the flow of energy had given organised labour the power to demand the improvements to collective life that had democratised Europe.

---

48   Alexander Werth, *France, 1940–1955*, New York: Henry Holt, 1956: 351.
49   Carew, *Labour Under the Marshall Plan*: 136.

The corporatised democracy of postwar Western Europe was to be built on this reorganisation of energy flows. ERP funds helped pay for building oil refineries and installing oil-fired industrial boilers, putting in place the infrastructure needed to convert from coal to oil.[50] The US encouraged the building of roads, gave ERP countries $432.5 million to purchase American vehicles, and subsidised Italian and French car manufactures. Western Europe had no significant oilfields, so the additional oil would come from the Middle East, in particular from the new fields in Saudi Arabia, where American companies and the US government were keen to increase production to provide funds to support the insecure oligarchy of Ibn Saud.

Scarce supplies of steel and construction equipment were shipped from the United States to the Persian Gulf, to build a pipeline from eastern Saudi Arabia to the Mediterranean, enabling a rapid increase in oil supplies to Europe. At the same time, Marshall Plan administrators devised a global pricing plan for oil. Oil was cheaper to produce in the Middle East and cheaper to transport from there to Europe, in comparison to the equivalent costs for US oil, the price of which was protected by government production quotas. Under the pricing plan, rather than allow Europe to benefit from cheaper oil, supplies from the Middle East were sold to Europe at the much higher price of imports from the US. The plan protected oil producers in America and the monopoly profits of the international oil companies, but would have made it difficult to switch Europe from coal, especially as the US companies supplying Middle Eastern oil would accept payment only in dollars. So ERP dollar funds were also used to pay for the European purchases of oil – an arrangement that secured the role of the dollar as the basis of the global financial system, built on the need to use dollars to acquire oil. Over 10 per cent of ERP funds were used to procure oil, representing the largest single use of Marshall Plan money. The ERP financed more than half the oil supplied to Marshall Plan countries by US companies during the period of the Plan (April 1948 to December 1951), making the oil companies among the largest beneficiaries of Marshall Plan aid.[51]

---

50   Raymond G. Stokes, *Opting for Oil: The Political Economy of Technical Change in the West German Industry, 1945–1961*, Cambridge, UK: CUP, 1994: 96. The European Cooperation Administration (the agency responsible for administering the ERP) spent $24 million on increasing refinery construction; and dollars freed by ECA funds from other expenses, such as oil purchases, were switched to refinery construction, along with ECA counterpart funds. David S. Painter, 'The Marshall Plan and Oil', *Cold War History* 9: 2, May 2009: 168. Building oil refineries represented an important means of reducing the severe shortage of dollars among European countries, as the ECA director Paul Hoffman reported to Congress, because it enabled them to import crude oil rather than more expensive refined products. Although an ostensible aim of the ERP was to address the dollar shortage, US oil companies successfully fought to limit the use of ERP funds to construct oil refineries. US Congress, House of Representatives, Committee on Interstate and Foreign Commerce, Petroleum Study, Progress Report, 15 May 1950, 81st Congress, 2nd Session.

51   David Painter, 'Oil and the Marshall Plan', *Business History Review* 58: 3, 1984: 362; Painter, 'Oil and the Marshall Plan': 164–5; Nathan Citino, 'Defending the "Postwar Petroleum

Spurred by these American subsidies, oil increased its share of Western Europe's energy consumption from 10 per cent in 1948 to almost one-third by 1960. The diversion of steel to build pipelines and of Marshall Plan funds for this purpose was justified in part by the need to undermine the political power of Europe's coal miners.[52]

OIL IN THE AGE OF COAL

If coal played a critical role in forging democracy, what difference did it make to replace coal with oil? Like coal, oil sometimes enabled workers to assemble themselves into new social forces. Although the refinery strike of 1945–46 was the first nation-wide oil strike in the United States, in California, the country's leading oil-producing region for the first third of the twentieth century, petroleum workers had led the struggles during and after the First World War not only for better pay and conditions, but also for a broader social transformation. They fought for the public ownership of the oil industry as the basis of 'a true democracy' in which '*government* shall be so formed as to benefit the great mass of the common people . . . against the material interests of the remaining few'.[53] They failed to have the industry placed under public control, but they forged a new kind of community-based labour movement deeply involved in local and state politics, and better able than unions in other industries to survive the political repression that followed.[54]

The political strength that oil workers could acquire depended on the ways in which oil was used and the vulnerabilities its use created. Before the twentieth century, the main use for petroleum was to provide artificial lighting, in the form of kerosene (also known as paraffin) for oil lamps, and to supply lubricants for machinery. It was widely distributed, mostly in small amounts, and supplied in reusable metal cans to individual consumers. With the exception of Russia, no country in the nineteenth century converted oil into a significant source of mechanical power to drive industry and transportation. Unlike coal, therefore, oil was not concentrated into vital channels on

---

Order": The US, Britain, and the 1954 Saudi-Onassis Tanker Deal', *Diplomacy & Statecraft* 11: 2, 2000: 137–160; Fred Block, *The Origins of International Economic Disorder: A Study of United States International Monetary Policy from World War II to the Present*, Berkeley: University of California Press, 1977.

52 James Forrestal, 'Diaries of James V. Forrestal, 1944–1949', vols 9–10, 6 January 1948, in 'James V. Forrestal Papers, 1941–1949', Princeton: Seeley G. Mudd Manuscript Library. See also ibid., vols 7–8, 2 May 1947; Painter, 'Oil and the Marshall Plan': 361–2.

53 *Kern County Union Labor Journal*, 10 November 1917 and 18 May 1918, cited in Nancy Quam-Wickham, 'Petroleocrats and Proletarians: Work, Class and Politics in the California Oil Industry 1917–1925', PhD dissertation, Department of History, University of California, Berkeley, 1994: 13–14.

54 Quam-Wickham, 'Petroleocrats and Proletarians'.

which other processes depended, and oil regions did not become industrial centres. The places where oil was produced were often remote from large markets, most of which were found in the regions that had industrialised using coal. Even there, lamp oil was increasingly a product for rural areas rather than towns and cities, which were illuminated with coal gas and, by the end of the nineteenth century, with electricity. The weakness of these link-ages and the limited role of oil as a concentrated source of mechanical energy restricted the potential political force of those who produced the oil – except, as we will see, in Russia.

These weaknesses can be seen in the largest oil-producing region outside America and Russia before the First World War – the Austrian province of Galicia, part of modern Poland and Ukraine. The Galician oil wells extended eastwards from Cracow in a 300-mile arc towards the border of Romania. By the 1890s steam-powered percussion drills had replaced the hand-digging of wells, accessing deeper layers of oil-bearing rock and causing a surge in production in the following decade. The increased supply threatened the large firms that controlled the European kerosene market, the Standard Oil Company and its main European rival, Deutsche Bank in Germany. However, Galicia lacked a network of navigable waterways or railways for transporting its oil to Germany and other important markets, an isolation that the large companies could use to weaken both local Galician oil firms and the work-force. Starting in 1904, oil workers organised a series of strikes over condi-tions of work and collective rights, including the demand for an eight-hour day. The local firms were vulnerable to the strike and willing to negotiate, but the large foreign operators refused to deal with the strikers. When the work-ers responded by sabotaging the oilfields, disabling the pumps that moved oil to storage reservoirs and allowing it to flow into local streams, the Austrian government sent seven infantry battalions to protect the pumps and pipelines. By refusing to negotiate and prolonging the strike, the large firms were able both to defeat the workers and to put the smaller producers out of business. In fact, rumours circulated that Standard Oil had financed the 1904 strike with this dual aim.[55]

In the twentieth century, as the spread of electric lighting began to limit the growth in demand for kerosene in industrialised countries, oil companies were forced to look for new uses for their product. The solution was to convert the oil from a means of illumination into a source of mechanical power. At first it was used in boilers as a direct substitute for coal to drive reciprocating steam engines, in the form of fuel oil. The development of the internal combus-tion engine, which spread rapidly after 1900, gave oil a use for which it had

---

55   Alison Fleig Frank, *Oil Empire: Visions of Prosperity in Austrian Galicia*, Cambridge, MA: Harvard University Press, 2007: 140–72.

no readily available substitute, both in the lightweight gasoline engine and the more powerful diesel engine.[56]

In the Russian-controlled Caucasus, oil workers were already able to benefit from this development. The oilfields of Baku, in modern Azerbaijan, concentrated around the city and occupying an area of no more than 12 square miles, produced more than half the world's petroleum for a brief period at the start of the twentieth century. Linked by a rail line and pipeline to the Black Sea port of Batumi and by waterways and railways to the rest of Russia, the oil industry launched the protests that culminated in the Revolution of 1905. Labour unrest in the south Caucasus began in 1901–02 with strikes and demonstrations led by the pipeline, refinery and port workers of Batumi, culminating in a large strike by oil workers at the Rothschild plant in which 14 protesters were killed. The labour organisers, including the young Joseph Stalin, stayed in touch with allies in Baku.[57] The wider Revolution began with a strike of Baku oil workers in July 1903, which spread along the railway line to the marshalling yards and workshops at Tiflis (now Tbilisi), the midpoint of the Transcaucasus Railway, then to Batumi, and then 'like a brushfire across southern Russia'.[58] It was the country's first general strike, which, as we have seen, led Rosa Luxemburg to recognise the new power of workers connected, as she put it, by individual 'economic' grievances rather than 'political' organisation.[59] In December 1904 the Baku oil workers announced a second general strike, from which the 1905 Revolution was launched.

As the Revolution unfolded, local observers reported that 'labour troubles have been felt in Baku more severely, perhaps, then in any other part of Russia'.[60] Stalin later claimed that the advanced organising skills of the oil workers of Baku and the intensity of their conflict with the oil industrialists gave him an experience that qualified him as 'a journeyman for the revolution'.[61] In fact, however, the leaders of the striking oil workers broke with the local Bolsheviks

---

56   The first oceangoing ship to be equipped with a diesel engine was an oil tanker, the *Vulcanus*, built for the Royal Dutch company and launched in December 1910. Frederik Carel Gerretson, *History of the Royal Dutch*, 4 vols, Leiden: E. J. Brill, 1953–57, vol. 4: 54–5.

57   Ronald Grigor Suny, *The Making of the Georgian Nation*, 2nd edn, Bloomington: Indiana University Press, 1994: 162–4; Robert Service, *Stalin: A Biography*, Cambridge, MA: Belknap Press of Harvard University Press, 2005: 48–50.

58   Robert W. Tolf, *The Russian Rockefellers: The Saga of the Nobel Family and the Russian Oil Industry*, Stanford, CA: Hoover Institution Press, Stanford University, 1976: 156.

59   Luxemburg, *Mass Strike*: 44.

60   Report from Mr Vice-Consul Urquhart, Baku, appended to Mr Consul Stevens, 'Report for the Year 1905 on the Trade and Commerce of Batoum and District', 26 March 1906: 13, in United Kingdom Parliamentary Papers, House of Commons, vol. cxxvii, Command Paper 2682, no. 3566 Annual Series, Diplomatic and Consular Reports, Russia, 1906.

61   Stalin's words, from a 1926 speech to railway workers, are cited in Ronald Grigor Suny, 'A Journeyman for the Revolution: Stalin and the Labour Movement in Baku, June 1907–May 1908', *Soviet Studies* 23: 3, 1972: 373.

and negotiated with the owners of the oil industry the first labour contract in Russian history, winning the right to a nine-hour day, sick pay, free fuel and elected factory representatives. Their political demands were for 'the convocation of a constituent assembly on the basis of universal, equal, direct, and secret suffrage' and 'freedom of speech, assembly, press, strikes, and unions'.[62]

The power of the oil workers reflected the fact that the Baku industry at the turn of the century was organised and connected in ways that more closely resembled the contemporary coal industries of northern Europe than oil production elsewhere or in later periods. More than a hundred enterprises produced oil in the space of a few square miles, creating a dense network of derricks, open storage pits and steam engines, crisscrossed with pipes carrying oil and supplying water, steam and natural gas, and with high-tension cables distributing electricity. A short distance away, on the Caspian coast, were over a hundred refineries, with their own large workforces, and from there the oil was carried by steamship and rail across the Russian Empire. The proximity of wells, workshops, pumps, power supplies and refineries created a concentrated labour force with the ability to disrupt supplies of energy across a broad region.[63]

A second way in which Baku production resembled that of the contemporary coal industry was that its oil was used primarily not for illumination, but to produce steam power. The heavy crude of Baku contained relatively low amounts of the more volatile hydrocarbons refined into kerosene, and yielded a higher proportion of residual oil more suitable for use in steam boilers. The Caucasus lacked the supplies of coal and timber found in Pennsylvania and other oil regions, a deficiency that encouraged the use of oil to produce combustion heat. Engineers in Baku had developed an atomising spray for burners that enabled the efficient use of oil to fuel steam engines in ships and railways. The Russian Caspian fleet converted from coal to oil in the 1870s, and Russian railways began to switch in the 1880s. By 1890, all Russian trains except those in the coal region of the Donets basin and in Siberia ran on fuel oil, and its use had spread to the metallurgical industry and to factories in the north. Over the following decade, oil accounted on average for an estimated 41 per cent of commercial primary energy consumption in Russia.[64] The oil strikes that

62   Solomon M. Schwarz, *The Russian Revolution of 1905: The Workers' Movement and the Formation of Bolshevism and Menshevism*, transl. Gertrude Vakar, Chicago: University of Chicago Press, 1967, Appendix 6: 'The Baku Strike of December, 1904: Myth and Reality': 303; Beryl Williams, '1905: The View from the Provinces', in Jonathan Smele and Anthony Haywood, eds, *The Russian Revolution of 1905*, London: Routledge, 2005: 47–8.

63   Tolf, *Russian Rockefellers*: 145–7. My analysis in this and the following paragraph draws on Richard Ryan Weber, 'Power to the Petrol: How the Baku Oil Industry Made Labor Strikes and Mass Politics Possible in the Russian Empire (and beyond)', MA thesis, Program in Liberal Studies, Columbia University, May 2010.

64   Tolf, *Russian Rockefellers*: 70–1; N. L. Madureira, 'Oil in the Age of Steam', *Journal of Global History* 5: 1, 2010: 79.

launched the 1905 Revolution were able to paralyse transportation networks and industrial activity across the Empire, much as coal strikes could in north-western Europe.

Unlike north-western Europe, Russia was a multi-ethnic empire. Its ethnic divisions were reflected and employed in the organisation of the Baku oil indus-try – and in the defeat of the 1905 Revolution. Unskilled labour in the indus-try was carried out partly by local Azeris and partly by migrant workers from Iran, from both Persian- and Azeri-speaking communities. The skilled work-force was chiefly Russian and Armenian. The managers and local owners of oil businesses and other commercial enterprises were mostly Armenians, many of whom had prospered in the oil boom. A local British observer described Baku as 'commercially and ethnologically the Johannesburg of Russia', compar-ing it to the gold-mining boomtown of the Transvaal.[65] The South Africa war had recently consolidated a system of imperial self-government based on a racialised labour regime, developed in the mining industry, from which Britain would derive ideas for 'self-determination' in the oil-producing regions of the Arab world (see Chapter 2).

The Russian imperial government responded to the revolutionary strikes by unleashing the Black Hundreds, ultranationalist counter-revolutionary forces whose principal weapon was the pogrom – the organised use of mob violence against ethnic minorities. The first round of ethnic violence in Baku, in January 1905, was unsuccessful and 'gave renewed impetus to the labour movement'. The following September, however, the Black Hundreds stormed the city, set fire to the oilfields, and stirred up and armed the Muslim Azeris against the Christian Armenians. Thousands were killed, the oil industry was crippled and the workers' revolutionary demands were defeated.[66]

Despite the signs that oil might be turned into an instrument for build-ing political freedoms, the patterns of labour mobilisation, transportation and energy use found in Baku at the turn of the twentieth century proved to be an exception. The use of ethnic divisions to organise oil production proved more common, and would later be employed throughout the Middle East.[67] The abil-ity to weaken the labour force by dividing it into separate racial groups, with managers, skilled workers and unskilled workers housed and treated separately, reflected the different distribution of oil production across the world compared

65   James Dodds Henry, Baku: An Eventful History, New York: Arno Press, 1977 [1905]: 12; Arthur Beeby-Thompson, The Oil Fields of Russia, London: Crosby Lockwood & Son, 1904: 125–6; Hassan Hakimian, 'Wage Labor and Migration: Persian Workers in Southern Russia, 1880–1914,' International Journal of Middle East Studies 17: 4, 1985: 443–62.

66   Report from Mr Vice-Consul Urquhart: 13; Tolf, Russian Rockefellers: 156–60; Henry, Baku, 149–218.

67   See Robert Vitalis, America's Kingdom: Mythmaking on the Saudi Oil Frontier, 2nd edn, London: Verso, 2009.

to coal, and its development after rather than before the rise of modern industry. Oil production often grew rapidly, in regions remote from large populations, to serve distant users in places already industrialised with coal – a fact that encouraged the producers to import workers from different places and then perpetuate the forms of ethnic division. This difference, however, was only one of several factors that made oil production increasingly unlike the production of coal. Oil was produced using distinctive methods, and transported over longer and often more flexible routes, for reasons connected in part to the different physical and chemical form of the carbon it contains. To understand further why the politics of oil differed from those of coal, we must turn to these factors.

OIL FLOWS

Since oil comes to the surface driven by underground pressure, either from water trapped beneath it or from gas trapped above, sometimes assisted by the action of pumps, its production required a smaller workforce than coal in relation to the quantity of energy produced.[68] Workers remained above ground, closer to the supervision of managers. As the carbon occurs in liquid form, the work of transporting energy could be done with less human labour. Pumping stations and pipelines could replace railways as means of transporting energy from the site of production to the places where it was used or shipped abroad. These methods of transport did not require teams of humans to accompany the fuel on its journey, to load and unload it at each junction, or to continuously operate engines, switches and signals. In fact, oil pipelines were invented as a means of reducing the ability of humans to interrupt the flow of energy. They were introduced in Pennsylvania in the 1860s to circumvent the wage demands of the teamsters who transported barrels of oil to the rail depot in horse-drawn wagons.[69] Baku borrowed the innovation in the following decade from the American oil drillers, for the same reason. Pipelines were vulnerable to sabotage. During the 1905 Revolution in Russia, for example, the British consul in Batumi reported that 'a considerable number of pipes have been holed by the revolutionaries and have thereby been rendered useless'. But they were more difficult to incapacitate than the railways that carried coal, and could be quickly patched up. The damage, the consul reported, 'will not take long to repair and the line will in all probability be at work shortly'.[70]

---

68   As oil is extracted the pressure in the reservoir drops. Pumps may then be used to bring more oil to the surface, or to increase the reservoir pressure by driving water or gas into secondary wells.

69   Daniel Yergin, *The Prize: The Epic Quest for Oil, Money, and Power*, New York: Simon & Schuster, 1991: 33.

70   Mr Consul Stevens, 'Report for the Year 1905': 8.

In addition, diesel oil and petrol are lighter than coal and vaporise more easily, and their combustion leaves little residue compared with the burning of coal. For these reasons, as Lewis Mumford noted in 1934,

> they could be stowed away easily, in odds and ends of space where coal could not be placed or reached: being fed by gravity or pressure the engine had no need for a stoker. The effect of introducing liquid fuel and of mechanical stokers for coal, in electric steam plants, and on steamships, was to emancipate a race of galley slaves, the stokers.[71]

The fluidity and relative lightness of oil made it feasible to ship it in large quantities across oceans. In contrast, very little coal had historically crossed oceans.[72] In 1912, Britain exported one-third of its coal and was responsible for two-thirds of the world's seaborne exported coal; but almost 90 per cent of its exports went to the adjacent regions of Europe and the Mediterranean.[73] Over the course of the twentieth century, the proportion of coal exported internationally stabilised at about 15 per cent. By contrast, following the development of the oil tanker in the late nineteenth century, oil could be moved cheaply between continents. From the 1920s onwards, about 60 to 80 per cent of world oil production was exported. So much oil was moved across oceans that, by 1970, oil accounted for 60 per cent of seaborne cargo worldwide.[74]

---

71   Lewis Mumford, *Technics and Civilization*, New York: Harcourt, Brace, 1934: 235.

72   The main exception was high-quality steam coal from South Wales, essential for the navy and fast liners, which was shipped to British overseas coaling stations (H. Stanley Jevons, *The British Coal Trade*, London: E. P. Dutton, 1915: 684). In fact, half the coal Britain shipped outside Europe in the decade 1903–13 went to just two places – Río de la Plata in South America and the Suez Canal (Rainer Fremdling, 'Anglo-German Rivalry in Coal Markets in France, the Netherlands and Germany, 1850–1913', *Journal of European Economic History* 25: 3, 1996: Table 2). Historically, long-distance coal shipments from Britain could be used as ballast or make-weight, and benefited from low rates for back-carriage (William Stanley Jevons, *The Coal Question*, London: Macmillan, 1865: 227).

73   H. S. Jevons, *British Coal Trade*: 676–84. The economic historian Charles Kindleberger, an architect of the Marshall Plan who had headed a section on military supplies in the Office of Strategic Services in 1942–44, recalled that, at the outbreak of the Second World War,

> coal was regarded as something that didn't move across big bodies of water. It was shipped to British coaling stations but you wouldn't expect international transoceanic trade as a regular thing. And yet when the war came along, and we needed to get coal to Europe we started to move coal out . . . They were loading it in clam shell buckets on to barges in Puget Sound to go to Europe, a landing in Texas, Portland, Maine, everywhere.

Richard D. McKinzie, 'Oral History Interview with Charles P. Kindleberger', Independence, MO: Harry S. Truman Library: 108–9, at www.trumanlibrary.org/oralhist/kindbrgr.htm.

74   In 2005, 86 per cent of world coal production was consumed within the country of production. International Energy Agency, 'Coal in World in 2005', at www.iea.org. For oil, see Podobnik, *Global Energy Shifts*: 79; for the 1970 figure (which refers to ton-miles of crude oil and oil products), see United Nations Commission on Trade and Development, *Review of Maritime Transport 2007*, Geneva: UNCTAD, 2007. In 1970 coal accounted for less than 5 per cent of seaborne trade.

Compared to carrying coal by rail, moving oil by sea eliminated the labour of coal heavers and stokers, and thus the power of organised workers to withdraw their labour from a critical point in the energy system. Transoceanic shipping operated beyond the territorial spaces governed by the labour regulations and other democratic rights won in the era of widespread coal and railway strikes. In fact shipping companies could escape the regulation of labour laws altogether – as well as the payment of taxes – by registering their vessels in Panama or under other 'flags of convenience', removing whatever limited powers of labour organising might have remained. (When oil production later moved offshore, in places like the Gulf of Mexico, the rigs were treated as vessels and also registered under flags of convenience, enabling even the production site to operate free of local taxes and labour laws.)

Unlike railways, ocean shipping was not constrained by the need to run on a network of purpose-built tracks of a certain capacity, layout and gauge. Oil tankers frequently left port without knowing their final destination. They would steam to a waypoint, then receive a destination determined by the level of demand in different regions. This flexibility carried risks: in March 1967 it was one of the causes of the world's first giant oil spill, the Torrey Canyon disaster off the coast of Cornwall, which helped trigger the emergence of the environmental movement, a later threat to the carbon-fuel industry.[75] But the flexibility further weakened the powers of local forces that tried to control sites of energy production. If a labour strike, for example, or the nationalisation of an industry affected one production site, oil tankers could be quickly rerouted to supply oil from alternative sites.

In other words, whereas the movement of coal tended to follow dendritic networks, with branches at each end but a single main channel, creating potential choke points at several junctures, oil flowed along networks that often had the properties of a grid, like an electricity network, where there is more than one possible path and the flow of energy can switch to avoid blockages or overcome breakdowns.

These changes in the way forms of fossil energy were extracted, transported and used made energy networks less vulnerable to the political claims of those

---

75   The *Torrey Canyon*, an oil tanker owned by a Bermuda-based subsidiary of the Union Oil Company of California, registered in Liberia, chartered to BP, built in 1959 and rebuilt in 1966 in a Japanese shipyard to increase her size from 66,000 to 119,000 deadweight tons, ran aground off the coast of Cornwall, England, in March 1967. The tanker had set sail without knowing its final destination, and lacked detailed navigation charts for the coast of south-west England. The damage to the coastline and to wildlife was exacerbated by the lack of methods to handle large oil spills. The British government tried to set fire to the oil by having air defence forces bomb it with napalm, creating further damage and inadvertently revealing both their possession of the controversial weapon and the inaccuracy of the bombers (more than a quarter of the bombs missed their target). John Sheail, 'Torrey Canyon: The Political Dimension', *Journal of Contemporary History* 42: 3, 2007: 485–504; Cabinet Office, *The Torrey Canyon*, London: HMSO, 1967.

whose labour kept them running. Unlike the movement of coal, the flow of oil could not readily be assembled into a machine that enabled large numbers of people to exercise novel forms of political power.

PRODUCING SCARCITY

There was another set of ways in which the different properties of oil compared to coal affected its democratic potential. The fluidity of oil and its relative ease of distribution presented those who controlled oil resources and their distribution networks with a new problem. In both the coal and the oil industries, producers always sought to avoid competition. Competing with rival firms over prices or market share destroyed profits and threatened a company with ruin. In the case of coal, the high cost of transporting supplies across oceans ensured that producers faced competition only within their own region. They avoided competition either by forming cartels, as in France, Germany and the United States, or by creating organisations to regulate prices and production, such as the postwar European Coal and Steel Community. In Britain, producers were ruined by competition, and in 1946 were taken over by the state.

Oil companies faced a much larger difficulty in avoiding competition. With the advent of the bulk oil tanker in the 1890s, it was no longer enough to control production and distribution in only one region. Since oil could travel easily between continents, petroleum companies were always vulnerable to the arrival of cheaper oil from elsewhere. This vulnerability, seldom recognised in accounts of the oil industry, created another set of limits to the democratising potential of petroleum.

The solutions that oil companies developed to this problem might be called a method of sabotage. In the coal age, workers had discovered the power that could be built from the ability to interrupt, restrict or slow down the supply of energy. The challenge facing large oil companies was to do something similar: to introduce small delays, interruptions and controls that, by limiting the flow of energy, would enhance their control. Émile Pouget's pamphlet of 1909 on sabotage had concluded by suggesting that the capitalist class were perhaps the real saboteurs. A decade later, following the publication of an English translation of the pamphlet in Chicago, the American economist Thorstein Veblen developed this idea.[76] Large business corporations, Veblen wrote, depended for their profits on a form of sabotage. Their goal was not to maximise production, but to raise prices by restricting output to ensure a shortage. The 'pettifogging

---

76 Thorstein Veblen, *An Inquiry Into the Nature of Peace and the Terms of Its Perpetuation*, New York: Macmillan, 1917, rev. edn 1919: 167–74; *On the Nature and Uses of Sabotage*, New York: Oriole, 1919; and *The Industrial System and the Captains of Industry*, New York: Oriole, 1919. Veblen's argument has more recently been developed by Shimshon Bichler and Jonathan Nitzan, *The Global Political Economy of Israel*, London: Pluto Press, 2002.

tactics of Standard Oil', for example, demonstrated how profits far exceeding the earning capacity of invested assets flowed from the 'power of inhibition' exercised by large business.[77] This 'capitalisation of inefficiency' was especially profitable with a commodity such as oil, which was relatively cheap to produce but becoming so vital to industrialised society that great profits could be made if the supply was restricted. The goal of oil companies was to place themselves in control of the conduits, processing points and bottlenecks through which oil had to flow, to restrict the development of rival channels, beginning with oil wells themselves, and to use this command of obligatory passage points to convert the flow of oil into profits.

The two world wars of the twentieth century helped restrict the supply and movement of oil, but between the wars both domestic firms in the United States, where most world oil was then produced, and the handful of oil companies seeking to control international trade, needed a new set of mechanisms to limit the production and distribution of energy. The devices they developed included government quotas and price controls in the United States, cartel arrangements to govern the worldwide distribution and marketing of oil, consortium agreements to slow the development of new oil discoveries in the Middle East, and political agencies to manage the threat of those in the Middle East and elsewhere who opposed the oil companies' system of sabotage. These controls shaped the development of the transnational oil corporation, which emerged as the leading long-distance machinery for maintaining limits to the supply of oil. One could think of this development as the formation of what has been called a 'technological zone' – a set of coordinated but widely dispersed regulations, calculative arrangements, infrastructures and technical procedures that render certain objects or flows governable.[78]

The following chapters explore how this was done, beginning with the efforts in the early twentieth century to prevent and then constrain the production of oil in the Middle East, and the technical and political arrangements that made this possible. After the Second World War, as we will see, when significant quantities of oil began to flow from the Middle East (almost half a century after its discovery there), further devices were added to this machinery for the production of scarcity. While powers to limit the production of oil in the Middle East continued to develop, two further techniques emerged for transforming

---

77   Thorstein Veblen, 'On the Nature of Capital', *Quarterly Journal of Economics* 23: 1, 1908: 104–36.

78   Andrew Barry, 'Technological Zones', *European Journal of Social Theory* 9: 2, 2006: 239–53. Other raw materials presented similar problems of regulating global production to prevent competition. None of them, however, were as cheap to produce and transport as oil, or usable in such vast quantities, so they did not generate the same scale of need for techniques for the production of scarcity. On the constructing of political machines, see also Andrew Barry, *Political Machines: Governing a Technological Society*, London: Athlone Press, 2001.

carbon-energy abundance into a system of limited supplies. The first was the new apparatus of peacetime 'national security'.[79] The Second World War had given US oil companies the opportunity to reduce or shut down most of their production in the Middle East. In 1943, when Ibn Saud demanded funds to compensate for the loss of oil revenues, the oil companies persuaded Washington to extend Lend Lease loans to the Saudi Arabian monarch. These payments for *not* producing oil were presented as a necessity for America's national security. They marked the start of a postwar politics in which the collaboration of local governments in restricting the flow of oil, and US antagonism towards those who tried to increase its supply, was organised as though it were a system for 'protecting' a scarce resource against others.

The second method of preventing energy abundance involved the rapid construction of lifestyles in the United States organised around the consumption of extraordinary quantities of energy. In January 1948, James Forrestal, recently appointed as the country's first secretary of defense under the new National Security Act, discussed with Brewster Jennings, president of Socony-Vacuum (later renamed Mobil Oil, now ExxonMobil), how 'unless we had access to Middle East oil, American motorcar companies would have to design a four-cylinder motorcar sometime within the next five years'.[80] In the following years the US automobile companies helped out by replacing standard six-cylinder engines with the new V-8s as the dream of every middle-class family, doubling the average horsepower of American passenger car engines within less than a decade.[81] While Forrestal spoke, the Morris Motor Company in Britain was preparing to challenge the successful four-cylinder Volkswagen Beetle with the four-cylinder Morris Minor, Citroën to do the same with the two-cylinder

---

79   Critical accounts of US international oil policy tend to accept 'national security' as the concept with which to frame the history of oil, exposing its true meaning either in terms of the logic of capitalist expansion that confronts an inevitable scarcity of resources – as in Michael Klare, *Resource Wars: The New Landscape of Global Conflict*, New York: Henry Holt, 2001, and *Rising Powers, Shrinking Planet: The New Geopolitics of Energy*, New York: Metropolitan Books, 2008 – or in terms of the need for an imperial power to secure the conditions for capitalist expansion – as in Simon Bromley, *American Hegemony and World Oil*, University Park, PA: Pennsylvania State University Press, 1991, and 'The United States and the Control of World Oil', *Government and Opposition* 40: 2, 2005: 225–55. Explaining oil in terms of the logics of capitalist expansion leads such accounts to overlook the socio-technical work that must be done to turn the multiple struggles over oil into the singular narrative of the unfolding and stabilising of the logic of capital. On the ability of the US oil majors to frame their programme in terms of 'national security', and the reproduction of this perspective in scholarship, see Vitalis, *America's Kingdom*.

80   Forrestal, 'Diaries', vols 9–10. He made the same argument at a Cabinet meeting on 16 January 1948 (ibid., 2,026).

81   Tom McCarthy, *Auto Mania: Cars, Consumers, and the Environment*, New Haven: Yale University Press, 2007: 107–8. Paul Sabin's study of the California oil industry traces the building of the 'infrastructure of consumption' that produced the scarcity of oil (Paul Sabin, *Crude Politics: The California Oil Market, 1900–1940*, Berkeley: University of California Press, 2004). On the history of American attitudes towards energy, see David E. Nye, *Consuming Power: A Social History of American Energies*, Cambridge, MA: MIT Press, 1999.

2CV, and the German engine maker BMW with its first postwar passenger car, the one-cylinder Isetta 250. The European vehicles outsold and outlasted the badly engineered American cars, but the latter helped engineer something larger. They manufactured the carbon-heavy forms of middle-class American life that, combined with new political arrangements in the Middle East, would help the oil companies keep oil scarce enough to allow their profits to thrive.

The ability of organised workers to assemble a political machine out of the networks and nodal points of a coal-based energy system had shaped the kinds of mass politics that emerged, or threatened to emerge, in the first half of the twentieth century. The rise of oil reorganised fossil-fuel networks in ways that were to alter the mechanics of democracy. The possibilities for making democratic claims were altered in both the countries that depended on the production of petroleum and those that most depended on its use.

Much more could be said about the role of the major oil companies and car manufacturers in helping to produce and popularise ways of living based on very high levels of energy consumption. This is a question not of balancing the history of oil production and distribution with an analysis of its consumption, so much as understanding that production involved producing both energy and the forms of life that were increasingly dependent on that energy.

CHAPTER 2

The Prize from Fairyland

The story of oil in the Middle East usually begins in the wrong place: with the discovery of oil at Masjid-i-Suleiman in 1908. After seven years of unsuccessful exploration, lugging their heavy equipment on wagons and mules across harsh and inhospitable terrain, a small team of drillers working for a maverick British investor on the desert plateau of south-west Persia struck a large source of oil. The discovery led to the creation of one of the world's largest oil companies, later known as BP, and launched the development of a modern petroleum industry in the world's richest oil region. This tale of heroic explorers discovering unimagined wealth in a desolate territory overlooks the fact that oil was already known to exist in more convenient places in the Middle East, and that a principal reason for searching in the barren hills of Persia was not to launch the region's oil industry, but to delay its development.

The main feature of Middle Eastern oil throughout the twentieth century was that there was always too much of it. To be more precise, there was too much of it in too few locations. To have plentiful supplies of a source of energy is not necessarily a problem. Where there is abundant water, timber, solar energy or grassland, widely distributed across space, collective life can thrive. Those who harness and supply the energy can earn a living and perhaps a profit from doing so. With energy from fossil fuels, as we saw in the case of coal, the quantity of energy available can increase exponentially. For geological reasons, however, the sites at which these large volumes are available happen to be relatively few. This combination of extraordinary abundance and limited locations gave rise to the problem.

Firms that organised the supply of fossil fuels could frequently collaborate to restrict their availability. With coal, as we have seen, for several decades they were forced to share this ability to sabotage the flow of energy with those who mined and transported it, enabling coal workers and their allies to assemble an unusual political power. In the case of oil, the capacity to slow down or interrupt the supply of energy on a large scale was much harder to organise. Oil workers found it difficult to carry out a successful sabotage – a difficulty that would impede their efforts to build with oil an enduring mechanism for advancing democratic political claims.

The companies that managed the production and distribution of oil also faced greater challenges than coal companies in restricting the flow of energy. However, in the Middle East and other regions they could benefit from the relative dearth and isolation of sites initially known to produce oil, take advantage of the distance that separated these places from those countries (already industrialised with coal) where most of the oil was consumed, develop their own ability to act at both ends of that separation, maintain or block the conduits that connected the two ends, and do all this with the help of narrowly focused political and military support.

The oil companies were smaller and potentially weaker than the workforces whose labour they sought to control. But their power of action expanded along the network of drilling sites, pipelines, terminals, refineries, distribution points, boardrooms, investment houses and government offices that grew with the producing and marketing of oil. In the months that followed the discovery of oil at Masjid-i-Suleiman in 1908, for example, the fledgling British company – the future BP – was unloading steel pipe to build a pipeline from the oil field to the coast, planning a telephone line to follow the path of the pipeline, contracting with local tribesmen to guard the route, designating a firm of agents to handle the local storage and shipping of oil, drafting a prospectus in Britain to attract investment in the venture, and arguing unsuccessfully with the Admiralty that the prospectus be allowed to claim government support for an oil industry in Persia as a future source of fuel for the Royal Navy.[1] These narrow but well supervised networks of distribution, affiliation, assertion and control became far more extended than those of earlier forms of energy, even coal, reflecting the more fluid and transportable properties of oil and the much larger profits to be made from restricting its supply. Oil workers were not just more isolated and disconnected than coal workers had been; they were isolated at the ends of a much more extended network.

After assuming that the aim was to discover oil rather than delay its development – and thus beginning, for reasons I will outline, in the wrong place – the conventional story of Middle Eastern oil makes a second mistake: it misrepresents the protagonists. The main players in most accounts are the large oil companies and their governments, which in turn are often represented by a few heroic men, whose 'driving energy and enthusiasm' propel the struggle for what Daniel Yergin in his epic history of oil, quoting Winston Churchill, calls 'the prize': mastery over the world's petroleum.[2] This approach leaves out the role of those producing the oil, whose power must be weakened or diverted whenever it threatens access to the prize. It also minimises something else: the oil, whose energy is the force that oil firms seek to master and whose location, abundance, density and other properties shape the methods and apparatus of its control. This apparatus, composed of machinery, men and women, knowhow, finance and hydrocarbons, is what we refer to in shorthand as the 'oil firm'. It might help

---

1   Ronald W. Ferrier, *The History of the British Petroleum Company*, vol. 1: *The Developing Years: 1901–1932*, Cambridge, UK: CUP, 1982: 92–133.

2   Daniel Yergin, *The Prize: The Epic Quest for Oil, Money, and Power*, New York: Simon & Schuster, 1991: 12.

to think of the firm, in a technical sense, as a parasite: an entity that feeds off something larger, the flows of energy. If it thrives and becomes very large, as several oil firms did in the course of the twentieth century, the reasons may lie less in the enthusiasm and willpower of its leaders and more in the way it adapts to the processes off which it lives, and which it diverts to its own enlargement.[3] If the flows of energy appear blocked or dysfunctional, this may reflect more the ordinary methods of parasitism than an unresolved struggle for mastery.

A third misunderstanding finds its way into most accounts of oil in the Middle East. Petroleum companies were never strong enough to monopolise the flow or stoppage of oil by themselves. They needed outside help, both military and financial. To draw on the resources of well-armed states and government treasuries, Western oil companies began to describe their control of overseas oil as an 'imperial' interest of the state, or in later language as a 'strategic' interest, and thus somehow beneficial to the public well-being. Imperially minded political leaders often supported this view, for a variety of purposes, while others rejected it. Historians of oil usually echo the imperial account.

Such accounts jump from the fact that industrial societies (especially the United States) were developing ways of living that consumed ever-increasing amounts of energy to the conclusion that the control of oil by giant oil companies best served that way of life, even when the companies' paramount aim was to impede the flow of energy and increase its cost, and when various alternative methods of supplying oil, and of organising collective life, were possible. In the last third of the twentieth century, when the governments of the producer countries began to share control of the oil, a similar claim was made about the 'national' interest of those countries.

Rather than assume that the control of Middle Eastern oil was an imperial or strategic interest of Britain, Germany, the United States or other countries, or that it served the national interest of producer states, we will ask who mobilised these claims and for what purposes, and how they conflicted with other, sometimes more democratic claims to the control of oil, including the claims of those whose labour produced it. Those claims did not emerge until later, for oil company obstruction and other delays postponed the building of large oil industries in most of the Middle East. But from the start, for the imperial powers the access to Middle Eastern oil was connected with the threat of democracy.

A VERITABLE LAKE OF PETROLEUM

At the beginning of the twentieth century, hundreds of enterprises were involved in prospecting for, producing, shipping and distributing supplies of oil in different parts of the world. Among these, a handful of firms were devising methods

---

3   Michel Serres, *The Parasite*, Minneapolis: University of Minnesota Press, 2007.

for controlling the supply of oil over great distances. These enterprises took different forms, corresponding to different methods and points of control. Some were producers of oil, organised like mining companies with workers' camps and teams of engineers, and in many cases operating the new rotary drilling equipment that replaced the hammer-action of the older percussion drills and could penetrate thousands of feet below ground. Three such firms each came to dominate a distant region of supply – Royal Dutch in Sumatra, Burmah Oil in Rangoon, and the Nobel Brothers in Baku. Others were banking houses that controlled the flow of investment capital needed to build the railways and pipelines that could monopolise the shipping of oil, including Deutsche Bank in Berlin, Rothschild's in Paris and the Mellon family of Pittsburg, the founders of Gulf Oil. Another firm, the Shell Transportation Company, expanded in the 1890s by adopting and developing another means of transporting oil in bulk, the ocean-going tanker. The world's largest operator, the Rockefeller-controlled Standard Oil, began as a refinery business and built its domination of the American market by first monopolising the refining industry (with the help of faster refining techniques, using large quantities of steam power generated by fuel oil from the refinery), then controlling pipelines and shipping routes, and finally taking charge of distribution, replacing independent importers and wholesalers with Standard's own worldwide networks of storage tanks, horse-drawn delivery wagons and reusable tin cans.

Before the 1880s there had been only one significant oil-exporting region in the world, the Oil Lands of north-western Pennsylvania. By controlling the refineries, and later the pipelines, through which Pennsylvania's oil flowed, Standard Oil had been able to dominate sales of kerosene and other petroleum products across America and around the world. By the end of the nineteenth century, however, European firms had developed large commercial oil production at five locations outside North America: in Baku, Burma and Sumatra, and in two regions of Central Europe, Austrian Galicia and Romania. The development of technologies for transporting oil that took advantage of its liquid form and eliminated most manual labour from the movement of energy – steel pipelines, high-pressure steam pumps, bulk tankers and large storage tanks – rendered local monopolies in any world region vulnerable to supplies from each of these sites. After a series of unsuccessful efforts to absorb or destroy the main firms producing at these rival locations, Standard Oil came to terms with them. During the first decade of the twentieth century, the American firm and a few large European companies created arrangements to restrict the production of oil and control its worldwide marketing – and simultaneously to address the threat of oil from the Middle East.

Two alliances were formed, one to manage Asian trade and the other for Europe. In 1902, Royal Dutch joined forces with Shell and Rothschild, which had oil interests in Baku and Romania, to form an alliance that later became Royal Dutch/Shell. In 1905 the Shell group forced Burmah Oil, which supplied the vast Indian market, to agree to a division of Asian sales, an agreement to which Standard also adhered. The European markets were organised in a similar way. In 1906, Rothschild joined with the other large Caspian producer, Nobel, and with Deutsche Bank, its partner in Romania, to form the European Petroleum Union, a cartel to manage the western European kerosene and fuel-oil markets. The cartel then agreed with Standard Oil to divide up European sales, the US company accepting a limit of 80 per cent and the European side sharing the rest.[4]

At the same time, the large companies turned their attention to the Middle East. It was not enough to divide up the marketing of oil from the world's five or so existing oil regions. The firms continued to face the risk that a rival enterprise might develop a large new source of petroleum, menacing the world with additional supplies. The greatest danger lay in the Middle East, where oil companies knew of several potential sites. A related threat was that Russian producers at Baku on the Caspian Sea – the world's most prolific oil region at the start of the century, but also the one most isolated from large markets – would find an easier way to ship their oil abroad, in particular shortening the route to Asia by building a pipeline to the Persian Gulf (see map, pp. 116–7). To block these threats, the three largest European oil firms purchased rights to explore for oil in the Middle East: Deutsche Bank in 1904 in northern Iraq (at that time, the Ottoman provinces of Mosul and Baghdad, part of what Europeans called Mesopotamia), Burmah Oil the following year in Persia (or Iran, as it would be known after 1935), and the Shell group in 1908–10 in Egypt.

Oil politics proceeded in a peculiar way. Since the object of the largest companies was more often to delay the development of new oil regions, they had to take control of key sites. It was not always necessary to control the oilfields themselves. The companies had learned from Standard Oil that it was easier to control the means of transportation. Building railways and pipelines required negotiating rights from the government, which typically granted the further right to prevent the establishing of competing lines. After obtaining the rights, the aim was usually to delay construction, but without losing the right. Iraq became the key place to sabotage the production of oil. It would retain that role through much of the twentieth century, and reacquire it in a different way in the twenty-first century. The story of Iraq illustrates how this process began.

Of the three sites in the Middle East, Iraq was the most promising and accessible. Local producers around Mosul had mined oil from hand-dug pits for centuries, refining it in local stills and supplying the lamp oil market of

4 Gregory Nowell, *Mercantile States and the World Oil Cartel, 1900–1939*, Ithaca, NY: Cornell University Press, 1994: 56–61; Robert W. Tolf, *The Russian Rockefellers: The Saga of the Nobel Family and the Russian Oil Industry*, Stanford, CA: Hoover Institution Press, 1976: 183–90; Yergin, *The Prize*: 121–33.

Baghdad. Around 1870 the governor of Baghdad had built a larger refinery north of the city, at Baquba. In 1888 the Ottoman sultan took over the rights to the oil as a monopoly of the imperial court, and three years later asked Calouste Gulbenkian, a young Armenian petroleum engineer whose father had developed a business importing kerosene from Baku, to prepare a report on the Mosul oilfields.[5] Thanks to the availability of previous surveys of the region's potential oil sites, Gulbenkian was able to submit the report without himself visiting the area. (He later built one of the world's largest personal fortunes through the rights he negotiated to the oil of Iraq, without ever setting foot in the country.[6]) A British geological survey of 1899 confirmed the area's potential as a petroleum region, noting that where the Tigris River cut through the low limestone hills, the cliffs 'exude long threads' of crude oil 'which pollute the river for nearly 3 miles'. Remarking on the accessibility of the region, the report noted that 'the oil could be at once shipped into light steamers and barges' down the Tigris, which 'offers a natural outlet towards the Persian gulf'.[7] That year, the Ottoman government proposed to manufacture a second outlet for the oil, by offering for sale a concession to build a railway connecting Mesopotamia to Europe. The leading German oil firm, Deutsche Bank, began to negotiate for the concession. After a German technical commission of 1901 described Mosul as 'a veritable "lake of petroleum" of almost inexhaustible supply', Deutsche Bank moved ahead with plans to ensure that oil from this 'lake' was unable to reach European markets, where it would threaten the large investments it was making in Romanian oil. In 1903 it purchased the rail concession, and the following year an exclusive right to the oil of Mosul and the neighbouring province of Baghdad. The bank then stalled on building the railway, and made little effort to develop the oil.[8]

The petroleum fields of Egypt occupied an even more accessible location, on the coast of the Red Sea near the entrance to the Gulf of Suez. 'A very large proportion of the shipping of the world passes within two miles of our wells, which are situated within a few hundred yards of deep water', reported the Shell group's geologist after the company bought up shares in the fields. The existence of oil deposits had been known for thirty years, but French opposition to British control of Egypt helped prevent their development before 1904, when the two governments settled their dispute over Egyptian state revenues. A Department of Mines was set up that year to auction exploration rights, which speculators

5   Stephen Hemsley Longrigg, *Oil in the Middle East*, London: OUP, 1968, 13–14.

6   Ralph Hewins, *Mr Five Per Cent: The Story of Calouste Gulbenkian*, New York: Rinehart, 1958: 30.

7   F. R. Maunsell, 'The Mesopotamian Petroleum Field', *Geographical Journal* 9: 5, May 1897: 530, 532.

8   Edward Mead Earle, *Turkey, the Great Powers, and the Bagdad Railway: A Study in Imperialism*, New York: Macmillan, 1923: 15; Dietrich Eichholtz, *Die Bagdadbahn: Mesopotamien und die deutsche Ölpolitik bis 1918*, Leipzig: Leipziger Universitätsverlag, 2007: 32.

quickly bought up. The largest investor was the English financier Ernest Cassel, who had built a fortune managing the supply of capital for the construction of the Aswan Dam in Egypt and speculating in the agricultural land watered by the scheme, and now hoped to make another fortune buying up and selling investment rights in oil. Cassel's local investment firm, the National Bank of Egypt, set up the Eastern and African Concessions Syndicate to hold its oil leases. The aim was to monopolise the oil rights not just for Egypt but for the entire Ottoman Empire.[9]

Like Deutsche Bank in Turkey, Shell had no strong interest in developing the Egyptian oilfields. It invested in Cassel's syndicate in Egypt as a way to join his scheme to control oil rights to the entire region – a scheme that focused, the company noted, on 'the great economic and political struggle for the oilfields of Mesopotamia.'[10] The British administration in Cairo accused Shell of trying to restrict the development of Egypt's oilfields: 'Your company, in its natural desire to establish a virtual monopoly', wrote Edward Cecil, Britain's senior financial official in Cairo, 'is anxious to control large areas of undeveloped land, and possibly to restrict temporarily the production of petroleum.'[11] When Shell objected to the government's proposed solution – to enforce 'continuous working clauses' in its leases and encourage rival companies to work the oilfields – the British administration responded with a remedy that Britain would later oppose throughout the Middle East: in 1913, it nationalised Shell's subsidiary company in Egypt.[12]

THE PROTECTION OF INDIAN INVESTMENTS

Despite their accessibility, neither the banks of the Tigris nor the shores of the Red Sea provided the site for the first large oilfield in the Middle East. In 1905, Burmah Oil took over the monopoly rights that another British speculator had acquired to search for oil in Persia. As in Egypt and Ottoman Iraq, however, Burmah's aim in rescuing this failing venture was not to open up the production of Middle Eastern oil.

Persia lay between the world's most productive oilfields of that period, at Baku on the Caspian Sea, and Burmah Oil's protected markets in India. The two large oil producers in the Caspian region, Rothschild and Nobel, had made plans to construct a pipeline running south from Baku to the Persian Gulf, but

---

9   Frederik Carel Gerretson, *The History of Royal Dutch*, vol. 3, Leiden: E. J. Brill, 1953–57: 240–1; Colonel John Ardagh, 'The Red Sea Petroleum Deposits', *Proceedings of the Royal Geographical Society and Monthly Record of Geography* 8: 8, 1886, 502–7.

10   Gerretson, *History*: 242.

11   Letter from E. H. Cecil to Waley Cohen, December 1912, in Geoffrey Jones, *The State and the Emergence of the British Oil Industry*, London: Macmillan, 1981: 118.

12   Jones, *Emergence*: 120–1.

put them aside in favour of the shorter line westward to Batumi on the Black Sea (see Chapter 1). In 1901, the price of Caspian oil collapsed. Since Baku's isolation from major markets was a main cause of the collapse, the Russian government revived the plan for a trans-Persian pipeline, with the support of Rothschild and Nobel. The oil rights that the British speculator, William Knox D'Arcy, purchased that year from the Shah of Persia included an agreement that, so long as he proceeded with exploration, the government would allow no other company to build a pipeline to carry oil to the country's southern shore. The power to block the construction of a Russian pipeline to the Persian Gulf helped keep D'Arcy's speculative venture afloat.[13]

D'Arcy seemed to share the belief that Persia was a less promising location than Mesopotamia. After securing the Persian concession, he began competing with Deutsche Bank to obtain the Mesopotamian rights from Turkey. The drilling team he sent to the region in 1901 chose as its first exploration site a place called Chiah Surkh, near Kasr-i Shirin, which lay not on the desert plateau of southern Persia, in fact barely in Persia at all, but on the border of Mesopotamia, about fifty miles north-east of Baghdad and closer to the Caspian than the Gulf, in an area that a frontier adjustment of 1914 would transfer to the future state of Iraq. The site offered a foothold in Mesopotamia, along with a more immediate advantage. The Baku oil firms might have bypassed D'Arcy's monopoly of pipelines to the southern shore of Persia by using a route that crossed into Iraq at Khanaqin, on the main Tehran–Baghdad road, reaching the Gulf via southern Iraq. Kasr-i-Shirin lay on the same route (see map opposite), a few miles up the road from Khanaqin. By drilling there rather than in southern Persia, D'Arcy blocked the potential bypass route for a pipeline from Baku, securing his ability to obstruct any increase in Caspian exports to India.

After two years of drilling the team struck oil, but the twenty-five barrels a day that trickled from the well were not enough to interest the large oil companies to whom D'Arcy had hoped to sell his venture. Instead he agreed to share his rights in Persia with Burmah Oil, which suspended operations at the site near Baghdad and moved the drillers and their equipment hundreds of miles to the south-east, up the valley of the Karun River into the mountains of Khuzestan.[14]

---

13 A. A. Fursenko, *The Battle For Oil*, Greenwich, CT: Jai Press, 1990: 130–3; Ferrier, *History*, vol. 1: 43–4; Nowell, *Mercantile States*.

14 Masjid-i-Suleiman was not as remote as heroic histories of the petroleum industry suggest. It lay in the valley of the Karun, the largest river in southern Iran, and the country's only navigable waterway. A British company, Lynch Brothers, ran a steamship on the river, monopolising the route from the Gulf to Isfahan. The problem for a prospective oil industry, however, was that the river's winding course took 500 miles to traverse the 150 miles to the sea, and steam ships could not cross the rapids below Ahwaz, so cargoes (including oil before the completion of the Anglo-Persian pipeline) had to be unloaded and carried past the rapids on a small railway (built in 1891), and then reshipped. M. Th. Houtsma, A. J. Wensinck and T. W. Arnold, eds, *The Encyclopaedia of Islam*, 1st edn, vol. 2, Leiden: E.J. Brill, 1913–36: 779–80.

THE PETROLEUM DEPOSITS OF MESOPOTAMIA.

A SECOND BAKU IN THE MAKING.

ACCORDING to all indications, the near future will witness the opening of the extensive oilfields of Mesopotamia, which have been mentioned in Babylonian railway, at last be opened for widespread use and international trade. The rôle to be played by Mesopotamian oil in the world's market may be of great

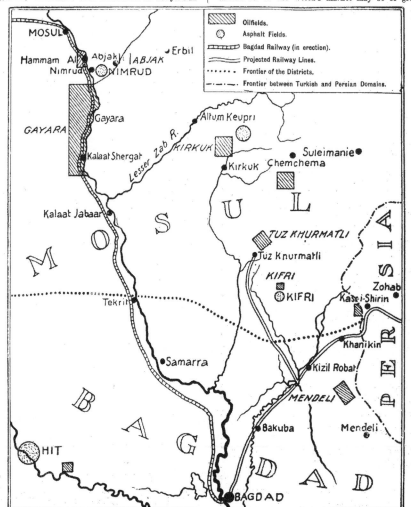

scriptures as well as in the Bible, and which in the form of asphalt contributed to the erection of the magnificent buildings of Babylon and Assyria.

The rich oil treasures of Mesopotamia will, with the aid of modern technical science and the new Bagdad magnitude and importance. The subject is also of political importance, as it is of great interest both to Germany and England, and if only the German bank which participates in the erection of the Bagdad railway line obtains concessions, the influence of Germany

The oilfields and railways of Mesopotamia mapped in the journal *Petroleum Review*, 23 May 1914

D'Arcy was able to find an investment partner thanks in part to the support of a group of largely Indian-based British imperialists, who were attempting to expand the reach of Britain's Indian empire by establishing greater control over local potentates of the Persian Gulf, and by encouraging local British monopolies in trade, steam navigation, and other enterprises. Led by Lord Curzon, the new Indian viceroy, they popularised the idea that Britain was engaged in an imperial struggle with Russia in which Persia and the Gulf formed a vital frontier. In his book *Persia and the Persian Question*, Curzon had warned repeatedly about the dangers of allowing Russia to build a railway to the Persian Gulf, and on taking office he had signed a protection agreement with the ruler of Kuwait to prevent the building there of a Russian pipeline or railway terminus. In an effort to portray Russia as a military threat rather than a commercial rival, Curzon failed to mention that a principal purpose of such a railway or pipeline would be to export oil from Baku. This omission was not due to ignorance. Before his appointment to India, while serving as a member of parliament, Curzon had travelled to the Caucasus and Persia, and after witnessing the oil boom in Baku in 1890 he became a shareholder and director of the Persian Bank Mining Rights Corporation, which spent three years trying to develop oil production in Persia a decade before D'Arcy's efforts.[15] When the D'Arcy initiative discovered oil, Curzon's colleague Lord Kitchener, commander-in-chief of the Indian army and another proponent of India's imperial expansion, had a telegram sent to the head of the Indian military detachment guarding D'Arcy's site enquiring whether the reports of the discovery were true, in order to decide whether to buy shares in the venture.[16]

Later historians like to repeat the views of men like Curzon and Kitchener, describing the events of this period as the unfolding of the 'Great Game' – a long struggle on the imperial border between the British and Russian empires. Although Kipling used the phrase 'Great Game' in *Kim*, his 1901 tale of espionage adventures on India's north-west frontier, he employed it to refer to the game of life, not to Anglo-Russian rivalry. The term was not used in diplomatic documents or public discussion, and only became popular among historians much later, in the Cold War era.[17] This later creation of scares about Soviet expansion connected with an American attempt to challenge British control of Iranian oil, first established by D'Arcy (see Chapter 5), depended on attributing to the Russians a centuries-long interest in expanding to the Gulf, for which the anachronistic phrase 'Great Game' provided a convenient shorthand.

---

15   David Gilmour, *Curzon: Imperial Statesman*, New York: Farrar, Straus, & Giroux, 2003: 76.

16   William Strunk, 'The Reign of Shaykh Khaz'al Ibn Jabir and the Suppression of the Principality of Arabistan', PhD thesis, Department of History, Indiana University, 1977: 152.

17   M. E. Yapp, 'The Legend of the Great Game', Proceedings of the British Academy, 2001, vol 111.

In the early twentieth century, many political figures in Britain disagreed with the view of the Indian imperialists about Russia, arguing that both sides, British and Russian, might gain from improved trade between the Caucasus and India.[18] This was particularly true since the largest Russian oil exporters were foreign, and included strong British interests. In 1901, 30 per cent of capital invested in Baku oil came from abroad, and over two-thirds of that was British.[19] With the pipeline to the Gulf blocked by the D'Arcy oil concession, the Baku oil industrialists tried an alternative project – a rail line from the Caspian to Karachi, which British and French financiers supported but the imperialists governing India again obstructed.[20] (Others could have benefited from increased Russian supplies to India, as a railway might have carried sugar and grain as well as kerosene. Food supplies would have alleviated the deadly famines that British commercial policy helped inflict on India, and that Curzon's cost-cutting imperial management exacerbated, including the mass starvation of 1899–1902 that took between 5 and 10 million lives.[21]) For Britain's Indian imperialists, expanding India's commercial and political empire into the Gulf required the blocking of Russian commercial expansion. A speculative investment in Persian oil, even one that failed, was a useful means to these ends. They helped arrange for Burmah Oil to invest in D'Arcy's scheme and keep alive his monopoly rights both to Persian oil and to the building of a trans-Persian pipeline.

For Burmah Oil, the D'Arcy project looked particularly useful. Under great pressure from Shell, whose oil exports from Baku were eroding its protected sales in India, Burmah was about to acquiesce to the 1905 agreement with Shell's Asiatic group, limiting its share of the Indian market. In deciding to take over D'Arcy's failing venture, Burmah wanted to keep the concession afloat as a means to prevent others from producing oil in the Middle East, or pumping it there from the Caucasus, which would only add to its problems in India. After further exploration failures, the firm cut back its Persian commitments to a minimum, 'to maintain a covering interest and no more'.[22] As the company later acknowledged, 'it was primarily the protection of its Indian investments that took the Burmah Oil Company into Persia'.[23]

---

18   Briton Cooper Busch, *Britain and the Persian Gulf, 1894–1913*, Berkeley: University of California Press, 1967.

19   Jones, *Emergence*, 56.

20   D. W. Spring, 'The Trans-Persian Railway Project', *Slavonic and East European Review* 54: 1, 1976: 60–82.

21   Mike Davis, *Late Victorian Holocausts: El Niño Famines and the Making of the Third World*, London: Verso, 2001: 158–78.

22   Ferrier, *History*: 43–4.

23   Cited in Ferrier, *History*: 69. Ferrier interprets 'the protection of its Indian investments' to mean insuring against exploration failure in Burma. As Nowell points out in *Mercantile States*, he fails to mention the Baku pipeline, despite previously discussing it in detail.

Burmah's partner in Persia, the D'Arcy enterprise, remained committed to finding oil and recovering its investment. In May 1908, despite orders from Burmah to begin winding down its drilling operations, the exploration party discovered the large field at Masjid-i-Suleiman. Perhaps worried by the great size of the discovery, Burmah still tried to go slow, recalling the head of the drilling team to Britain and then demanding that he drill further exploratory wells before starting production. 'For why I do not know', complained D'Arcy, 'as if they all failed, it could not affect existing facts. I suppose when they have made Musjid [sic] like the top of a Pepper Pot they will be happy.'[24] Burmah took a year to incorporate the Anglo-Persian Oil Company, the firm later known as BP, which acquired D'Arcy's concession rights in exchange for shares in Burmah. With little interest in developing its new source of supply, the company took another three years to lay an eight-inch pipeline to carry the oil 140 miles to the shoreline, on the border of Iraq at Abadan, and to build there a set of rudimentary stills with which to refine it.

We have now assembled an alternative account of the beginnings of the modern oil industry in the Middle East. The story begins not with heroic prospectors in the barren hills of Persia, but with rival firms and their allies attempting to win 'the great economic and political struggle' for the oil of Mesopotamia. The goal of the large firms was not to develop important new sources of oil, but to delay their development; for some it was also to obstruct the export of oil from the large Russian fields at Baku. To achieve these goals, the oil companies were learning to portray their needs as furthering the imperial interests of the state, and thus contributing to the well-being of the nation.

A SCHEME TO KEEP PRODUCT OUT OF THE MARKET

As soon as it discovered oil, the much-delayed venture in Persia encountered two further problems. First, Anglo-Persian faced a 'flank attack' from rival companies attempting to destroy it (or so the company claimed) by opening up a competing production site nearby.[25] Deutsche Bank had decided to develop its oil concession in Mesopotamia, in collaboration with Shell.

The events that followed are often told as the story of the Baghdad Railway – the final episode in the imperial rivalry among European powers that is said to have triggered the First World War. While financiers, contractors, shippers, and cotton and grain merchants were all initially interested in a plan for a rail line that would connect Mesopotamia and the Persian Gulf to Europe, most

---

24   Ferrier, *History*: 92.

25   Marian Kent, 'The Purchase of the British Government's Shares in the British Petroleum Company, 1912–1914', in, *Moguls and Mandarins: Oil, Imperialism, and the Middle East in British Foreign Policy, 1900–1940*, London: Frank Cass, 1993: 36.

accounts never mention that Deutsche Bank eventually built the railway to serve primarily as a pipeline on wheels.

The Ottoman government had other goals for the railway. It saw it partly as a means for the easier movement of troops. By settling refugees from military defeats in other parts of the empire along the route, it also hoped to use the railway to increase the production of grain – its primary source of revenue, an income disrupted since the 1870s by the arrival of cheap grain from America. The first section of the route, known as the Anatolian Railway, connecting Istanbul with central Anatolia, had been built in the 1890s. The line failed to make a profit, but subsidies from the Ottoman government, costing more than the total agricultural tax revenue of the region the railway served, guaranteed Deutsche Bank and other bond-holders a return on their investment.[26] For the German bank and its allies, however, financing the remainder of the route to Baghdad was impossible until they linked it with the production of oil in Mesopotamia. Since initially they had no interest in developing a new source of oil, they used the exclusive railway and petroleum concessions to prevent others from developing it. Only when Anglo-Persian found oil across the border in Persia did the project move ahead, in tandem with a plan to create a new way to sell the unwanted oil in Europe. At that point the British firm tried to block the scheme. Not realising that extending the line to Baghdad was primarily an oil project, and that large oil firms were often interested less in producing oil than in sabotaging its production, scholars have found it hard to follow the story of the Baghdad Railway – or the reasons for the blockages, delays and collaborations that were somehow to be blamed for the outbreak of the Great War.

As in Persia, the initial goal in acquiring exclusive rights to Mesopotamian oil and the means of transporting it to Europe was to block the production of oil. After obtaining the oil concession in July 1904, the Germans stalled on building the railway and on drilling for oil. The 'dilatory handling of the whole affair', Deutsche Bank acknowledged twenty years later, 'was carried out for tactical reasons'.[27] By March 1907, the Ottoman government was contesting the oil contract on the grounds that Deutsche Bank 'had not fulfilled certain

---

26 Donald Quataert, 'Limited Revolution: The Impact of the Anatolian Railway on Turkish Transportation and the Provisioning of Istanbul, 1890–1908', *Business History Review* 51: 2, 1977: 139–60, and *Workers, Peasants and Economic Change in the Ottoman Empire: 1730–1914*, Istanbul: Isis Press, 1993. On wheeled pipelines, and a later effort to exploit the oil of Mosul, see Fırat Bozçalı, 'The Oil Pipeline on Wheels', MA thesis, Center for Near Eastern Studies, New York University, 2009. My account of the Baghdad Railway draws on Sam Rubin, 'Iron and Steel, Oil and Grain: The Baghdad Railway and the Worlds it Built', MA thesis, Department of Middle Eastern, South Asian and African Studies, Columbia University, 2011.

27 Eichholtz, *Die Bagdadbahn*: 32. Marian Kent suggests that the delay in developing the oil was due to the weakness of Deutsche Bank's claims to the oilfields. But the claim was weakened only after the Young Turk Revolution, so this does not explain the delay from 1904 to 1908. *Oil and Empire: British Policy and Mesopotamian Oil, 1900–1920*, London: Macmillan, 1976: 24.

of its provisions, notably with respect to test borings'.[28] The following year, however, the Young Turk Revolution brought to power a government initially more disposed towards Britain, at the same time as the British venture found oil in Persia.

The Germans quickly resumed construction of the railway. To put themselves in a position to threaten the new Anglo-Persian production, they began looking for somewhere to sell the anticipated supplies of unwanted oil, the income from which would help finance the railway. The solution was a plan to break the hold of Standard Oil over the supply of kerosene in Europe. The European Petroleum Union of 1906 had secured one-fifth of the market for European companies. To attack Standard's remaining share, Deutsche Bank in Germany and allied oil interests in France organised domestic legislation in the two countries to create government-regulated monopolies of the lamp oil market.[29]

Meanwhile Deutsche Bank itself suffered a flank attack, which it attributed to Standard Oil. An American syndicate calling itself the Ottoman-American Development Company negotiated a preliminary concession to build a rival railway, a more ambitious line 2,000 kilometres in length, running from the Mediterranean coast of northern Syria through Aleppo and Sivas to Mosul, and on to the Persian frontier at Khanaqin – where Anglo-Persian had been drilling – with rights to any mineral resources found within forty kilometres of the track. A Berlin newspaper reported that the head of the syndicate, a retired US admiral named Colby M. Chester, was 'a straw man of the Standard Oil Company', while Deutsche Bank warned that the concession was not a plan 'for bona fide railroad development but a scheme for controlling certain undeveloped oil fields in order to keep their product out of the market' – a tactic that the bank would have little difficulty in recognising.[30]

The Rockefeller group's involvement remained a rumour, although we know that John Worthington, the head geologist and oil scout for Standard Oil, visited the Middle East in 1910 and reported favourably to the company concerning the oil prospects of Mesopotamia. Given the extraordinary efforts of Standard Oil to prevent the development of rival oilfields in every corner of the world at that time, its absence from the battle over Mesopotamian oil would be surprising. American officials were puzzled that the Colby syndicate would put down a large deposit on such an ambitious scheme without undertaking any prelimi-

28   'Consul General at Berlin (Coffin) to Secretary of State', 4 August 1920, US Department of State, *Papers Relating to the Foreign Relations of the United States 1920*, Washington, DC: US Government Printing Office, 1948–, 2: 660. Referred to in the following notes as FRUS 1920.

29   Nowell, *Mercantile States*: 61–76, uncovers the details of the lamp oil monopoly and its relationship to the Mesopotamian oil concession.

30   John A. DeNovo, 'A Railroad for Turkey: The Chester Project, 1908–1913', *Business History Review* 33: 3, 1959: 313.

nary surveys. The US State Department sent a diplomat from Washington to meet with Chester's son, the syndicate's representative in Istanbul, to explore supporting the concession as an instrument for expanding American trade in the Ottoman Empire. Unaware that the concession agreement might be intended not for an expansion of trade but its decrease, the diplomat was astonished to discover that, on the day he arrived in Istanbul to meet him, the son had left the country for Vienna. The Germans used their influence with Ottoman officials to have final approval for the American concession denied.[31]

In the meantime, a consortium of British financiers close to the new government in Istanbul created a London-based joint-stock company called the Turkish Petroleum Company. The group was led by Ernest Cassel, whose plans to organise a monopoly of all the region's oil rights, starting from Egypt, we have already encountered. In 1912 Cassel's group arranged for Deutsche Bank, which still held the rights to the Mesopotamian oil, and its European ally Shell, which included the oil interests of the French Rothschilds, each to take a nominal 25 per cent share in the oil company. The financiers, who called their investment firm the National Bank of Turkey, and gave several prominent members of the new Turkish government seats on its board, retained the other half of the company.[32]

The oil and railway scheme could now threaten the Anglo-Persian Oil Company. The latter's control of the Persian oilfields, intended to block rival firms from threatening the large Indian market of its parent company, Burmah Oil, would be circumvented by the development of Mesopotamian oil. Unable to defeat the flank attack, Anglo-Persian's alternative was to join it. For this it needed the help of the British government, which could use the Ottoman Public Debt Administration (the consortium of foreign creditors created after the state bankruptcy of 1875) to veto the increase in customs duties with which Turkey would service the loans needed for the railway. Anglo-Persian warned the government that if the Shell group – a rival in seeking Admiralty contracts for fuel oil – obtained control of Mesopotamian oil, it would lower prices to drive Anglo-Persian out of business, or into a merger with Shell, and then raise prices and 'open up this potentially vast source of supply only gradually'. A

---

31   DeNovo, 'Railroad for Turkey': 318. On John Worthington, see Edgar Wesley Owen, *Trek of the Oil Finders: A History of Exploration for Petroleum*, Tulsa, OK: American Association of Petroleum Geologists, 1975: 1,282.

32   Gerretson, *History*: 243–48; Marian Kent, 'Agent of Empire? The National Bank of Turkey and British Foreign Policy', *Historical Journal* 18: 2, 1975: 367–89, and *Oil and Empire*. The Ottoman government might have preferred to cancel the original oil concession, but negotiating a new concession would have allowed Standard Oil or Russian oil interests to press their demands for oil and railway deals. It would also have triggered provisions of the Turkish mining law that required test drillings to determine the value of a new concession before negotiating its terms – a delay the government would have been anxious to avoid. 'Consul General at Berlin (Coffin) to Secretary of State', 4 August 1920, FRUS 1920, 2: 661.

Foreign Office official objected to 'the attitude of Anglo-Persian, who have hitherto posed as being ultra-imperialist', but were now threatening to sell out to Shell if the government did not help them out.[33] Supporters of Anglo-Persian in the Foreign Office, persuaded by this argument, forced Cassel's British investment consortium to transfer to them their 50 per cent share in the venture.

To protect Anglo-Persian more fully, Britain also negotiated an agreement with the German and Turkish governments that the railway would stop short of the Persian Gulf, at Basra, and secured a monopoly on river transportation from Basra to the Gulf for the shipping interests of the India shipping magnate James Mackay, Lord Inchcape. The British government portrayed this monopoly, and the long delays caused in obtaining it, as essential to keeping imperial communications in British hands. However, a British company, Lynch Brothers, already controlled steam navigation from Baghdad to the Gulf. *The Times* in London had dismissed the pretence of entrepreneurs and imperialists that the Baghdad Railway threatened to become 'a high road to India', and it was widely understood that Britain's communications and trade with India would continue to use maritime rather than overland routes. The advantage of forcing Lynch to cede its shipping monopoly to Inchcape was that Inchcape was also a director of Anglo-Persian.[34] The arrangement protected not the flow of Britain's imperial trade towards the Persian Gulf and India, but a point of blockage. Through Inchcape, Anglo-Persian retained the power to prevent Mesopotamian oil from reaching the protected markets of Asia.

In the summer of 1914, at the same time as the kerosene monopolies were being finalised in Germany and France, the Turkish Petroleum Company agreement was signed in London, and the Ottoman government agreed to lease to the new company all 'petroleum resources discovered, and to be discovered' in the provinces of Mosul and Baghdad.[35] On the eve of the Great War, the world's four largest petroleum companies after Standard Oil – German, French, Anglo-Dutch and British – had agreed to share the rights to the oil of Mesopotamia.

The outbreak of the war postponed any development of the concession. This was hardly a problem. Limiting the production of oil was a central purpose for agreeing to share it. The final paragraph of the 1914 agreement was a famous 'self-denying clause', under which Europe's principal oil companies promised not to undertake oil production anywhere in the Ottoman Empire (except Egypt

33   Marian Jack, 'The Purchase of British Government's Shares in the British Petroleum Company, 1912–1914', *Past and Present* 39: 1, 1968: 142, 147.

34   Earle, *Turkey, the Great Powers, and the Bagdad Railway*: 255–63; Stuart A. Cohen, *British Policy in Mesopotamia, 1903–1914*, Reading: Ithaca Press, 2008: 198.

35   'Turkish Grand Vizier (Said Halim) to German Ambassador in Turkey (Wangheim), Constantinople', June 28, 1914, FRUS 1920, 2: 662.

and Kuwait, which together with southern Persia were already under British control), unless jointly through the Turkish Petroleum Company.[36]

FAIRYLAND

While dealing with the flank attack in Mesopotamia, the Anglo-Persian Oil Company had encountered a second difficulty: no one would buy its oil. The Persian crude was found to contain high levels of sulphur, whose smell, along with the film it produced on glass when burned, made the oil unsuitable for use as kerosene for illumination. There was no market for the company's product, and with no dividend in sight investors were unwilling to provide the funds to complete the production facilities. The only hope for Persian oil was to sell it not as an illuminant but as fuel oil for steam or diesel engines. Since there were few oil-powered engines in use anywhere near southern Persia, the company faced bankruptcy.

The solution to this difficulty was for D'Arcy and Burmah Oil to translate their weaknesses and needs into an imperial interest. This was a tactic the company used at every opportunity. The government of India had been paying for a detachment of soldiers to guard the company's oil drillers. After the discovery of oil, the British minister in Tehran, Arthur Hardinge, suggested that the company should assume the cost of the guard, or replace it with a cheaper local force. In rejecting the suggestion, D'Arcy replied that he and his partners

> are endeavouring to develop and have already met with marked success in laying the foundations of this new industry, an industry to be worked entirely by British initiative, in British hands, and by British capital, and one which we have every reason to believe should be looked upon with favour, if not indulgence by the British Government, since it may in the near future become a source of valuable oil for our navy.

Anglo-Persian tried the same tactic to cope with the larger problem of creating a market for its products. It appealed again to the British government, asking it to create a demand for its oil by purchasing two long-term contracts for fuel oil, one for the Indian Railways and the other for the Royal Navy. Both the India Office and the Admiralty rejected the proposal. The Indian railways ran on coal, of which India had plenty. The Admiralty, on the other hand, had already converted most of its fleet to run at least partially on oil, and was now considering whether to build ships that could run on oil alone. There were

---

36   The text of the agreement over the TPC is published as an appendix to Edward Mead Earle, 'The Turkish Petroleum Company: A Study in Oleaginous Diplomacy', *Political Science Quarterly* 39: 2, 1924: 277–9.

many other sources of oil available, however, including the Egyptian wells on the Gulf of Suez that lay directly on one of the world's main shipping lanes, were already under British control, produced 100,000 tons of oil in 1914 and went on to produce millions more; and Mexico, where in 1910 a British company discovered the largest oilfields in the world at that time.[37] Despite the rejection from the Admiralty, in the prospectus that Anglo-Persian drafted to launch its shares on the stock market the company claimed that it already had Admiralty support. When the Admiralty found out, it blocked the document's publication. Anxious to attract investment in the share offering, the company still alluded in its prospectus to the alleged military significance of its oil for fuelling the Royal Navy. A few years later, the Admiralty changed its mind.

Starting with Winston Churchill's account in *The World Crisis*, published in 1923, historians have echoed the company's claim in its prospectus, playing up the importance of Anglo-Persian to Britain's imperial interests to explain the Admiralty's change of mind. 'Fortune', wrote Churchill, discussing the outcome of the company's appeal for help, 'brought us a prize from fairyland beyond our brightest hopes.' Appointed first lord of the Admiralty following the Moroccan Crisis of 1911, Churchill was fighting for an unprecedented increase in the cost and destructive power of the Royal Navy – an expansion that helped drive Europe three years later into an unexpected and disastrous war. The main expense was a fleet of fast battleships equipped with steam turbines (high-speed engines developed to drive the new electric generators and then adapted for marine use) and powered by fuel oil instead of coal. These in turn required the construction of large oil depots in Britain to store sufficient reserves of fuel to fight a six-month war, a fleet of tankers to import the fuel reserve, and the purchase of the oil supplies, which, as Churchill explained, were 'in the hands of vast oil trusts under foreign control'.[38] The trusts in question were Standard Oil, based in the country that was Britain's securest ally, and the Anglo-Dutch Shell group, so the real problem was less their foreign ownership than their monopoly power. In converting the navy to oil, the Admiralty was making itself vulnerable to the growing power of the oil monopolies.

The Admiralty was also vulnerable to another new power. In 1903, in response to the rising force of the labour movement, the British government had introduced a system of state pensions, followed in 1908–12 by national unemployment and disability insurance, healthcare programmes and other improvements to collective welfare. To pay for these measures, parliament had initially cut back the Naval Estimates – the annual budget of the largest of the

---

37   Jones, *Emergence*: 68, 85.

38   Winston Churchill, *The World Crisis, 1911–1918*, abridged and revised, ed. Martin Gilbert, London: Penguin, 2007: 75–6.

armed forces – placing them under closer scrutiny and rules of accounting. It then raised taxes on the rich, who provoked a constitutional crisis by making an unsuccessful attempt to use the House of Lords to block the increase. The Admiralty's costly plan to switch the motive power of the Royal Navy to steam turbines powered exclusively by oil, aggravated by the monopoly-pricing of oil, faced strict new budgetary limits and was liable to encounter insuperable parliamentary opposition. Churchill needed a way to get around this novel democratic obstacle.

The plight of Anglo-Persian provided a solution. The beleaguered company was offering a long-term supply contract at a price so low that Churchill could announce it as a gift from fairyland. He then went to great lengths to arrange the award of the prize in a way that evaded parliamentary scrutiny of its terms. The Admiralty structured the advance payment that the company needed to stay in business as a purchase of 51 per cent of its shares (for which the Admiralty received none of the normal rights to oversee the company's business, giving it no power to attack the system of monopoly). With the help of the government law officers, Churchill presented the purchase to parliament for its approval not as a financial bill, which would go for examination before a select committee, but as a policy document or White Paper, declaring at the same time that the contract to supply oil around which the deal was built was a commercial arrangement whose details could not be made public. The wide denunciations of the secrecy of the deal, introduced to parliament on 17 June 1914, were silenced by the outbreak of war.[39]

The rescue of Anglo-Persian provided a means to evade public scrutiny of the cost of the switch from coal to oil, but did nothing to address one of the causes of those expenses – the monopolistic control of oil prices. On the contrary, by advancing the company a loan and arranging for it to share in the project to hinder the development of Mesopotamian oil, the British government enabled Anglo-Persian to become one of the leading members of the emerging international oil cartel. If Britain's dependence on coal had provided a means for the labour movement to build more democratic forms of politics, the conversion to oil provided imperialists like Churchill with the means to evade those democratic demands.

THE STRUCTURE

There was a larger sense in which oil offered a way to limit popular claims, reflected in another reason why the Admiralty changed its mind about Anglo-Persian and committed itself to the internal combustion engine. In 1910–11, coal miners in south Wales went on strike demanding the payment of a

---

39   Jack, 'Purchase of British Government's Shares'; Ferrier, *History*: 105–6.

minimum wage. The strike launched the Great Unrest of 1910–14 – the most intense period of industrial action Britain had seen.

Before moving to the Admiralty, Churchill had been in charge of the Home Office, where he was responsible for policing the first wave of the Great Unrest, and warned of the 'new force' trade unions had acquired by the coordination of industrial action among coal miners, railwaymen and dockers.[40] Working with Nevil Macready, a general at the War Office who began his career as a military police officer in the colonial occupation of Egypt, Churchill introduced new methods to break picket lines and defeat strikes, using cavalry and armed infantry not as an accessory to local police forces but as the main instrument of order.[41] In August 1911, when the strikes moved from the coal mines to the railways, Churchill deployed troops to maintain control of the rail lines (and to police electric power stations), violating a rule that military force could be deployed only at the request of local civil authorities – a rule confirmed by parliament following the Featherstone massacre of 1893, when soldiers had shot and killed striking coal miners. Labour leaders in parliament pointed out that the government could have ended the rail strike immediately by ordering the railway companies to concede the strikers' main demand – that they recognise the right of national unions to represent railway workers – and attacked Churchill for his 'diabolical part' in provoking unrest by substituting 'military rule' for civil government.

Churchill justified using the army by referring to the nature of railways. The military authorities required 'full discretionary power to move troops along the lines of railway', he argued in parliament, something impossible to do if they had to request civilian permission at each point along the route. Since railways had created 'immense populations of working people . . . concentrated together' in large cities, entirely dependent on trains to supply fuel and food, the strike threatened a 'degeneration . . . of all the structure, social and economic, on which the life of the people depends'. Railway lines allowed him to evoke the existence of a vulnerable economic and social 'structure', something non-local whose protection required local civilian authority to be subordinated to a coordinated military power.

With one opposition MP shouting 'martial law' and another suggesting 'they have all gone mad', Churchill resorted to his customary bombast, asking 'whether in the history of the world a similar catastrophe can be shown to have menaced an equally great community', and turning to fifteenth-century Iraq for an answer. He compared the dangers threatened by the railway strike to

40   Randolph S. Churchill, *Winston S. Churchill: Young Statesman 1901–1914*, London: Heinemann, 1967: 365.

41   Anthony Mór-O'Brien, 'Churchill and the Tonypandy Riots', *Welsh History Review* 17: 1, 1994: 67–99.

the devastation that followed the breaking of the great Nimrod Dam on the Euphrates.[42]

Events in another part of the Arab world, however, provided the opportunity the government used to overcome the intransigence of the railway owners and concede the strikers' demands. The Great Unrest in Britain coincided with an even greater unrest in Morocco. France had sent troops there to help suppress a popular uprising against the sultan, whose debts to European financiers had led to the imposition of heavy taxes.[43] When Germany challenged the incipient French seizure of almost the last uncolonised corner of Africa, Britain responded by threatening war against Germany and began making preparations for a European conflict, including detailed planning of the use of railways for mobilising troops.[44] The decision to prepare for war allowed the government to order the railway companies to negotiate with the unions – and Churchill to request a move from the Home Office to the Admiralty. Supporting the French occupation of Morocco and responding to Germany's protests with a threat of war allowed Churchill's militarism, checked by the resilience of railway unions at home, to move to a larger stage.

The south Wales coal strikes that had launched the Great Unrest were a particular threat to the navy. The Welsh coalfields produced steam coal, a hybrid grade of fuel combining the high calorific value of anthracite with an ability to generate heat quickly, making those fields the only source of fuel for coal-fired battleships. At the Admiralty, Churchill immediately set up the Royal Commission on Fuel and Engines, to examine switching the Royal Navy's ships from coal- and oil-fired steam engines to internal combustion engines dependent on oil. The political unrest in the Welsh coalfields influenced Admiralty thinking. It provided another incentive for the decision to abandon coal in favour of oil, and the consequent change in policy towards Anglo-Persian.[45] In committing the Royal Navy to a new source of energy, the government was making itself vulnerable to the monopolistic powers of the oil companies. At the same time, it was freeing itself from the political claims of the coal miners.

---

42 'Employment of Military', Hansard, HC Deb, vol. 29, 22 August 1911, cc. 2,282–378.

43 Edmund Burke, *Prelude to Protectorate in Morocco: Precolonial Protest and Resistance, 1860–1912*, Chicago: University of Chicago Press, 1976. For contemporary views of British and French aggressiveness, see E. D. Morel, *Morocco in Diplomacy*, London: Smith, Elder, 1912.

44 Churchill, *World Crisis*: 41.

45 Jack, 'Purchase of British Government's Shares': 154. Similar unrest among a different group of coal miners had shaped Admiralty planning a decade earlier. In 1903, the Commission on Fuel Oil had recommended only a partial switch from coal to oil, partly because the Great Pennsylvania Coal Strike of 1902, a turning point in American labour struggles, had caused a domestic switch to oil and a reduction in US oil exports, raising Admiralty concerns about the security of supply. Geoffrey Miller, *Straits: British Policy Towards the Ottoman Empire and the Origins of the Dardanelles Campaign*, Hull: University of Hull Press, 1997: Chapter 27.

As we have seen, Persia was not the only place where the Admiralty could obtain oil. The great discoveries in Mexico had made it the third-largest producing country in the world by 1914. A British firm, Mexican Eagle, controlled 60 per cent of production and had become one of the world's largest oil suppliers. The Admiralty signed a supply agreement with the company in July 1913, but rejected its attempt to win a long-term agreement in exchange for a government purchase of its shares – a deal similar to one Anglo-Persian was negotiating.[46] The firm was in a battle to control Mexican oil production with Standard Oil, which tried to undermine the British company by helping to finance the overthrow of the government of Porfirio Díaz, triggering the Revolution of 1910–20.[47] By the time the Admiralty was deciding on oil contracts, revolutionary forces were in control of the oilfields, and Emiliano Zapata and other rebel leaders were demanding land reform, workers' rights and other revolutionary changes.

Persia too was in the midst of revolution, the Constitutional Revolution of 1905–11. A year-long series of strikes, protests and sit-ins had forced the Shah in 1906 to accept a constitution and *majlis*, or parliament. Persian oil workers from Baku, returning home after the 1905 Russian Revolution, contributed their revolutionary experience. The Organisation of Iranian Social Democrats, based in Baku and linked with the Russian Social Democrats, was active in popular assemblies that sprang up throughout the country, and formed a party, the Mujahidin, that had acquired an estimated 86,000 members by 1907. It called for the redistribution of land, an eight-hour working day, the right to strike, and universal male suffrage in place of the limited representation of large landowners, merchants and clerics in the new *majlis*.[48] One of the leaders of this progressive movement, Sayyid Hasan Taqizadeh, visited London after being expelled from Iran, and was invited by a group of left-wing MPs to address a meeting in the House of Commons, where he sought Britain's support for the Revolution against Russian threats to intervene and restore the autocratic power of the Shah.[49] But Britain acquiesced in Russia's undermining of the Revolution, and later backed the rise of an army officer, Reza Khan, who seized power in 1921 and created a new autocracy that was to rule the country until the Islamic revolution of 1979. London also took advantage of the weakening control of the central government to create a militia to police the south, the South Persia

46   Merrill Rippy, *Oil and the Mexican Revolution*, Leiden: Brill, 1972: 153; Jones, Emergence: 76.

47   Kenneth Grieb, 'Standard Oil and the Financing of the Mexican Revolution', *California Historical Quarterly* 50: 1, 1971.

48   Janet Afary, 'Social Democracy and the Iranian Constitutional Revolution of 1906–11', in John Foran, ed., *A Century of Revolution: Social Movements in Iran*, Minneapolis: University of Minnesota Press, 1994.

49   Mansour Bonakdarian, 'The Persia Committee and the Constitutional Revolution in Iran', *British Journal of Middle Eastern Studies* 18: 2, 1991: 190.

Rifles, replacing the detachment of Indian troops that had previously guarded the Anglo-Persian Oil Company's operations. Compared to the great unrest in the Mexican oilfields, and in the coal districts of south Wales, the oil regions of southern Persia and of neighbouring Mesopotamia offered a means of obtaining energy that appeared to require far fewer concessions to democratic political claims.

Churchill's prize was not a gift from fairyland, but an energy source to be produced by oil workers in Persia and Mesopotamia – or Iran and Iraq as they were soon to be known. The threat and subsequent outbreak of war presented Britain with an opportunity to end the Great Unrest at home. By the end of the war, taking control of the oilfields of Mesopotamia would supply a further means of weakening the new force of organised labour. While weakened at home, however, the political claims constructed through the supply of energy would come to include those of oil workers abroad. In the same process, the narrow but vital economic 'structure' that an imperial government claimed special powers to police – the network of energy flows – would now expand from the railway lines and coalfields of Britain to encompass the oilfields of the Middle East.

To understand the place of Middle Eastern oilfields in the history of democratic politics, it is necessary to undo the conventional story of the beginnings of the region's oil industry. In place of heroic pioneers on a remote and empty plateau, we have traced a history of rival firms seeking exclusive powers to build or block the paths of railways and pipelines, intended to obstruct more than to develop the supply of oil. The battles were played out amid the revolutionary struggles of Tehran and Istanbul, and in relation to the political upheavals in Britain and other coal-based imperial powers. Facing new levels of scrutiny in parliaments that were beginning to represent mass political parties, the oil firms and their allies in finance and government were learning to frame their interests as imperial needs of the state. And imperial statesmen were becoming spokesmen for the vulnerable structures of energy supply, as a means of countering the powers of those fighting for a more egalitarian collective life.

CHAPTER 3

Consent of the Governed

The First World War was the first great carbon-fuelled conflict. Coal-fired facto-ries produced munitions, armaments and motor-driven vehicles that multi-plied the capacity of humans to kill. The mechanisation that harnessed fossil fuels did not reduce the use of human labour. By connecting human combat to much greater stores of energy, machines created new powers of action, greatly extending the physical limits of human and animal power. Armies became war machines that continuously deployed their mechanical and human elements in ever-greater quantities over large areas and prolonged campaigns. The mass production and deployment of the machinery of death allowed European states to sustain a war of attrition that massacred millions in Europe, and to extend the fighting to Africa and the Middle East, where hundreds of thousands more were killed by fighting, famine and mass deportation. The expanding apparatus of war required coal and oil, steel and nitrate-based explosives, but also food, fodder and clothing. The more the conflict extended, therefore, the more dependent it became on those whose labour in coal mines, munitions factories, wheat fields and cotton plantations made it possible. Extended warfare destroyed the pre-war relations of political authority in most of the regions where it was fought, above all in the Middle East. At the same time, it lent additional force to demo-cratic political claims that drew their effectiveness from the new dependence of the powerful on the flow of carbon energy.

In the Middle East, the Ottoman Empire initially stayed out of the war, but then sided with Germany against the imperial powers that had been slowly dismembering it. A British army from India, composed mainly of Indian troops, invaded and occupied Iraq, while British forces combining with an Arab army took control of most other Arab provinces of the Ottoman Empire, starting with the Hejaz in western Arabia and moving north to take Palestine and the rest of Greater Syria (modern Jordan, Syria and Lebanon). An industrialised state like Britain could now fight a war of extraordinary violence, extent and duration, bringing much of the Middle East under its control. However, the destructive scale of the conflict was to make it harder to assemble a postwar imperial order.

Industrialised warfare confirmed the importance of petroleum as a fuel for transportation rather than illumination. After the war, this presented the large oil companies with a problem. On the one hand, they could now use the risk of a future war to argue, as the Anglo-Persian Oil Company had begun to claim, that their efforts to control the global supply of oil were important not for their own profits but for the security of the imperial state. Organising the monopolistic control of oil in the world that emerged from the war, as we will see, was going to require the increased support of imperial governments. On the other hand, if oil supplies were as vital and as vulnerable as the leading oil companies now claimed, their governments could conclude that the cartel system these rival firms wished to rebuild might not be the cheapest or most reliable way of securing the oil. Perhaps the government of a major power should produce its own oil, or encourage the development of smaller, independent oil companies, or even return to the original system where each country enabled its own oil industry to develop. Over the following years, each of these alternatives threatened at various moments to develop. But the large oil companies were able to re-establish their prewar monopoly, minus the defeated Germans, delaying the emergence of a rival arrangement for a further five decades.

Governing the global supply of oil, like most things that we call 'global', rested on the control of a comparatively small number of sites – a few dozen major oilfields, pipelines and terminals, and the handful of bulk tanker fleets that journeyed between them. Towards the end of the war, two important sites were removed from the direct control of the large oil companies. In 1917, the revolutionary government in Mexico re-established the principle that ownership of the country's oil resources, which were then among the most abundant in the world, lay with the state rather than the surface landowners, converting the ownership claims of foreign oil companies into concessions from the government. The Russian Revolution of the same year led to the nationalisation of the oil producers of the Caucasus, after Soviet forces recaptured the oilfields from British-backed local governments in 1920. In both cases the international oil firms responded by trying to deprive the state-controlled oilfields of investment and markets.[1] The curtailment of Mexican and Russian production eased the problem of curbing the global supply of oil. In the years following the Great War, the competition to manage the global oil network focused on one undecided site, as it had on the eve of the war: the oilfields of Iraq.

TRANSLATING DEMOCRACY

To limit the development of Mesopotamian oil, it was no longer possible just to seek a concession from a government in Istanbul. As we will see in Chapter 4, the Anglo-Persian Oil Company and the British government were to resuscitate the old Ottoman concession of 1914, held in the name of the London-based Turkish

1   Robert W. Tolf, *The Russian Rockefellers: The Saga of the Nobel Family and the Russian Oil Industry*, Stanford: Hoover Institution Press, 1976: 196–212; Merrill Rippy, *Oil and the Mexican Revolution*, Leiden: E. J. Brill, 1972: 160–2; N. Stephen Kane, 'Corporate Power and Foreign Policy: Efforts of American Oil Companies to Influence United States Relations With Mexico, 1921–1928', *Diplomatic History* 1: 2, 1977: 170–98; Daniel Yergin, *The Prize: The Epic Quest for Oil, Money, and Power*, New York: Simon & Schuster, 1991: 232–3, 238–43.

Petroleum Company, as part of the means of gaining control (and of attempting to exclude Standard Oil). But they needed the help of another device, more effective than a joint-stock company existing as no more than papers signed in prewar London. Following the upheavals of the war, they required a method for dealing with political forces in the Middle East, forces that were no longer organised under the authority of Ottoman administration. Mechanised military power was available, but was too expensive and ineffective to furnish the main method of control. The device that emerged was called 'self-determination'.

A handful of industrialised states in the global north had brought much of the world under the control of imperial government. The resources that made modern imperialism possible had also given groups of organised workers in industrialised regions an unusual power to make successful political claims, thanks to their novel ability to shut down the supply of energy. The new call for self-determination seemed at first to be a way of generalising this ability to make effective democratic claims to people in other parts of the world. In practice, however, it did something different. The doctrines and devices of self-determination turned an apparently democratic impulse into a set of universal claims that circulated rapidly around the world, but also very thinly. The claims had certain important uses, but only at specific sites. At the same time, the mechanism of self-determination could be used to defeat the kinds of democratic claims being successfully advanced in Europe.

Most historians assume that the principle of self-determination was an American idea. Many also acknowledge its connection with the Revolution in Russia. 'In early 1918', Daniel Yergin writes, 'to counter the powerful appeal of Bolshevism, Woodrow Wilson had come out with his idealistic Fourteen Points and a resounding call for the self-determination of nations and peoples after the war.'[2] This way of describing self-determination reflects the fact that it indeed became an American idea; that is, it became both American and an idea. First, the publicity machinery known as 'public diplomacy' circulated President Wilson's speeches around the world – speeches that criticised 'secret diplomacy' (the clandestine agreements among European powers for the annexation of territory) but initially made no mention of self-determination. After Wilson adopted the latter term, political movements in Europe, Asia and Africa responded by invoking the name of the American president and the authority of the United States when making claims for an end to wartime occupation or independence from imperial control – claims that Wilson himself seldom supported.[3] Second, this machinery, by making the speeches 'resound', made self-determination into an idea. It became something that travelled quickly and

---

2   Yergin, *The Prize*: 188.
3   Erez Manela, *The Wilsonian Moment: Self-Determination and the International Origins of Anticolonial Nationalism*, Oxford: OUP, 2007.

far because it was somehow nonmaterial, an ideal more than a reality, a future hope rather than a material practice.

What we call ideals are ways of speaking, and of referring to the words of others, that acquire this general, disembodied circulation. While appearing to be nonmaterial, with the incorporeal form we attribute to ideals or principles, terms like self-determination and democracy acquire their lightness and transportability through specific practices. To understand their effectiveness we need to follow the work done to strip such terms of the varied circumstances that produce them, to translate and mistranslate multiple claims into a common idiom, and to build the acoustic machinery of their circulation.

We can trace this work by following the emergence and transformation of the claim to self-determination in the period of the First World War. The genealogy will take us to southern Africa, to changes in the methods of imperial rule, to the labour movements that played a new role in both democratic politics and mechanised warfare, and back to the Middle East, where the battle over 'self-determination' was to be most intensively fought.

Woodrow Wilson's rhetoric was responding not just to the powerful appeal of Bolshevism, but to Lenin's declaration the day after taking power in October 1917 that 'any nation that desires independence' should be allowed 'to determine the form of its state life by free voting'. Lenin was stating not a general right (the demand was subordinate to the need to end the rule of capitalists, as the new Soviet state set about doing in Baku and other places) but the wrong of imperialism, in which powerful states seized and annexed the territory of weaker nations. Following the declaration, Lenin's government published the secret wartime agreements that Imperial Russia had made with Britain and France to divide among themselves the territories of the Ottoman Empire.[4] Lenin's declaration, moreover, echoed wider campaigns, emerging across several continents, against the violence and injustices of empire. His views on imperialism had been influenced by the writings of English and German political economists, including J.A. Hobson, who published his classic work *Imperialism* in 1902 and whose concerns provide a connection between Lenin and Wilson.[5]

Hobson's understanding of imperialism as a political and economic movement took shape in response to the violent British colonial conflict that preceded the First World War: the South African war of 1899–1902. The discovery of

---

4   V. I. Lenin, 'Second All-Russia Congress of Soviets of Workers' and Soldiers' Deputies: Report on Peace', in *Collected Works*, vol. 26: *October 1917–January 1918*, Moscow: Progress Publishers, 1960, available at Marxists Internet Archive, www.marxists.org/archive. See also A. J. Mayer, *Wilson vs. Lenin: Political Origins of the New Diplomacy, 1917–1918*, Cleveland: World Publishing Company, 1969; Antonio Cassese, *Self-Determination of Peoples: A Legal Reappraisal*, Cambridge, UK: CUP, 1995: 14–18.

5   V. I. Lenin, 'Plan of the Book Imperialism', *Collected Works*, vol. 39: *Notebooks on Imperialism*, Moscow: Progress Publishers, 1974: 230–9. The same volume contains his 'Notebook on Hobson' and 'Notebook on Brailsford'.

the Witwatersrand gold fields in 1884, containing the world's largest deposits of gold, had allowed the rapid expansion of international trading mechanisms based on gold reserves, and had enabled London to maintain its dominant place in those mechanisms, despite losing ground to Germany and the United States as a producer and exporter of manufactured goods.[6] The gold-mining boom led to a conflict between the white Afrikaner republics and the large British mining firms, which sought the support of the more powerful political apparatus of the British colonial state to address the problems of creating and policing the industrial labour force on which the mineral-based international monetary order depended.[7] Gold occurs in the earth in such tiny particles that its extraction needs enormous quantities of labour. Since its value depends on maintaining a constant price, producing gold on an industrial scale required methods for greatly reducing labour costs. The large British firms were run by American mining engineers, who introduced from US mines in California and Venezuela the system of mining camps organised around a rigid racial division of the labour force (the system that would later play an important role in the oil industry).[8]

Like other members of the radical wing of English liberalism, Hobson had supported the Afrikaner republics that Britain defeated in the South African war and condemned the 'methods of barbarism' of British militarism, including the introduction of what Britain called concentration camps, in which tens of thousands of black and Afrikaner civilians died.[9] Britain's annexation of the Boer republics led to the formation in 1910 of the Union of South Africa as a self-governing dominion within the British Empire. The development of self-government in South Africa, which became a method of empowering whites and further disempowering nonwhites, would shape the wider solution to the claims of subject populations after the First World War.

Visiting the country on the eve of the South African war, Hobson saw in the struggle between the Dutch settlers of the Transvaal and the large British mining interests that pushed for its annexation the physical dynamic of imperialism. The continuous expansion of imperial rule, and the increasing military expenditure this required, were not the result of psychological or racial drives, as orthodox British opinion held. They were driven by the needs of those

---

6   Marcello de Cecco, *The International Gold Standard: Money and Empire*, 2nd edn, New York: St Martin's Press, 1984: 22–38.

7   See Shula Marks and Stanley Trapido, 'Lord Milner and the South African State', *History Workshop* 8, 1979: 50–80, which supports in broad terms Hobson's analysis in *The War in South Africa: Its Causes and Effects*, London: J. Nisbet, 1900.

8   Y. G.-M. Lulat, *United States Relations with South Africa: A Critical Overview from the Colonial Period to the Present*, New York: Peter Lang, 2008: 31–47. On oil, see Robert Vitalis, *America's Kingdom: Mythmaking on the Saudi Oil Frontier*, 2nd edn, London: Verso, 2009.

9   W. T Stead, *Methods of Barbarism: The Case for Intervention*, London: Mowbray House, 1901.

who, in distinction to manufacturers and merchants, were now known as 'capitalists': financiers and large banking houses, unable to find profitable investments at home – because, in Hobson's analysis, the majority of the population earned too little to create a demand for additional goods. Finance capital instead flowed overseas, investing funds in mining and other capital-intensive methods of producing raw materials, and in building the railways required to carry these materials for shipment back to Europe. When their ventures caused local conflict or financial distress, the investors portrayed them as 'imperialism' and used their influence in the offices of state to have public funds spent on military protection for these supposedly public interests.[10]

For the instigators of the South Africa war, the annexation of the Boer republics and the creation of the Union of South Africa provided the prototype for a new form of empire, based on the principle of self-government. Alfred Milner, the high commissioner for southern Africa, and the young administrators he recruited, hoped to transform Britain's colonies into a commonwealth of self-administered territories. Reinforced with programmes to improve the health and industrial discipline of the population, self-government would strengthen the empire and redistribute to the colonies more of the cost of maintaining it. Only the white settler populations were to participate in electing and running the administration of these self-managed dependencies. Milner brought to southern Africa the experience he had gained in the British occupation of Egypt, where he helped transform a short-term military occupation into an 'experiment' in indefinite European control, and then articulated the reasons why 'the game of Egyptian independence', as he called it, depended on 'the controlling hand' of the European.[11] As the programme of imperial rule drawn up by Milner's group following their return from South Africa to London explained, 'the faculty of government is reserved to the European minority, for the unanswerable reason that, for the present, at any rate, this portion of its citizens is alone capable of the task'. The principle of self-rule was not, therefore, in contradiction with the idea of empire. On the contrary, the need for self-government could provide, paradoxically, a new justification for overseas settlement and control, because only the European presence in colonised territories made a form of self-rule possible: 'the more backward races', such as the people of Egypt or India, were to be included in the imperial Commonwealth 'for the very reason that they are as yet unable to govern themselves'.[12] Without the presence of a European minority, these progressive imperialists argued, no non-European people could be trained for a future role in their own government.

---

10   J. A. Hobson, *Imperialism: A Study*, London: James Nisbet & Co., 1902; P. J. Cain, *Hobson and Imperialism: Radicalism, New Liberalism, and Finance 1887–1938*, Oxford: OUP, 2002.

11   Alfred Milner, *England in Egypt*, 11th edn, London: Edward Arnold, 1904: 358.

12   Lionel Curtis, *The Problem of the Commonwealth*, London: Macmillan, 1915: 60, 198.

The South African model was to have a strong influence on the postwar reorganisation of imperial power, especially in the Middle East. Jan Smuts, the Afrikaner military and political leader who fought the British but then negotiated the incorporation of the Boer republics into the Union of South Africa, allied himself with Milner's group and helped articulate the new imperial programme. Smuts befriended Hobson on his visit to South Africa, and continued afterwards to correspond with him and read his work.[13] While using radical allies to fight the gold-mining magnates, Smuts himself was no radical. He called on British troops to crush a general strike led by white gold miners in 1913, in which twenty miners were killed, and the following year imposed martial law to defeat a second general strike, deporting its leaders back to the United Kingdom – most white miners being recent immigrants, mainly from the exhausted copper and tin mines of Cornwall.[14] At the same time he began systematising the racial segregation of labour, introduced into the organisation of the mining industry by the engineers brought from the US by the large South African mining companies – a racial structure that would define the politics of the new state.

After commanding the South African military occupation of German South-West Africa in 1915 and the British conquest of the German colonies of East Africa the following year, General Smuts met up with his 'old friend' Hobson when he arrived in England in 1917 to join the war cabinet and participate in framing the postwar settlement. Working with Milner and his disciples in London, Smuts would guide the formulation of the 'ideal' of self-determination later attributed to Woodrow Wilson.[15]

MINES OF MOROCCO AND RAILWAYS OF MESOPOTAMIA

The vision of a white-ruled, self-governing empire faced opposition on several fronts. In South Africa, the Bambatha rebellion of 1906 in Natal, which began as a protest against taxes imposed by the self-governing colony, demonstrated

13   Jan Christiaan Smuts, *Selections from the Smuts Papers*, ed. W. K. Hancock and Jean Van Der Poel, vol. 2, Cambridge, UK: CUP, 1966–73: 50–5, 304, 440–4, 530–2.

14   Jonathan Hyslop, 'Martial Law and Military Power in the Construction of the South African State: Jan Smuts and the "Solid Guarantee of Force" 1899–1924', *Journal of Historical Sociology* 22: 2, 2009: 234–68. Five years earlier Smuts had proposed replacing the Cornish miners with Afrikaaners. 'I agree with you as to your Cornishmen', wrote John X. Merriman, the leader of the Cape Colony; 'the sooner they leave South Africa the better for all of us – overpaid, insolent fellows with their family ties across 6,000 miles of water.' Smuts, *Selections*, vol. 2: 344.

15   Smuts, *Selections*, vol. 3: 464. Smuts came to London to attend the imperial war cabinet, a meeting of leaders of British dependencies, but stayed on as a member of the war cabinet, a small committee of the Westminster government set up to direct the war. On Smuts see also Mark Mazower, *No Enchanted Palace: The End of Empire and the Ideological Origins of the United Nations*, Princeton: Princeton University Press, 2009: 28–65.

the resistance to the new forms of colonial self-rule.[16] In the same year, the Dinshaway incident in Egypt, Britain's second-most-populous colonial territory after India, stimulated the organisation of a national movement in opposition to foreign rule and to the prerogatives of the European settler community.[17] While organising the struggle of the Indian community against the labour and immigration laws that Smuts had introduced in the Transvaal, Mohandas Gandhi had begun to articulate a different claim of *swaraj*, or self-rule, defined not as the political independence of the state but as the cooperative self-sufficiency of the community, to be won through the methods of passive resistance. In 1912, prominent black South Africans founded what was to become the African National Congress, initially under the name of the South African Native National Congress. In Britain itself, the outbreak of the First World War produced an increased opposition to the new imperialism of men like Milner and Smuts, and designs for a more democratic postwar world.

The proposals for postwar democracy took their shape from the controversies that were developing over imperialism and the struggle for material resources. The work of Hobson, echoed and extended in the writings of leading critics of imperialism like H. N. Brailsford and E. D. Morel, made it possible to trace the causes of war to the uncontrolled flow of finance overseas, the resulting competition for exclusive control of economic resources outside Europe, and the growth of arms manufacturers and military cliques with a vested interest in war.

In a book published on the eve of the conflict in 1914, *The War of Steel and Gold*, Henry Brailsford mapped these connections. Forty years earlier, he wrote, the failure of speculative loans from British and French bankers to the government of Egypt had led Britain to occupy the Nile valley. This let loose the scramble among European powers for other African territories.[18] The Berlin Act of 1885 had created for the first time a legal structure to regulate the acquisition of colonies by European states, and articulated a philosophy of colonialism based on the responsibility of civilised states for the 'moral and material well-being' of inferior races. It also acknowledged the 'right of the indigenous populations to dispose of themselves', meaning that colonialism was to be based upon the consent of colonised populations, a consent acquired through treaties

16   Shula Marks, 'Class, Ideology, and the Bambatha Rebellion', in Donald Crummey, ed., *Banditry, Rebellion, and Social Protest in Africa*, Oxford: James Currey, 1986: 351–72.

17   In response to a fight in the village of Dinshaway, provoked by five British officers shooting the villagers' domestic pigeons for sport, in which a fleeing soldier had died of sunstroke, the British authorities tried fifty-two villagers before a military tribunal. Four men were sentenced to death and hanged in front of their fellow villagers.

18   Henry Noel Brailsford, *The War of Steel and Gold: A Study of the Armed Peace*, 10th edn, London: G. Bell & Sons, 1918.

with native rulers.[19] The forced labour, mutilations, mass killings and deaths from starvation and disease that took the lives of millions of Africans in the Congo Free State, a colony created under the Berlin process and a model for labour methods transferred to neighbouring colonies, had been exposed in the writings of Edmund Morel.[20] This demonstration of 'high Imperialist finance in a peculiarly brutal form' proved the failure of the Berlin framework for obtaining the consent of the colonised and the need for a more robust mechanism for regulating the exercise of European economic power abroad.[21]

Events in the decade leading up to the First World War, in Brailsford's account, confirmed the problem. Seeking greater control over Egypt, where local opposition to the colonial occupation was mounting, Britain reached an accord with France in 1904 whereby France recognised the British occupation of Egypt in exchange for a secret British commitment to support its seizure of Morocco. Berlin responded to the incipient French control of Morocco by provoking a crisis with France over access to Moroccan resources, claiming that German companies had obtained rights to exploit iron ore and other minerals. The Algeciras Conference of 1906 only partially resolved the dispute, and in 1911, following a rebellion in Morocco, France sent troops to occupy the country. As Franco-German relations deteriorated, Germany reacted by blocking French finance from sharing control of the Baghdad Railway and the oil reserves to which it would provide access. The origins of the Great War turned not on a breakdown of the balance of power in Europe, Brailsford wrote, but on 'the mines of Morocco and the railways of Mesopotamia'.[22]

Rather than restoring the balance between competing imperial powers and re-establishing the Berlin arrangement, Brailsford proposed an 'economic

---

19   Siba N. Grovogui, Sovereigns, *Quasi Sovereigns, and Africans: Race and Self-Determination in International Law*, Minneapolis: University of Minnesota Press, 1996; William Roger Louis, 'The First World War and the Origins of the Mandates System', in *Ends of British Imperialism: The Scramble for Empire, Suez and Decolonization: Collected Essays*, London: I. B. Tauris, 2006: 225–6; Antony Anghie, 'Finding the Peripheries: Sovereignty and Colonialism in Nineteenth-Century International Law', *Harvard International Law Journal* 40: 1, 1999: 51–7.

20   E. D. Morel, *King Leopold's Rule in Africa*, London: Heinemann, 1904; and *Red Rubber*, London: T. Fisher Unwin, 1906. In 1904 Morel founded the Congo Reform Association with Roger Casement; see Adam Hochschild, *King Leopold's Ghost: A Story of Greed, Terror, and Heroism in Colonial Africa*, Boston: Houghton Mifflin, 1998.

21   Brailsford, *War of Steel and Gold*: 71.

22   Ibid.: 37. Reviewers found Brailsford's book – published just before the war in May 1914, when few people expected a conflict – 'pessimistic and cynical' (Brailsford, *War of Steel and Gold*: 8). For recent scholarship on the expectation of war and its causes, see Annika Mombauer, 'The First World War: Inevitable, Avoidable, Improbable or Desirable? Recent Interpretations on War Guilt and the War's Origins', *German History* 25: 1, 2007: 78–95. On German mining interests in Morocco, see Joanne Stafford Mortimer, 'Commercial Interests and German Diplomacy in the Agadir Crisis', *Historical Journal* 10: 4, 1967: 440–56. On the blocking of French financial participation in the Baghdad Railway (and of Ottoman recognition of French sovereignty over Algeria and Tunis), see Marian Kent, 'Agent of Empire? The National Bank of Turkey and British Foreign Policy', *Historical Journal* 18: 2, 1975.

structure' to replace the Berlin Act and more directly manage the exploitation of natural resources overseas. The Algeciras mechanism for sharing access to Moroccan minerals and other investments, destroyed by Britain's clandestine agreement to support the French occupation, offered a model for an alternative to such 'secret diplomacy' and imperial control. It was a source, as we will see, of the idea of the mandate system that would frame access to Mesopotamian oil after the war.[23]

The War of Steel and Gold had gone through ten editions by 1918. In the third edition, published in May 1915, Brailsford elaborated the idea of an economic structure into the proposal for a League of Nations. This would be more than a 'League to Enforce Peace', in which the great powers agreed to use collective force against aggressor states – the proposal for 'peace with a punch' that William Taft, the former Republican president of the United States, advocated a few months later, and that his successor, Woodrow Wilson, adopted in an address before Taft's organisation in May 1916.[24] As an economic structure, the League that Brailsford and other socialists proposed would be 'a permanent authority . . . to internationalize the export of capital'. It would manage competition for concessions, control essential trade routes, ship canals and free ports, and allocate shares according to agreed proportions for investment in all mineral and railway concessions. The League or its member governments would monitor these investments to prevent slavery, sweating or the systematic ill-treatment of workers; to prevent usurious lending to states, as happened with the loans to Egypt, Turkey and Morocco, whose failure had triggered the sequence of events leading to the current world crisis; and to stop imperial interests from financing revolution, as they were reported to have done in the revolutions of 1908 in Turkey and 1911 in Mexico – a reference in the former case to the oil interests represented by Ernest Cassel, and in the latter to the role of Standard Oil.[25] In other words, the League was to be an economic mechanism to replace, not war between states, but its taproot – the conflict over material resources.[26]

---

23   Brailsford, *War of Steel and Gold*: 249. The Ottoman Public Debt Administration, through which European creditors collaborated in managing international investment in Turkey, provided another model. The agreement over Morocco, a set of secret clauses in the Anglo-French accord of 1904, was published in the French press in November 1911, and the following spring by E. D. Morel in *Morocco in Diplomacy*, London: Smith, Elder & Co., 1912. Morel's book was republished after the outbreak of the war by the National Labour Press as *Ten Years of Secret Diplomacy: An Unheeded Warning*, and went through five large editions by 1918. See F. Seymour Cocks, *E. D. Morel: The Man and His Work*, London: Allen & Unwin, 1920: 199.

24   'The League to Enforce Peace', *Advocate of Peace* 77: 7, July 1915: 168–70; 'Peace with a Punch', *New York Times*, 1 July 1915: 3; Thomas J. Knock, *To End All Wars: Woodrow Wilson and the Quest for a New World Order*, New York: OUP, 1992: 57 (where the claim that Wilson spoke of self-determination in these wartime speeches is repeated).

25   On Cassel, see Chapter 2, above. On Mexico, see Kenneth J. Grieb, 'Standard Oil and the Financing of the Mexican Revolution', *California Historical Quarterly* 50: 1, March 1971: 59–71.

26   Brailsford, *War of Steel and Gold*.

A MACHINE TO CONTROL FOREIGN POLICY

These proposals for a postwar politics built on the dismantling of imperialism and new methods of controlling the exploitation of minerals and the flow of international finance circulated and grew over the following three years. In books, journals and congresses, British socialists drew up proposals for an alternative to European colonisation. The Union of Democratic Control, run by Morel (who was to defeat the secretary of state for the colonies, Winston Churchill, in the parliamentary elections of 1922) and including Hobson and Brailsford among its inaugural members, campaigned for parliamentary control of foreign policy to eliminate the secret diplomacy that allowed imperial interests to govern international relations.[27] In 1915 a conference of the Independent Labour Party supported the creation of a 'machinery for the democratic control of foreign policy', together with a system for the international management of colonial territories under which, as the *New Statesman* proposed in 1916, Europe would 'hold those territories in trust for civilization'.[28]

In the summer of 1917, encouraged by the role of Russian workers in bringing a progressive government to power and the prospect of a rapid end to the war, the labour movement began to formulate concrete proposals for the postwar settlement, drafting a document called the Memorandum on War Aims. Drawing on the ideas of Hobson, Brailsford and others, the goal of the movement was to extend the democratisation it had begun to win at home to areas under Europe's economic and political control overseas. It was driven not so much by altruism (and was ambivalent about whether non-European peoples were ready to govern themselves) as by the understanding that imperialism abroad limited and undermined whatever democratic gains were made at home.

The Labour Memorandum called for 'the complete democratization of all countries', which required 'the placing of foreign policy, just as much as home policy, under the control of popularly elected Legislatures'. Within Europe, postwar boundaries should be determined on 'the general principle of allowing all people to settle their own destinies'.

Outside Europe, to democratise imperial power the Memorandum proposed two innovations. First, the League of Nations, with a representative international legislature, would replace European states as the administrator of dependent territories. In the former Ottoman territories of the Near East people were to 'settle their own destinies' as in Europe, but if that proved impractical the territories should be administered not by European states but

---

27   H. Hanak, 'The Union of Democratic Control during the First World War', *Historical Research* 36: 94, November 1963: 168–80.

28   Carl F. Brand, *British Labour's Rise to Power*, Stanford: Stanford University Press, 1941: 63, 72.

by an international commission acting under the League. In tropical Africa, the League would take control of not just the former German-ruled territories, as other groups had proposed, but all European colonies, and would administer international investment and trade. Where the Act of Berlin a generation before had committed European powers to protect the 'moral and material well-being' of the colonised, the Memorandum introduced a language of social improvement or development, and an economic mechanism for its promotion: in administering investments in mining, railways and other enterprises, the League was to ensure that all revenues were expended on 'the welfare and development' of the people themselves.

Second, the Memorandum called for an international agreement to enforce legislation protecting workers against exploitation, including the regulation of factory conditions and hours of work and the prevention of sweating. The labour movement adopted the Memorandum on War Aims at a special conference on 28 December 1917. Two months later the same proposals were adopted by a meeting of socialist and labour leaders from all the allied European states.[29]

These democratic plans for an alternative to imperialism go unmentioned in most accounts of the League of Nations and the system of mandate rule imposed under the League's authority on the postwar Middle East. As we will see in Chapter 5, they were to reappear in a new form after the Second World War, when Britain and the United States created, in the United Nations, not just a successor to the League, but two new institutions intended to control international finance and investment, the International Monetary Fund and the World Bank, and attempted to create a third institution to manage the international oil industry – although with none of the democratic elements that the labour movement proposed during the First World War. The impact of the socialists' plans at the time they were formulated can still be traced in the postwar settlement, not in the main architecture of the League of Nations but in the efforts taken to marginalise the attempt to subject imperial power to democratic control.

When the Allied powers created the League at the peace conference in Paris after the war, they established two additional international arrangements, corresponding to the two demands of the left, appended as Articles 22 and 23 of

---

29 'British Labor's War Aims: Text of a Statement Adopted at the Special National Labor Conference at Central Hall, Westminster, on December 28, 1917', *International Conciliation* 4: 123, February 1918: 45–56 (the summary of the text published in *The Times*, 28 December 1917: 7, omitted the demand for the international regulation of working conditions). 'Labour War Aims: Views of Inter-Allied Conference', *The Times*, 25 February 1918: 3. The only significant difference between the Memorandum approved by the Labour conference in December 1917 and the version approved by the Inter-Allied Socialist and Labour Conference in February concerned the mode of administering African territories. Henry R. Winkler, 'British Labor and the Origins of the Idea of Colonial Trusteeship, 1914–1919', *Historian* 13: 2, 1951: 161–2.

the Covenant of the League. Article 22 created the system of mandates in the Middle East and Africa, and Article 23 created the International Labour Office. The negotiations over the concrete form of these two arrangements were deliberately removed from the main work of creating the League, allowing the imperial powers to control the outcome and limit their effectiveness. The functions that the left proposed as the main instruments of a democratised international order were reduced to appendages. The International Labour Office proceeded to introduce international labour regulations along the lines proposed in the labour movement memorandum.[30] The mandate system appeared to derive from the Labour proposals of 1917–18, but these were transformed by turning the demand for democratisation into the very different principle of self-determination, or 'the consent of the governed'.

THEY ARE UNFORTUNATELY THE WORKERS

The British war cabinet could not at that moment easily ignore the labour movement's demand that it agree on a concrete list of democratic war aims. Following the horrendous battlefield losses of 1917 and the withdrawal of revolutionary Russia from the war, and short of ships to bring American armed forces to Europe, the government needed to intensify the 'combing out' of the protected industrial workforce to put more men onto the battlefields and into the shipyards.

Wartime labour protests were by then a serious concern. Industrialised warfare required the organisation of coal supplies and manufacturing as much as weapons and troops on the battlefield. Trade unions had agreed to a suspension of the right to strike for the duration of the war. When the government introduced conscription (for the first time in the country's history) in 1916, it protected key industries like munitions and shipbuilding from compulsory military service, but began 'combing out' male industrial workers wherever it determined that a manufacturing process could be run with a smaller or less skilled workforce. Workers were unable to change jobs without their employer's consent, and suffered from rising prices and inadequate supplies of food and housing. Control broke down, and in the spring

---

30   The Treaty of Versailles (Part I of which – the first twenty-six articles – formed the Covenant of the League) spelled out details in Part XIII, on Labour (Articles 387–99). The preamble to this section called for urgent improvements in the conditions of labour, such as 'the regulation of the hours of work . . . the prevention of unemployment, the provision of an adequate living wage, the protection of the worker against sickness, disease and injury . . . recognition of the principle of freedom of association . . . and other measures'. 'The Versailles Treaty June 28, 1918: Part XIII', Avalon Law Project: Documents in Law, History, and Diplomacy, at avalon.law.yale.edu/imt/partxiii.asp. On the ILO, see Markku Ruotsila, '"The Great Charter for the Liberty of the Workingman": Labour, Liberals, and the Creation of the ILO', *Labour History Review* 67: 1, April 2002: 29–47.

of 1917 a strike by munitions workers led to wider conflicts, with 200,000 workers on strike.[31]

One week after the Labour conference in December 1917, the government summoned a meeting of trade union leaders to negotiate its proposals for further manpower reductions in protected industries, hoping to avoid the mass strikes of the previous spring. Addressing the meeting on 5 January 1918, the prime minister, Lloyd George, issued the first statement from any Allied leader listing the aims of the war, providing a justification for continuing the fighting. Given the fear that the war was turning against the Allies, the speech was also a veiled indication to Germany of the terms upon which Britain would negotiate peace. Delivered without consulting Allied governments and with opposition from the Foreign Office, which resisted any compromise with Germany, the statement on war aims was drafted for the war cabinet by the South African leader Jan Smuts, together with a leading figure from Milner's South African coterie, the prime minister's secretary Philip Kerr.[32] The response to the labour movement's demand for a democratised structure of international relations was authored by the South-African-formed imperialists.

The government statement echoed Labour's list of war aims, but translated them into a new vocabulary, one that transformed the democratisation of transnational relations into the principle of 'self-determination'. Organised labour, Lloyd George began, having been called on to maintain the might of armies in the field, was entitled to know for what cause they were sacrificing. The postwar territorial settlement, he said, must be based on 'the right of self-determination or the consent of the governed'. The Labour document had spoken neither of self-determination nor of a right. It had called for a process, the democratisation of all countries, and proposed mechanisms for advancing it, by placing overseas investment under international control. Democracy had been won at home not by manufacturing the consent of the governed, but by developing the means to withhold consent – in particular through the threat of the general strike.

The international organisation Lloyd George proposed was intended to pursue the control of arms and the peaceful settlement of disputes, not the larger management of imperial economic relations. In place of the international control of imperialism, the prime minister proposed that the 'general principle of national self-determination' should apply not only to the settlement of Europe but to Africa, although only to the former German colonies. In those

---

31   George H. Cassar, *Lloyd George at War, 1916–1918*, London: Anthem Press, 2009: 42–3.

32   'Man-Power: Ministers' Conference with Labour, More Men from Munitions', *The Times*, 4 January 1918: 6. David R. Woodward, 'The Origins and Intent of David Lloyd George's War Aims Speech', *Historian* 34: 1, November 1971: 38. Alfred Milner was another member of the eight-man war cabinet. After serving under Milner in South Africa, from 1910 to 1916 Kerr edited *The Round Table*, the journal of the Milner group.

places, he explained, populations lived under the rule of chiefs or councils who were 'competent to speak' for them. In other words, self-determination would be a process of recognising (and in practice, of helping to constitute) forms of local despotism through which imperial control would continue to operate. It would produce a mechanism of consent. This was an updating of the principle enshrined in the General Act of Berlin, the 'right of the indigenous populations to dispose of themselves'. It rephrased the old colonial principle of self-disposition, which sought to found imperial authority on the power of native chiefs, who signed agreements with colonising powers.[33] In the case of the Middle East, the prime minister shifted to a vaguer formulation: Arabia, Armenia, Mesopotamia, Syria and Palestine, he said, were 'entitled to a recognition of their separate national conditions'. Since Britain was making other plans for these areas, the shift to generalities was made explicit: 'the exact form of that recognition', he said, 'need not here be discussed'.[34]

Three days later President Wilson, surprised by Britain's unilateral statement of war aims, issued his famous list of Fourteen Points, enumerating the principles that should govern the peace settlement. He made no mention of a right to self-determination. The first object of the Fourteen Points was the commercial principle of the open door, reflecting the American argument that to reduce the chance of war international financiers and trading firms should share access to overseas territories rather than arrange exclusive imperial concessions (an argument America would later use to require that the agreement Britain and France made after the war to share the oil of Mesopotamia be renegotiated to allow the participation of Standard Oil). Wilson added in his fifth point that the interests of subject populations should have 'equal weight' with these legitimate imperial interests, but said nothing about self-determination. When he began to use the latter term in discussing the postwar settlement, it was to reiterate the Berlin principle and argue that subject peoples should have a say in choosing which Western power would govern them, as the imperial state prepared them for autonomy or self-rule.[35] When the nationalist leaderships of the main Arab countries declared their independence after the war – Egypt

---

33   Grovogui, *Sovereigns*: 80.

34   'British War Aims: Mr Lloyd George's Statement, Justice For Small Nations, Alsace Lorraine, Reparations Vital', *The Times*, 7 January 1918: 7. On the 'decentralised despotism' of the new methods of colonial rule, see Mahmood Mamdani, *Citizen and Subject: Contemporary Africa and the Legacy of Late Colonialism*, Princeton: Princeton University Press, 1996.

35   Wilson first used the phrase 'self-determination' in a speech on 11 February 1918, analysing the German and Austrian responses to his Fourteen Points. He used the phrase only in passing, however, and did not include it in the summary of four principles that should guide the peace settlement. On the difference between self-determination and Wilson's principle of self-government, see Trygve Throntveit, 'The Fable of the Fourteen Points: Woodrow Wilson and National Self-Determination', *Diplomatic History* 35: 3, 2011: 445–81.

in March 1920, Syria in the same month – Wilson refused to recognise them.[36] The United States did not support Iraqi nationalism, and when the US consul in Baghdad supported anti-British activities, possibly on behalf of the Standard Oil Company, Washington was annoyed and almost decided to remove him.[37]

The plan for the League of Nations and the mandate system was given concrete form by Smuts, in a pamphlet entitled 'The League of Nations: A Practical Suggestion'. This confirmed the translation of the demand for democracy into a mechanism for producing the consent of the governed. In the future government of the territories and people formerly belonging to Russia, Austria and Turkey, Smuts wrote, the League should apply 'the rule of self-determination, or the consent of the governed to their form of government'. The document also confirmed the understanding that, for the colonised areas of the world, even those formerly under German rule, not even this principle was to apply. The German colonies in Africa, Smuts explained, 'are inhabited by barbarians, who not only cannot possibly govern themselves, but to whom it would be impracticable to apply any idea of political self-determination in the European sense . . . The disposal of these Colonies should be decided on the principles which President Wilson has laid down in the fifth of his celebrated Fourteen Points.'[38] In other words, any political claims the colonised population made would have to be weighed against the interests of the colonial power. According to the balancing machinery specified in Wilson's fifth point, those colonial interests 'must have equal weight'. Smuts could think of the peoples of German-ruled Africa as barbarians, perhaps, because of the sustained resistance they had shown to the colonisation of their lands since the 1880s, which in South-West Africa had led to the deliberate German extermination of the Herero and Nama peoples in the genocide of 1904–7.[39]

As we have seen, South Africa was a laboratory for the development of the self-governing colonial state, so it is no surprise that the country provided a critical source of expertise for transforming the pressure for democratisation into a new framework for imperialism. Smuts and other architects of the unified South Africa had fought a series of battles to define the self that would exercise the new

---

36   Robert Lansing, US secretary of state, was concerned about how self-determination would affect Britain: 'What effect will [the principle of self-determination] have on the Irish, the Indians, the Egyptians and the nationalists among the Boers? Will it not spread discontent, disorder and rebellion?' 'Self-determination and the Dangers', memo by Lansing, 30 December 1918, cited in William Stivers, 'International Politics and Iraqi Oil, 1918–1928: A Study in Anglo-American Diplomacy', *Business History Review* 55: 4, 1981: 536.

37   Stivers, 'International Politics and Iraqi Oil': 536.

38   Jan Smuts, 'The League of Nations: A Practical Suggestion', in John Dugard, ed., *The South West Africa/Namibia Dispute: Documents and Scholarly Writings on the Controversy Between South Africa and The United Nations*, Berkeley: University of California Press, 1973: 30.

39   David Olusoga and Casper W. Erichsen, *The Kaiser's Holocaust: Germany's Forgotten Genocide and the Colonial Roots of Nazism*, London: Faber & Faber, 2010.

powers of government. The great advantage of the doctrine of self-government or self-determination, in contrast to the arguments for democracy, was that the self to which it referred was very weakly defined. In the South African case, the struggles over the constitution of the new state were fought over the control of labour, as the colony sought to build the strength of the European settler class against the power of the mining magnates, on one side, who preferred indentured Asian labour, and the native African population on the other. The white population needed to be strengthened, it was felt, against both an economic threat, as Europeans could not subsist on the wages of African mine workers, and against a threat to their vitality, as poverty caused whites to degenerate in racial quality. The South African Native Affairs Commission had drawn up plans for systematic segregation, extending the racialised structures of the Transvaal gold-mining industry to the country as a whole. Blacks were to be allocated separate levels of pay, areas of settlement, and schools, subjected to pass laws controlling the movement of workers into urban areas, and governed under separate Native Councils. After the war, the Smuts government completed the main principles of segregation, including removing blacks from skilled industrial employment, removing them from most areas of the country to reservations, and 'retribalising' them under separate native rulers.

J. A. Hobson had written to Smuts before the war to criticise the plans to deny the African population any political rights in the new South African state. J. X. Merriman, the leader of Cape Colony, agreed with Smuts's fear that the Liberals in London 'will create some trouble on this delicate subject' and that 'any general Native franchise' was 'impossible to dream of' at present. He warned Smuts, however, that black South Africans 'are unfortunately the workers and in every country the future belongs to the worker'. He warned of the 'evil signs' of 'an intermingling that bodes ill for the future', especially since the best Natives were 'above, in many cases far above, our lowest stratum of Europeans'.[40] Merriman had previously written to Smuts: 'I do not like the Natives at all and I wish we had no black man in South Africa. But there they are, our lot is cast with them by an overruling Providence and the only question is how to shape our course so as to maintain the supremacy of our race and at the same time do our duty.'[41]

The problem of non-European claims was solved by the doctrine of 'separate development'. Since the future appeared to belong to the workers – an acknowledgement of the novel and growing powers of miners and other organised industrial workforces – they could not simply be ignored. Instead, their claims were deferred into the future, by designating them as populations whose rights were suspended because they were in need of 'development'. The mandate

---

40   John X. Merriman, letter to Smuts, 19 July 1908, in Smuts, *Selections*, vol. 2: 446–7.
41   Smuts, *Selections*, vol. 2: 239.

system that provided the justification for colonialism after the war was to be based on the same principle, and in fact the language of 'mandates' would be quickly replaced with doctrines of development. As the practice of development grew under mandate rule and in the later twentieth century, it always carried this racial structure. Even after the adjective was dropped, the term 'development' would always mean 'separate development'. Populations were designated as undeveloped in relation to the European races, were to acquire the know-how of development from Europeans and Americans, and were to be denied the democratic rights enjoyed by 'developed' peoples, a denial explained by their need for development.

The advancing of democratic claims requires a machinery, but the League was created with no democratic mechanisms. Its apparatus, the mandate, was a device first developed just before the war as a means of managing the imperial struggle over Morocco. Drawing on the experience of organising shared access to the trade of China, America had proposed at the Algeciras Conference of 1906 a mechanism to guarantee competing imperial powers equal access to Moroccan trade. The Act of Algeciras established international control of the ports of Morocco by having a native police force in all the ports paid for, officered and managed by the foreign powers. To gain the consent of France, the imperial power with the largest interests in Morocco, a compromise was reached that gave France, together with Spain, which controlled the country's northern coast, effective control of the police force, but under a 'mandate' from the other imperial states. The two European states would be recognised jointly as 'the mandatory of all the powers for the purpose of at once maintaining order and preserving equal opportunities for all of them'.[42]

In 1914, Brailsford had proposed the Moroccan agreement as a model for international collaboration over access to non-European regions.[43] In a first sketch of the mandate idea the following year, Hobson referred to this precedent as a mechanism for shared international control in place of colonialism, and from Hobson it was borrowed and weakened by Smuts, then taken up by Woodrow Wilson.[44] George Beer, an American ally of the Milner group and part of a committee asked by Wilson's aide, Colonel House, to collect views on the postwar settlement, wrote a report on 'The Future of Mesopotamia' in January 1918, and proposed the Algeciras mandate as a model for the colonial rule of Iraq. The administration of former Ottoman territories, he suggested,

---

42   Letter from Secretary of State Elihu Root to Baron Speck von Sternberg, German ambassador in Washington, 17 March 1906, cited in Pitman B. Potter, 'Origin of the System of Mandates Under the League of Nations', *American Political Science Review* 16: 4, November 1922: 580.

43   Brailsford, *War of Steel and Gold*: 249.

44   J. A. Hobson, *Towards International Government*, New York: Macmillan, 1915: 141; Potter, 'Origin of the System of Mandates': 577–81.

should be entrusted 'to different states acting as mandatories of the League of Nations', an arrangement similar to the Six Powers Group in China and the Algeciras Act of 1906.[45]

When the draft Covenant of the League was published, the labour movement in Britain condemned the proposals. The organisation was not a democratic body based on parliaments, as the Labour party and other European socialists had proposed, but an alliance of governments, with authority concentrated in the Council of the League controlled by the five powers that had won the war.[46] The weakened system of mandates had no effective monitoring mechanism or means of enforcement, and even the open-door principle of the 'equal treatment' of competing claims to trade and investment had been rephrased as merely their 'equitable treatment'. Brailsford wanted the mandates to be subject to 'searching and continuous inspection by Officers of the League', and to constitute, 'above all things, an economic structure' responsible for allocating shares of raw materials such as coal, iron, oil, cotton, wool, phosphates and grain. 'The oil of Mosul', for example, 'would have been distributed to all who need [it]' in proportions fixed by a standing council of the League.[47] The mandate system approved in Paris, Hobson argued, would 'furnish the political machinery for the completion of the process by which Western Europe has absorbed in colonies and protectorates so large a section of the earth'.[48]

The translation of democracy into self-determination enabled the survival of European control, including the control of oil. At the same time, in adopting the principle of self-determination, the imperial powers appeared to be acting with a new idealism. Woodrow Wilson would continue to be associated with this ideal, so that almost a century later, US plans to invade Iraq with the claim of intending to establish an Arab democracy could be discussed as a reassertion of Wilsonian 'idealism'. The view of Wilson on the part of those who had fought for a practical democratisation of international relations was rather different. 'If history makes any comment upon his statesmanship', a Labour Party newspaper wrote in 1919, 'it will be to condemn him as the weakest and most incompetent person whom a malignant fate ever entrusted with the power to interfere in human affairs.'[49]

The industrialised world brought into being with the energy from coal was also a colonising world. While the coal enabled an extraordinary concentration

45   George Louis Beer, 'The Future of Mesopotamia', in Louis Herbert Gray, ed., *African Questions at the Paris Peace Conference, with Papers on Egypt, Mesopotamia, and the Colonial Settlement*, New York: Macmillan, 1923: 424–5.

46   Carl F. Brand, 'The Attitude of British Labor Toward President Wilson during the Peace Conference', *American Historical Review* 42: 2, 1937: 246.

47   Henry Noel Brailsford, *After the Peace*, London: L. Parsons, 1920: 110, 119.

48   Hobson, quoted in David Long, *Towards a New Liberal Internationalism: The International Theory of J. A. Hobson*, Cambridge, UK: CUP, 1996: 158.

49   *Labour Leader*, 22 May 1919, cited in Brand, 'Attitude of British Labor': 252.

of production and population at the sites, close to the coal mines, where industrialisation had first occurred, the need for materials unavailable in the industrial regions, such as cotton, sugar, rubber and gold, encouraged the expansion of mining, plantations and colonial settlement across wide areas of the non-European world, along with railways, banking firms, investment capital and imperial armies. The mining and transportation of coal had created the possibility of a more democratic politics. The attempt to expand democratic control along the production and transport routes of these other materials proved more difficult. Democracy was becoming an ideal, a lightweight claim, translated into doctrines of self-determination.

CHAPTER 4

Mechanisms of Goodwill

At the end of the First World War, the prospect seemed unlikely that Britain would keep control either of Mesopotamia (or Iraq, as it would now be known) or of the other Arab territories it had occupied during the conflict. The Ottoman system of authority had been destroyed, and in every part of the region both local oligarchies and popular groups were organising alternatives. Yet British forces were to remain in Iraq for four decades, helping British oil companies, in collaboration with French and American firms, to take control of the country's oil, and subsequently of the entire oil production of the Middle East. The foreign oil firms were to continue in command of the region's main economic resource for more than half a century, until the beginning of the 1970s.

Among the processes that helped sustain this extraordinary control of twentieth-century energy resources, two were important from the beginning. First, as we have seen, the oil firms were concerned not simply with the supply of oil but with limiting its production and slowing the development of the petroleum industry. This impeded the ability, using the infrastructure of oil, to build effective methods for advancing egalitarian political claims. Second, the new mandate system under which Britain and France initially organised their justification for ruling much of the Arab world was set up as what the British representative to the Mandates Commission of the League of Nations called a 'dual mandate'. The European powers claimed both a mandate to civilise the native population and a mandate to rule the natives in the interests of civilisation.[1] By the interests of civilisation they meant the economic interests of the West, which frequently meant the interests of its oil companies. In the case of Iraq, the formal mandate under the League was short-lived, but the dual mandate endured under different terms. The first part continued under the name of 'self-determination', or what Lord Milner, who served as British secretary of state for the colonies after the war, called the attempt to 'rule subject races through their chiefs'; the second continued under the name of 'development', or the principle that subject peoples had no right 'to deny their bounties to those who need them'.[2]

---

1 Frederick Lugard, *The Dual Mandate in British Tropical Africa*, 5th edn, Hamden, CT: Archon Books, 1965.
2 Ibid.: 61, 194.

POSTWAR REVOLUTIONS

By the end of the war, Britain had more than a million soldiers in the Middle East, occupying Egypt and Sudan and the arc of Ottoman territory that stretched from Palestine in the west through northern Syria to the provinces of Mosul, Baghdad and Basra. Facing popular pressure at home to demobilise the troops, Britain soon discovered that even this vast body of armed men was unable to maintain control of the occupied territories.

In Syria, a British-backed Arab military government was nominally in power, but when Britain withdrew its support to allow France to occupy the country under the terms of a postwar deal between the two powers, popular committees took control of Damascus and other large towns. On 7 March 1920, meeting as the Syrian General Congress, they declared the country independent. The invading French army seized control by force, but opposition re-emerged in the Great Syrian Revolt of 1925–27.[3]

In Palestine, a month after the Syrian declaration, large demonstrations were launched against the British occupation. The protests demanded independence and a halt to Zionist immigration, which the British had decided to support as a means of creating a European settler population through whom it might retain a territorial hold on the eastern Mediterranean. Britain had originally planned to retain only the Palestinian port of Haifa, using the enclave as the terminus for a railway or pipeline to carry oil from Iran to the Mediterranean.[4] As it became clear that Palestinians' opposition to the seizure of their territory would require a larger military presence, Britain had opted to support the Zionist project to build up a Jewish colony in Palestine. Its military occupation could then be justified as necessary to support the self-determination of the European settlers, and to mediate the conflict that resulted as the settlers attempted to acquire Palestinian lands.

In Egypt, the popular uprising began a year before, in the Revolution of 1919. Strikes paralysed transportation and government administration in Cairo, while the rural population sabotaged the machinery of its wartime impoverishment – the railway system used to requisition food supplies and labour.[5] The

---

3   James L. Gelvin, *Divided Loyalties: Nationalism and Mass Politics in Syria at the Close of Empire*, Berkeley: University of California Press, 1998: 87–137. Following the withdrawal of Russia from the war, Britain and France had abandoned their wartime deal, the Sykes-Picot agreement, and negotiated a new understanding. France gave up Mosul to Britain in exchange for Britain's agreement to the French invasion and occupation of Syria and a share of Mosul's oil.

4   'Notes of a Meeting Held at Mr Lloyd George's Residence', in US Department of State, *Papers Relating to the Foreign Relations of the United States: The Paris Peace Conference, 1919* 5: 807.

5   See Abd al-Rahman al-Rafi'i, *Thawrat sanat 1919: Tarikh misr al-qawmi min sanat 1914 ila sanat 1921*, 2 vols, Cairo: Maktabat al-Nahda al-Misriya, 1946; Reinhard Schulze, *Die Rebellion der ägyptischen Fallahin 1919*, Bonn: Ballbek Verlag, 1981. On rural impoverishment

following March, two days after the declaration of independence in Damascus, members of Cairo's suspended Legislative Assembly, meeting at the home of the leading nationalist, passed a resolution declaring the British protectorate over Egypt null and void, and proclaiming the independence of 'the Egyptian territories' (al-bilad al-misriya), defined as the countries of Egypt and Sudan.[6] By August 1920, Britain was offering to accept a form of Egyptian independence provided it retained military control of the Suez Canal, whose need for 'protection' provided the pretext for a continued military presence. Britain abandoned a proposal for a constitution under which the various foreign colonies in Egypt would be directly represented in the upper house of the legislature, proposing instead to retain the power to veto the implementation of any laws it deemed to be 'operating inequitably' against the European settler communities in the country.[7]

In Iraq, which saw the most prolonged fighting of the war, resistance emerged more gradually. In the same month as the declarations in Damascus and Cairo, a group of twenty-nine delegates of an incipient nationalist movement met in Baghdad and declared the country's independence. Iraqi nationalists were encouraged by events next-door in Iran, where British attempts to impose a form of protectorate were meeting resistance, and by the Soviet success that spring in driving the British from Baku.[8] In July, an uprising in the middle Euphrates valley, triggered by the increased taxation with which the occupying British army tried to recoup its costs, turned into Thawrat al-Ishrin – the Revolution of 1920. Britain took more than six months to put down the rebellion, which demonstrated the increasing difficulty and expense of imperial rule.

THE WILSONIAN ATTITUDE

It was to these challenges that the doctrine of self-determination, or native rule, offered a solution. British officials in London, discussing the crisis in Iraq and preparing to send an official from the Indian administration, Sir Percy Cox, to Baghdad as high commissioner, expressed a fear that he 'might adopt a

---

and the railways, Ellis Goldberg, 'Peasants in Revolt: Egypt 1919', *International Journal of Middle Eastern Studies* 24: 2, May 1992: 261–80; and Nathan Brown, *Peasant Politics in Modern Egypt: The Struggle Against the State*, New Haven: Yale University Press, 1990. On the urban strike wave, Joel Beinin and Zachary Lockman, *Workers on the Nile: Nationalism, Communism, Islam, and the Egyptian Working Class, 1882–1954*, Princeton: Princeton University Press, 1987: 84–120.

6   Al-Rafi'i, *Thawrat sanat 1919*, vol. 2: 106–8.

7   Alfred Milner, 'Report of the Special Mission to Egypt', December 9, 1920, National Archives of the UK: Public Record Office (referred to hereafter as PRO), Cabinet Office Records, CAB/24/117: 13, 23–6.

8   Ali al-Wardi, *Lamahat ijtima'iya min tarikh al-'iraq al-hadith*, vol. 5, *Hawla thawrat al-'ishrin*, 2nd edn, London: Kufan, 1991: 45–54.

more Wilsonian attitude than we wished him to'.[9] The term 'Wilsonian' referred not to the ideas of self-determination recently attached to the American president, but to the views of the man Cox was sent to relieve, Arnold Wilson. An officer in the Indian army, Wilson had first come to the Middle East in 1907 as the head of the force of twenty Indian cavalry sent to protect the Anglo-Persian drilling party searching for oil at Masjid-i-Suleiman. (After Cox relieved him of his duties in postwar Iraq, he became the manager for the oil company's operations in the Gulf).[10] During the war Wilson served under Cox as a political officer in Iraq, and when the war ended he stood in for his superior as acting civil commissioner in Baghdad, in charge of the largely Indian administration (both British officers and Indian subordinates) assembled to manage the occupation of the country. After the war, the administration began 'governing Mesopotamia as though it were an Indian province'.[11] As the popular insurgency against British rule gathered momentum in the summer of 1920, Wilson informed his superiors in London that they faced two choices: 'either to hold Mesopotamia by force, or to clear out altogether'. This view, said Lord Curzon, 'left him with an unpleasant impression of Colonel Wilson's incapacity to deal with the situation'. London wanted instead 'the middle course of retaining our position in the country with the goodwill of the people'.[12] Postwar imperialism needed a mechanism of goodwill – a machinery for producing the consent of the governed.

Those trying to find a way of maintaining British power in postwar Iraq faced the problem not of Wilsonian self-determination so much as of the 'Wilsonian' view of imperialists like Arnold Wilson, whether Indian-trained colonial officers overseas or hard-line cabinet members at home, who wanted Britain to establish direct rule over Iraq, perhaps by encouraging the immigration of settlers from India as Britain was attempting to do in East Africa, and to maintain or extend control over countries like India and Egypt. Britain had generally not built its imperial control in Asia and Africa by the immediate annexation of local states. Although imperial power depended on the frequent use of armed violence, and trading ports and other strategic footholds were often seized by force, its expansion had typically proceeded by a method of infiltration and the gradual usurpation of command. This required the preservation of local forms of authority and legal order, even as they were being undermined from within. After the Indian uprising of 1858, and with the extension of

9 'Minutes of Inter-Departmental Conference on Middle Eastern Affairs', 16 June 1920, PRO, Foreign Office Records, FO 371/5227-0002: 5.

10 Arnold Wilson, SW. Persia: A Political Officer's Diary, 1907–1914, London: Oxford University Press, 1941.

11 Edwin Montagu, Secretary of State for India, 'Mesopotamian Administration', 23 July 1920, PRO, CAB 24/109.

12 'Minutes of Inter-Departmental Conference on Middle Eastern Affairs': 5, 3.

imperial rule over Africa after 1882, Britain developed more elaborate doctrines and practices of native rule.[13]

The most common method of controlling territories without incurring the degree of opposition and expense that came with immediate annexation had come to be called 'protecting' them. When the British government of India extended its empire to incorporate Ottoman territories of the Persian Gulf, it signed protection agreements with local emirs similar to those it had previously made with the princely states of India. The agreements acknowledged the authority of the local ruler, who in turn ceded part of that authority to the imperial power, often including control over the country's external trade or natural resources.[14] By the early twentieth century, textbooks of international law attempted to formalise the doctrine of protection by distinguishing between protectorates over 'real states', such as the one France established over Morocco in 1912, and 'so-called protectorates', such as those European states were acquiring over what were called African 'tribes', through a treaty with their chiefs. The political systems of Africa were no less real than others, but distinguishing certain protected territories as 'real states' rationalised the fact that, while virtually every newly occupied territory was now described as a protectorate, certain countries remained powerful enough to demand powers of self-government, but were denied independence – or, as it was then called, membership in the 'family of nations'. Protectorates offered a provisional family membership. Lassa Oppenheim's *Treatise on International Law*, in its third edition of 1920–21, remarked that, while protected states were real states, 'all of them are non-Christian states of such a civilisation as would not admit them to full membership of the Family of Nations, apart from the protectorate under which they now are'.[15] Like the principle of self-determination that was to replace it, the doctrine of protection allowed imperial powers to acknowledge a claim of independence, while insisting that for less developed peoples (or, as they were sometimes still called, non-Christians), the only way to advance that claim was under European control.

In the past, the imperial power usually offered protection not to a territory or population but to the ruler, who was to be protected against removal

---

13   Nicholas Dirks, The Hollow Crown: *Ethnohistory of an Indian Kingdom*, 2nd edn, Ann Arbor: University of Michigan Press, 1993; Mahmood Mamdani, *Citizen and Subject: Contemporary Africa and the Legacy of Late Colonialism*, Princeton: Princeton University Press, 1996; Karuna Mantena, *Alibis of Empire: Henry Maine and the Ends of Liberal Imperialism*, Princeton: Princeton University Press, 2010.

14   Anthony Anghie, 'Finding the Peripheries: Sovereignty and Colonialism in Nineteenth-Century International Law', *Harvard International Law Journal* 40: 1, 1999: 48–51.

15   Lassa Oppenheim, *A Treatise on International Law*, vol. 1, *Peace*, 3rd edn, ed., Ronald F. Roxburgh, London: Longmans, Green, 1920: 168. On quasi-sovereignty and protectorates, see Siba N. Grovogui, *Sovereigns, Quasi-Sovereigns, and Africans: Race and Self-Determination in International Law*, Minneapolis: University of Minnesota Press, 1996.

not only by rival powers but by his own subjects. During the First World War, however, Britain took control of countries in the Middle East with no ruler on whom it could rely. In destroying the Ottoman Empire by force, it had eliminated the authorities over whom it might have established claims of protection. To cope with this problem, it tried to create a new form of protection. In 1914, at the outbreak of the war, Britain made Egypt a protectorate without seeking the agreement of the sovereign power.[16] Declaring Ottoman suzerainty to be terminated, it announced a protectorate not over the Ottoman viceroy, who was deposed and replaced with an uncle, but over the country and its population. It would 'adopt all measures necessary for the defence of Egypt', Britain said, 'and protect its inhabitants and interests'.[17]

British officials in Cairo envisaged the protectorate over Egypt as a prototype for incorporating other Ottoman territories into the empire. In the course of the war, Britain planned to create further protectorates where Arab uprisings had weakened or destroyed prewar Ottoman authority. The expeditionary force sent from India to southern Iraq in 1914, ostensibly to protect the Anglo-Persian oilfields, had the larger aim of securing the Indian government's ties with local Arab powers in the event of a popular uprising against the Turks.[18] In March 1917, London ordered its representatives in Iraq to hold Basra under British rule and establish in Baghdad 'an Arab state with local ruler or government under British protectorate in everything but name'.[19] As in Palestine, the initial plan had been to keep control only of the key points for the shipment of oil. A riverfront town on the Shatt al-Arab waterway (the confluence of the Tigris and Euphrates), Basra offered a base for securing the Anglo-Persian oil terminal on the opposite bank of the river a few miles downstream at Abadan, and for constructing a pipeline to Palestine. Until the end of 1917, the British were still debating whether to hold Baghdad or try to keep British influence under loose Ottoman authority.[20] The Ottomans held onto Mosul, the third province that would later be added to form Iraq, until the end of the war. One week after the armistice in November 1918, British forces entered Mosul, but the status of that oil-rich region was not decided until later.

---

16   When it occupied the country in 1882, to suppress a popular revolt against Anglo-French control of the government's finances, Britain left Egypt nominally under the rule of the Ottoman sultan and his local viceroy. In government correspondence at the time, ministers referred to the dual control as 'Anglo-French protection'. See Sir E. Malet to Earl Granville, Cairo, telegram, 7 May 1882, PRO, FO 407/20.

17   Milner, 'Report': 7.

18   Stuart A. Cohen, *British Policy in Mesopotamia, 1903–1914*, Reading: Ithaca Press, 2008: 221–9.

19   Cited in Peter Sluglett, *Britain in Iraq: Contriving King and Country, 1914–1932*, New York: Columbia University Press, 2007: 15.

20   Reidar Visser, *Basra, the Failed Gulf State: Separatism and Nationalism in Southern Iraq*, Münster: Lit Verlag, 2005: 59.

ECONOMY IS THE TEST OF POLICY

In constructing a machinery of consent, the British sought a mode of government that would deal with two forms of opposition: the local opposition to
foreign military occupation, but also the challenge of Labour members of
parliament and other critics of imperialism at home, who were opposed to the
cost of empire and the prolongation of compulsory military service after the
war. Arthur Hirtzel, a senior official at the India Office in London, said that the
problem in Iraq was how to create 'some administration with Arab institutions
which we can safely leave while pulling the strings ourselves; something that
won't cost very much, that Labour can swallow consistent with its principles,
but under which our political and economic interests will be secure.'[21]

The emergence of an independent state in Syria, prior to the French occupation, had shown that local administration and national leadership could quickly
emerge from the destruction of the Ottoman order. In Iraq much of the local
Ottoman administration remained in place. This administration 'had given to
the dwellers in towns some semblance of Civilisation', the British conceded.
'There were law courts, from which there was an appeal to Constantinople;
and there was an electoral system under which not only municipalities were
worked, but members were sent to the Turkish Parliament. Iraq was, in fact,
a part – like any other – of the Ottoman Empire.'[22] However, a system of law,
municipal administration and representative government were not enough. The
British needed a 'native ruler', someone whose weakness would allow them to
offer protection, and thus maintain indirect control.

Britain's solution was 'the creation of an Emir'. The high commissioner,
Percy Cox, acknowledged that this was an anachronism. 'The immediate selection of an Emir connoting the establishment of dynasty', he wrote, 'is . . . a problem of the greatest difficulty at the present epoch.' He suggested a republic with
an elected president, provided the League of Nations would allow Britain to
nominate the first holder of the office. Britain considered supporting the most
powerful local figure, Sayyid Talib, the prewar ruler of Basra, but decided he was
too independent to use.[23] (His main British supporter in Iraq, St John Philby,
went on to support the emergence of a local ruler to the south, Ibn Saud, the
emir of Najd, who subsequently expanded his territory into the Kingdom of
Saudi Arabia.) A committee in London recommended that the emir's selection
be postponed for some years and that the British high commissioner fill his
place, but Cox felt that this would make the idea of the sovereignty and thus

---

21   Cited in Sluglett, *Britain in Iraq*: 31.
22   Montagu, 'Mesopotamian Administration'.
23   Sir Percy Cox, 'Note on the Mesopotamia–Persia Situation', 30 July 1920, PRO, CAB
24/110; Visser, Basra.

the self-determination of Iraq 'difficult to interpret'. Britain solved its problem by selecting a 'native ruler' from outside Iraq, and looked to the two emergent powers of Arabia for a candidate. After considering Ibn Saud of Najd, they opted for Emir Faisal, son of the Hashemite ruler of Hejaz.[24]

The financial burden of colonialism reflected this difficulty in replacing Ottoman administration with 'native' rule. While postwar budgets were tight, and provided a reason for scaling back in Iraq, Britain had cost-saving devices like the use of cheap Imperial battalions from India, the levying of an Iraqi armed force, and the deployment of air power. Using aircraft to bomb Iraqi towns and villages helped suppress the 1920 revolt and subsequent uprisings with speed, but air power was unreliable. The secretary of state for India, for example, found the proposal to rely on air power 'difficult to reconcile' with reports of 'the difficulty of keeping aircraft serviceable in a tropical climate'.[25] The colonial secretary, Winston Churchill, argued for a combination of air power and popular consent, using the former to demand the latter. He called for holding the country 'not by sheer force, but by the acquiescence of the people of Mesopotamia as a whole in a Government and Ruler whom they have freely accepted, and who will be supported by the Air Force, and by British organised levies, and by 4 Imperial battalions'. This would create, he argued, 'an independent Native State friendly to Great Britain, favourable to her commercial interests, and costing hardly any burden upon the Exchequer'. The secretary of state for war raised doubts about bombing people as a means of winning their consent.

> Punitive measures may have to be taken against disturbers of the peace; the only means at the disposal of the Air Force, and the means now in fact used, are the bombing of the women and children of the villages. If the Arab population realize that the peaceful control of Mesopotamia ultimately depends on our intention of bombing women and children, I am very doubtful if we shall gain the acquiescence of the fathers and husbands of Mesopotamia as a whole to which the Secretary of State for the Colonies looks forward.[26]

Wars of occupation were now prolonged, attritional and destructive. Mechanised warfare could be fought on a global scale, but only at great cost. Despite an occupying army in Iraq proportionally much larger and better armed than its forces occupying India, Egypt and other territories, the British

---

24   Cox, 'Note on the Mesopotamia–Persia Situation'.

25   'Minutes of Inter-Departmental Conference on Middle Eastern Affairs': 8.

26   Memorandum by Churchill, 4 August 1921, PRO, CAB 24/126, and Memorandum by secretary of state for war, 17 August 1921, PRO, CAB 24/127, cited in William Stivers, *Supremacy and Oil: Iraq, Turkey, and the Anglo-American World Order, 1918–1930*, Ithaca: Cornell University Press, 1982: 78. On bombing villages to secure payment of taxes and other British uses of air power, see Sluglett, *Britain in Iraq*: 264–70.

administration could not establish control. By 1919–20, Britain was facing revolt almost everywhere in the empire – in Ireland, India and Egypt, as well as Palestine and Iraq.

But the financial constraint also reflected the changed political order British imperialists faced at home. Parliament had forced the Admiralty and War Department to introduce new methods of reporting military expenditures. In June 1920, Labour MPs forced Churchill to reveal that the occupation of Mesopotamia was costing as much as £50 million annually.[27] The rise of the labour movement and the social measures adopted in response to its power had produced demands to reveal the actual costs of empire. This led to calls for the elimination of waste and for 'economy', which was declared in the press to be 'the supreme national need'. The debate on Iraq was summarised in *The Times*: 'economy . . . was the test of policy'.[28]

Against these difficulties, self-determination was not a problem for imperialism – it was a solution. From a financial point of view, it could work in Britain's favour. If the principle were defined to mean that occupied countries should be asked to consent to their occupation, and that mechanisms of native rule should be devised to produce that consent, then the new 'liberal internationalism' would provide a tool not for the undermining of imperial interests, but to ensure their survival.

CONTROL OF THE OIL AREA

Britain soon abandoned its initial plans for the postwar control of Iraq. In April 1920, Britain and France met at San Remo in Italy and reached an agreement to divide control of the Arab territories. To legitimise Britain's continued military occupation of Iraq and Palestine, and France's seizure of Lebanon and Syria by force immediately after the meeting, they claimed them as 'mandates' under the League of Nations, according to the scheme they had devised at the Paris peace conference a year before. They also signed a second agreement at San Remo to share the oil resources of Mosul. To justify taking control of the oil of Mosul, a territory Britain now claimed as part of Iraq, they referred to the London-based Turkish Petroleum Company's unratified Ottoman concession agreement of 1914 (see Chapter 2). Anglo-Persian Oil (the future BP) was to hold half the company, as agreed in 1914. Shell was to control the other half, by combining its original 25 per cent share with the old Deutsche Bank portion, which was to go to a French consortium under the control of Shell. To persuade the Iraqis to

---

27 'Persia and Mesopotamia', *The Times*, 10 June 1920: 17.

28 'Public Anger At Waste: Mesopotamia Debate To-Day, Urgent Coalition "Whip"', *The Times*, 23 June 1920: 16; 'Mesopotamia and Economy: Lord Curzon on Arab Rule, A Cabinet Committee', *The Times*, 26 June 1920: 16.

accept foreign control of the oil, Anglo-Persian and Shell agreed to allow 'the native Government or other native interests' in Iraq to purchase a holding in the company of up to 20 per cent.[29]

Neither the mandate nor the oil agreement survived for long. The Rockefeller Standard Oil interests defeated the petroleum agreement through carefully targeted threats against Anglo-Persian and the Shell group.[30] Standard's agents also tried to weaken the British in Baghdad, circulating attacks on British policy from the English press, which reappeared in nationalist speeches, and possibly funding the insurgents during the 1920 uprising – although the evidence was hard to pin down. 'I wish these Americans would do something', complained Lord Curzon, the foreign secretary, referring to the agents of Standard Oil, 'to justify our expelling them from Mesopotamia.'[31] Over the following year Washington itself came close to removing the US consul in Baghdad, who had acted as the sales agent for the Standard Oil Company of New York during the war, supplying the Ottoman forces in the city, when it discovered he was lending support to anti-British forces.[32]

After the Iraqi uprising was defeated, Standard Oil lent support to another anti-British force, the emergent republican government in Turkey – or so the British learned 'on good authority' in December 1921 – as an alternative method of driving the British out of Iraq. The oil company was suspected of 'inciting the Turks to attack Iraq in the hope of obtaining from them a share in the oil which they are unable to get so long as His Majesty's Government remain in control of the oil area.'[33] At the same time, an American firm that had earlier been linked

---

29   The San Remo Oil agreement, often omitted in historical accounts, can be found in US Department of State, *Papers Relating to the Foreign Relations of the United States, 1920*, Washington, DC: US Government Printing Office, 2, 1935: 655–8. On Shell's control of the French share, see Gregory Nowell, *Mercantile States and the World Oil Cartel, 1900–1939*, Ithaca, NY: Cornell University Press, 1994: 80–160.

30   In 1911 the US Supreme Court dissolved the Standard Oil trust and split it into numerous companies. The two largest, Standard Oil of New Jersey (later Exxon) and Standard Oil of New York (later Mobil, then merging with Exxon to form ExxonMobil in 1999), remained under the Rockefeller family's control, and are referred to here as 'Standard Oil'. The Rockefeller firms attacked Anglo-Persian with the threat of signing a rival oil concession in northern Iran, and Shell by undermining its plans for a government-sanctioned oil monopoly in France, a revival of the prewar Franco-German kerosene monopoly project mentioned in Chapter 2. A new French oil consortium was formed to hold the French share of Iraqi oil, Compagnie Française des Pétroles, in which Standard Oil and its French allies held the largest share, with smaller shares for independent French oil companies, and even for Anglo-Persian and Shell. Under pressure from the left in parliament, the French government later took a 35 per cent share in the consortium. Nowell, *Mercantile States*: 135–44, 160–222.

31   'Foreign Influences Behind Arab Uprising', 12 August 1920, PRO, FO 371/5228-0002. The claim about the uprising is repeated in Winston S. Churchill, 'Foreign Incitement of the Turks to Attack Iraq', 13 December 1921, PRO, CAB 24/131.

32   Stivers, 'International Politics and Iraqi Oil, 1918–1928: A Study in Anglo-American Diplomacy', *Business History Review* 55: 4, 1981: 536, and *Supremacy and Oil*: 109.

33   Churchill, 'Foreign Incitement of the Turks', CAB 24/131.

with Standard Oil signed an agreement with the new Ankara government to complete the prewar project for building a railway to Mosul and Baghdad, with rights to develop the oil of Mosul.[34] The pressure from Standard Oil forced Britain to rewrite the San Remo oil agreement to include the Americans as shareholders in the scheme.

The Iraqis themselves needed no help from Standard Oil in opposing British rule. The government the British set up in Baghdad under Emir Faisal, now designated king of Iraq, refused to recognise Britain's claim to rule on the basis of a 'mandate' from the League of Nations. In June 1921, barely a year after announcing the mandate, Cox informed London that it was 'out of date'. Britain agreed to replace it in October 1922 with a twenty-year treaty of alliance, recognising the sovereignty, if not yet the independence, of the new state. The colonial power continued to face opposition at home, where popular opinion was opposed to a long-term commitment in Iraq, and a month after signing the treaty the British government fell. Iraq was a central issue in the election that followed, and Churchill, an architect of the Iraq settlement, lost his seat to the socialist E. D. Morel – the wartime leader of the campaign for the democratic control of foreign policy. The new government in London amended the treaty with Iraq to reduce Britain's formal role in the country from twenty years to four.[35] Facing popular opposition in Iraq and parliamentary opposition at home, Britain attempted from 1923 to secure its position in Iraq at the lowest cost. The solution lay in resolving the control of oil, which was both the main reason for the continued British military presence and potentially the means to pay for it.

Following their agreement to include the Americans, the oil companies had taken almost two years to decide how to share control of the Turkish Petroleum Company, which they later renamed the Iraq Petroleum Company (IPC). Negotiations between IPC and the government of Iraq took two more years, and the companies took another decade to start producing oil in significant quantities. As usual, the delays reflected their preference for impeding the development of large new sources of supply. British officials in Baghdad helped Iraq negotiate a series of terms intended to prevent IPC from sitting on the concession and producing as little oil as possible, with increasing drilling obligations, minimum production levels, a timeline for the construction of a pipeline, and

34 John A. DeNovo, *American Interests and Policies in the Middle East, 1900–1939*, Minneapolis: University of Minnesota Press, 1963: 210–28. The American firm was the same Chester group whose Ottoman-American Development Company, mentioned in Chapter 2, was accused of being a front for the Standard Oil Company. The firm attempted to win Standard's support after the war, but seems to have been an instrument of Turkey's challenge to Britain rather than of Standard Oil.

35 Toby Dodge, *Inventing Iraq: The Failure of Nation-Building and a History Denied*, New York: Columbia University Press, 2003: 22–6.

the auctioning of undeveloped drilling blocks. In practice IPC was able to evade all these requirements, largely because it refused the one demand that might have enabled Iraq to monitor its compliance: an Iraqi share in its ownership. In granting a one-quarter share in IPC to Standard Oil and other American oil interests, the oil companies had eliminated the British government's proposal for Iraqi interests to hold 20 per cent of the venture. After months of negotiations in which IPC refused to yield on ownership, the Baghdad government gave way, and in March 1925 signed a concession agreement that gave it no share in the company. Desperate for the revenues from oil to begin, under pressure from the British, and perhaps warned that a League of Nations Commission deciding whether to award Mosul province to Turkey or Iraq would favour Iraq if the oil issue was finally settled, the Baghdad government consented to a deal that deprived it of any control over the development of the country's main economic resource.

Meanwhile, in the Red Line Agreement of 1928, the major oil companies finalised their shares of Iraq's oil and extended the consortium's arrangements for impeding the development of oil to the rest of the Middle East, by agreeing not to develop production elsewhere in the region without the consent of all its members.[36] At the same time, in response to what was called an 'oil offensive' from the Soviet Union (an attempt to sell more oil abroad and to escape the control of Shell and Standard Oil), the large international firms made a parallel deal to divide the world's markets among themselves, and to limit production to maintain prices.[37] They later agreed to try and keep those prices at the relatively high level at which oil was produced and sold in Texas. The 1928 arrangements also operated as a broader hydrocarbon cartel, covering the coal and chemical industries. The leading oil companies agreed with German and British chemical industry conglomerates to collaborate in controlling patents on the production of synthetic fuels.[38]

The League of Nations Commission proceeded to hand Mosul to Iraq, along with its rich deposits of oil, provided that the mandate be extended for twenty-five years, on the grounds that the Kurdish-speaking population of the province, who formed its majority, needed the protection of an imperial

---

36 Ronald W. Ferrier, *The History of the British Petroleum Company*, vol. 1: *The Developing Years: 1901–1932*, Cambridge, UK: CUP, 1982: 583–5. Under the agreement, Anglo-Persian, the Shell Group, French oil interests organised as the Compagnie Française des Pétroles (in which Standard Oil, Anglo-Persian and Shell were also part owners), and Standard Oil–led US interests organised as the Near East Development Corporation, each shared 23.75 per cent of the Iraq Petroleum Company, with the remaining 5 per cent held by Calouste Gulbenkian, the Ottoman-Armenian entrepreneur who had organised the original Turkish Petroleum Company. The Red Line was drawn to encompass all of the Middle East (excluding North Africa) except for regions already under the control of Anglo-Persian.

37 Alzada Comstock, 'Russia's Oil Offensive', *Barron's*, 30 January 1928: 17.

38 Nowell, *Mercantile States*: 223–79.

power. Tasked with deciding the future of Mosul according to the principle of self-determination, the Commission had interpreted this to mean conducting inquiries about whether the people of the region considered themselves Arabs or Turks. Those they consulted were more concerned with collective well-being and economic survival than with organising their multiple attachments into an ethnic category, which freed the Commission to allocate the province to Iraq on economic grounds, using the argument that Baghdad and Basra provinces depended on grain imports from the north.[39]

The annexation of Mosul required Britain briefly to amend the Anglo-Iraq treaty again, but the new twenty-five-year agreement included a provision for early termination of the mandate if the League of Nations agreed that Iraq's political development qualified it for membership. Within a year, British administrators were arguing for a rapid end to the mandate, anxious to keep in power the new governing elite that guaranteed its access to the oil and its right to maintain air force bases in the country. To that end, Britain falsified reports to the Mandate Commission, creating the impression of a state meeting mandate criteria for membership of the League. Again, an election in Britain was decisive. In May 1929 the Conservative government was defeated, in part because of the harm done by what an internal party warning called its 'militarist and adventurous foreign policy'. The new Labour government quickly agreed to suspend the 1927 treaty, and put Iraq forward for League membership by 1932.[40] The wartime plans of the Labour party platform in 1916 had long been abandoned. In place of 'the democratization of all countries', the mandate had installed a narrow elite in power, allied with the British.

NATURAL SPOKESMEN FOR THE MANY

Under the principle of self-determination, mechanisms were devised to produce the 'agreement' of occupied Arab countries to European control. In the case of Egypt, for example, after finally agreeing to negotiations in London with the nationalist elite in order to bring an end to the 1919 Revolution, the British party to the talks, led by Lord Milner, insisted that the nationalist leadership return to Egypt with the draft of a proposed treaty 'to explain to the public of that country the nature of the settlement . . . and the great advantages which Egypt would derive from it'. If it were favourably received, Milner explained, 'this would constitute a "mandate" from the people'. The procedure that the delegates adopted, Milner reported, 'was to invite small groups of representative

---

39   Sarah Shields, 'Mosul Questions: Economy, Identity and Annexation', in Reeva Simon and Eleanor Tejirian, eds, *The Creation of Iraq, 1914–1921*, New York: Columbia University Press, 2004; Quincy Wright, 'The Mosul Dispute', *American Journal of International Law* 20: 3, July 1926: 453–64.

40   Dodge, *Inventing Iraq*: 32–7.

Egyptians to meet them and to discuss the proposed settlement. The latter in turn reported to other groups in the provinces, whence resolutions of adherence were received . . . so that within a fortnight of their arrival it became evident that a substantial majority of the representative elements in the country were favourable' to the proposed treaty.[41] Similar procedures for obtaining consent were organised in Iraq. The mandate system was turned into a machinery of consent, where the imperial power signed treaties (except in Palestine, where control broke down) by which a minority of 'representative elements' in quasi-independent states assented to the British imperial presence. Mandates were transformed back into a form of protectorate.

The mechanisms of consent enabled imperial powers to deal with two forms of opposition: first, the partial sovereignty acknowledged in the signing of treaties allowed local elites to present themselves as nationalists, weakening more populist opposition. The power of a local oligarchy organised under forms of kingship, accompanied by the rule of large landowners, could be represented as an expression of 'self-determination'. As Frederick Lugard explained, 'The ideal of self-government can only be realised by the methods of evolution which have produced the democracies of Europe and America', that is, 'by representative institutions in which the comparatively small educated class shall be recognised as the natural spokesmen for the many'.[42] Second, the mandate framework provided a method for Britain to weaken its own domestic pressure to democratise foreign policy ('something Labour can swallow'), on the grounds that it was acting not as an imperial power but on a mandate from the League.

A further advantage of 'self-determination' was that the world could now be grasped in terms of political identities that were determined by race or ethnicity, a flexible concept that could refer to language, religion, shared history or, most often, simple geographical demarcation. Since no population was ethnically homogenous, this created the possibility of identifying or shaping groups as 'minorities'. The imperial power could then claim the duty to protect them as an endangered fragment of the population. In Egypt, Britain abandoned the protectorate, but in the 1920–22 negotiations over Egyptian independence claimed the right to a continued role in the country as protector of the European residents – whom it wanted initially, as we have seen, to be represented separately in the upper house of the legislature. In Palestine, Britain achieved the same position by creating a European minority – through facilitating Zionist settlement and suppressing local attempts to stop it, and then attempting to establish institutions in which the native population and the minority Zionist community were 'equally' represented. In fact Britain refused to create a legislative assembly in Palestine unless the Palestinian leadership accepted the terms

41   Milner, 'Report': 23, 35.
42   Lugard, *Dual Mandate*: 193.

of the mandate, which recognised Jewish 'national' claims in Palestine but did not recognise Palestinians as a national community.[43] After France invaded Syria (whose southern provinces Britain had retained to form Palestine and Transjordan), it divided the country into six further states. The various political affiliations of each geographical region were simplified into ethno-religious identifications: an Alawite state, a Druze state, a predominantly Christian state (Lebanon), the mixed Turkish, Alawite, and Armenian state of Alexandretta, and the Arab states of Damascus and Aleppo. The last two were reunited in 1924 as the state of 'Syria', into which the Druze and Alawite states were incorporated in 1936 and 1937. Alexandretta was handed to Turkey in 1939, leaving only Lebanon as a separate entity out of the original six statelets.[44] To ethnic groups that could not serve as the mode of control, no protection was offered. The Armenians failed to receive protection against Turkish atrocities, or to be granted a postwar state of their own. But refugees from the atrocities were welcomed into Syria and Lebanon by the French, as another Christian minority in need of imperial protection.[45]

MATERIAL OBLIGATIONS

The training of subject races in self-government represented only one half of the mandate that imperial powers could now claim. Alongside their 'moral obligations to the subject races', which included the training of native rulers, the introduction of a limited amount of schooling to 'assist progress without creating false ideals', and other carefully graduated processes of 'civilisation', the mandatory power claimed a set of 'material obligations'. These were obligations not to civilise native forms of rule, but rather to ensure that natives were ruled in the interests of civilisation.

Lord Lugard, the former British governor of Nigeria, explained the difference between the moral and the material sides of colonialism in his work *The Dual Mandate*, written just before he took up his appointment as the British representative to the Permanent Mandates Commission of the League, a position he held from 1922 to 1936. He wrote his classic text on native rule as both a guide to colonial officials and an attack on the attempt by the labour movement in Britain to subject imperialism to democratic control. The material part of the dual mandate was a duty to ensure the 'development of natural resources for the mutual benefit of the people and of mankind in general'. The imperial

43   Rashid Khalidi, *The Iron Cage: The Story of the Palestinian Struggle for Statehood*, Boston: Beacon Press, 2006: 31–48.

44   George Antonius, 'Syria and the French Mandate', *International Affairs* 13: 4, July–August 1934: 523–39.

45   Tsolin Nalbantian, 'Fashioning Armenians in Lebanon, 1946–1958', PhD thesis, Department of Middle Eastern, South Asian, and African Studies, Columbia University, 2010: 33.

power, Lugard argued, was the 'trustee, on the one hand, for the advancement of the subject races, and on the other hand, for the development of its material resources for the benefit of mankind'.[46]

The obligation to 'develop' the world's resources provided an answer to left-wing critics of empire, who were the target of Lugard's conclusion to his 600-page text. Since the First World War, these critics had been arguing that 'the British taxpayer was being called on to support the ambitions of chauvinists, and that the native races were misgoverned and robbed of their lands and their proper profits by the greed of exploiters'. There seemed to be 'an organised attempt', Lugard complained, 'to promulgate these doctrines among the Labour Party, and to persuade them that the existence of the Empire is antagonistic alike to their own interests and to those of the subject races'. The Research Department of the Labour Party, he suggested, 'would persuade the British democracy that it is better to shirk Imperial responsibility, and relegate it to international committees; that material development benefits the capitalist profiteer; and that British rule over subject races stands for spoliation and self-interest'.[47] The doctrine of the dual mandate provided an answer to these critics of empire. Imperialism, Lugard argued, was not an anti-democratic process. On the contrary, only through colonialism could the new democratic claims of the labour movement be met. 'The democracies of to-day claim the right to work', he noted; but without the raw materials produced in the colonies 'the satisfaction of that claim is impossible'. Imperial merchants, miners and manufacturers employed their technical skills, capital and energy overseas not as 'greedy capitalists' but 'in fulfilment of the Mandate of civilisation'.[48]

The doctrine of development provided a new rationale for imperial power, one that the Mandates Commission of the League was to play an important role in elaborating. At this point, in the 1920s, the doctrine referred only to the development of material resources. In the following chapter I will trace the emergence of a new object of development – 'the economy'.

---

46   Lugard, *Dual Mandate*: 58–9, 606.

47   Ibid.: 608. On the Mandates and development see Antony Anghie, 'Colonialism and the Birth of International Institutions: Sovereignty, Economy, and the Mandate System of the League of Nations', *New York University Journal of International Law and Politics* 34: 3, 2002,: 513–633. See also Priya Satia, 'Developing Iraq: Britain, India and the Redemption of Empire and Technology in the First World War', *Past and Present* 197: 1, 2007: 211–55. (T. E. Lawrence used the claim of 'development' to criticise the occupation: 'We say we are in Mesopotamia to develop it for the benefit of the world. All experts say that the labour supply is the ruling factor in its development. How far will the killing of ten thousand villagers and townspeople this summer hinder the production of wheat, cotton, and oil?' 'A Report on Mesopotamia', *Sunday Times*, 22 August 1920).

48   Lugard, *Dual Mandate*: 61.

CONCENTRATING THE WEIGHT OF FORCES

The Iraq Petroleum Company finally began drilling for oil in April 1927, almost a quarter of a century after the Ottoman government had given Deutsche Bank the first oil concession for Mesopotamia. Within a few weeks it had discovered a vast oilfield, in a highly porous limestone structure stretching for sixty miles to the north of Kirkuk. The company used the discovery as an excuse for further delays. It abandoned exploration elsewhere in Iraq and spent another seven years drilling test wells in the Kirkuk field, slowly determining the extent and peculiarities of the reservoir and producing a token 2,000 barrels of oil per day. It built roads, workshops and housing, creating accommodation for 2,000 Iraqi workers, 125 Europeans, and 30 Americans. It was unwilling to develop production, however, especially when the 1929 financial crisis brought on the Great Depression. The government of Iraq demanded that the company build a pipeline to export oil to the Mediterranean, but the company refused to do so until the government agreed to renegotiate the 1925 oil concession.

In 1931 Iraq's pro-British prime minister, Nuri al-Sa'id, agreed to a revision of the concession in exchange for a modest cash advance. The new agreement eliminated the government's right to tax the company's profits (a right distinct from the royalty payments on each barrel of oil produced) and removed the minimum drilling obligation and the requirement that the company periodically relinquish undeveloped parts of the concession area. The agreement expanded the concession area from the 192 square miles that the company had been required to select under the relinquishment provision to 32,000 square miles (from 50,000 hectares to over 8 million hectares). Having accepted what the State Department's oil expert later called 'one of the worst oil deals that has ever been signed', Iraq finally began to earn a modest income from oil.[49]

A pair of twelve-inch pipelines from Kirkuk to the Mediterranean was built in 1932–34, one line branching south to a British-controlled terminal at Haifa, the other north to a terminal at Tripoli under French control (see map, pp. 116–7). With twelve pumping stations, the first of the great Middle East pipelines – at that time the biggest welded pipeline in the world – the new conduit allowed oil production to increase forty-fold, from 2,000 to 80,000 barrels a day. This was only a fraction of what Iraq's wells could produce, but a plan to increase the pipeline capacity fourfold was delayed by the Second World War, and then limited to half that by the 1948 Palestine war, which closed the southern route to Haifa – although a larger replacement was then built, running north to the Syrian coast at Banias. Production was

---

49   Francisco Parra, *Oil Politics: A Modern History of Petroleum*, London: I. B. Tauris, 2004: 12–13. The 1931 agreement gave IPC control of the north-east of the country. When concessions for the north-west and the south were offered over the following decade, they were purchased by IPC, giving it control of almost the entirety of Iraq's oil.

doubled to 160,000 bpd in 1950, and doubled again in 1952 (by 1980 it would reach 2.5 million bpd).[50] Meanwhile, in July 1940, the railway line connecting Baghdad to Mosul was finished, completing the route of the Baghdad Railway, which had been intended as the region's first oil pipeline but had taken four decades to finish.

In building the infrastructure of oil, the petroleum companies were also laying out the infrastructure of political protest. The points of vulnerability, where movements could organise and apply pressure, now included a series of oil wells, pipelines, refineries, railways, docks and shipping lanes across the Middle East. These were the interconnected sites at which a series of claims for political freedoms and more egalitarian forms of life would be fought.

Britain had reoccupied Iraq in 1941, less than a decade after acknowledging the country's formal independence. Following the war, protests culminated in the popular uprising and student and worker strikes of 1948. The Communist Party of Iraq, which had emerged as one of the best-organised political movements in the region, demanded 'the evacuation of foreign troops, the unshackling of democratic freedoms [and] the provision of decent bread to the people'.[51] The party had 'concentrated the weight of its force in the colossal enterprises that were . . . most vital to the country' – the railways, the port of Basra and the oilfields. This focus on the most vulnerable points in the technical structures of a petroleum-based system of production 'constituted the key to its basic strategy'.[52]

In the railways, the party organised most of its resources at 'the most fundamental point in the entire system, the railway workshops at Schalchiyyah', where the main stores and all repair and maintenance work were concentrated. 'Stoppage of activity in this place for ten to fifteen days would have brought the movement of trains in the whole of Iraq to a complete standstill'.[53] In the British-controlled oilfields, the party focused its activities at an even more vital site – 'the point of bifurcation of the Kirkuk–Haifa and the Kirkuk–Tripoli pipelines, the K3 pumping station near Hadithah'.[54] A strike by oil workers in June 1946 demanding the right to a union, sickness and disability insurance, and a pension, was crushed by force, with ten workers killed and twenty-seven injured.[55] During the 1948 uprising, however, the oil workers succeeded in shutting down K3. Since the pumping station supplied the gasoline for other pumping stations, the union posted guards to ensure that not 'even a pint of gasoline' got out. The stoppage lasted two weeks, until the Company surrounded the site

50   Stephen Longrigg, *Oil in the Middle East: Its Discovery and Development*, 3rd edn, London: OUP, 1968: 70–83, 174–82; DeGolyer & McNaughton, *Twentieth Century Petroleum Statistics*, Dallas: DeGolyer & MacNaughton, 2009.

51   Prison letter from Comrade Fahd, early February 1948, cited in Hanna Batatu, *The Old Social Classes and the Revolutionary Movements of Iraq*, London: Saqi Books, 2004: 564.

52   Ibid.: 616.

53   Ibid.: 617.

54   Ibid.: 622.

55   Ibid.: 624.

with machine guns and armoured cars and cut off supplies of food. Unable to risk an armed confrontation, the strikers decided to march on Baghdad, more than 150 miles away. After three days of marching, with increasing support along the way, they 'entered Fallujah and fell into a police trap'.[56] The oil workers were sent back to K3, and the strike leaders to prison.

TROUBLEMAKERS

The other end of the Kirkuk–Haifa pipeline, in Palestine, provided another site of struggle. In the 1936–39 Arab revolt – the most sustained anticolonial uprising against the British in the twentieth century – a major target of the insurgency was the recently completed pipeline from Iraq. Initial efforts to weaken the British in August 1936 by organising a strike at the oil refinery at Haifa, and at the port, the railway and the Public Works Department, were defeated when the British brought in Royal Navy engineers to run the trains and Jewish workers to run the port and the refinery.[57] The pipeline was more vulnerable. Palestinian forces destroyed it for the first time near Irbid on 15 July 1936. They later blew it up several times near the villages of Kaukab al-Hawa, Mahane Yisrael, and Iksal, between 'Afula and Beisan, and at Tel 'Adas, al-Bira, 'Ard al-Marj, Tamra, Kafr Misr, Jisr al-Majami', Jinjar, Beisan and Indur.[58] Unable to protect the pipeline, the British created of a force of armed Jewish settlers to assist with its defence, and to guard the Haifa–Lydda railway line.[59] This British-officered force was the nucleus of the Zionist army that seized control of Palestine in 1948.

The construction of a pipeline to carry petroleum from the oilfields of Saudi Arabia to the Mediterranean produced another set of political calculations and opportunities. The Trans-Arabian Pipeline Company, a joint venture by the four US companies that owned Aramco – the firm that in 1933 had acquired exclusive rights to produce oil in Saudi Arabia – originally planned to terminate the pipeline near the British refinery at Haifa.[60] In 1946 they altered its

56   Ibid.: 625.

57   Zachary Lockman, *Comrades and Enemies: Arab and Jewish Workers in Palestine, 1906–1948*, Berkeley: University of California Press, 1996: 243.

58   Ghassan Kanafani, 'The 1936–39 Revolt in Palestine', New York: Committee for a Democratic Palestine, 1972: 109, available at www.newjerseysolidarity.org. Kanafani twice mentions the place name Bashan, which is presumably a translator's error and has been corrected to Beisan; Ain Dur has been corrected to Indur. 'Ard al-Marj refers to Marj ibn Amir.

59   Kanafani, 'The 1936–39 Revolt'. On the British–Zionist collaboration in defending the pipeline, see David Ben-Gurion, 'Our Friend: What Wingate Did for Us', *Jewish Observer and Middle East Review*, 27 September 1963: 15–16.

60   See map, pp. 116–7. Standard Oil of California (now Chevron) had acquired rights to Saudi oil in 1933, formed a joint venture with The Texas Company (Texaco) three years later, and expanded the venture in 1947 to include Standard Oil of New Jersey (Exxon), and Socony-Vacuum (Mobil). On the history of Middle East oil pipelines, see Rafael Kandiyoti, *Pipelines: Flowing Oil and Crude Politics*, London: I. B. Tauris, 2008: 49–83.

route to avoid Palestine and pass through the south-west corner of Syria, with a terminal on the Lebanese coast near Sidon. The reason given was the uncertain political future of Palestine, but this uncertainty may have included more than just the growing threat of Zionism to the country's stability. The British refinery, located at the terminus of the existing pipeline from Iraq, was the site of an additional threat to oil company control. Its workers organised a strike in February 1935, the 1936 strike mentioned above, and a thirteen-day strike for better wages in March 1947.[61] In the summer of 1947, Samuel Mikunis, secretary of the Communist Party of Palestine, testifying in Jerusalem before the United Nations Special Committee on Palestine, raised a series of objections to the local political powers exercised by the oil companies:

> The oil refinery at Haifa (The Consolidated Refineries Limited) is a foreign concern exempted from all payment of customs duties. Monopoly concessions have been granted to the Iraq Petroleum Company and to the Trans-Arabian Oil Company. These concessions include the right – free of royalties, taxes, import duties or other payments, charges or compensations – to lay pipelines through any part of the country, to expropriate land, to seize any wood, stone, water and other local materials required, to import cheap labour regardless of existing immigration laws, to pass freely the border of Palestine, to build and use their own harbours, railroads, aerodromes and wireless stations, to exact port taxes for harbouring and loading, and to keep their own police force. The population of Palestine does not derive even cheaper oil and petrol from these concessions, granted by the Government without any consultation of the people.[62]

Rerouting the pipeline through Syria provided a way to avoid this kind of political contestation. When the Syrian parliament refused to ratify the terms of the agreement with the pipeline company, arguing for improved transit fees and a less one-sided US position on Palestine, the oil companies had the CIA organise a coup to put a more accommodating colonel in power. The new military government suspended parliament and the constitution, and completed the pipeline agreement.[63] Events such as these engineered the postwar relationship between oil and democracy.

---

61   Lockman, *Comrades and Enemies*: 327, 331.

62   Testimony of Samuel Mikunis to the UN Special Committee on Palestine, 13 July 1947, UN General Assembly, A/364/Add.2 PV, at domino.un.org. Previously a movement of both Palestinian Arabs and Jewish settlers, in 1943 the Palestine Communist Party had split into Arab and Jewish movements, but the Jewish factions, including the one led by Mikunis, continued until late 1947 to oppose the Zionist plan for a Jewish state in favour of Arab–Jewish cooperation. Lockman, *Comrades and Enemies*: 303–51.

63   Douglas Little, 'Cold War and Covert Action: The United States and Syria, 1945–1958', *Middle East Journal* 44: 1, Winter 1990: 55–6; Irene Gendzier, *Notes from the Minefield: United States Intervention in Lebanon, 1945–1958*, 2nd edn, New York: Columbia University Press, 2006: 97–8.

In Lebanon, the United States pressured the government to sign a bilateral investment treaty that would exempt the oil companies from local labour law.[64] Labour protests beginning in the winter of 1943–44, demanding union rights and improved pay and conditions, had led to the passage of a labour code in 1946.[65] Kamal Jumblatt, the minister of national economy, represented a reformist faction that opposed generous concessions to foreign multinationals and favoured the development of domestic manufacturing. His deputy warned that an earlier pipeline and refinery, the Kirkuk–Tripoli line, which was the other branch from the K3 pumping station in Iraq, had provided little employment or local development. 'Two million tons of oil flow every year through Tripoli, but what does the huge installation represent in the economy of the town? Few perhaps know that a single cotton spinning and weaving plant in Tripoli itself employs four times as much labour as the whole Iraq Petroleum terminal and refinery together.'[66] In the final negotiations over the pipeline concession, the Americans secured Jumblatt's removal from office.[67] When the pipeline began operations, the US company used temporary employees and other measures to prevent the unionisation of the workforce.[68]

In the case of Saudi Arabia, Aramco imported the system of racial segregation and the corresponding inequality in pay, working conditions and housing that were familiar features of oil and other extractive enterprises in the United States, and were used to lower costs and inhibit labour organising and political action.[69] As production developed at the end of the Second World War, the Saudi workforce carried out a series of strikes demanding better treatment and pay and an end to racial discrimination. Known 'trouble makers' from Iraq were deported, as were workers from what had become Pakistan, after further protests in 1949. The company explained to the State Department that those deported were followers of 'the Communist line, particularly as regards evils of capitalism *and racial discrimination*'. A ten-day strike in 1953, after the company refused to recognise labour leaders as representatives of the workforce, led to a promise of reforms and the imposition of martial law in the oilfields, allowing Aramco

---

64   Gendzier, *Notes from the Minefield*: 111–14, 131–2.

65   Irene C. Soltau, 'Social Responsibility in the Lebanon', *International Affairs* 25: 3, July 1949: 307–17; Elizabeth Thompson, *Colonial Citizens: Republican Rights, Paternal Privilege, and Gender in French Syria and Lebanon*, New York: Columbia University Press, 2000: 277–81; Malek Abisaab, '"Unruly" Factory Women in Lebanon: Contesting French Colonialism and the National State, 1940–1946', *Journal of Women's History* 16: 3, 2004: 55–82.

66   Na'im Amiouni (Amyuni), 'A Short History of our Pre-War and Post-War Economic Problems', 3 July 1946, cited in Gendzier, *Notes from the Minefield*: 48.

67   Gendzier, *Notes from the Minefield*: 47–8, 145.

68   Ibid.: 112, 117.

69   Robert Vitalis, *America's Kingdom: Mythmaking on the Saudi Oil Frontier*, 2nd edn, London: Verso, 2009. Vitalis brings to light the importance of race to the organisation of oil production, the repeated efforts by Saudi and other workers to win a more egalitarian labour regime, and the tenacity with which the American company fought to preserve racial discrimination.

spokesmen to blame the government for simply enforcing its own anti-union policies. When the promises were not kept, a wave of protests, stoppages and boycotts followed, culminating in a general strike in June 1956. The workers' demands included the introduction of a political constitution; the right to form labour unions, political parties and national organisations; an end to Aramco's interference in the country's affairs; the closure of the US military base; and the release of imprisoned workers. Aramco's security department identified the strike leaders to the Saudi security forces, who imprisoned or deported the organisers.[70]

There were similar pressures in Iran, where Britain had assured its control of oil and of supply routes during the Second World War through an Anglo-Soviet invasion of the country. To gain support for the military occupation, Britain acceded to popular pressure to depose the shah, but secured a future for his methods of autocratic rule by replacing him with his son.[71] Struggles for better pay and working conditions in the oil industry and for an end to the system of racial discrimination in the management and accommodation of the workforce led to a series of strikes in 1945–46, including a three-day general strike in the refinery at Abadan and across the oilfields. A parliamentary delegation from Britain reported that the housing the Anglo-Persian Oil Company, now renamed Anglo-Iranian, ran for its workers 'looks like a penal settlement in the desert' with accommodation 'little better than pig-styes'. The government passed a Labour Law responding to some of the workers' demands, but also establishing state regulation of labour unions, then declared martial law in the oil region and attempted to crush the independent oil union.[72] In 1949–51 the union and its allies in the Tudeh Party (the communist party of Iran) re-emerged. As in Mexico in 1937, a reformist government tried to defuse the oil workers' power by nationalising the country's oil industry, although on terms more favourable to the foreign oil company than those demanded by the union and the communist party. There followed a violent confrontation between the oil workers and the Mossadegh government, which arrested the leaders of the oil union. Anglo-Iranian had no grounds on which to oppose the

---

70   Vitalis, *America's Kingdom*: 92–5, 119, 171–84 (Vitalis's italics). See also William Eddy, Letter to Children, 23 November 1953, William A. Eddy Papers, Box 8, Folder 7, Public Policy Papers, Department of Rare Books and Special Collections, Princeton University Library; and Alexei Vassiliev, *The History of Saudi Arabia*, New York: New York University Press, 2000.

71   Ervand Abrahamian, *Iran Between Two Revolutions*, Princeton: Princeton University Press, 1982: 164–5.

72   Katayoun Shafiee, 'Cracking Petroleum with Politics: Anglo-Persian Oil and The Socio-Technical Transformation of Iran, 1901–54', PhD thesis, Department of Middle Eastern and Islamic Studies, New York University, 2010; Fred Halliday, 'Trade Unions and the Working Class Opposition', *MERIP Reports* 71, October 1978: 7–13; Habib Ladjevardi, *Labor Unions and Autocracy in Iran*, Syracuse: Syracuse University Press, 1985: 61–9, 123–47; Ervand Abrahamian, *Iran Between Two Revolutions*.

nationalisation (Britain had nationalised its own coal industry five years earlier), and its effort to have the International Court of Justice declare Iran in violation of the concession agreement failed. In 1953 the CIA and the British intelligence services organised a coup, which removed Mossedegh from power and gave the Shah the power to defeat the nationalist movement and crush the labour movement and the left. The Anglo-US coup re-established foreign control over the country's oil – although Washington forced Anglo-Iranian, now renamed BP, to reduce its share of the oil monopoly to 40 per cent, with US and other foreign firms sharing the remainder.[73]

After the First World War, Britain had turned the doctrine of self-determination into a means for manufacturing a weakened but cost-effective mechanism of indirect rule in Iraq, securing for the handful of major international oil companies control of the region's oil. The oil firms delayed the development of the oilfields during the interwar period, protecting their monopoly control of world oil. After the Second World War, the construction of new energy networks replacing coal with oil was the basis for weakening the left in Europe and building there the corporatist forms of postwar democracy. Those networks had different political properties from the coal-centred energy arrangements they replaced. Although the oilfields, pumping stations, pipelines and refineries of the Middle East became sites of intense political struggle, they did not offer those involved the same powers to paralyse energy systems and build a more democratic order.

---

73   Ervand Abrahamian, 'The 1953 Coup in Iran', *Science and Society* 65: 2, Summer 2001: 185–215.

CHAPTER 5

Fuel Economy

We are learning to think of democracy not in terms of the history of an idea or the emergence of a social movement, but as the assembling of machines. Those who assembled the supply of coal into an apparatus for democratising the industrialised world had tried to extend its mechanisms to govern relations with non-European regions. Following the crisis of the First World War, they proposed devices to govern the international flow of finance and redirect its profits to beneficial ends. The imperial powers, in uneasy alliance with local forces, managed to forge an alternative device, one that replaced democratic claims with the process of 'self-determination' and substituted for the democratic control of international capital the emergent apparatus of 'development'.

The difficulty in governing the movement of money continued to be an obstacle to the growth of more egalitarian and democratic politics, an obstacle increasingly connected with the flow of oil. A generation later, in the wake of the failure of democratic governments in Europe and a second global war, another effort was made to devise a method for managing the international flow of finance, the arrangement known as the Bretton Woods system. Its development coincided with new forms of democratic politics in industrialised countries, based on the management of what had recently come to be called 'the economy'. Both the international financial arrangement and the apparatus of 'the economy' were devices for governing democracies; both systems, as we will see, were constructed in ways that took advantage of the rapidly increasing use of non-renewable carbon energy, which with the shift to the age of oil continued its exponential rate of growth. In order to grasp the changing relation between carbon energy and democracy in the second half of the twentieth century, we must explore the place of oil in these two machineries of government.

OIL TO DRIVE THE MONEY LENDERS FROM THE TEMPLE

The collapse of democracy in Europe in the 1920s and 1930s, the rise of fascism and the slide towards another world war were understood to have been caused by the collapse of methods for maintaining the value of money. In central and eastern Europe, countries were forced to abandon the attempt to base the value of their currencies on reserves of gold. One by one their domestic financial systems collapsed, middle classes were pauperised, the poor endured widespread unemployment, and interwar democracy was destroyed. 'The breakdown of the international gold standard', Karl Polanyi wrote in 1944, was 'the mechanism which railroaded Europe to its doom'.[1]

During the Second World War, Britain and the United States made plans to engineer a new mechanism for managing the international movement of money. At a meeting in July 1944 at the Mount Washington Hotel in Bretton Woods, a faded New Hampshire resort built in 1902 with the fortune of a Pennsylvania coal magnate, the forty-four Allied states reached agreement on a plan, setting up the International Monetary Fund and International Bank for Reconstruction and Development, today known as the World Bank. The Bretton Woods agreement abandoned a system that had been built on the wealth and technologies of coal and replaced it with one based on the movement of oil.

To prevent a repeat of the interwar financial catastrophe and another collapse of democracy, governments had to control those whose actions had caused it – the currency speculators. The discovery of the Witwatersrand gold-fields in southern Africa in the 1880s (see Chapter 3), and the consolidation there of the British gold-mining monopolies and their racialised labour regime, had allowed the expansion of international trade regulated by reserves of gold. It also encouraged the growth of large private banks, which profited from speculation in the value of national currencies. The goal of the Bretton Woods reforms was to eliminate the power of the bankers to speculate. In his address at the closing of the Bretton Woods talks, the Secretary of the US Treasury, Henry Morgenthau, said that the purpose of the new monetary system was to 'limit the control which certain private bankers have in the past exercised over international finance' and drive 'the usurious money lenders from the temple of international finance'.[2] To curb large-scale speculative movements of capital, the value of currencies was to be tied not to reserves of gold but to the exchange of goods, whose value reflected human and material wealth. Declaring that no people or government 'will again tolerate prolonged or wide-spread unemployment', Morgenthau argued that with the new international financial machinery 'men and women everywhere can exchange freely, on a fair and stable basis, the goods which they produce through their labor'.

The new system managed to limit the destructive power of private currency speculators for about two decades. It achieved this, however, by connecting the value of currencies not to the general flow of goods produced by the labour of men and women, but principally to the movement of oil. The speculators were able to weaken the mechanism in the late 1960s thanks to stresses created by the

---

1   Karl Polanyi, *The Great Transformation: The Political and Economic Origins of Our Time*, New York: Farrar & Rinehart, 1944: 20.

2   'Address by the Honorable Henry Morgenthau, Jr., at the Closing Plenary Session' (22 July 1944), in Department of State, ed., *United Nations Monetary and Financial Conference: Bretton Woods, Final Act and Related Documents, New Hampshire, July 1 to July 22, 1944*, Washington DC: US Government Printing Office, 1944: 7–10, available at www.ena.lu.

movement of oil, and destroyed it in the 1980s when they devised new ways to speculate in currencies.[3]

Currency systems are always material as well as calculative devices, built out of technical processes. The gold standard, the previous mechanism, had been initially made possible by coal and steam power, in ways we will examine later. Gold reserves could no longer provide the instrument to secure international financial exchange, because the European allies had been forced to send all their gold bullion to America to pay for imports of coal, oil and other wartime supplies. By the end of the war the United States had accumulated 80 per cent of the world's gold reserves. At Bretton Woods, the United States agreed to fix the value of the dollar on the basis of this gold, at $35 per ounce. The other participating countries agreed that the dollar would be the only reserve currency convertible at a fixed rate to gold, and that the value of their own currencies would be tied to the dollar, and thus indirectly to the American gold monopoly. However, the circulation of dollars soon began to outpace American accumulations of gold, in part because the gold miners of South Africa could not increase their production of gold as fast as world trade, fuelled by the easier flow of oil, began to grow.[4] In practice, what sustained the value of the dollar was that countries had to use the American currency to purchase the essential materials that formed the bulk of international trade, above all oil.

In both value and volume, petroleum had become the largest commodity in world trade. In 1945 the United States produced two-thirds of the world's oil, and more than half of the remaining third was produced in Latin America and the Caribbean.[5] Under the arrangements that governed the international oil trade, the commodity was sold in the currency not of the country where it was produced, nor of the place where it was consumed, but of the international companies that controlled production. 'Sterling oil', as it was known (principally oil from Iran), was traded in British pounds, but the bulk of global sales were in 'dollar oil'. The rest of the world had to purchase the energy they required using American dollars. The value of the dollar as the basis of international finance depended on the flow of oil.

The place of oil in international finance escapes most standard accounts of the postwar financial system. Yet it was clearly understood in postwar planning documents.[6] John Maynard Keynes and Harry Dexter White, the

---

3 Donald A. MacKenzie, *An Engine, Not a Camera: How Financial Models Shape Markets*, Cambridge, MA: MIT Press, 2006.

4 Barry Eichengreen, *Global Imbalances and the Lessons of Bretton Woods*, Cambridge, MA: MIT Press, 2007: 40–1.

5 Degolyer & MacNaughton, *Twentieth Century Petroleum Statistics*, Dallas: DeGolyer & MacNaughton, 2009.

6 See for example Cornelius J. Dwyer, 'Trade and Currency Barriers in the International Oil Trade', Walter J. Levy Papers, Box 22, Folder 4, Laramie, Wyoming: American Heritage Center, University of Wyoming, 1949. Dwyer was assistant chief, Petroleum Branch, Economic

architects of the Bretton Woods system, had argued for a third institution along-side the International Monetary Fund and the World Bank, to manage trade in oil and other essential raw materials.[7] Their proposals for rebuilding the inter-national financial system after the war included schemes to create stockpiles of oil, rubber, sugar and other commodities to prevent shortages, gluts and price swings. Even those opposed to Keynes – in particular the nascent neolib-eral movement, which objected to the government regulation of international banking – accepted the need to reduce financial speculation by tying the move-ment of money to trade in key commodities such as oil. Drawing on Benjamin Graham's proposal for 'a modern ever-normal granary', Friedrich Hayek, the intellectual leader of the movement, argued for an 'international commodity standard' to replace the gold standard, in which currency would be issued in exchange for 'a fixed combination of warehouse warrants for a number of stora-ble raw commodities'.[8] Both sides of the debate about preventing the speculative destruction of currencies believed that postwar financial stability, and thus the future of democracy, depended on managing the storage and exchange of key commodities. Increasingly the movement of just one commodity, petroleum, provided the mechanism that stabilised, or threatened to disrupt, the demo-cratic order.

The concern with oil was visible in the sequence of meetings that estab-lished the new arrangements. Between the talks at Bretton Woods in July 1944, which created the postwar financial regime, including the IMF and the World Bank, and those at Dumbarton Oaks in the autumn of the same year, where the allied powers formulated arrangements for a successor to the League of Nations, a third meeting was held: representatives of Britain and the United States met in Washington in early August to draw up a postwar petroleum order. The meeting finalised plans to establish a permanent body to be called

---

Cooperation Administration (the US government agency that administered the Marshall Plan). The neglect of oil in standard histories of the international financial system can be seen, for exam-ple, in Barry Eichengreen, 'The British Economy Between the Wars', in Rodrick Floud and Paul Johnson, eds, *The Cambridge Economic History of Modern Britain*, Cambridge, UK: CUP, 2004, and *Globalizing Capital: A History of the International Monetary System*, 2nd edn, Princeton: Princeton University Press, 1996; and in Francis J. Gavin, *Gold, Dollars, and Power: The Politics of International Monetary Relations, 1958–1971*, Chapel Hill: University of North Carolina Press, 2004.

7   Harry Dexter White argued for an 'international essential raw material development corporation' whose function would be 'increasing the world supply of essential raw materials and assuring member countries of an adequate supply at reasonable prices'. Harry Dexter White, 'United Nations Stabilization Fund and a Bank for Reconstruction and Development of the United and Associated Nations', preliminary draft, March 1942, Chapter III: 30. Harry Dexter White Papers, 1920–55, Box 6, Folder 6, Public Policy Papers, Princeton: Seeley G. Mudd Manuscript Library.

8   F. A. Hayek, 'A Commodity Reserve Currency', *Economic Journal* 53: 210/211, 1943: 176–84; Benjamin Graham, *Storage and Stability: A Modern Ever-Normal Granary*, New York: McGraw-Hill Book Company, Inc., 1937.

the International Petroleum Council. Just as the IMF was intended to limit the chaos caused by the speculative dealings of international banks, the parallel organisation for petroleum was intended to limit the trouble caused by international oil companies – and to pre-empt the oil-producing countries, especially in the Middle East, from taking control of the oil themselves. In an echo of the mandates established under the League of Nations to obstruct the demand for political independence in the Arab world, the International Petroleum Council was envisaged as a form of 'trusteeship' to facilitate Anglo-American control of Middle Eastern oil.

A TRUSTEESHIP OF THE BIG POWERS

The major oil companies cooperated with the scheme for an international oil body as an alternative to Keynes's wider plans for the international control of commodities – plans that were to be discussed at the inaugural meeting of the United Nations in April 1945. The head of Shell's US subsidiary warned that if the companies failed to support the International Petroleum Council they risked a 'master agreement made in San Francisco that proposes to cover all sorts of commodities with all sorts of countries'. In the special oil agreement, he said, 'we have something we have had a hand in making'.[9] The impetus to create a new regime governing Middle Eastern oil also came from the weakened position of the American international oil companies in their main overseas region, Latin America. There was alarmist talk from oil executives about the depletion of US reserves and new military needs for petroleum, which helped them win subsidies from Washington for developing Middle East production. But the real problem they faced was to the south.

Immediately before the war, the 'rude expropriations' of American interests in Bolivia and Mexico, as the State Department's petroleum adviser put it, and the move towards state monopolies or much stiffer concession terms in the rest of Latin America, had made it more difficult for US firms to make large profits there.[10] Postwar profits would have to be obtained increasingly from the Middle East, where large undeveloped oil resources continued to pose a threat, but pressure for national control of oil resources seemed easier to prevent. US companies had acquired concessions there in the interwar years, but made little effort to develop them. With declining wartime need for oil from the Middle East, they were able to scale back their modest operations. In 1945 the Middle

---

9   Minutes of National Oil Policy Committee, 18–19 April 1945, cited in Stephen J. Randall, *United States Foreign Oil Policy, 1919–1948: For Profits and Security*, Montreal and Kingston: McGill-Queen's University Press, 1985: 206.

10   Herbert Feis, 'The Anglo-American Oil Agreement', *Yale Law Journal* 55: 5, 1946: 1,174–5; Michael B. Stoff, 'The Anglo-American Oil Agreement and the Wartime Search for Foreign Oil Policy', *Business History Review* 55: 1, Spring 1981: 59–74.

East produced only 7.5 per cent of the world's oil, two-thirds of which came from the British-controlled oilfields in Iran.[11]

In building oil industries in Venezuela, Mexico and other parts of Latin America, the oil companies had been obliged to deal with sovereign states, independent for more than a century and increasingly able to negotiate more equitable oil agreements. In the Middle East, sovereign states were still forming out of older local and imperial forms of rule. The oil companies could portray their role there as the 'development' of remote and backward peoples, and impose less equitable arrangements.

The State Department wanted to prevent the US oil companies from causing the same problems for themselves in the Middle East that they had created in Latin America. An international framework, in agreement with Britain, would give corporate oil operations the appearance of a trusteeship, the new term for the old idea of the mandate. A petroleum agreement could frame Anglo-US control of the oilfields of the Middle East as a means of making the oil available to every country that needed it, and present this 'equitable' management as a principle that disqualified the claims of producer countries to control their own oil. A report for the State Department by the Office of Strategic Services suggested, 'The principle of equitable distribution and exploitation overrides to some extent the sovereign rights of the oil producing countries and presupposes a kind of trusteeship of the big Powers over the world's oil resources.'[12]

Initially Washington intended to have a government agency play the role of trustee. In 1943, the US Petroleum Administration for War established a government oil company, the Petroleum Reserves Corporation, to assume control of the oil reserves of Saudi Arabia. It planned to take majority ownership of the California-Arabian Oil Company, the American joint venture that owned rights to the oil. Washington also extended wartime Lend Lease aid to Saudi Arabia (relieving US oil companies of the need to subsidise the rule of Ibn Saud), and drew up plans to construct a US government-owned pipeline to carry oil from the Saudi oilfields to the Mediterranean. By taking control of the oil of Saudi Arabia, the State Department hoped to do a better job than the oil companies in preventing nationalisation, in part by funnelling financial support to the region's ruling families to use for 'development'.[13] After the First World War, the British government had envisioned its mandate over Iraq as a scheme for the 'development' of the country's material resources, to create a new form of protectorate and encourage the oil companies to invest in the stability of imperial power. Washington's plans for trusteeship were a new version of imperial development.

---

11   DeGolyer & MacNoughton, *Twentieth Century Petroleum Statistics.*

12   OSS, Research and Analysis Branch, 'Comments on a Foreign Petroleum Policy of the Unites States', cited in Randall, *United States Foreign Oil Policy*: 147.

13   Robert Vitalis, *America's Kingdom: Mythmaking on the Saudi Oil Frontier*, 2nd edn, London: Verso, 2009: 62–125.

The American owners of the Saudi rights, Standard Oil of California (later renamed Chevron) and Texaco (now merged with Chevron), blocked Washington's attempted takeover. To create the impression of an official American partnership with the Arab state, they changed the name of their joint venture from the California-Arabian to the Arabian-American Oil Company (Aramco). Rather than allowing the government to invest in the company, they raised the capital they needed for postwar expansion by arranging for the Standard Oil Companies of New Jersey and New York (now ExxonMobil) to buy a 40 per cent share in Aramco. They also defeated the pipeline plan, but then demanded government support for building themselves (see map overleaf).

Similar American plans for a 'trusteeship' over oil were unfolding in Iran, which Britain and Russia had occupied during the war. Attending a meeting with Churchill and Stalin in Tehran at the end of 1943, at which a tentative plan for creating the UN was agreed, President Roosevelt took up State Department ideas for framing the US role in postwar Iran as an international trusteeship. He described the team of fifty US administrative advisers already working in Iran as a 'clinic' that was 'demonstrating the practicability, and something of the form of the projected new "trusteeship"'.[14] Like the mandate for Iraq after the First World War, the trusteeship idea for Iran offered a way for the United States to challenge Britain's control of the oil, while pushing the American oil companies to take steps towards the country's broader 'development'. The State Department pressed the Standard Oil companies and another US firm to bid for oil concessions, but when American petroleum geologists failed to find good prospects in the south-east, and began surveying in the north near the border with the Soviet Union, Moscow responded by asserting its own claims to an oil concession in the north.

The reason why Middle Eastern oil should be placed under American control was sometimes hard to clarify. Herbert Feis, a former economic adviser at the State Department who had chaired its Committee on International Oil Policy in 1943, tried to explain to the public the need for the international oil agreement. 'Nations that lacked oil had to bargain or barter for it; they became dependent on the will and bounty of others', he wrote, adding with barely veiled sarcasm: 'the United States was unused to the idea'.[15] A senior economic policy-maker may have enjoyed pointing out, after leaving office, that for oil companies the principle of market exchange – bargaining for something and depending on this interaction with others – was an unfamiliar idea. The Cold War soon provided the oil companies with a way to deflect such cynicism.

---

14   Arthur Millspaugh, *Americans in Persia*, Washington, DC: Brookings Institution Press, 1946: 8, cited in Simon Davis, '"A Projected New Trusteeship"? American Internationalism, British Imperialism, and the Reconstruction of Iran, 1938–1947', *Diplomacy & Statecraft* 17: 1, 2006: 31–72.

15   Feis, 'Anglo-American Oil Agreement': 1,174.

Middle East oil in proven reserve is estimated at more than 26,000,000,000 barrels, as agai[n]
U.S. reserve of 20,000,000,000, enough to last 15 more years at present rate of consumption. B[rit]
ain monopolizes all the working Iran fields. Russia would like north Iran oil and Dutch ha[ve]
a great unexplored concession in northwest Iran. Britain controls Iraq oil (*see next page*)

'Middle East oil: Trouble erupts as great powers jockey for the power that petroleum provides',
Life, 11 June 1945

BAKU

CASPIAN SEA

U. S. S. R.

KUK

TEHRAN

TEXAS
(AT SAME SCALE)
□□□□□□□□□□□

MASJID-I-SULAIMAN

HAFT KEL

AGHA JARI

IRAN
100% British
□□□□□□

AN

GACH SARAN

BALUCHISTAN

PERSIAN GULF

RAS TANURA

ADRIYA

ATIF

MAM

ABQAIQ

BAHREIN
100% U.S.

QATAR
100% British
□

ARABIA
% U.S.
□□□

ARABIAN SEA

3,300 MILES
ABADAN-PORT SAID

S., French and Dutch have interests there. U. S. operates Bahrein (*see pp. 32–33*), has inside ck in Saudi Arabia (*pp. 34–37*) and shares the new Kuwait field with British. Only fields own above are those explored and working (but nonproducing Qatar and Kuwait are shown cause of importance). Proposed U.S. pipeline across Arabia is far shorter than water route.

The ambition of the State Department in establishing an oil agency to stand alongside the IMF and the World Bank, in the words of a departmental memo, was to create a 'worldwide system of actual administrative control of the world's petroleum resources'.[16] The Anglo-American Petroleum Agreement, drawn up in 1944 to provide the framework for the post-war petroleum order, called for 'the efficient and orderly development of the international petroleum trade', and said this required 'international agreement' among producing and consuming countries – a clear alternative to the unilateral actions of the Latin Americans. Article 1 of the agreement laid out the new formula for the defeat of any further efforts by producer countries to control their own oil: supplies of petroleum should be made available in international trade to all countries 'on a competitive and nondiscriminatory basis' and 'within the framework of applicable laws and concession contracts'; thereby, 'the interests of producing countries should be safeguarded with a view to their economic advancement'. In other words, the large oil companies would represent the interests of all countries in managing access to oil, on the basis of the existing system of concession agreements, while compensating producer countries by contributing to their development. To further these goals the agreement proposed the creation of a body called the International Petroleum Commission, to collect statistics and publish reports. Feis, the former economic adviser, dismissed the agreement as a proposal 'to create no more than a continually active conference room, attended by a staff of experts, and supplied with a multigraph machine'.[17] He was right, but failed to note that holding multilateral meetings and duplicating endless statistical reports would help make oil 'international', countering any claims that producer countries might make to treat the oil as a national resource.

FAILURE OF LONG-RANGE PLANS

The international petroleum agreement was never implemented. The rivalry between Britain and America over the control of oil was unresolved. The major oil companies forced the revision and weakening of the agreement, and domestic US oil companies blocked its ratification in the Senate. Meanwhile the plans for trusteeships over the oil of Iran and Saudi Arabia were dropped, and the United States found a simpler way to claim control of the region's oil, and thus secure the circulation of dollars.

The British had one main goal in the oil negotiations: to organise the production and flow of oil in a way that would rebuild the value of the pound sterling, as a second international reserve currency alongside the dollar. Britain wanted an agreement that would allow it to exclude American oil imports from

---

16   Randall, *United States Foreign Oil Policy*: 138.
17   Feis, 'Anglo-American Oil Agreement', 1,187.

British markets (the so-called sterling area, consisting of most countries of the British Empire, plus Iraq, Kuwait, and other Persian Gulf territories). It also hoped to strengthen the pound by increasing postwar British oil production in the Middle East. Since there was, as usual, more oil available than could be produced without lowering prices and reducing the large flows of company income on which the value of sterling increasingly depended, it also sought to limit any postwar expansion of US production in the Middle East.

Britain's attempt to defend the pound sterling as a rival international currency was a struggle over oilfields. When the heads of the Trans-Arabian Pipeline Company, the non-profit joint venture set up by the US oil companies to ship Saudi oil to Europe, were deciding the route for the pipeline, they initially planned to terminate it in Palestine, a state to which Britain, before the war, had promised independence by 1949. After the UN voted instead to partition Palestine into three states (one Arab, one Jewish, and an internationalised city of Jerusalem), but provided no way to carry out the break-up of the country or the eviction of the Arab population from the Jewish state, allowing the Zionist movement to seize most of it by force, the oil companies changed their minds. They briefly considered a southerly route terminating on the northern coast of the Sinai Peninsula, in Egypt. Egypt, however, remained within the British sphere of influence. That raised a further problem besides the question of the troubles in Palestine. Egypt was a member of the sterling area. In fact, Egypt and Iraq were the only non-Commonwealth members of this exchange mechanism.[18] The American oil companies wanted to use the route of the pipeline to undermine the sterling area. To assist with this financial engineering, they diverted the pipeline north into Syria and Lebanon. Meanwhile the British built a rival pipeline at the same time, to increase the flow of sterling oil from Iraq to the Mediterranean. But whereas the Americans built a thirty-inch line, the British line was half that size (carrying about one-third as much oil), 'the limitation of diameter to 16-inch being enforced by the inability of sterling-area manufacturers to produce larger pipe and the equal impossibility of obtaining dollars'.[19] The battle over the postwar international monetary system was being fought in pipeline routes and in rival diameters of pipe.

Oil was so large a component of its international trade that a 1955 report on the treatment of oil in Britain's trade accounts suggested that 'the international

---

18   For an explanation of the currency mechanism see Elliot Zupnick, 'The Sterling Area's Central Pooling System Re-Examined', *Quarterly Journal of Economics* 69: 1, February 1955: 71–84. Egypt agreed to leave the sterling area in July 1947, hoping to convert its sterling balances, accumulated in London during the Second World War, into dollars. Shortly after, however, Britain broke the terms of the agreement by suspending the convertibility of Egypt's sterling balances. Frederick Leith-Ross, 'Financial and Economic Developments in Egypt', *International Affairs* 28: 1, 1952: 29–37.

19   Stephen Longrigg, *Oil in the Middle East: Its Discovery and Development*, 3rd edn, London: OUP, 1968: 79–80.

ramifications of the oil industry (including its tanker operations) are so large and so complex as almost to constitute oil [as] a currency in itself'.[20] Europe and other regions had to accumulate dollars, hold them and then return them to the United States in payment for oil. Inflation in the United States slowly eroded the value of the dollar, so that when these countries purchased oil, the dollars they used were worth less than their value when they acquired them. These seigniorage privileges, as they are called, enabled Washington to extract a tax from every other country in the world, keeping its economy prosperous and thus its democracy popular.

In February 1945, on his way home from a second conference of the Big Three powers, at Yalta, President Roosevelt stopped in Egypt and held meetings with three regional monarchs – the rulers of Saudi Arabia, Egypt and Ethiopia. The meeting with Ibn Saud is taken to mark the sealing of a special relationship with Saudi Arabia, concerned with Middle Eastern oil. This was not the reaction of William Eddy, the agent in the Office of Strategic Services (a forerunner of the CIA) who helped arrange the meeting and went on to a career in the CIA under the cover of working as a political agent for Aramco. Six months later, a fellow US agent in the region was bemoaning to Eddy the failure of their hopes for 'a long range plan for Saudi Arabia' after 'we all worked like dogs on it in Washington' – a reference to their failure to win large-scale US support for the country.[21] The programme of Lend Lease aid enjoyed by Saudi Arabia and Iran during the war was cancelled, the Saudi request that America not support the Zionist programme for making Palestine into a Jewish state was ignored, and wartime plans for trusteeships and large-scale development programmes for Iran and Saudi Arabia were dropped.[22]

Later on, President Truman would refuse to extend a programme of Marshall Aid to the Middle East, offering instead the Point IV programme. America would not be able to share capital or material wealth with the world's 'underdeveloped areas', Truman explained, for those resources 'are limited'. As a consolation, Washington would offer them ideas. US businesses would be encouraged to share their 'imponderable resources in technical knowledge', which 'are constantly growing and', in contrast to material wealth, 'are inexhaustible'. Technical knowhow would enable countries to use their existing material resources to produce more food, clothing and mechanical power.[23] The idea of

20   Steven Gary Galpern, *Money, Oil, and Empire in the Middle East: Sterling and Postwar Imperialism, 1944–1971*, Cambridge, UK: CUP, 2009: 15.

21   'Letter to Eddy from Paul H. Alling, Legation of the United States of America, Tangier, Morocco, August 9, 1945', William A. Eddy Papers, Box 8, Folder 6, Public Policy Papers, Department of Rare Books and Special Collections, Princeton University Library.

22   See Vitalis, *America's Kingdom*: 79–86; Simon Davis, '"Projected New Trusteeship"'.

23   Harry S. Truman, 'Inaugural Address', 20 January 1949, available at the American Presidency Project, www.presidency.ucsb.edu. Linda Wills Qaimmaqami argues that Truman's business-led model of development helped precipitate the nationalisation of oil in Iran: 'The Catalyst of Nationalization: Max Thornburg and the Failure of Private Sector Developmentalism in Iran, 1947–51', *Diplomatic History* 19: 1, 1995: 1–31.

development would play a subsidiary but important role in US relations with the non-West, but its role would be to manage the difference between extraordinary levels of affluence for some and modest levels of living for the vast majority of the world, rather than to offer effective means of addressing those differences.

Meanwhile, another way of managing relations with the non-West, including the oil states of the Middle East, was emerging. Following the Yalta talks, the US had begun planning to move armed forces rapidly from Europe to the Pacific theatre, and wanted arrangements for landing rights and refuelling in the Middle East. This concern, rather than cementing a new relationship over oil, was the main reason for Roosevelt's meeting with Ibn Saud. Unable to get further large-scale financial support from Washington, Aramco and Ibn Saud settled for the building of an airport at Dhahran, which was to serve as a US air base. By the time the funds for the base were approved, the war in the Pacific was over and the US Department of War had decided that the airfield was 'of doubtful military usefulness'. Aramco, however, realised that playing on fears of military vulnerability offered a method for securing continued subsidies from Washington.[24] With the abandoning of larger development plans, oil companies could now begin to recast their interests not as a 'trusteeship' over the world's oil but, in a parallel language, as necessary for securing 'strategic' concerns.

A larger opportunity soon emerged for creating a strategic frame in which to place American oil interests, and thus to organise postwar international finance. As the Second World War ended, the dispute with the USSR re-emerged over oil concessions in Iran, triggered by American oil prospecting near the Soviet border. Over the following months, the United States turned the dispute over Iranian oil into an international crisis. This gave American officials the opportunity to make Iran into a different kind of clinic – a place in which to incubate a new context to support American oil policy in the Middle East, and an expansion of American power more generally. At the height of the Iranian oil concession crisis, in February 1946, George Kennan dispatched the famous Long Telegram from Moscow, his 'psychological analysis' arguing that the Soviet Union acted not on the basis of rational calculation of its interests but through the complex psychology of a paranoid commitment to absolute power, and thus to filling 'every nook and cranny available to it in the basin of world power'. To counter this threat, Kennan argued, democratic states had to become, in effect, less democratic, and operate more like the state that was said to threaten them. This pervasive threat could not be effectively countered by 'the sporadic acts which represent the momentary whims of democratic opinion', but only by policies that were 'no less steady in their purpose, and no less variegated and resourceful in their application' than those of the paranoid Russian state. The threat required 'the adroit and vigilant application

---

24   Vitalis, *America's Kingdom*: 82.

of counter-force at a series of constantly shifting geographical and political points'. The feeble whimsy of democratic politics was to be replaced by an all-encompassing imperial vigilance. Democratic weakness was also to be countered at home, by taking incisive measures 'to solve internal problems of our own society, to improve self-confidence, discipline, morale and community spirit of our own people'.[25]

Opponents of this programme to transform American rivalry with the Soviet Union into a global political, cultural and psychological battle labelled it the 'Cold War' – the term that the neoliberal critic Walter Lippmann had borrowed from George Orwell's essay warning of the oligarchic and technocratic state that would emerge from a condition of permanent war.[26] The critics lost, the Cold War was constructed, and ordinary corporate ambition to control resources overseas, in the increasingly difficult context of postwar decolonisation and the assertion of national independence, could now be explained by invoking and elaborating this global 'context'. In the Middle East, devices like the mandate and the trusteeship, and grandiose plans for development, were no longer necessary. US officials and oil executives could explain why American oil companies needed to control production in the region by referring to its 'strategic importance' in a situation of permanent war, without mentioning corporate profits or the need to restrict the supply of oil from the Middle East. Academic analysis could then repeat the language of strategic necessity, helping to build the Cold War into a long-term device for managing American interests overseas, for organising financial flows through the control of oil, and for countering democratic threats to social discipline and community spirit at home. This way of talking about oil continues even today.

I concluded Chapter 1 with the Marshall Plan and the construction of the Cold War in Europe. After networks of coal production had enabled the assembling of forms of democratic agency that allowed the advancement of new claims for political justice, the Marshall Plan helped engineer a political and financial setup in Western Europe that was less vulnerable to such claims, by making Europe increasingly dependent on oil and the dollar. These arrangements were to be based on the development and control of Middle Eastern oil, and the trading of that oil in dollars. Thus the sites of democratic contestation and vulnerability were shifted to the Middle East.

---

25   George Kennan, 'The Chargé in the Soviet Union to the Secretary of State', 22 February 1946, US Department of State, *Papers Relating to the Foreign Relations of the United States, 1946*, Washington DC: US Government Printing Office, 1946, 6: 696–709, and (revised and published under the pseudonym 'X'), 'The Sources of Soviet Conduct', *Foreign Affairs* 25: 4, 1947: 566–82, at 575, 576.

26   George Orwell, 'You and the Atomic Bomb' (1945), in Sonia Orwell and Ian Angus, eds, *The Collected Essays, Journalism and Letters of George Orwell*, New York: Harcourt, Brace & World, 1968; Walter Lippmann, *The Cold War: A Study in US Foreign Policy*, New York: Harper, 1947.

The Anglo-American Petroleum Agreement, envisioned as the basis for an international petroleum commission to operate alongside the Bretton Woods institutions, had attempted to extend this engineering of democratic politics by providing the Anglo-American control of Middle Eastern oil with a collective international framework. The 1945–46 crisis in Iran, emerging as the US tried to challenge Britain's dominant position in Middle Eastern oil and consolidate the dollar-oil mechanisms, allowed the extension of an alternative framework to govern the control of oil and the management of democracy: the Cold War.

Postwar democracy in the West appeared to depend upon creating a stable machinery of international finance, an order assembled with the help of oil wells, pipelines, tanker operations and the increasingly difficult control of oil workers. The fact that flows of oil were the basis for intersecting networks of global energy supply and global currency movements helped introduce a disjuncture that would become increasingly apparent by the end of the 1960s, leading to the energy, dollar and Middle East crises of 1967–74. The following chapter will consider those interlocking crises. Before that, let us explore a second dimension of postwar carbon democracy, a dimension that was also linked to oil and would also be transformed in the 1967–74 crises: the mid-twentieth century politics of 'the economy'.

THE CARBON ECONOMY

John Maynard Keynes, the economist who played a leading role in devising the postwar apparatus for tying the value of money to the movement of oil, helped formulate and describe another innovation of the mid-twentieth century: the modern apparatus of calculation and government that came to be called 'the economy'. A further set of connections between oil and mid-twentieth-century democratic politics concerns the role of economic expertise. Like twentieth-century democracy, twentieth-century economic expertise developed in a specific relationship to the hydrocarbon age.

Keynes's main contribution to the making of this object was to devise new ways of describing and managing the domestic circulation of money. In a memorable passage in *The General Theory*, his classic treatise of 1936, he explained the difference between the market devices of *laissez-faire* economics and the modern need for government to organise the circulation of money by picturing banknotes buried in disused coalmines:

> If the Treasury were to fill old bottles with bank notes, bury them at suitable depths in disused coal mines which are then filled up to the surface with town rubbish, and leave it to private enterprise on well-tried principles of *laissez-faire* to dig the notes up again . . . there need be no more unemployment and, with the help of the

repercussions, the real income of the community, and its capital wealth also, would probably become a great deal greater than it actually is.[27]

British coal production peaked in 1913. By the time Keynes began writing *The General Theory*, twenty years later, the country's coal mines were being exhausted at an unprecedented rate. William Stanley Jevons, the author of an earlier revolution in British economic thinking, the mathematical calculation of individual utility of the 1870s, had published a book warning of the coming exhaustion of coal reserves. Keynes was reading that book as he published *The General Theory*, and gave a lecture on Jevons in 1936 to the Royal Statistical Society.[28] It is indicative of the transformation in economic thinking in which Keynes played a role that the exhaustion of coal reserves no longer appeared as a crisis. The management of coal reserves could now be replaced in the mind, and in the textbooks of economics, with reserves of currency. In the era that Keynes's thinking helped to define, the supply of carbon energy was no longer a practical limit to economic possibility. What mattered was the proper circulation of banknotes.

The shaping of Western democratic politics from the 1930s onwards was carried out in part through the application of new kinds of economic expertise: the development and deployment of Keynesian economic knowledge; its expansion into different areas of policy and debate, including colonial administration; its increasingly technical nature; and the efforts to claim an increasing variety of topics as subject to determination not by democratic debate but by economic planning and knowhow. The Keynesian and New Deal elaboration of economic knowledge was a response to the threat of populist politics, especially in the wake of the 1929 financial crisis and the labour militancy that accompanied it and that re-emerged a decade later. Economics provided a method of setting limits to democratic practice, and maintaining them.

The deployment of expertise requires, and encourages, the making of socio-technical worlds that it can master. In this case, the world that had to be made was that of 'the economy'. This was an object that no economist or planner prior to the 1930s spoke of or knew to exist. Of course, the word 'economy' existed prior to the 1930s, but it referred to a process, not a thing. It meant government,

---

27   John Maynard Keynes, *The General Theory of Employment, Interest, and Money*, London: Macmillan, 1936: 129.

28   William Stanley Jevons, *The Coal Question: An Inquiry Concerning the Progress of the Nation and the Probable Exhaustion of Our Coal-Mines*, London: Macmillan, 1865. Jevons's son, H. Stanley Jevons, returned to the question of the exhaustion of coal reserves in *The British Coal Trade*, London: E. P. Dutton, 1915. He revised his father's estimate of the date of the possible exhaustion of British coal mines from one hundred years to 'less than two hundred years' (756–7). John Maynard Keynes, 'William Stanley Jevons 1835–1882: A Centenary Allocation on his Life and Work as Economist and Statistician', *Journal of the Royal Statistical Society* 99: 3, 1936: 516–55. Lecture delivered on 21 April 1936. *The Coal Question* is quoted on p. 517.

or the proper management of people and resources, as in the phrase 'political economy'.[29] The economy would now become the central object of democratic politics in the West – a process that paralleled the emergence of 'development' outside the West. The economy became an object whose management was the central task of government, requiring the deployment of specialist knowledge.

CIVILISATION IS THE ECONOMY OF POWER

Most thinking about the relationship between economics and the economy continues to reflect the influence of the great Austrian-born social theorist Karl Polanyi. Polanyi argued that the economy emerged as an institutional sphere separate from the rest of society in the nineteenth century. Before this moment of separation, the economy was absorbed or embedded in wider social relations. It follows, he argued, that the formal rules of classical, Ricardian economics relate only to a particular historical period, when market exchanges ceased to be a minor aspect of broader social relations and became an apparently self-regulating system to which other social spheres were subordinated. Moreover, he argued, classical political economy helped to achieve this separation of the market system from society, in particular by formulating ways of treating land, labour and money as though they were merely commodities – a set of fictions that were essential to the formation of the economy as its own institutional sphere.[30] Treating money, in particular, as though it were a commodity, in which speculators could trade, Polanyi suggested, had later led to the collapse of European democracies.

The consensus that the economy became a distinct object of intellectual knowledge and government practice in the late eighteenth or the nineteenth century overlooks a surprising fact. No political economist of that period refers to an object called 'the economy'. In the sense of the term we now take for granted, referring to the self-contained structure or totality of relations of production, distribution and consumption of goods and services within a given geographical space, the idea of the economy emerged more than a century later, in the 1930s and 1940s. Both in academic writing and in popular expression, this meaning of the term came into common use only during the years around the Second World War.

---

29   This and other sections of this chapter draw on Timothy Mitchell, 'Economists and the Economy in the Twentieth Century', in George Steinmetz, ed., *The Politics of Method in the Human Sciences: Positivism and Its Epistemological Others*, Durham, NC: Duke University Press, 2005: 126–41.

30   In *The Great Transformation* (1944), Polanyi describes the emergence of 'society' in the nineteenth century as a system of regulations and controls attempting to limit the spread of market relations. In later writings, he describes the latter as the emergence of 'the economy'. Karl Polanyi, Conrad M. Arensberg and Harry W. Pearson, *Trade and Market in the Early Empires: Economies in History and Theory*, Glencoe: Free Press, 1957.

From the works of Thomas Mun and William Petty in the seventeenth century to Adam Smith in the late eighteenth, political economy was not concerned with the structure of production or exchange within an economy. In *The Wealth of Nations*, Adam Smith never once refers to a structure or whole of this sort. When he uses the term 'economy', the word carries the older meaning of frugality or the prudent use of resources: 'Capital has been silently and gradually accumulated by the private frugality and good conduct of individuals . . . It is the highest impertinence and presumption . . . in kings and ministers, to pretend to watch over the oeconomy of private people.'[31] The objects of political economy were the proper husbanding and circulation of goods and the proper role of the sovereign in managing this circulation. An earlier tradition of writing on the economy or management of the large household or estate was extended to discussions of the management of the state, imagined as the household of the sovereign. The term 'economy' came to refer to this prudent administration or government of the community's affairs.[32] Political economy referred to the economy, or government, of the polity, not to the politics of an economy.

As countries moved from the agrarian world of the eighteenth century to an increasingly industrial and urban life in the nineteenth, the phrase 'political economy' continued to refer to the management or government of a polity, even as writers debated the need for new forms of government. The German-American journalist Friedrich List, whose *National System of Political Economy* (1856) is sometimes read as a precocious study of 'the national economy' in its twentieth-century sense, wrote in these terms. Popularising American arguments about the need for government policies to encourage and protect the development of industry, List contrasted 'the financial economy of the state', which referred 'to the collection, to the use, and the administration of the material means of a government', with 'the economy of the people', which referred to 'the institutions, the regulations, the laws, and the circumstances which govern the economical conditions of the citizens'. The term 'economy' denoted the forms of administration, regulation, law and social circumstance that defined the processes known as government.[33]

The book Keynes had been reading on the coal question, published by William Jevons in 1865, illustrates the meanings of economy before the twentieth-century invention of 'the economy', and their relation to the growth of coal and

---

31   Adam Smith, *An Inquiry into the Nature and Causes of the Wealth of Nations*, London: Methuen, 1950 [1776]: 327–8.

32   Keith Tribe, *Land, Labour, and Economic Discourse*, London: Routledge & Kegan Paul, 1978: 80–109; Michel Foucault, *Security, Territory, Population: Lectures at the Collège de France 1977-1978*, London: Palgrave Macmillan, 2007.

33   Friedrich List, *Das Nationale System der Politischen Oekonomie*, Stuttgart and Tübingen: J. G. Cotta'scher Verlag, 1841. English translation, *National System of Political Economy*, transl. G. A. Matile, Philadelphia: J. B. Lippincott & Co., 1856: 281.

steam power. Jevons suggested that the economy or prudent management of resources applied especially to the resource that had made industrial civilisation possible. He contrasted the vast dissipation of force and matter that occurs in nature with the tiny fraction of power whose economy was the basis of civilisation. 'Material nature presents to us the aspect of one continuous waste of force and matter beyond our control', he wrote. 'The power we employ in the greatest engine is but an infinitesimal portion, withdrawn from the immeasurable expanse of natural forces.' However, he continued, 'while the sun annually showers down upon us about a thousand times as much heat-power as is contained in all the coal we raise annually, yet that thousandth part, being under perfect control, is a sufficient basis for all our economy and progress'. Quoting the German chemist Justus von Liebig, he described this efficient management and control of the power of fossil fuels as the basis of the work of civilisation. 'Civilization, says Baron Leibig, is *the economy of power*, and our power is coal. It is the very economy of the use of coal that makes our industry what it is; and the more we render it efficient and economical, the more will our industry thrive, and our works of civilization grow.'[34]

CALCULATION IN THE AGE OF COAL

Nineteenth-century writing about political economy reflects the world of coal mines and steam engines. The mines and the engines, however, did more than provide objects of reflection. They helped form a world of calculation, circulation and control of which the doctrines of political economy became a part. The gold standard provides a good example of this. As Britain's overseas empire grew, and with it the national debt that funded colonial wars, the country needed a system of money that could increase greatly in quantity and travel over large distances, yet retain its value. The solution was to introduce token money: coins whose value resided not in the metal itself, of which the actual worth was slightly less than the value the coin represented, but in stores of gold held by the government that issued them. Token coinage had to be too expensive to counterfeit, yet affordable enough to manufacture in large quantities. The development of coal-powered, steam-driven rolling mills and presses made it possible to solve this problem. In the Great Recoinage of 1816–17, which inaugurated the use of silver coins as token money, the eight coining presses at the Royal Mint in London produced up to 250,000 coins per day.[35] Steam-powered coinage allowed Britain gradually to implement the gold standard (the rest of

---

34   Jevons, *Coal Question*: 122, 125; emphasis in original.
35   Great Britain, Committee on the Royal Mint, Report from the Select Committee on the Royal Mint, London: HMSO, 1849: 74; Angela Redish, 'The Evolution of the Gold Standard in England', *Journal of Economic History* 50: 4: 789–805.

Europe followed only after 1870), which contributed to the dominant role of British finance in world trade. It also contributed to the development of new ways of knowing about questions of money and wealth. The coining and circulation of money on a large scale produced new problems, including inaccuracy in striking coins and coins losing weight through usage. The problems were the object of repeated investigation, including a Royal Commission of 1849, and of an innovative statistical study by Jevons, who organised a survey of the age and weight of coins held by banking houses from which he calculated the average rate of wear.[36] In other words, an industrial, coal-fired coinage system generated forms of circulation, storage, accounting and investigation, one of several such developments though which an empirical science of political economy could emerge.

Other forms of steam-powered machinery laid out other forms of circulation, calculation and control. During his stay in America in the 1820s, Friedrich List became briefly involved in coal mining in Pennsylvania, and joined a venture to build a rail line to carry coal to its consumers. On his return to Germany, he began to champion an expanded use of railways, not just as lines connecting two points, but as webs of commerce and communication that could engineer a common space of exchange. 'The needs of industry and communication', he wrote in 1836, 'will compel the railway systems of the larger Continental nations to form a net-like shape, concentrating on the main points in the interior and radiating from the centre to the frontiers'.[37]

Coal production itself generated a new space of calculation and debate. Jevons wrote his study of the rate of exhaustion of coal supplies to draw popular attention to the use of statistical methods, by showing how the new tools he had helped develop to analyse tables of statistical information could be applied to questions of the day.[38] He wanted to show that statistics could be used to measure a natural law, the Law of Social Growth. He took estimates of remaining supplies of coal in Britain published by the geologist Edward Hull and statistics from the Mining Record Office to estimate the annual rate at which British coal consumption was increasing. Hull had estimated that, at the current consumption rate of 72 million tons a year, the country's recoverable coal was sufficient to last more than a thousand years. While acknowledging that consumption had doubled over the last twenty years, and that if it continued to increase at the same rate supplies would be exhausted in only 172 years, Hull argued that

---

36   See Sandra J. Peart, "'Facts Carefully Marshalled" in the Empirical Studies of William Stanley Jevons', *History of Political Economy* 33, 2001, annual supplement: 252–76.

37   List, 'Deutschlands Eisenbahnsystem in militärischen Beziehung' (1836), cited in Keith Tribe, *Strategies of Economic Order: German Economic Discourse, 1750–1950*, Cambridge, UK: CUP, 1995: 63; translation of the term netzartig ('net-like') modified.

38   Peart, "'Facts Carefully Marshalled'"; Margaret Schabas, 'The "Worldly Philosophy" of William Stanley Jevons', *Victorian Studies* 28: 1, 1984.

supplies from America and 'greater economy' in 'the getting and using of the mineral' would extend Britain's supply, and that one should not suppose 'that any part of the Creator's universe has been regulated on so short-sighted a plan, that it shall become disorganized because some of the elements necessary to its economy have failed'.[39]

Jevons set out to dispel these 'plausible fallacies' of the geologists. To understand and measure progress, he argued, what matters is not the absolute amount by which production of a good increases, which tells us nothing, but the rate – the increase relative to the increase in a previous period. If the amount of coal a country produces increases in one year by a million tons, but that increase is smaller than the increase in the preceding year, then although its total production has increased, the rate of increase has declined. 'In statistical matters', he explained, one must cultivate the habit of treating all quantities 'relatively to each other'. The rate of growth indicated not a fixed annual increase of consumption, but a geometric process of growth, in which the amount of each year's increase would be greater than the previous year. Describing the novel social experience that coal and steam power had created, the experience that today we would call 'exponential growth', in which practically infinite values are reached in finite time, Jevons showed how quickly even very large stores of coal might be depleted. Applying his methods to the consumption data of the Mining Record Office, Jevons arrived at a figure by logarithmic calculation of 3.5 per cent annual growth. At that rate, the supplies of coal identified by Hull would last not for a thousand years, but only for one hundred.[40]

Jevons then showed that problems would arise much sooner, perhaps within twenty or thirty years. It was erroneous to think that 'some day our coal seams will be found emptied to the bottom, and swept clean like a coal-cellar', or that the country's fires and furnaces would 'be suddenly extinguished, and cold and darkness will be left to reign over a depopulated country'. Long before that, the rising cost of coal as its recovery became more difficult would cause 'the climax of our growth' and 'the end of the present progressive condition of the kingdom'.

From these calculations he drew an immediate and practical conclusion. In the few remaining decades while the country's revenue was expanding and wealth accumulating, efforts had to be made 'to raise the character of the people'. Pointing out the undeniable fact that 'the whole structure of our wealth' was built upon 'a basis of ignorance and pauperism and vice', he argued for a reduction in the employment of children in manufacture and a general system of education to dispel 'the ignorance, improvidence, and brutish drunkenness of our lower working classes'. Instead of spending current material wealth on 'increased

---

39   Edward Hull, *The Coal-Fields of Great Britain*, 2nd edn, London: Edward Stanford, 1861: 236, 238–9, 243.

40   Jevons, *Coal Question*: 4, 170, 236–40.

luxury and ostentation and corruption', the country should spend it on creating 'the increased efficiency of labour in the next generation'. He concluded with the warning that 'we are now in the full morning of our national prosperity, and are approaching noon. Yet we have hardly begun to pay the moral and social debts to millions of our countrymen which we must pay before evening.'[41]

Three themes emerge from Jevons's writing on coal, which we will follow forward to understand what was different for the making of the economy under the subsequent dominance of oil. First, the supply of carbon energy, like the industrial circulation of coinage and the development of railway lines, formed a concentrated movement of materials that, as a process, was reported, measured, tracked across time and compiled into tables. As problems and disputes arose, methods of inspection and information-gathering increased. The Mines Inspection Act of 1850, for example, led to the appointment of government inspectors of coal mines, who in 1854 began to compile the system of Mining Records, making available the statistics on which Jevons based his work. Second, these statistics made possible the mathematical measurement of progress, rates of growth, and the depletion of resources. The questions of material limits, the exhaustion of nature and future decline became matters of increasing concern. Third, with the consequences of modern industrial and urban life, a parallel concern developed with the measurement and amelioration of the moral condition of the poor, and its relationship to the efficiency of labour.

Following Jevons, the development of social statistics took two different paths. One was research on the measurement of poverty, the living conditions of the poor, and industrial accidents. By the end of the nineteenth century, almost all industrialised states had bureaus of labour statistics, created in response to the economic crises of 1873–95 and to the growing political strength of labour organisations. The information they collected on the life of the working classes shaped the new measures of social welfare, such as retirement pensions and various forms of industrial and medical insurance, and helped to implement the new programmes. The wartime campaign to generalise these measures, as we saw in Chapter 3, led to the creation of the International Labour Office as part of the Treaty of the Versailles at the end of the First World War.

The second path was research on race development and eugenics. The work of Francis Galton on the statistical analysis of heredity, inspired by the evolutionary theory of his half-cousin Charles Darwin, first appeared in 1865, but was unable to win wider support until the 1890s. Towards the end of the century, governing classes in Europe and America became alarmed by evidence of what was considered the deterioration of racial quality, revealed in Britain by the difficulty of recruiting physically healthy soldiers for the South African war, and elsewhere by fears that the poor and the less physically fit were reproducing

---

41   Ibid.: v, xxiii–xxvi.

faster than the racially strong part of the population, leading to the risk of 'race suicide'.[42] Galton and his followers proposed controlled breeding to improve racial quality, and to counter the effects of the widening of voting rights. People are not 'of equal value, as social units', Galton warned, 'equally capable of voting, and the rest'.[43] To advance the study and improvement of racial quality, Galton developed new statistical methods. In fact, modern, mathematical statistics with its methods of correlation, regression and error analysis, was developed for the purpose of the eugenics movement.[44] The work was continued by Galton's student, Karl Pearson, whose drive to universalise mathematical statistics was particularly successful in its influence in economics in the early twentieth century, where Irving Fisher and others 'were soon refining the method of correlation to use it as a test of the quantity theory of money'.[45] The monetarists simplified their theories to fit the ultra-empiricism of statistical correlation, looking for a single indicator that could reveal the role of the money supply in determining economic cycles. By the 1920s American economists were 'correlating furiously and indiscriminately and with an inverse correlation between zeal and discretion', wrote Jacob Viner. 'As might have been anticipated in a world full of nonsense correlations, the results were grotesque.'[46]

NATURAL RESOURCES AND RACIAL VIGOUR

In the early decades of the twentieth century, a battle developed among economists, especially in the United States, that shaped the future of economic knowledge and its relation to nature and the material world. The battle was to have important consequences for the way questions of natural resources entered democratic debate. One side wanted economics to start from natural resources and flows of energy, the other to organise the discipline around the study of prices and flows of money. The battle was won by the second group, who created out of the measurement of money and prices a new object: the economy.

---

42   G. R. Searle, *A New England? Peace and War 1886–1918*, Oxford: Clarendon Press, 2004: 375–6.

43   Theodore M. Porter, *The Rise of Statistical Thinking, 1820–1900*, Princeton: Princeton University Press, 1986: 130.

44   Donald Mackenzie, *Statistics in Britain, 1865–1930: The Social Construction of Scientific Knowledge*, Edinburgh: Edinburgh University Press, 1981; Porter, *The Rise of Statistical Thinking*: 129–46, 270–314; Alain Desrosières, 'Managing the Economy: The State, the Market, and Statistics', in Theodore Porter and Dorothy Ross, eds, *The Cambridge History of Science*, vol. 7: *Modern Social Sciences*, Cambridge, UK: CUP, 2003.

45   Porter, *Rise of Statistical Thinking*: 314.

46   Jacob Viner, 'The Present Status and Future Prospects of Quantitative Economics', *American Economic Review*, March 1928 (supplement), reprinted in J. Viner, *The Long View and the Short*, Glencoe: Free Press, 1958: 451, cited in Thomas M. Humphrey 'Empirical Tests of the Quantity Theory of Money in the United States, 1900–1930', *History of Political Economy* 5: 2, 1973: 307.

In the emergent profession of academic economics, many economists were concerned to measure the exhaustion of the earth. In the United States, leading economists like Richard T. Ely, a founder of the American Economics Association, and his student Thorstein Veblen, whose theory of capitalism as a system of 'sabotage' we encountered in Chapter 1, became preoccupied with questions of natural resources and their depletion, with excess or 'conspicuous' consumption, and with the dissipation and conservation of 'energy'. Economics, in their view, was to be a study not of the laws of markets but of material flows and resources.[47] These men lost the battle to shape the discipline they helped found to the rival forces of the price theorists, led by men like Irving Fisher. Economics became instead a science of money; its object was not the material forces and resources of nature and human labour, but a new space that was opened up between nature on one side and human society and culture on the other – the not-quite-natural, not-quite-social space that came to be called 'the economy'.

Many new devices and arrangements made it possible, during the first half of the twentieth century, to develop the forms of calculation and practices of representation that enabled people to talk about and manage the circulations of money that represented the 'national economy'. Rather than describe all the work that went into building it, we can illustrate some of the mundane and interconnected ways in which it came into being with the example of Irving Fisher – the man whom the *New Palgrave Dictionary of Economics* in 1987 called 'the greatest economist America has produced'.[48]

A disciple of the work of William Jevons, Fisher is remembered as the man who built the first working model of the economy. The model consisted of a tank of water fitted with cisterns, pipes, valves, levers and stoppers. He used this hydraulic-mechanical apparatus in his lectures at Yale as an experimental device to investigate how a shock to demand or supply in one of ten different commodities affected the overall level of water, or prices, in a general equilibrium system. A more practical example of the work of making the economy was Fisher's invention of the 'Index Visible', a device for managing information on small cards that is known today as the Rolodex, which he patented in 1913. He set up a company in his house in New Haven, the Index Number Institute,

---

47   Veblen argued that business should be run by engineers rather than businessmen, for engineers understood material processes and were orientated towards the more efficient use of resources, whereas businessmen were concerned only with profits. In response to the great anthracite coal strike of 1902, a movement among engineers in the US wanted to take control of the 'economic', not just of the 'technical', efficiency of business, and called for an alliance between engineers and organised labour. Donald R. Stabile, 'Veblen and the Political Economy of the Engineer: The Radical Thinker and Engineering Leaders Came to Technocratic Ideas at the Same Time', *American Journal of Economics and Sociology* 45: 1, 1986: 41–52.

48   James Tobin, 'Irving Fisher (1867–1947)', in J. Eatwell, M. Milgate and P. Newman, eds, *The New Palgrave: A Dictionary of Economics*, vol. 2, London: Macmillan, 1987: 369–76.

where assistants working in the basement used the new equipment, along with the index formulas Fisher had devised, to calculate the first indices of commodity prices and the purchasing power of the dollar. The *New York Times* and other newspapers published his price indexes every week, together with a commentary by Fisher, enabling 7 million readers to follow and participate in the price movements that would come to be called the economy.

There were many other mechanisms for removing nature and material resources from economics and turning it into a science of prices – not as simple as the Rolodex, or as uncontroversial. For example, Fisher became a champion of eugenics. His mentor at Yale was William Graham Sumner, America's leading social Darwinist. In 1906, Fisher helped establish the Race Betterment Society, and in 1922 founded and became the first president of the American Eugenics Society. Racial improvement formed a logical part of his economic theory. Human labour was a form of wealth or capital stock. Like non-human capital, it was a resource that could be improved or left to degenerate. The progress of society depended on the decisions individuals took about whether to consume in the present or invest for the future. These decisions were affected by an individual's self-control, life expectancy, thrift and degree of foresight – something that inferior races, and degenerate members of a superior race, lacked.[49]

Appointed to President Theodore Roosevelt's National Conservation Committee, set up in 1908 to address growing concerns over the exhaustion of natural resources, Fisher produced a report arguing that the most important means of conserving nature was not for the government to regulate its exploitation, but to take measures to prevent 'racial degeneracy', since 'one of the first symptoms of racial degeneracy is decay of foresight', while 'the more vigorous and long-lived the race, the better utilization can it make of its natural resources'. Economics would withdraw from studying the capacities and resources of nature and attend instead to the capacities and resources of the human. Fisher advocated establishing a federal Department of Health as the main instrument of racial improvement, but economics too could work on the enhancement of human capabilities. It could extend individual powers of foresight by developing prosthetic devices like the Rolodex and the newspaper commodity price index, and subsequently by elaborating the entire machinery of calculation called the economy.[50]

---

49   Mark Aldrich, 'Capital Theory and Racism: From Laissez-Faire to the Eugenics Movement in the Career of Irving Fisher', *Review of Radical Political Economics* 7: 3, 1975: 33–42.

50   After his stint on the National Conservation Committee, Fisher taught a new course at Yale on 'National Efficiency', which was described as a 'study of natural resources, racial vigor, and social institutions'. William J Barber, 'Irving Fisher of Yale', *American Journal of Economics and Sociology* 64: 1, 2005: 49.

MONEY ECONOMY

In the discipline of economics, the easiest place to trace the appearance of the idea that the economy exists as a general structure of economic relations would be in the publication of John Maynard Keynes's *General Theory of Employment, Interest and Money*, in 1936. Although tending to employ phrases like 'economic society' or 'the economic system as a whole', where today one would simply say 'the economy', the *General Theory* conventionally marks the origin of what would come to be called macro-economics.[51]

The economy was formed as a new object in the context of broader developments. Jan Tinbergen, a pioneer of the mathematical measurement of 'the economy', developed his first econometric model in response to a Dutch government request for policies to combat the depression.[52] Keynesian theory was also a response to the experience of mass unemployment and depression, and to the emergence of fascist, Soviet, New Deal and other general economic programmes that addressed not just individual human behaviour but the interaction of aggregate and structural factors such as employment, investment and money supply. Also important was the emergence after the First World War of the welfare and development programmes for European colonies (Keynes's first job was in the Revenue, Statistics and Commerce Department of the India Office), in response to the growing threats to colonial rule.

These broader events were not just the context for the emergence of a new conception of the economy. While the possibility of making the economy in the mid-twentieth century arose out of these events, economics was itself involved in the reconfiguring of social and technical worlds that gave rise to the economy, as we have seen with the work of Fisher. We can mention two larger aspects of this reconfiguration: new forms of circulation of money; and the weakening of European empires and other forms of imperial control, accompanied by the creation of 'national economies'.

The interwar period saw a significant alteration in the forms of circulation of money in countries such as Britain and the United States. The most dramatic change was the increase in the use of money – in particular paper money – for everyday transactions. Before the First World War, Keynes had remarked on how seldom people in Britain used token or paper money for financial transactions. He could think of only two purposes for which he himself regularly used money – to purchase railway tickets and pay his domestic servants.[53] Most everyday transactions were settled by running an account or writing a cheque. In the United

51   Michael Bernstein, *A Perilous Progress: Economics and Public Purpose in Twentieth-Century America*, Princeton: Princeton University Press, 2001; Philip Mirowski, *Machine Dreams: Economics Becomes a Cyborg Science*, Cambridge, UK: CUP, 2002.

52   Mary S. Morgan, *The History of Econometric Ideas*, Cambridge, UK: CUP, 1990: 102.

53   John Maynard Keynes, *Indian Currency and Finance*, London: Macmillan, 1913.

States, federal bank notes had been introduced by the National Currency Act of 1863, but their supply was limited. Their use remained unpopular, and they competed with a range of other regional bank notes and local scrips.[54] Again, local accounts and personal cheques were by far the most common ways to settle transactions. During the war the situation began to change, with the rapid increase in the printing of money, and the relaxation and later abandonment of the gold standard in most countries. The creation of the US Federal Reserve in 1913, and similar reforms in other countries, led to a standardisation of bank notes and the widespread and rapid acceptance of the use of paper money.

This transformation in the use and circulation of money illustrates how economic knowledge helped to form its new object. In the first place, economists developed new theories of money, entering into the political battles over questions of currency reform, the gold standard, and government control of exchange rates and money supply. Keynes's first published work, *Indian Currency and Finance* (1913), was a practical contribution to this politics, and was followed by the publication of *A Treatise on Money* (1930). In the United States, the conflict between Irving Fisher's quantity theory of money and the 'real bills' doctrine of J. Laurence Laughlin and his students shaped the creation of the Federal Reserve system.[55] The conceptions and calculative technologies provided by economists were built into the new financial institutions. In other words, economists developed practical tools for measuring and managing the value of money that became part of the novel day-to-day machinery of monetary circulation that was soon to be recognised as 'the economy'.

The next step was to begin to see this new mechanism of money circulation as a system in its own right, rather than just another 'market'. Following the publication of *A Treatise on Money* (1930), Keynes made a decisive break with the ideas of his predecessors at Cambridge, Marshall and Pigou, as well as with the work of Fisher and Frisch. Earlier theorists, he argued, had treated money as simply a neutral signifier of value, and thus saw no essential difference between a system of exchange using money and a barter system. In the earliest surviving drafts of *The General Theory*, which date from 1932–33, and in fragments of his Cambridge lecture notes from the same period, he discusses the differences between the 'real-exchange economy' or 'neutral' economy of classical economic theory, and the 'money economy' of the real world of the present.[56] These notes represent his first use of the concept of 'the economy' in its contemporary sense.

---

54   Viviana A. Zelizer, *The Social Meaning of Money: Pin Money, Paychecks, Poor Relief and Other Currencies*, Princeton: Princeton University Press, 1997.

55   Perry Mehrling, 'Retrospectives: Economists and the Fed: Beginnings', *Journal of Economic Perspectives* 16: 4, Autumn 2002: 207–18.

56   John Maynard Keynes, *The Collected Writings of John Maynard Keynes*, ed. Donald Moggridge, London: Macmillan, 1971–89, vol. 13: 396–412, 420–1; vol. 29: 54–5; Robert Skidelsky, *John Maynard Keynes*, vol. 2: *The Economist as Saviour, 1920–1937*, London: Macmillan, 1992.

Keynes's breakthrough was to conceive of the new totality not as an aggregation of markets in different commodities, but as the circulation of money: the economy was the sum of all the moments at which money changed hands.

THE NATIONAL ECONOMY

A further step in the making of this economy was to construct mechanisms for measuring all the instances of spending and receiving money within a geographical space – the new national income accounts. Before the interwar period, attempts to calculate national wealth or 'national dividend' had come up against a series of insuperable obstacles. There was the problem of counting the 'same' goods or money twice. For example, commodities sold at wholesale could not be counted again, it was thought, when sold at retail. Income earned as a professional salary should not be included in national wealth a second time when paid as wages to the servants. And, as Alfred Marshall pointed out, there was the problem of accounting for all the waste that was incurred in the production of wealth – not only the depreciation of tools and machinery, but also the exhaustion of the country's natural resources.[57]

After the First World War, the Dawes Committee, set up to estimate Germany's 'capacity to pay' economic reparations, discovered the lack of not just reliable data concerning national income but of a manageable conception of what one was trying to count. In both Germany and the US there were extensive interwar efforts to remedy this problem.[58] It took two decades to solve it. The solution was not to count things more accurately, but to re-conceive the object being counted. No longer was the goal to count the nation's wealth or dividend, but rather its aggregate 'national income' – the sum of every instance of money changing hands. Each such instance represented income to the recipient, however productive or unproductive the activity and regardless of the waste incurred. The work of Keynes again played a critical role, and he and his students worked closely with the Treasury in London to design the methods of estimating national income.

In the United States, Simon Kuznets of the National Bureau of Economic Research systematised the new methods. In 1942 the US Department of Commerce began publishing national economic data, and in his 1944 budget speech President Roosevelt introduced the idea of 'gross national product'.[59]

---

57   Alfred Marshall, *Principles of Economics*, 8th edn, London: Macmillan, 1920: 523.

58   J. Adam Tooze, 'Imagining National Economies: National and International Economic Statistics, 1900–1950', in Geoffrey Cubitt, ed., *Imagining Nations*, Manchester: Manchester University Press, 1998: 212–28. See also J. Adam Tooze, *Statistics and the German State, 1900–1945: The Making of Modern Economic Knowledge*, Cambridge, UK: CUP, 2001.

59   Daniel Bell, *The Coming of Post-Industrial Society: A Venture in Social Forecasting*, New York: Basic Books, 1976: 331–2.

Kuznets warned that 'a national total facilitates the ascription of independent significance to that vague entity called the national economy'.[60] The warning was of no use. The subsequent elaboration of the GNP of each economy made it possible to represent the size, structure and growth of this new totality. The making of the economy provided a new, everyday political language in which the nation-state could speak of itself and imagine its existence as something natural, spatially bounded and subject to political management.

The emergent national economy was dependent upon a 'nationalisation' of political and administrative power – the emergence of large-scale, techno-scientific governmental practices based upon the vastly expanded administrative machinery of post-1930s national governments. It also contributed to the making of these nationalised machineries of government, in which economics superseded law as the technical language of administrative power.[61]

For orthodox, pre-Keynesian economics, the sphere of economic behaviour was the individual market. This was the abstraction in terms of which the relations between costs, utilities and prices were to be analysed. When Keynes's *General Theory* replaced this abstraction, which had no geographical or political definition, with the 'economic system as a whole', it was a system defined by a set of geopolitical boundaries. The system was represented in terms of a series of aggregates (production, employment, investment and consumption) and synthetic averages (interest rate, price level, real wage, and so on), whose referent was the geographic space of the nation-state. This 'national' framing of the economy was not theorised, but introduced as a commonsense construct providing the boundaries within which the new averages and aggregates could be measured.[62] Subsequently, the division of economics into the separate fields of macro- and micro-economics inscribed this commonsensical reference to the nation-state in the structure of the discipline, where it remained unnoticed. Thinking of the national economy as simply 'the macro level' provided a substitute for a theoretical analysis of its geopolitical construction. In place of a study of the institutional forms of the state, economics reproduced this institutional structure within the structure of the discipline.

The forming of the economy in terms of the nation-state was related to the re-casting of the international order. The dissolution of the European and Japanese empires before and after the Second World War destroyed an older framing of political power in terms of position in an imperial order. Here too the economy provided a new way of organising geopolitical space. Previously

---

60   Simon Kuznets, *National Income and Its Composition, 1919–1939*, Vol. 1, New York: National Bureau of Economic Research, 1941: xxvi.

61   Theodore J. Lowi, 'The State in Political Science: How We Become What We Study', *American Political Science Review* 86: 1, 1992: 1–7.

62   Hugo Radice, 'The National Economy: A Keynesian Myth?' *Capital and Class* 8: 1, 1984: 121.

it had made little sense to talk of, say, the British economy, so long as Britain's economic realm was thought to include India and its other colonies. More generally, a world that was pictured as consisting outside Europe of a series of extensive but discontinuous European and other empires could not easily be imagined to contain a large number of separate economies, each coinciding with a self-contained geographical space and consisting of the totality of economic relations within that space.

The collapse of empire and the growing hegemony of the United States created a new order, consolidated first by the League of Nations and then by the UN, the World Bank and the International Monetary Fund, in which the world was rendered in the form of separate nation-states, with each state marking the boundary of a distinct economy. Again, the new macro-economics took these imagined objects as its untheorised referents: international trade was measured in terms of aggregates (imports and exports of goods and capital) and averages (terms of trade, exchange rates) that were defined in terms of the transactions between national economies.[63] Economic expertise, institutionalised in the World Bank, the IMF and other new agencies, helped construct the new global political order through the publication of statistics and the proliferation of political programmes defining as their object these separate economies.

The framing of the Keynesian national economy was part of a programme to limit and reduce the operation of market competition, through increased management of finance, trade and migration, and above all through the prevention of a global market in labour. It can thus be seen as a successor to the colonial order – an earlier and much older system of limiting market forces by means of monopoly, managed trade, the control of labour, and political repression, which began to collapse in the interwar period. Seen in this light, the making of 'the economy' should be connected with a parallel development that also sought to frame politico-economic relations to exclude the operation of market competition: the development of the large corporation, including its largest and most powerful variant, the multinational oil corporation.

Joseph Schumpeter argued that economists had more justification than natural scientists for using mathematical models to describe the world they studied.[64] This was because the economic world, unlike the natural world, was actually constructed out of numerical phenomena – prices, measures of quantity, interest rates, and so on. He saw this as an argument for the further development of quantitative and formal methods of economic analysis. This affinity between the methods of economics and the make-up of the world it studied was certainly a strength, but it was a strength that had further consequences.

---

63   Ibid.
64   Joseph Schumpeter, 'The Common Sense of Econometrics', *Econometrica* 1: 1, January 1933: 5.

It made it relatively easy for economic knowledge to become involved in the everyday making of the objects of economic analysis.[65] As a result, there could never be any simple divide between the models and representations developed by academic economics and the world it claimed to represent.

These transformations created in the twentieth century a political and material world densely imbued with the expertise, calculative techniques and conceptual machinery of modern economics. The so-called material world of governments, corporations, consumers and objects of consumption was arranged, managed, formatted and run with the help of economic expertise. The readiness with which it seemed that this world could be manipulated and modelled by economics reflected not simply that it was a naturally 'quantitative' world, as Schumpeter suggested. It reflected this imbrication of the concepts and calculations of economic science in the world it was studying.

FUEL MONEY

We can now connect the assembling of 'the economy' with the transition from a coal-based energy system to a predominantly oil-based one. The conception of the economy depended upon abundant and low-cost energy supplies, making postwar Keynesian economics a form of 'petroknowledge'.

The conceptualisation of the economy as a process of monetary circulation defined the main feature of the new object: it could expand without getting physically bigger. Older ways of thinking about wealth were based upon physical processes that suggested limits to growth: the expansion of cities and factories, the colonial enlargement of territory, the accumulation of gold reserves, the growth of population and absorption of migrants, the exploitation of new mineral reserves, the increase in the volume of trade in commodities. All these were spatial and material processes that had physical limits. By the 1930s, many of those limits seemed to be approaching: population growth in the West was levelling off, the colonial expansion of the United States and the European imperial powers had ended and was threatened with reversal, coal mines were being exhausted, and agriculture and industry faced gluts of overproduction. The economy, however, measured by the new calculative device of national income accounting, had no obvious limit. National income, later renamed the gross national product, was a measure not of the accumulation of wealth but of the speed and frequency with which paper money changed hands. It could grow without any problem of physical or territorial limits.

Oil contributed to the new conception of the economy as an object that could grow without limit in several ways. First, oil declined continuously in price. Adjusting for inflation, the price of a barrel of oil in 1970 was one-third of

---

65 Michel Callon, *The Laws of the Markets*, Oxford: Blackwell, 1998.

what it had sold for in 1920.[66] So although increasing quantities of energy were consumed, the cost of energy did not appear to represent a limit to economic growth. (In fact, economists explained the growth of their new object without reference to the consumption of ever-increasing quantities of physical energy, measuring only the input of capital and labour. This left an unexplained 'residual' growth, which for a long time they tried to attribute to factors outside their economic models that they called 'technology'.[67])

Second, thanks to its relative abundance and the ease of shipping it across oceans, oil could be treated as something inexhaustible. Its cost included no calculation for the exhaustion of reserves. The growth of the economy, measured in terms of GNP, had no need to account for the depletion of energy resources. The leading contributions to the academic formulation of the economy – Keynes's *General Theory*, Hicks's *Value and Capital*, Samuelson's *Foundations*, and the Arrow-Debreu model – paid no attention to the depletion of energy.[68] The economics of growth of the 1950s and 1960s could conceive of long-run growth as something unrestrained by the availability of energy.[69] Moreover, the costs of air pollution, environmental disaster, climate change and the other negative consequences of using fossil fuels were not deducted from the measurement of GNP. Since the measurement of the economy made no distinction between beneficial and harmful costs, the increased expenditure required to deal with the damage caused by fossil fuels appeared as an addition rather than an impediment to growth.[70] In all these ways, the availability and supply of oil contributed to the shaping of the economy and its growth as the new primary object of mid-twentieth-century politics.

The abundance of hydrocarbon energy contributed to the new forms of calculation in further ways, two of which were of particular significance. One was the industrialisation of agriculture. To earlier economic thought, land appeared as a primary source of wealth and as a limited resource, unable to

---

66   The price of oil fell from $31 a barrel in 1920 to $9 in 1970 (in 2006 prices). The average price per decade also declined, from $18 per barrel in the 1920s, to $15 per barrel in the 1930s and 1940s, $14 per barrel in the 1950s and $12 per barrel in the 1960s. *BP Statistical Review of World Energy 2007*, available at www.bp.com.

67   Dale W. Jorgenson, ed., *The Economics of Productivity*, Cheltenham: Edward Elgar, 2009. Robert U. Ayres and Benjamin Warr show that including a measure for energy, or rather exergy – energy when converted into useful work – provides a better accounting for all US growth since 1900. Ayres and Warr, 'Accounting for Growth: The Role Of Physical Work', *Structural Change and Economic Dynamics* 16: 2, 2005: 181–209.

68   Keynes, *General Theory*; John Hicks, *Value and Capital*, Oxford: OUP, 1939; Paul A. Samuelson, *Foundations of Economic Analysis*, Cambridge, MA: Harvard University Press, 1947; Kenneth J. Arrow and Gerard Debreu, 'Existence of an Equilibrium for a Competitive Economy', *Econometrica* 22: 3, 1954: 265–90.

69   Geoffrey M. Heal and Partha S. Dasgupta, *Economic Theory and Exhaustible Resources*, Cambridge, UK: CUP, 1979: 1.

70   Herman E. Daly, *Steady-State Economics: The Economics of Biophysical Equilibrium and Moral Growth*, San Francisco: W. H. Freeman, 1977.

increase at the rate of population growth and liable to degeneration and exhaustion. The introduction of synthetic fertilisers after the First World War, manufactured from natural gas, and of chemical herbicides and insecticides after the Second World War, appeared to remove these natural limits to growth. The other contribution was the rise of synthetic materials, manufactured with hydrocarbons, which appeared as a direct answer to resource depletion. In 1926, a meeting of the Institute of Politics in Williamstown, Massachusetts, brought together mining engineers, geologists and chemists to talk with political scientists about the threat of resource depletion. The mining engineers warned about the threat of exhaustion of key minerals; but the chemists disagreed, arguing that the new synthetic materials developed during the First World War would make it possible to create any resources that ran short by artificial means. 'The mining engineers argued that when present stocks of important materials are exhausted, our civilization will be profoundly dislocated', according to a report on the meeting. 'The experts in chemistry, on the other hand, were pervaded with a striking optimism.' Acknowledging the possibility of temporary shortages, 'they looked forward with assurance to replacing exhausted materials with others equally suited to human needs.' The difference of view extended to political issues. The mining engineers warned that 'the natural distribution of resources is distinctly unequal, so that a condition approaching monopoly exists in many essential resources', oil being the most obvious example. The chemists, on the other hand, 'felt that synthetic products would, in many cases, break up national monopolies, and restore a really competitive situation'.[71]

If oil played a key role in the making of 'the economy', it also shaped the project that would challenge it, and later provide a rival method of governing democratic politics: the 'market' of neoliberalism. A group of European intellectuals under the leadership of Friedrich Hayek launched the neoliberal movement at a colloquium in Paris, organised in August 1938, to discuss the work of Walter Lippmann criticising the New Deal, as a movement against this new object of planning, the economy, and against planning itself as a method of concentrating and deploying expert knowledge. Neoliberalism proposed an alternative ordering of knowledge, expertise and political technology – the political apparatus that it named 'the market'. This was not the market of David Ricardo or William Jevons, but a term that began to take on new meanings in the hands of the nascent neoliberal movement. Drawing on Lippmann's warnings in *The Phantom Public* and *The Good Society* about the dangers of public opinion and the need to expand the areas of concern that are reserved to the decisions of experts, neoliberalism was envisioned by

---

71   Henry M. Wriston, 'Institute of Politics', *American Political Science Review* 20: 4, 1926: 853–4.

Hayek and his collaborators as an alternative project to defeat the threat of the left and of populist democracy.

The development of neoliberalism was delayed by the war and the programmes of postwar reconstruction. Its political challenge to the Keynesian apparatus got gradually underway a decade later, in modest form, with the founding of a think tank in London in 1955 called the Institute of Economic Affairs. The launch was triggered by the first postwar crisis in the oil-currency system: Britain's attempt to preserve the sterling area as a mechanism of currency regulation, despite the loss of its control of the hub of that mechanism, the Anglo-Iranian Company's oilfields in Iran. The desperate measures with which London tried to retain the pound's value despite the loss of the oil wells through which its value had been manufactured provided the point of vulnerability where the neoliberal movement first began to construct an alternative to the economy.

Likewise in the US, the origins of the neoliberal movement were tied to the struggles over the postwar issues of oil and the regulation of international financial speculation. The State Department's plans for American oil policy in 1945 were blocked by the Petroleum Industry War Council, whose foreign policy committee was chaired by Albert Mattei, president of the Honolulu Oil Corporation. Mattei warned the officials attempting to create an international body to regulate postwar oil development, 'we are going to come in with constructive suggestions, and if you don't accept our suggestions we are going to tear your playhouse down'.[72] He went on to help kill the Anglo-US Petroleum Agreement. A powerful northern California Republican, Mattei was a founding board member in 1946 of the Foundation for Economic Education – the original inspiration for Hayek's Institute of Economic Affairs in London. One of its first publications was Henry Hazlitt's *Will Dollars Save the World?*, an attack on the Marshall Plan and the forms of state planning in Europe on which it was based, as well as the ideas about the dollar and other currencies that it reinforced. Hazlitt called for the US to go on the real, not just the formal gold standard, and for others to follow.[73]

The oil wells and pipelines of the Middle East, and the political arrangements that were built with them, helped make possible the assembling of the Keynesian economy and the forms of democracy in which it played a central part. Democratic politics developed, thanks to oil, with a peculiar orientation towards the future: the future was a limitless horizon of growth. This horizon was not some natural reflection of a time of plenty; it was the result of a particular way of organising expert knowledge and its objects, in terms of a novel world

---

72   Stephen J. Randall, *United States Foreign Oil Policy 1914–1948*, 2nd edn, Montreal and Kingston: McGill-Queen's University Press, 2005: 199–200.

73   Henry Hazlitt, *Will Dollars Save the World?* New York: Appleton-Century, 1947. His analysis of Europe began with an attack on allied control of the German economy, based on the arguments of the ordoliberal Wilhelm Röpke.

called 'the economy'. Innovations in methods of calculation, the use of money, the measurement of transactions and the compiling of national statistics made it possible to imagine the central object of politics as an object that could increase in size without any form of ultimate material constraint.

We have now expanded the meaning of the term 'carbon democracy'. At first it referred to the central place of coal in the rise of mass democracy, and then to the role of oil, with its different locations, properties and modes of control, in weakening the forms of democratic agency that a dependence on coal had enabled. Oil has now taken on a larger significance in our understanding of democracy. In the postwar period, democratic politics was transformed not only by the switch to oil, but by the development of two new methods of governing democracies, both made possible by the growing use of energy from oil. One of these was an arrangement for managing the value of money and limiting the power of financial speculation, which was said to have destroyed interwar democracy – a system built with the pipelines, oil agreements and oligarchies that organised the supply and pricing of oil. It was accompanied by the construction of the Cold War, which provided a framework for the policing of the postwar Middle East that replaced the need for mandates, trusteeships, development programmes and other scaffoldings for imperial power. The other new mode of governing democracies was the manufacture of 'the economy' – an object whose experts began to displace democratic debate and whose mechanisms set limits to egalitarian demands. In the years 1967–74, as we will see in Chapter 7, the relations among these disparate elements were all transformed, just as they are being transformed again today. To understand the so-called 'oil crisis' of that period, we must first understand how political forces in the Middle East brought the postwar petroleum order to an end.

CHAPTER 6

Sabotage

While operating as part of an international financial system, and as the energy that made it possible to imagine the limitless growth of 'the economy', oil was a fluid that petroleum workers in production fields in different parts of the world recovered from beneath the ground, stored in tanks, processed in treatment plants, pumped into pipelines, loaded onto tankers and transported across oceans. The drilling rigs, pumps, pipelines, refineries and distribution networks of the oil industry were not as vulnerable to stoppages or sabotage as the carbon energy networks of the coal age. Nevertheless, as the Middle East replaced Latin America as the world's second-most-productive oil region after the United States, the possibilities for local disruption increased.[1]

Governments eventually came to power in Iraq, Algeria, Syria and Libya that were independent of British and French political influence, while the two American client states, Iran and Saudi Arabia, began attempting to loosen foreign control of their oil. These changes allowed local disputes and disruptions to be built into something more effective. Interrupting or reducing the supply of oil could become an instrument to be used for larger political purposes, aimed at altering the control of oil or changing other aspects of the political order in the Middle East. The construction of this instrument is usually described in terms of the emergence of a new political consciousness: the growth of a more assertive Arab nationalism. Equally important, however, were the practical forms of recalcitrance: the rerouting of oil supplies, the building of new refineries, and the acts of sabotage that made possible the first sustained challenge to the way Western oil companies managed the flow of oil.

REVOLUTION IN IRAQ

During the 1960s, the oil-producing states of the Middle East sought a way to take national control of their oil reserves without suffering the fate of Iran a decade earlier. When the government of Muhammad Mossadegh nationalised the assets of the Anglo-Iranian Oil Company in 1951, Iran had taken over the production of oil but was unable to sell it. The British blockaded exports from the refinery at Abadan, persuading tanker fleets and major oil companies to

---

1 Oil production in the Middle East and North Africa surpassed that of Latin America and the Caribbean in 1953, and of the US ten years later. DeGoyer & MacNoughton, *Twentieth Century Petroleum Statistics*, Dallas: DeGolyer & MacNaughton, 2009.

refuse to handle the oil. Anglo-Iranian made up the lost supplies by doubling production in the neighbouring oilfields of Kuwait, which became the largest producer in the Middle East. Since oil formed a large part of Iran's export revenues, the blockade threw the country into economic crisis, leaving the government an easy target for the Anglo-American-organised military coup of August 1953. The coup removed Mossadegh's parliamentary-based government, restored and enhanced the oligarchic rule of the shah, and exposed the left to violent repression.

Iraq was the next focus of the struggle between the oil firms and the producer countries. Like Iran it had a large agrarian population, while its cities were growing with the migrant poor driven from the countryside by the concentration of land in the hands of large landowners whose control over rural life and livelihoods had been consolidated under the British. In the oilfields, the railway yards and the textile mills, the workforce had formed active trade unions. The leadership of these and other popular political forces came largely from the Communist Party of Iraq, the largest and best-organised party in the country. The left campaigned for jobs, housing and other improvements to collective welfare, for ending the private control of large estates that caused misery in the countryside, for democratic rights in place of political repression and for ending foreign control of the oil industry.[2]

As the control of oil became the focus of popular political forces, it led to their undoing. The power of sabotage – the capacity to block or slow the flow of oil, a capacity that had previously been monopolised largely by the international oil companies – would be organised not by the workers who operated the oil industry, but by the state. When nationalist army officers led by Abd al-Karim Qasim overthrew the British-backed monarchical government in 1958, they relied initially on the Communists for popular support while trying to unify the country around a campaign for the control of oil. For Qasim and his successors, taking state ownership of the country's petroleum resources would offer a way to finance social reforms while bypassing those modes of wealth-creation that make the well off vulnerable to egalitarian demands. Oil revenues would remove the need to create national wealth through a radical redistribution of land and a large increase in manufacturing.

In other parts of the world (in much of East and South Asia, for example), effective agrarian reform was a critical instrument for building more egalitarian and democratic ways of life. Limiting the size of farms to the area that a family could work on its own removed from the wealthy the option of earning

---

2   Hanna Batatu, *The Old Social Classes and the Revolutionary Movements of Iraq: A Study of Iraq's Old Landed and Commercial Classes and of its Communists, Ba'thists, and Free Officers*, Princeton: Princeton University Press, 1978: 764–865; Joe Stork, 'Oil and the Penetration of Capitalism in Iraq', in Petter Nore and Terisa Turner, eds, *Oil and Class Struggle*, London: Zed Press, 1980: 172–98.

large rentier incomes from land, obliging those seeking to accumulate wealth to build it through the development of manufacturing. Such a change has a double effect, creating more equality (and smaller, more productive farms) in the countryside, while making those with capital gradually vulnerable to the power of an industrial workforce. Democratisation has generally depended on engineering such forms of vulnerability. The vulnerability arises not because manufacturing allows workers to gather and share ideas, or form what is called a 'social movement', but because it can render the technical processes of producing concentrations of wealth dependent on the well-being of large numbers of people.

The new Iraqi government attempted a redistribution of large agrarian estates, but struggled to implement the programme in the face of landlord opposition and a succession of serious droughts. It set the upper limit on landholding at 250 hectares (over 600 acres) of irrigated land, and double that area of rain-fed land.[3] In East Asia, governments driven by the fear that peasants and their allies might try to emulate the Communist revolution in China carried out land reform programmes that set limits on owning irrigated land as low as three hectares. Retaining their large estates, those with capital in Iraq had no need to take the difficult path of earning wealth through manufacturing, and would later enjoy the opportunities in trade, contracting and other services required by a government steadily enriched by oil. While manufacturing depends on complex human–mechanical processes that are vulnerable to sabotage, giving large industrial workforces the ability to make effective political demands, national control of oil would place its revenues in the hands of the state, gradually strengthening the powers of government and reducing its initial dependence on popular forces.[4]

Among the four large oil-producing countries of the Middle East in that period – Iran, Iraq, Saudi Arabia and Kuwait – Iraq's situation was peculiar. It was the country where the companies that controlled the world's major oil regions least wanted to produce more of it. The industry was under the management of the Anglo-Iranian Oil Company, now renamed British Petroleum.

3   Edith Penrose and E. F. Penrose, *Iraq: International Relations and National Development*, London: Ernest Benn, 1978: 240–8.

4   Studies of the impact of oil on democracy fail to consider these questions. Michael L. Ross, 'Does Oil Hinder Democracy?' *World Politics* 53: 3, April 2001: 325–61, for example, demonstrates a negative correlation between oil exports as a percentage of GDP and degree of democracy, as estimated in the Polity data set. The data are derived from an evaluation of the institutional procedures by which the candidate for chief executive is selected, elected and held accountable. The narrowness of this conception of democracy, the unreliability of its measurement, and the assumption that diverse institutional arrangements can be compared and ranked as embodying differing degrees of a universal principle of democracy, are among the many problems presented by the data. Ross is unable to establish reasons for the statistical relationship between oil exports and Polity data ranking, or to account for places, such as Venezuela and Indonesia, that experienced a different relationship between the development of oil and the emergence of more democratic forms of rule.

From the creation of the Iraqi oil industry in the 1920s, BP had sought to develop the country's oil more slowly than production in neighbouring countries. The company produced oil on behalf of a consortium, the Iraq Petroleum Company, in an arrangement similar to that in the neighbouring countries (including Iran after 1953). BP's partners in Iraq, however, included not only other members of the 'seven sisters', the cartel formed by BP, Shell and the five major US oil firms, but the French oil consortium Compagnie Française des Pétroles (known today as Total) and its ally Calouste Gulbenkian, the go-between who had built the consortium. Raising production in Iraq increased the market share of the French and Gulbenkian, whereas growth in the other three countries was shared only among the cartel.[5] As a result, oil production in Iraq grew at a much slower rate than among its neighbours.

BP delayed the completion of the pipeline to export the oil, deliberately drilled shallow wells to avoid discovering additional supplies, and plugged wildcat wells that yielded large finds to conceal their existence from the government. Although Iraq's reserves were comparable to those of the other three countries, its production in the 1950s and 1960s was kept at about half the level of the others, or less. BP and its partners used Iraq as the swing producer, with a large undeveloped capacity that was increased only to meet exceptional demand.[6]

Compared to Iran, where nationalisation had already been defeated, Iraq's position was even weaker. The bulk of its oil was exported by pipeline through Syria to the Mediterranean, so it did not control the point of shipment. It had a small refinery to process oil for domestic consumption, but the main refinery supplying regional markets was placed at the Mediterranean end of the pipeline, leaving Iraq no independent means of processing oil for export.

RELINQUISHMENT

When Qasim and his fellow army officers overthrew the British-backed monarchical government in 1958, they realised that these weaknesses would enable the major oil companies to defeat any attempt to nationalise the industry. Qasim's initial goal was to construct the equipment to overcome this vulnerability. He proposed that the Iraq Petroleum Company (IPC) lay a pipeline from the Mosul oilfields in the north to Basra in the south, and build a refinery there for export. The oil companies refused. They had no wish to give Iraq the ability to process

---

5   Independent companies had a token share in the Iran consortium, but in Iraq the CFP/Gulbenkian share was a much more significant 27.5 per cent. The operating companies in Kuwait and Saudi Arabia were not, strictly speaking, consortiums, but jointly owned subsidiaries of the parent companies.

6   *Twentieth Century Petroleum Statistics*; John Blair, *The Control of Oil*, New York: Pantheon Books, 1976: 81–5; Gregory Nowell, *Mercantile States and the World Oil Cartel, 1900–1939*, Ithaca: Cornell University Press, 1994: 270–5.

and export its own oil. Unknown to Qasim, moreover, there was already more than enough oil in the south. IPC estimated that the North Rumaila field near Basra might be the largest or second-largest oilfield in the world. In negotiations with the Iraqi government, however, BP kept this secret, noting that it would not be prudent at this stage 'to mention latent possibilities of greater Rumaila development'.[7]

The annual dividend BP paid its shareholders had grown from 16 pence per share in the early 1950s to 43 pence in 1954, or 43 per cent of the original value of each share. Given the postwar economic austerity in Britain and the demand of Iraq and other producer countries for a greater share of the income, the senior minister at the British Treasury had become embarrassed by the level of shareholder profits, and demanded in private that it be reduced. 'It is impossible to go on with these *stooges*', he wrote in an internal memo, threatening to publicly repudiate the directors of 'this unpatriotic organization'. BP refused to bend, pointing to the criterion that mattered most: its rival, Shell, paid higher returns. The 43 per cent return was soon surpassed; BP increased its dividend to 75 pence per share in the late 1950s, and to 117 pence in 1960.[8] Since increased production would lower prices and threaten this extraordinary rate of surplus income, BP was anxious not to see a new field like North Rumaila developed.

Unable to nationalise IPC, Iraq planned to develop a national oil industry alongside it. It proposed that the company relinquish part of the concession area, which covered almost the entire country. Under the original concession agreement of 1925, IPC had been required to relinquish all except about 0.5 per cent of the concession area within thirty-two months of starting exploration, but the consortium had forced the government to remove this provision from the revised agreement of 1931. BP and its partners now agreed to discuss giving up 50 per cent of the area – an offer later increased to 54 per cent – provided the area given up was expressed in square miles rather than as a percentage of the total (to make it more difficult for other countries to demand an equivalent deal).[9] The companies also insisted on deciding which areas to relinquish. Iraq was willing to let IPC keep all currently producing wells and areas with proven reserves, but wanted a say in which remaining areas were given up, so as to have

---

7   United Kingdom, Foreign Office, 'Searight's Account of His Interview with the Prime Minister', 9 April 1959, FO 371/141062, and 'IPC Believes Rumaila Oilfield Has Huge Potential', 14 June 1961, FO 371/157725, National Archives of the UK: Public Record Office: Foreign Office: Political Departments: General Correspondence from 1906 to 1966, referred to in subsequent notes as FO 371, followed by the piece number. For a detailed history of the negotiations between IPC and the government of Iraq, see Samir Saul, 'Masterly Inactivity as Brinkmanship: The Iraq Petroleum Company's Route to Nationalization, 1958–1972', *International History Review* 29: 4, 2007: 746–92.

8   James Bamberg, *History of the British Petroleum Company*, vol. 3: *British Petroleum and Global Oil, 1950–1975: The Challenge of Nationalism*, Cambridge, UK: CUP, 2000: 131, 135.

9   'IPC Negotiations with Iraqi Government', 30 July 1959, FO 371/141068.

attractive prospects to offer other companies with which it might work. The Foreign Office in London feared that Iraq might respond by annexing Kuwait, previously a dependency of Basra province. By depriving BP of the Kuwaiti oilfields it had used to replace Iranian supplies when it imposed its embargo on Iran in 1951, Baghdad could make it harder for BP to impose an embargo on Iraq in the event of nationalisation.[10] To the disquiet of officials at the Foreign Office, who found Iraq's proposals on relinquishment 'not in fact unreasonable', the oil companies rejected them.[11]

A PREFERENCE FOR CRISIS

The oil companies preferred to provoke a crisis. As the Foreign Office noted, the IPC owners 'may prefer to have 75 per cent taken away from them than to surrender 54 per cent, in view of implications in other areas'.[12] Forcing Iraq to act unilaterally would give the impression that IPC had no say in the matter, and make it harder for other countries to request similar arrangements. More importantly, it would enable the IPC partners to threaten litigation against any company that agreed to work in the confiscated areas, as BP had done successfully in Iran in 1951. Unable to reach an agreement, in December 1960 Iraq passed Law 80, cancelling the 1931 concession agreement and expropriating 99.5 per cent of the concession area, leaving IPC its producing wells but not the fields it had refused to develop, including North Rumaila. Its remaining 0.5 per cent share corresponded to the area it would have been allowed to retain under the original 1925 concession. The oil companies resolved 'to wait out Qasim', in the words of the authorised history of BP, 'hoping for a change of government'.[13]

The US and Britain, it seems, had already decided to eliminate Qasim. The CIA's attempt to kill him in February 1960 failed, as had an effort to assassinate him the previous year, but he was removed from power and murdered in the military coup of February 1963.[14] The US supplied the new government with the names of more than a hundred leftists for its death squads to hunt down,

---

10   'Nationalization of IPC', 1 April 1959, FO 371/141061.

11   'IPC: Points Causing Breakdown in IPC Meeting', 2 October 1959, FO 371/141069.

12   'IPC Relinquishment', June 1959, FO 371/141066.

13   Bamberg, *History of British Petroleum*, vol. 3: 167.

14   Penrose and Penrose, *Iraq*: 288; Thomas Powers, 'Inside the Department of Dirty Tricks: Part One, An Isolated Man', *Atlantic Monthly*, August 1979; Roger Morris, 'A Tyrant 40 Years in the Making', *New York Times*, 14 March 2003: A29; Malik Mufti, *Sovereign Creations: Pan-Arabism and Political Order in Syria and Iraq*, Ithaca: Cornell University Press, 1996: 143–4. Brandon Wolfe-Hunnicutt assesses the evidence from these sources and explains the shifting battle in the US government between those open to working with Qasim and those arguing for his elimination: 'The End of the Concessionary Regime: Oil and American Power in Iraq, 1958–1972', PhD thesis, Department of History, Stanford University, 2011: 26–90.

many of them prominent intellectuals, and Britain reported within a week that the 'winkling out' of the Communists was succeeding and 'the army has the situation under control'.[15] Large numbers of the leadership and rank-and-file of the country's popular political movement were killed, and thousands more imprisoned. James Akins, an American diplomat in Kuwait, from where the US was said to have liaised with the coup plotters, returned to Baghdad following the coup. 'We were very happy', he later recalled. 'They got rid of a lot of communists. A lot of them were executed, or shot. This was a great development.'[16] The military government requested that IPC turn over a disused pumping station to house political prisoners, asking the oil company 'to help equip the station and build it up into a concentration camp' capable of holding 1,200 political prisoners. IPC preferred not to become involved in the construction of a concentration camp – the term used by the government – but agreed to supply piped water to the desert prison.[17]

With Qasim out of the way and the left and the labour movement eliminated or 'under control', America and Britain were disappointed to discover that IPC was still uncooperative. The British embassy in Baghdad told London that 'the whole basis of the IPC concession here is out of date' and should be replaced with a partnership with an Iraqi state enterprise.[18] IPC, however, demanded that the new regime rescind the expropriation of its concession area. While continuing to pump the limited supplies of oil it wanted from Iraq, the consortium persuaded the US government to pressure independent oil companies not to take up any oil contracts offered by Iraq as long as the dispute over Law 80 was unresolved, and meanwhile delayed settling the dispute.[19]

The method of provoking a crisis and delaying its resolution was aided by a series of regional crises. In 1966, Syria tried to obtain higher transit fees from IPC for using the pipeline that carried Iraqi oil to the Mediterranean. Rather than pay the higher fees, IPC preferred to halt the pumping of oil through the pipeline. The closure lasted from November 1966 until the following March, and reduced

---

15 'Assessment of Iraqi Regime', 14 February 1963, FO 371/170502. On the list of names, see Wolfe-Hunnicutt, 'The End of the Concessionary Regime': 84–6.

16 Frontline, 'The Survival of Saddam', Interviews: James Akins, at www.pbs.org/wgbh/pages/frontline/shows/saddam/interviews/akins.html. See also Douglas Little, 'Mission Impossible: The CIA and the Cult of Covert Action in the Middle East', Diplomatic History 28: 5, 2004: 663–701.

17 'IPC Considers Options', 12 September 1963, FO 371/170505.

18 'Assessment of the Iraqi Regime', 14 February 1963, FO 371/170502.

19 'US Government Concerned About the Non-Cooperative Position Seemingly Adopted by IPC', 15 May 1963, FO 371/170504; see also FO 371/175777 and FO 371/17578. After Iraq asked the Italian company ENI for technical support in the event of nationalisation, the British embassy in Rome tried to pressure the Italian government to prevent ENI's collaboration (FO 371/157725). In February 1964, the US and Britain again asked the Italian government to dissuade ENI from taking up any oil contracts in Iraq (FO 371/175777). See also Wolfe-Hunnicutt, 'End of the Concessionary Regime': 144–74.

Iraq's oil income by two-thirds.[20] BP was happy to shut down Iraqi production, as this offered a way to deal with the problem of oversupply, while causing a further crisis with Iraq. In June 1967, Israel launched the Six-Day War against Egypt and Syria, and in protest the Syrian government cut the pipeline again.

The strategy of crisis and delay gained the major oil companies a decade, but came to an end in the aftermath of the 1967 war. In August 1967, Iraq rescinded a proposal to restore the large North Rumaila field to IPC, a plan favoured by the Oil Ministry but blocked by nationalist opposition to the role of the international oil companies. Over the following months the government made agreements for the state-owned Iraq National Oil Company, established in 1964, to develop the country's oil resources with partners not susceptible to pressure from the oil majors or the US government. In December 1967 it agreed a joint venture with a French state-owned oil company, and the following April it invited bids for technical support to develop North Rumaila and build a pipeline to a new refinery at Basra, to be operated not as a partnership but as an enterprise run directly by the Iraq National Oil Company. An offer from the Soviet Union was finalised a year later, after a coup in July 1968 that brought to power right-wing army officers allied with the Ba'th Party. Iraq was now able to build the independent capacity to process and export oil that Qasim had first sought in 1959.[21]

Arab states that had developed oil industries outside the jurisdiction of the world's seven large oil firms had already established national control. Syria nationalised its small petroleum industry in 1964, Algeria took majority ownership of its French-built industry in February 1971, and Libya began to nationalise foreign-owned oil production in December 1971. The following year, Iraq became the first Middle Eastern producer to wrest control of oil from the dominant Anglo-American cartel. When production from the Rumaila field began in April, IPC cut its production in the north by 50 per cent. After preparing austerity measures and taking two leaders of the Communist party into the cabinet to ensure popular support, on 1 June 1972 the Ba'thist government nationalised the Iraq Petroleum Company.[22]

BOXED IN

In the oil-producing states the powers of sabotage over which oil workers and oil firms had struggled were being increasingly taken over by governments – which were equipping themselves with the palace guards and intelligence services that

---

20   George Ward Stocking, *Middle East Oil: A Study in Political and Economic Controversy*, Nashville: Vanderbilt University Press, 1970: 270–99; Marion Farouk-Sluglett and Peter Sluglett, *Iraq Since 1958: From Revolution to Dictatorship*, 3rd edn, London: I. B. Tauris, 2001: 99–100.

21   On the details of these developments, see Wolfe-Hunnicutt, 'End of the Concessionary Regime': 209–62.

22   Bamberg, *History of British Petroleum*, vol. 3: 171, 469–70.

by the late 1960s made them immune to further foreign- or domestic-organised military coups. In industrialised countries, the 'power of inhibition' underwent a different change.[23] The rise of oil had weakened the old alliance of coal, which brought together miners, railwaymen and dockworkers, allowing them unprecedented power. By 1948, spurred by the role of the Marshall Plan in subsidising the switch from coal to oil, the era of the mass strike was over. In its place emerged a new method of making political claims, based on new ways of interrupting industrial processes.

In 1958 the French sociologist Serge Mallet studied workers at the CalTex oil refinery at Bec d'Ambes on the Gironde Estuary, near Bordeaux. CalTex was a joint venture created by the owners of Aramco to market oil from Saudi Arabia, originally operating in Africa and Asia. In 1947, when construction began on the Tapline to bring Saudi oil to Europe, CalTex took over the former Texaco refinery near Bordeaux, which had been destroyed during the war, and rebuilt it with Marshall Plan funds to handle the new shipments from Saudi Arabia. So the Bec d'Ambes refinery was part of the equipment installed to manufacture a less recalcitrant labour force in Europe.

Ten years later, unaware of this history, Mallet described the formation at Bec d'Ambes of what he called the 'new working class'.[24] The oil refinery exemplified a form of industrial production, dating from the 1930s but spreading rapidly since the 1950s, based on the automated processing and synthesising of materials. Unlike the old assembly-line methods in which workers directly constructed objects, Mallet argued, in a refinery or petrochemical plant workers supervised a flow of substances and managed the automated assembling of complex new materials. In oil refining, synthetic chemicals, electrical energy and telecommunications, workers were now managers, governing automated, computer-controlled processes. The same methods of automated processing were spreading to car manufacturing, railways, steel making, and even coal mining. Work was becoming technicised, eliminating many of the differences between manual labour and lower management: 'Between the operator of a cracking unit who, in a white collar, watches over the continuous flow of oil and the diverse pressures to which it is subjected and the engineer or higher level technician who supervises him, there is no longer a difference in kind, simply a difference of hierarchical situation.'[25]

---

23   Thorstein Veblen, 'On the Nature of Capital', *Quarterly Journal of Economics* 23: 1, 1908: 106.

24   Serge Mallet, *The New Working Class*, translation of *La nouvelle classe ouvrière* (1969), transl. Andrée Shepherd and Bob Shepherd, Nottingham: Bertrand Russell Peace Foundation for Spokesman Books, 1975: 85–118.

25   Serge Mallet, *Essays on the New Working Class*, ed. and transl. Dick Howard and Dean Savage, St Louis: Telos Press, 1975: 41.

The rise of forms of labour based on the supervision of continuous, automated processes did not eliminate industrial action. It produced a new form of strike. Rather than attempting to shut down an enterprise indefinitely through a total stoppage of work – an action difficult to sustain given its impact on the income of strikers – workers were now able to use their technical knowledge and critical role in automated processes to bring about 'the systematic disorganization of production' by causing limited work stoppages, 'spread out along the production process at the most sensitive places'. Brief interruptions aimed at vulnerable points or critical moments within an industrial process could paralyse an industry for months, without workers feeling the impact on their household income.[26]

From the 1880s to the 1940s, workers had built the power to sabotage critical processes at the level of national coal-based energy systems. They had used this power to organise mass parties and win radical improvements in their conditions of social vulnerability. By the 1950s and 1960s, the location, scale and duration of effective sabotage had shifted, now focusing on critical points and flows in complex chemical, metallurgical, communication and other processes. Its more localised scale made this power appear less revolutionary. But the strike waves of the later 1960s, Mallet argued – including the great upheavals of 1968, in which his writings became influential – suggested workers could use this power to acquire greater control of production.

By the late 1960s, as a struggle over the control of energy supplies unfolded in the Middle East, in the industrialised world the efforts among the forces of labour to protect or improve levels of income and conditions of work had intensified. The conflicts were found in the new manufacturing processes, but also in an older industry where the coordinated flow of materials could still be successfully interrupted: transportation. Disruptions to railways, shipping and docking, and increasingly aviation, accounted for 35 to 40 per cent of world labour unrest in the 1950s and 1960s. Shipping and docking, where stoppages had the most power to affect multiple upstream and downstream processes, accounted for more than half this unrest.[27]

The most effective challenge to these struggles once again made use of oil. A generation earlier, the switch to oil as a source of fuel for motive power was decisive in the defeat of the coal miners. The vulnerability of rigid regional energy networks carrying coal had been overcome with flexible, transoceanic energy grids, which isolated the producers of primary energy from those who put it to work in the main industrial regions. Once again, the fix that petroleum offered

26   Ibid., 43.
27   Beverly Silver, *Forces of Labor: Workers' Movements and Globalization Since 1870*, Cambridge, UK: CUP, 2003: 98–100.

was partly spatial, and was based on the introduction of more fluid processes.[28] This time, the transoceanic separation rested on the use of cheap oil to transport a standardised metal box.

This second change was made possible by containerisation. The introduction of metal shipping containers of standard dimensions that could be carried by road, rail and sea allowed goods to be moved in bulk without using labour to unload, stack and reload the individual merchandise as it switched from one mode of transport to another. Much as the fluidity of oil allowed energy to move easily over great distances because it could be pumped onto tankers, eliminating coal heavers and engine stokers, the shipping container made the movement of solid, manufactured goods into a fluid, uninterrupted process. Earlier attempts to introduce the use of containers had failed because different shippers preferred different sizes, making it difficult to stack the containers or build trucks, trains and ships to an optimum size. The escalation of the American war against the Vietnamese people in 1965 produced a logistics crisis as the supply of military goods overwhelmed Saigon's port facilities, leading the US military to introduce containerisation and speed the adoption of standard container dimensions. In 1969, shipping companies introduced huge new custom-built ships that could carry more than 1,000 containers in their holds and on deck. Containers eliminated most of the skilled labour and unionised power of dockworkers, and helped bring a halt to the 'unprecedented advance' in the conditions of labour in industrialised countries in the two decades after 1945.[29]

The container did more than reorganise relations of control at the narrow point where dockworkers could exercise power. Combined with the cheap oil of the 1960s, it made possible the moving of manufacturing overseas, just as the supply of energy used in industrialised countries had earlier been outsourced. After delivering military supplies from the US to Vietnam, the container ships returned empty. Looking for ways to earn additional income, the shippers began to stop in Japan and pick up manufactured goods to carry back to the US, cutting dramatically the cost of shipment and creating the boom in Japanese exports to the US.

Industrial labour could now be threatened with lower costs and unemployment, caused by outsourcing production to Japan and other countries with less unionised, lower-paid workforces. In the decade after 1966, the volume of international trade in manufactured goods increased at double the rate of the volume of global manufacturing.[30] The expansion of global shipping increased the demand for oil, helping create conditions that contributed

---

28   On the 'spatial fix', see David Harvey, *Spaces of Capital: Towards a Critical Geography*, Edinburgh: Edinburgh University Press, 2001.

29   Marc Levinson, *The Box: How the Shipping Container Made the World Smaller and the World Economy Bigger*, Princeton: Princeton University Press, 2006: 4.

30   Levinson, *The Box*: 11, 184–8.

to an increase in oil prices. The jump in oil prices in 1973–74 interrupted the development of outsourcing, as savings from containerisation were suddenly offset by much higher fuel costs for transoceanic shipping. In 1976, however, stable energy prices and the introduction of a new generation of even larger container ships allowed the growth of outsourcing to resume. At the same time, as we will see, the oil crisis and its market laws provided the 'shock' to explain the ending of improvements in conditions of labour, and a gradual reappropriation of the political powers and more egalitarian forms of life won over preceding decades.

INSTITUTIONALISED USELESSNESS

In 1964, the British government had tried to encourage the new military government in Baghdad to settle the dispute with the foreign owners of the Iraq Petroleum Company by offering it something in exchange: weapons. At a meeting with the Iraqi prime minister to discuss the oil law passed by the Qasim government before its overthrow the previous year, the British ambassador 'took the opportunity of making a reference to our supplying Iraq with arms and equipment'. Reporting that he 'merely juxtaposed the two things', he told London that its plan to use the sale of military equipment to gain concessions in the oil dispute was unlikely to succeed, since 'they are really doing us a favour in buying arms from us'. The Iraqis were supporting Britain's weakening trade balance by 'paying large sums in sterling', he explained, and at the same time were 'well aware of our desire that they should not seek alternative sources of supply'. A month later the Foreign Office noted in the same file that Iraq was now purchasing arms from the Soviet Union, and that 'partly as a result of poor after-contract performance by major British firms', Britain would 'have to fight hard to persuade the Iraqis to continue to buy British'.[31]

Although the ambassador pretended that oil and weapons were merely juxtaposed, in fact the two fit together in a particular way: one was enormously useful, the other importantly useless. As the producer states gradually forced the major oil companies to share with them more of the profits from oil, increasing quantities of sterling and dollars flowed to the Middle East. To maintain the balance of payments and the viability of the international financial system, Britain and the United States needed a mechanism for these currency flows to be returned. This was especially a problem for the US, since the value of the dollar was fixed in relation to gold, and provided the basis for the Bretton Woods financial system. Arms were particularly suited to this task of financial recycling, for their acquisition was not limited by their usefulness. The

---

31   'Roger Allen, Ambassador in Baghdad, to Foreign Office', 8 February 1964, FO 371/175780; cover note added 12 March 1964.

dovetailing of the production of petroleum and the manufacture of arms made oil and militarism increasingly interdependent.[32]

The conventional explanation for the rapid increase in arms sales to the Middle East, beginning in the mid-1960s, relies on the arguments offered by the arms salesmen, and by the governments that supported their business. Since the arms trade encouraged the militarisation of Middle Eastern states, its growth shaped the development of carbon democracy. To understand this dimension of the relationship between oil and democracy, we need to unpack the justifications used for selling weapons and provide an alternative account.

The purchase of most goods, whether consumable materials like food and clothing or more durable items such as cars or industrial machinery, sooner or later reaches a limit where, in practical terms, no more of the commodity can be used and further acquisition is impossible to justify. Given the enormous size of oil revenues, and the relatively small populations and widespread poverty of many of the countries beginning to accumulate them, ordinary goods could not be purchased at a rate that would go far to balance the flow of dollars (and many could be bought from third countries, like Germany and Japan – purchases that would not improve the dollar problem). Weapons, on the other hand, could be purchased to be stored up rather than used, and came with their own forms of justification. Under the appropriate doctrines of security, ever-larger acquisitions could be rationalised on the grounds that they would make the need to use them less likely. Certain weapons, such as US fighter aircraft, were becoming so technically complex by the 1960s that a single item might cost over $10 million, offering a particularly compact vehicle for recycling dollars. Arms, therefore, could be purchased in quantities unlimited by any practical need or capacity to consume. As petrodollars flowed increasingly to the Middle East, the sale of expensive weaponry provided a unique apparatus for recycling those dollars – one that could expand without any normal commercial constraint.

Since 1945, the United States had relied upon the 'institutionalised waste' of peacetime domestic military spending to soak up surplus capital and maintain the profitability of several of its largest manufacturing corporations.[33] It

---

32   Nitzan and Bichler offer an important study of this relationship. They locate its dynamic in the dominant place of arms manufacturing among leading US corporations and the superior profitability of arms exports over supplying domestic government demand. However, they downplay the role of dollar recycling and the deliberate wastefulness of military sales, especially in the case of oil states for which alternative spending options were limited. Jonathan Nitzan and Shimshon Bichler, 'The Weapondollar-Petrodollar Coalition', in *The Global Political Economy of Israel*, London: Pluto Press, 2002: 198–273.

33   Thorstein Veblen noted the role of 'conspicuous waste' in *The Theory of the Leisure Class: An Economic Study of Institutions*, New York: Macmillan, 1899: 36–42, but did not connect it with military spending, even in his subsequent discussion in *Imperial Germany and the Industrial Revolution*, New York: Macmillan, 1915.

enhanced this mechanism of waste with spending on the Korean and Vietnam wars. When projections for expenditure on Asian warfare began to drop in the later 1960s, America's two dozen giant military contractors were in urgent need of new outlets for their hardware. No longer able to rely on increased purchases by the US government, they sought to transform the transfer of weapons to foreign governments, previously a relatively small trade financed mostly through US overseas development aid, into a commercial export business.[34] The financiers concerned with dollar recycling now had a powerful ally.

Meanwhile, for the autocrats and military regimes of the Middle East, arms purchases provided a relatively effortless way to assert the technological prowess of the state. More importantly, once the West turned the supply of arms from a form of government-to-government aid into a commercial business, a space opened for middlemen to operate as brokers between the local state and the foreign firms. Members of ruling families, their in-laws and their political allies were well placed to fill this role, allowing a part of the revenues from oil, recycled as arms purchases, an easy diversion into prodigious levels of private accumulation.

After 1967, Iraq turned to France and the Soviet Union for arms, rewarding the countries that were helping it develop a national oil industry. For Britain and the US, the main recycling point was Iran, which imported almost three times as much weaponry as Iraq in the decade after 1967.[35] In 1966, the shah of Iran agreed to a large purchase from General Dynamics of its new F-111 fighter-bomber, an aircraft that was over budget, failing to meet performance targets, and frequently crashing in test flights.[36] He then persuaded the Western oil consortium to increase production by 12 per cent a year to finance this and future military spending. The following year the companies were able to increase production by double that amount, thanks to the Arab oil embargo during the June 1967 Arab-Israeli war, but in 1968 and 1969 Iran demanded even larger increases in revenue. As the supply of weapons and equipment accelerated, increasing numbers of arms contractors, bankers, construction companies, consultants, public relations firms and military officers began to profit from the flow of finance, building themselves into the capillaries and arteries through which it flowed. US banks and arms manufacturers, aided by their British,

---

34   See Nitzan and Bichler, 'Weapondollar-Petrodollar Coalition': 206–10, where the core arms firms are identified. In the 1950s about 95 per cent of US arms exports were financed by government aid; by the 1990s the figure was about 30 per cent. Ibid.: 216.

35   Arms Transfers Database, Stockholm International Peace Research Institute, at www.sipri.org/databases/armstransfers.

36   The smaller naval variant of the aircraft, the F-111B, had so many faults it was cancelled soon after going into production and replaced with the Grumman F-14, the plane eventually delivered to Iran in a deal that saved Grumman from bankruptcy. Marcelle Size Knaack, *Encyclopedia of US Air Force Aircraft and Missile Systems*, vol. 1, Washington, DC: Office of Air Force History, 1978: 222–63; Anthony Sampson, *The Arms Bazaar*, London: Hodder & Stoughton, 1977: 249–56.

French and Italian counterparts, transformed the export of weapons into one of the West's most profitable export industries.[37]

Since arms sales were useful for their uselessness, and there was no precedent for the volume of weapons sold, they needed a special apparatus of justification. The work of transforming the superfluous consumption of weaponry on a gargantuan scale into necessity was performed by a new rhetoric of insecurity, and by a series of US actions to produce or sustain the required experience of instability and uncertainty.

The old rhetoric of the postwar period about a communist threat to American interests in the Middle East was proving hard to keep alive. Having finally found a foothold in the oilfields of the Gulf, the Soviet Union had failed to threaten supplies of oil to the West, despite the warnings of Cold War experts. Soviet aid in exploiting the vast reserves of North Rumaila, offered in 1968, would allow Iraq to produce oil from a field whose development Western companies had spent four decades trying to delay (or seven decades, if one counts back to the days of the Baghdad Railway). Instead of threatening the security of the West's oil supplies, the Soviet Union was threatening to increase them.

The Arab defeat in the June 1967 war weakened Arab nationalists and strengthened the conservative, Western-backed regimes in the Gulf. The defeat also hastened a financial crisis in Britain. The brief Arab oil embargo and the closing of the Suez Canal interrupted the supply of Britain's sterling oil from the Gulf, creating a balance of payments crisis that forced the Labour government to devalue the pound and abandon its postwar effort to maintain sterling as an international trading and reserve currency. To address the financial crisis, Britain announced in January 1968 that it would end its role as an imperial power in the Middle East, withdrawing all military forces from the sheikhdoms of the Gulf within four years.[38]

Militarists at right-wing think tanks in Washington, in particular the new Center for International and Strategic Studies, began to warn that the British withdrawal would create a 'power vacuum' in the region. In reality it was thanks to the creation of a vacuum, or at least a 'deflation' in local power, that Britain could justify ending its military presence in the Gulf. Since the 'revolutionary Arabs' had been 'completely deflated' by the 1967 defeat, the Foreign Office noted, the sheikhdoms of the Gulf could survive without a

37   Nitzan and Bichler, 'Weapondollar-Petrodollar Coalition': 198–273; James A. Bill, *The Eagle and the Lion: The Tragedy of American-Iranian Relations*, New Haven: Yale University Press, 1988.

38   Steven G. Galpern, *Money Oil and Empire in the Middle East: Sterling and Postwar Imperialism, 1944–1971*, Cambridge, UK: CUP, 2009: 268–82.

British military presence.[39] The State Department official responsible for the Arabian peninsula agreed, arguing that the claim of the US ambassador in Tehran that hostile forces were ready to fill 'a vacuum' in the Gulf caused by the British departure was 'overdrawn if not inaccurate'. He pointed out that the major Arab powers, Egypt, Syria and Iraq, 'are pinned down elsewhere by the Israelis and Kurds' (whose rebellion in northern Iraq was funded by Israel), while the conservative Arab states saw an armed Iran 'more as a threat than a reassurance'.[40]

The shah of Iran seized the opportunity of Britain's departure to portray the large Iranian military purchases already underway as a scheme to turn Iran into the region's policeman. The only significant threat the shah faced was the growing number of domestic political opponents his government hunted down and imprisoned, a form of police work that had no need for most of the weapons he wished to purchase. He nevertheless demanded to buy ever more sophisticated and expensive arms, and to be given the increased oil revenue and large US government loans to pay for them. The US ambassador relayed to Washington the arguments the shah picked up from the American arms manufacturers, reporting his view that increased arms sales 'would benefit US industry (he mentioned DOD [was] obliged to bail out Lockheed), substantially help difficult US balance of payments situation, and serve our own vital strategic interests in Gulf and Middle East'.[41]

The arms manufacturers helped promote the doctrines of regional insecurity and national military prowess, instructing their agents to discuss arms sales not as commercial arrangements but in terms of strategic objectives. In September 1968, Tom Jones, the chief executive of Northrop Corporation, wrote to Kim Roosevelt (the former CIA agent who had engineered the overthrow of Mossadegh in 1953, and whose consulting firm now facilitated arms sales to the shah) about trying to sell Iran Northrop's P530 lightweight fighter, for which it had been unable to find buyers: 'In any discussions with the Shah', Jones explained, 'it is important that they be kept on the basis of

---

39 Foreign Office Minute, May 1971, FCO 8/1311, cited in William Roger Louis, 'The Withdrawal from the Gulf', in *Ends of British Imperialism: The Scramble for Empire, Suez and Decolonization: Collected Essays*, London: I. B. Tauris, 2006: 877–903, at 888. For a similar US assessment, see Central Intelligence Agency, 'National Intelligence Estimate 34-69-IRAN', 10 January 1969, in US Department of State, *Papers Relating to the Foreign Relations of the United States, 1969–76*, vol. E-4: *Documents on Iran and Iraq, 1969–1972*, ed. Monica Belmonte and Edward C. Keefer, Washington DC: US Government Printing Office, Document 1, available at history.state.gov, referred to in subsequent notes as FRUS.

40 William D. Brewer, 'Memorandum from the Country Director for Saudi Arabia, Kuwait, Yemen and Aden to the Country Director for Iran', 27 February 1970, FRUS, Document 51; Douglas Little, 'The United States and the Kurds: A Cold War Story', *Journal of Cold War Studies* 12: 4, 2010: 71.

41 DOD refers to the Department of Defense. Douglas MacArthur, 'Embassy in Iran to the Department of State', 19 March 1970, FRUS, Document 55.

fundamental national objectives, rather than allow it to take the appearance of a sales plan.'[42]

In 1969 the newly elected administration of Richard Nixon inadvertently offered the arms manufacturers and their clients a new term for these 'fundamental national objectives' – the so-called Nixon Doctrine. On a trip to south-east Asia in July, the president made some off-the-record remarks to the press at a stopover in Guam, intended to reassure the American-backed military dictatorships of the region that his promise to begin withdrawing forces from Vietnam did not imply any overall change in US policy, which would continue to rest on arming and assisting its client states to fight the threat of popular and democratic movements – or what Washington called 'subversion' – with the US intervening overtly only when local counterinsurgency programmes failed. The remarks about the limited role of direct intervention also provided cover for the action on which the Nixon government was secretly embarking, behind its public promise – a large escalation of the war against Vietnam and its extension into Cambodia and Laos. Since the reassurance about continuing to arm client states was off the record and could not be quoted directly, the US press started referring to it in shorthand as the Guam Doctrine, and then simply as the Nixon Doctrine, a term later adopted by Nixon's foreign policy team. This continuation of longstanding American military relations with client states was heralded in the American media as marking a new direction in American policy, a claim subsequently echoed in almost all academic scholarship on US foreign policy and the Middle East.[43]

The advantage of turning existing US counterinsurgency policy into a 'doctrine' was that rulers like the shah, and his allies in American arms firms and think tanks, could now appeal to it and demand to be given the same role as the south-east Asian dictatorships. Insisting that Washington either subsidise his weapons purchases with Congressional loans or pressure the American oil companies to pump more Iranian oil to pay the arms bills, the shah told the US ambassador 'he could not understand why we did not want to help him implement [the] Nixon doctrine in [the] Gulf area where our and our allies' interests were also threatened'.[44]

Deploying the Nixon doctrine enabled the shah and his supporters to overcome opposition in the State Department and other parts of the US government. By 1972 the American ambassador to Tehran was writing to Henry Kissinger, the national security advisor, criticising those in Washington who argued that

42   Cited in Sampson, *Arms Bazaar*: 248.

43   Jeffrey Kimball, 'The Nixon Doctrine: A Saga of Misunderstanding', *Presidential Studies Quarterly* 36: 1, 2006: 59–74. Mahmood Mamdani, *Good Muslim, Bad Muslim: America, the Cold War, and the Roots of Terror*, New York: Pantheon, 2004: 63–118, traces the continuity in US counterinsurgency strategy.

44   MacArthur, 'Telegram 1019'.

the US should do what was possible 'to prevent Iran, in our studied wisdom, from overbuying'. Using a back-channel communication to bypass the State Department, he warned that Britain, France and Italy were competing for arms contracts, and insisted 'there is no reason for us to lose the market, particularly when viewed over the red ink on our balance of payments ledger'. In the margin of the message Kissinger added a handwritten note: 'In short, it is not repeat not our policy to discourage Iranian arms purchases'.[45]

Facing a collapse in the value of the dollar, and increased lobbying from the arms firms, the Nixon administration decided to sell the shah all the weapons that he and his American lobbyists were demanding, allowing the sales to circumvent the normal governmental reviews and creating what a Senate report called 'a bonanza for US weapons manufacturers, the procurement branches of three US services, and the Defense Security Assistance Agency'.[46] Since Congress was unwilling to finance additional military sales credits, and the large New York banks were beginning to voice concerns about the shah's ability to maintain payments on the money they were lending him to buy weapons, the US government also began to push for an increased price of oil to pay for them.[47] The decision to weaponise the oil trade with Iran, and later other oil states, was announced as an extension of the 'Nixon Doctrine' to the Gulf, supplying the extraordinary levels of arms transfers with the equipment needed to explain them. Subsequent histories of these events faithfully reproduce this apparatus of justification.

As we will see in the following chapters, the Nixon administration also blocked the efforts of the UN and the Arab states, and at times even its own State Department, to settle the Palestine question, helping to maintain the forms of instability and conflict on which American 'security' policy would now increasingly depend. In Kurdistan, the other conflict keeping Arab states 'pinned down', Washington was unable to prevent Iraq from reaching a settlement with the Kurds in 1970, but responded to this threat of stability in the Gulf two years later by agreeing with Israel and Iran to reopen the conflict with renewed military support to one of the Kurdish factions. The aim was not to enable the Kurds to win political rights, according to a later Congressional investigation, but simply to 'continue a level of hostilities sufficient to sap the resources of our ally's neighboring country [Iraq]'.[48]

The arms sales to Iran and their supporting doctrine played no important role in protecting the Gulf or defending American control of the region's oil. In fact the major US oil companies lobbied against the increased supply of weapons

45   Harold Saunders, 'Memorandum for Dr Kissinger', 14 July 1972, FRUS, Document 212; see also Wolfe-Hunnicutt, 'End of the Concessionary Regime': 273.

46   Bill, *The Eagle and the Lion*: 200.

47   On the New York banks, see MacArthur, 'Telegram 1019'.

48   Bill, *The Eagle and the Lion*: 205; Little, 'The United States and the Kurds': 74–85.

to Iran and the doctrine used to justify them. They argued that political stability in the Gulf could be better secured by America ending its support for Israel's occupation of Arab territories and allowing a settlement of the Palestine question. The Nixon administration had also initiated a large increase in the sale of arms to Israel, although weapons sent to Israel were paid for not with local oil revenues but by US taxpayers. Arming Iran, an ally of Israel, the companies argued, only worsened the one-sidedness of America's Middle East policy. The oil companies also objected to the extraordinary level of weapons sales to Iran because the increased oil revenues Tehran required to pay for the weapons would force them to switch more production away from the Arab states, weakening the companies' relations with those states and benefiting the European oil firms and independent US firms that shared production in Iran. It might also lead Iran to demand an even higher share of profits.[49]

The absurdity of the scale of arms sales to the oil states later became apparent, when the hyper-armed Iranian state was brought down by street protests and a general strike led by oil workers in the 1979 revolution, and when the tens of billions of dollars Saudi Arabia spent on weapons left it helpless in 1990 against Iraq's occupation of Kuwait. Whatever the excess, however, the arms sales also militarised the oil states, with continuing consequences for local populations. The Kurds of Iraq had already discovered this in the 1960s, when the government used its British-supplied weapons against them, and would discover it again when Iran and the US abruptly cut off support for the Kurdish insurgency in 1975. Protesters in Iran felt the consequences when the government deployed American-supplied helicopters to fire on political demonstrations in 1978–79, and in countless other episodes. The militarisation also lined up numerous interests in the US that preferred to see regional crises unresolved and wars in the Middle East prolonged.[50]

REORGANISING THE POWER OF SABOTAGE

Iraq had assembled the political power to take control of its oil by developing an oilfield, a pipeline and a refinery. Taking full control of oil required more: not just the ability to produce oil independently of the major American and British oil companies, but the coordinated ability to cut back production as a means of putting pressure on the companies. Up to this point, producer states had been individually demanding an increased volume and share of production. They now sought to construct the collective capacity to limit production. Libya was the first producing country to achieve this, but the ability to cut back was assembled out of wider acts of sabotage.

---

49   Wolfe-Hunnicutt, 'End of the Concessionary Regime': 242–3.
50   Nitzan and Bichler, 'Weapondollar-Petrodollar Coalition'.

To reach refineries and markets in Europe, where most of it was consumed, oil from the Middle East was carried in pipelines running from Iraq and the Gulf to the Mediterranean, and in oil tankers along another narrow conduit, the Suez Canal. These conduits and the points where they branched, narrowed or terminated were among the most significant parts of the energy system. Their control was a leading concern of the handful of transnational oil companies that, until the 1970s, still dominated the production of oil in the Middle East. This control was not simply a question of keeping the conduits open. The oil majors also wanted the power to limit the flow of oil, in order to deal with the persistent threat of oversupply, and thus declining prices and lower profits. They tried to limit the development of independent conduits outside their control that would undermine their agreements on production quotas and price-fixing. And they needed to maintain a grid of alternative supply routes and sources. These would function like an electrical grid, so that particular production sites or transmission routes could be shut down or bypassed if they were disrupted or subject to disputes.

Until the late 1960s, this management of oil flows remained largely intact, surviving a series of crises in the 1950s and early 1960s. It even survived the Soviet threat. This was not the imaginary threat discussed in public, ever since the Soviet attempt to keep American oil companies out of northern Iran had been used in the manufacturing of the Cold War in 1946 – namely that the Soviet Union might try to seize the oilfields of the Middle East, imagined as a continuation of the 'Great Game' of Russian expansion to the south, whose invention we encountered in Chapter 2. The more serious concern was that the USSR might find a way to connect its Caspian oilfields and the extensive new fields of the Volga region and western Siberia to customers in western Europe, thereby subjecting the multinational oil companies to the threat of price competition. In the 1950s, after recovering from the wartime destruction of the Caspian fields, the Soviet Union began trying to export oil to Europe. The multinationals blocked these sales, relying on their control of distribution channels and on the US government, which pressured NATO members on 'security' grounds not to allow Soviet oil into Western Europe.[51] With the containment of the Soviet threat, the main challenge to the oil majors in the 1960s had been the rise of smaller, independent producers, refiners and distributors. These had begun to build a small share of the oil trade by undercutting the prices fixed by the cartel of major companies, forcing the majors to discount downstream

51 Sweden provided the main exception to this embargo. It was not a member of NATO, and its coal, iron and steel, and petroleum refining conglomerate, A. Johnson and Co., was powerful enough to act independently of the oil multinationals and trade with the Russians. Hans de Geer, 'Trading Companies in Twentieth-Century Sweden', in Geoffrey Jones, ed., *The Multinational Traders*, New York: Routledge, 1998: 141–4; and Peter R. Odell, *Oil and World Power*, Harmondsworth: Penguin, 1979: 48–71.

prices (in refining and distribution) and rely increasingly on their enormous profit margins from production in the Middle East.[52]

From the late 1960s the situation began to change. In the June 1967 Arab-Israeli war, the Iraq–Syria pipeline was cut again, the Suez Canal was blocked to shipping, oil workers in Bahrain shut down two refineries, and a general strike by oil workers in Libya stopped exports from Tripoli. The Arab states imposed an embargo on oil supplies to the US and other states that supported Israel's attack, including Britain and West Germany. Iraq proposed that the embargo be extended for three months from 1 September, on the grounds that only by restricting supplies during winter would the embargo have an effect. Iraq also called for the nationalisation of local oil-production companies. But Saudi Arabia succeeded in getting the embargo lifted, while the Libyan government ended the oil strike and imprisoned its leaders.[53]

In May 1969, a Palestinian resistance group blew a hole in the Tapline, the pipeline that carried oil from Saudi Arabia to the Mediterranean, where it passed through a part of Syria now occupied by Israel. Although such acts of sabotage were normally repaired within a few hours, Israel refused to allow Aramco to repair the pipe unless it agreed to pay Israel a fee for protecting it. The dispute kept the pipeline closed for four months.[54] Israel was simultaneously maintaining the closure of the other major conduit for carrying oil to Europe, the Suez Canal. Its invasion of Egypt in 1967 blocked the Canal, and its rejection of UN and American proposals for a peace settlement based on a return to the pre-1967 borders kept the waterway closed.

Although the story is little known, the blocking of the Canal enabled Israel itself to become an oil conduit. The Israeli government collaborated with Iran to build a pipeline from Eilat to Ashkelon, financed in secret by West Germany. The pipeline carried Iranian oil from the Red Sea to the Mediterranean, bypassing the Suez Canal, allowing Iran to loosen the control of the major oil companies over its oil industry. It also enabled Israel to export oil it took from an Egyptian oilfield in Sinai, which its forces had seized in the war.[55] To evade the

---

52   Stocking, *Middle East Oil*, 416–33.

53   John Wright, *Libya: A Modern History*, Baltimore: Johns Hopkins University Press, 1982: 105; M. S. Daoudi and M. S. Dajani, 'The 1967 Oil Embargo Revisited', *Journal of Palestine Studies* 13: 2, 1984: 71–2, 80. The Saudis had already allowed Aramco – the US company that controlled the Trans-Arabian Pipeline, or Tapline, which carried oil from the Saudi fields to the Mediterranean – to resume pumping oil, even though a few miles of its route cut across the northeast corner of the Golan Heights, the part of southern Syria now under Israeli occupation.

54   The Tapline Company agreed to pay for the repair and cleanup and to cover the cost of protecting the pipeline. James Feron, 'Israel in Accord with Aramco on Repair of Damaged Tapline', *New York Times*, 11 July 1969: 7; 'Israeli Jets Strike Military Targets in Egypt and Jordan', *Washington Post*, 17 September 1969: A26.

55   Uri Bialer, 'Fuel Bridge across the Middle East: Israel, Iran, and the Eilat-Ashkelon Oil Pipeline', *Israel Studies* 12: 3, 2007: 29–67. The pipeline replaced a smaller one, built using 200 kilometres of pipes, together with pumps and other equipment stolen from Egypt during Israel's 1956

oil majors' control of marketing, Iran and Israel sold the oil through a Swiss-registered joint venture, Trans-Asiatic Oil Ltd, shipping most of it via Romania to Spain, where the fascist government under Franco had successfully excluded the international oil companies from operating.[56] Meanwhile, Egypt tried to build a pipeline to bypass the Suez Canal on the other side, connecting the Gulf of Suez to the Mediterranean, but its efforts to open a conduit outside the control of the oil majors were blocked by the British government.[57]

The closing of the Suez Canal also hastened another weakening of the oil majors' control over supply routes. Western Europe began to obtain significant supplies of oil from the Soviet Union, evading the embargo the transnational companies had tried to enforce since the Second World War. Following the first closing of the Suez Canal in 1956, the Italian state oil company, ENI, led by Enrico Mattei, had begun to obtain oil from the Russians. In 1968 the Soviet Union completed a pipeline to the Baltic Sea, terminating at Ventspils on the Latvian coast. Soviet oil could now be shipped cheaply to northern Europe.[58]

These disruptions and alterations to the flow of Middle Eastern oil had further effects. Since the grant of the first oil concession in southern Iran in 1901 – which was partly motivated, as we saw in Chapter 2, by an earlier effort to block the export of Russian oil – Western oil companies had controlled the flow of oil from the Middle East, using this control to manage its price around the world. Seven decades later, within three years of the upheavals of the 1967 war, that ability had been destroyed.

On 1 September 1969, a group of army officers seized control in Libya and removed the monarchy from power. They released from prison the thirty-six-year-old leader of the 1967 oil strike, Mahmud Sulaiman al-Maghribi, and appointed him initially as prime minister and the following April, after Captain Muammar Qaddafi emerged as leader of the coup and took al-Maghribi's place as prime minister, as head of a team to renegotiate the terms of the country's

---

invasion of Sinai, and used to bring smaller quantities of Iranian oil to the refinery at Haifa. The post-1967 pipeline secured supplies to Israel, but was also intended to reduce Europe's dependence on Arab oil.

56   In the 1970s, the trader who handled the Israeli pipeline oil, Marc Rich, used it to break the contract system for oil sales and create the spot market in oil, which would end the method of pricing oil through agreements within and among the large oil companies and allow the development of speculative markets in oil futures. Previously part of the Bretton Woods mechanism for limiting the global threat of financial speculators, oil would itself become a medium of financial speculation. Daniel Amman, *The King of Oil: The Secret Lives of Marc Rich*, New York: St Martin's Press, 2009: 64–86.

57   Elie Podeh, 'Making a Short Story Long: The Construction of the Suez-Mediterranean Oil Pipeline in Egypt, 1967–77', *Business History Review* 78: 1, 2004, 61–88.

58   Marshall I. Goldman, 'The Soviet Union', in Raymond Vernon, ed., *The Oil Crisis*, New York: Norton, 1976: 130. Enrico Mattei also maintained contacts with the FLN in its independence struggle against the French in hydrocarbon-rich Algeria (P. H. Frankel, Mattei: *Oil and Power Politics*, London: Faber & Faber, 1966: 120).

contracts with foreign oil companies.[59] Talks with Exxon and Occidental made no headway, until Libya's position was reinforced by a Syrian bulldozer. On 3 May 1970, a mechanical excavator laying telephone cable in southern Syria near the Jordanian border cut the Tapline. The Saudis called the incident 'planned sabotage'.[60] Using the interruption in supplies to negotiate higher transit fees, Damascus refused to allow repairs and kept the line closed for nine months.[61] Two weeks after the pipeline was ruptured, the Syrian oil minister met with his Libyan and Algerian counterparts (Algeria was demanding a revision of its oil agreement with France), and agreed to 'set a limit to the lengthy and fruitless negotiations' with the oil companies, implement their demands for a higher share of the oil income by unilateral action if necessary, and set up a fund for mutual support in any confrontation with the oil companies.[62] With 500,000 barrels a day of Saudi supplies to Europe cut off, Libya was able to pressure Occidental Petroleum, a relatively small California-based company with no alternative sources of oil, to agree to a new tax rate, breaking the united front among oil companies. Libya became the first producer country to use an embargo on supplies to win an increase in the level of taxation of oil production.

POSTED NOTES

Reinforced by the interruptions in supply from the Gulf, the Libyan embargo had broken the ability of the oil companies to dictate to the countries with large oil reserves the tax they would pay on their profits from the production of oil.

Since the 1930s, world oil prices had been governed by the international oil companies, which attempted to limit the supply of oil from the Middle East, in collaboration with a system of government production quotas and import controls in the United States. Overseas, the cartel agreement made between the seven major international oil corporations in 1928, in response to the large discoveries in Iraq and to the 'oil offensive' from the Soviet Union, established exclusive territories for each company and set quotas intended to maintain world prices at the level of US prices.[63] From 1932 the Texas Railroad Commission set

---

59   Joe Stork, *Middle East Oil and the Energy Crisis*, New York: Monthly Review Press, 1975: 153–7.

60   Francisco Parra, *Oil Politics: A Modern History of Petroleum*, London: I. B. Tauris, 2004: 122.

61   'Hopes Rise for Tapline Repair', *Washington Post*, 6 December 1970: 25; 'Pipeline in Syria is Reopened After Nine Months', *New York Times*, 30 January 1971: 3; Paul Stevens, 'Pipelines or Pipe Dreams? Lessons From the History of Arab Transit Pipelines', *Middle East Journal* 54: 2, 2000: 224–41.

62   'Chronology: May 16, 1970–August 15, 1970', *Middle East Journal* 24: 4, 1970: 500.

63   Alzada Comstock, 'Russia's Oil Offensive', *Barron's*, 30 January 1928: 17. See also Chapter 4.

quotas to regulate domestic US production.[64] As production in the Middle East began to increase after the Second World War, threatening to lower the price of oil, Congress pressured the major oil companies to protect US oil prices by limiting imports from the Middle East. In 1954 the Oil Policy Committee, an industry-government body, established regular US import quotas, formalised by a proclamation by President Eisenhower in 1959, limiting imports to 9 per cent of domestic demand.[65] The blocking of imports allowed domestic US production to continue expanding despite the availability of oil at much lower costs of production in the Middle East. As a result, American oil reserves were exhausted more quickly than those of other regions. By 1971, US production had started to decline, as the volume of reserves in the lower forty-eight states passed their peak. Declining production, coupled with continually rising demand, meant that the US no longer had the surplus capacity required to regulate prices.

In 1960, in response to the drop in demand for non-US oil caused by Eisenhower's import quotas, Venezuela and Saudi Arabia – together with the other three large Gulf producers, Iraq, Kuwait, and Iran – set up the Organization of Petroleum Exporting Countries (OPEC). For Venezuela, where a revolution had overthrown the military government and brought an elected government to power, the aim was to imitate the collective arrangement among US states for restricting production, in order to negotiate an increased share of oil revenues and conserve supplies, and thus to allow an orderly process of economic growth and avoid a premature depletion of reserves. Initially the Middle East producers were trying to maintain their tax revenues from oil by increasing the volume of production. Only a decade later were they in a position to increase revenues by adopting the US method of limiting the volume of production.[66]

Part of the difficulty facing the producer states in negotiating the tax revenues to be paid by the production companies was that, before the mid-1960s, there was no 'market' price for crude oil. US prices were established by government production and import quotas, while elsewhere most crude was transferred by the large firms to their own refining affiliates, or traded from one major to another at low prices under long-term contracts. The level of tax paid to the

---

64 The Texas quota system was reinforced by the federal Connally Act, known as the 'Hot Oil' Act, of 1935. Harold F. Williamson, *The American Petroleum Industry*, 2 vols, Evanston: Northwestern University Press, 1959–63, vol 2: 543–4. Thirty years later, OPEC took the Texas system as a model for its system of international quotas. Anthony Sampson, *The Seven Sisters: The Great Oil Companies and the World They Made*, London: Hodder & Stoughton, 1975: 92.

65 Williamson, *American Petroleum Industry*: 543–4. 'Overland' imports were exempt from the import quota, to protect Canadian suppliers whose pipelines gave them no alternative market. Mexican suppliers had no pipelines to carry oil to the US, but took advantage of the same exemption: tankers that had previously shipped Mexican oil to New Jersey were diverted to Brownsville, Texas, from where the oil was carried in tanker trucks twelve miles south across the Mexican border and then re-imported overland. Richard H. K. Vietor, *Energy Policy in America Since 1945: A Study of Business–Government Relations*, Cambridge, UK: CUP, 1984: 130.

66 Parra, *Oil Politics*: 89–109.

producer countries was calculated in reference to an artificial figure called the 'posted price' – a benchmark set by the oil firms, with the tax per barrel set at 50 per cent of that figure. Following Eisenhower's introduction of import quotas, the companies lowered the posted price, thereby reducing their tax payments to the producer states. When the latter responded with the creation of OPEC, the companies agreed after 1960 to leave the benchmark at a fixed level. This guaranteed the producer states a set income per barrel of oil produced, even as the price of oil outside the US began to decline due to competition from independent oil companies and from the Soviet Union. Since the posted price was not adjusted for inflation, however, the real tax rate per barrel of oil fell, especially in the later 1960s when the value of the dollar began a rapid decline.

Meanwhile, a group of independent, mostly German oil dealers started to publish regular figures on the price of refined oil products in Europe. An American oil economist, Morris Adelman, was able to take these figures, deduct known costs for refining and shipping, and infer for the first time an approximate 'market price' for Middle Eastern oil (it would take another decade to create a functioning global oil market). His figures showed that in 1960 the oil companies were producing oil at a cost of 10¢ cents per barrel, including a 20 per cent return on invested capital, and earning a profit above that return of 68¢ per barrel. For the major oil companies, Adelman later remarked, 'a market price was an uninvited intruder'.[67]

The general public failed to notice the intruder for almost a decade – an ignorance from which the oil companies continued to benefit. Negotiations over rates of taxation on the extraordinary profits that international firms were earning from Middle Eastern oil took the form of attempts to raise the posted price. Unaware that the 'posted price' was simply a device for calculating tax rates, the news media and the public assumed these were negotiations over the price of oil. The companies could then portray the increased taxation of their windfall profits from oil as an increase in its 'price' – an increase that they would be obliged to pass on to the consumer.

Following the success of Libya in winning a new tax rate in 1970, OPEC was in a position to challenge the setting of tax rates by the major US and European companies. Iran led the OPEC states in demanding a general increase in the posted price, along with an increase in the tax level based on that price from 50 to 55 per cent. This represented an attempt by the producer countries not to increase the price of oil, but to return real tax rates to the levels they had enjoyed before inflation, Israel's closing of the Suez Canal and other factors had pushed up the oil price in the later 1960s.

---

67 Morris Adelman, 'My Education in Mineral (Especially Oil) Economics', *Annual Review of Energy and the Environment* 22, 1997: 21; and *The Genie Out of the Bottle: World Oil Since 1970*, Cambridge, MA: MIT Press, 1995: 41–68.

Supported by the State Department, which arranged for the Justice Department to waive anti-trust regulations, the companies met together and decided to accept an increase in the benchmark. Undersecretary of State John Irwin had circulated a memo following the Libyan deal pointing out that, given the import quotas that made crude oil prices in the US much higher than in Europe, an increase in Middle East prices would be to America's benefit:

> Many claim that access to cheaper energy sources has given European producers an advantage over goods produced in the United States, particularly in certain industries such as petrochemicals. The Libyan settlements will increase energy costs to Europe (and probably to Japan) and could reduce whatever competitive advantage those areas enjoy over the US because of access to lower cost oil.[68]

By April 1971, the companies had agreed with OPEC to raise the posted price from less that $2 per barrel to more than $3. The price at which oil from the Gulf actually traded remained at just over half the posted price, rising from about $1.30 to $1.70 per barrel – still below the level of the mid-1950s in nominal terms, and well below that level when adjusted for inflation. Meanwhile, refined oil products were selling in Europe at a price of more than $13 per barrel, 60 per cent of which represented government taxes in the consumer country. Following the 1971 OPEC tax increase, in other words, European states were still earning about four times as much revenue from each barrel of oil as the OPEC states.[69]

The 50 per cent increase in tax rates was only a temporary measure. It ensured the OPEC countries a higher share of oil profits, but the system of allowing international companies to earn all the profits from oil and then attempting to tax those profits was itself coming to an end. Led by Iraq, the large producer states had gradually built the infrastructure and the expertise to take control of production themselves. Iraq announced its nationalisation of the British-controlled Iraq Petroleum Company in 1972. Iran had already warned the oil companies that, when the 1954 consortium agreement expired in 1979, it would expect a radically different arrangement.[70] Saudi Arabia negotiated a gradual transfer of ownership of Aramco to the state, threatening the company

---

68 Cited in Tore T. Petersen, *Richard Nixon, Great Britain and the Anglo-American Alignment in the Persian Gulf: Making Allies out of Clients*, Brighton: Sussex Academic Press, 2009: 38.

69 Parra, *Oil Politics*: 110–34; V. H. Oppenheim, 'Why Oil Prices Go Up (1): The Past: We Pushed Them', *Foreign Policy* 25, Winter 1976–77: 24–57; Morris Adelman, 'Is the Oil Shortage Real? Oil Companies As OPEC Tax-Collectors', *Foreign Policy* 9, Winter 1972–73: 86.

70 'Telegram 7307 From the Embassy in Tehran to the Department of State, December 23, 1971, 1300Z', Documents on Iran and Iraq 1969–1971, Document 155, available at history. state.gov.

with the same fate as the Iraq Petroleum Company if it refused to negotiate. By the end of 1972, the other large producers in the Gulf, Kuwait and Iran, were making similar arrangements.

GOLD FINISH

Facing the loss of their control of the oilfields in the Middle East, the international oil companies now needed a means of generating a large increase in the price of oil. A much higher price would enable them to open up new production sites in less accessible areas, such as the North Sea and Alaska. It would also allow them to realise a greater share of profits from the downstream refining and marketing, compensating for the loss of profits from producing Middle Eastern oil.

There were three changes that would allow the reorganisation of the mechanisms for pricing oil. First, following the successful collaboration developed to raise the Libyan oil price, the producer states had to take over from the oil companies the system of restricting production, to prevent surplus oil from lowering the price. This would be easier for a group of sovereign states to achieve than for a cartel of oil companies liable to anti-trust investigation if they were seen to be forcing prices up.

Second, the international firms, which would process and market oil for the new state-run production companies, had to find ways to sell more oil and protect it against rival sources of energy. To raise the price of oil, it was not enough for those producing it to make the supply scarce. A higher price would simply drive consumers to switch to cheaper alternatives. The oil companies needed ways to 'sabotage' the supply not only of oil, but also of coal, natural gas and nuclear power. For this reason, as we will see in the following chapter, what is now remembered as the 1973–74 oil crisis was first discussed not as a problem of oil, but as an 'energy crisis'. Since oil was the largest commodity in world trade and shaped the international flow of dollars, the transition to a new petroleum order also began as a financial crisis.

Third, to maintain demand for oil as its price increased, the international oil companies needed to open up new markets. The largest market to which their access was restricted was the United States. The US import quotas helped prevent lower-priced Middle Eastern oil from competing with domestic production, which in the first half of 1971 was selling for $3.27 a barrel – almost double the new price of oil from the Persian Gulf. However, the import controls had become a mechanism of the postwar international financial system, protecting the value of the dollar. By restricting imports of oil into the United States, Washington reduced the flow of dollars abroad, limiting the accumulation of dollar reserves overseas. Later it tried to give further support to the dollar's value by interventions in the London gold market. When these two mechanisms proved insufficient, a third technique was added: the rapid increase in arms exports to oil-producing countries, especially Iran.

The oil companies needed an alternative to the use of oil (and escalating arms sales) to control dollar flows. The quota on US oil imports was denying them access to the world's largest petroleum market, and the drive to sell arms to Iran was putting pressure on them to increase production there. The solution for which the oil companies had begun to argue was to abandon Bretton Woods.[71]

In March 1967, Chase Manhattan Bank, the Rockefeller financial house closely tied to Standard Oil of New Jersey (Exxon), proposed that the United States abandon the gold standard. The American Bankers Association condemned the proposal, and Chase quickly offered a retraction. Questioning the automatic convertibility of dollars into gold was considered a threat to the stability of the postwar international monetary system and to America's political and financial authority. Eight months later, however, Eugene Birnbaum, senior economist at Standard Oil, published a report entitled *Changing the United States Commitment to Gold*. The report called for the US to end the Bretton Woods system unilaterally by rejecting the obligation to convert dollars into gold. Birnbaum's arguments were critical to making the idea of abandoning Bretton Woods acceptable.[72]

A year after Birnbaum's report, in November 1968, America's decade-long effort to support the value of the dollar collapsed. The US tried to transform Bretton Woods into a mechanism that allowed the gold peg to float. In an effort to combat inflation by lowering domestic oil prices, Washington began removing the controls on oil imports in 1970, but this caused more dollars to flow abroad. By the following year, the US had used up most of its non-gold reserves, and only 22 per cent of its currency reserves were backed by gold. When European banks requested payment for their dollars in gold, the US defaulted. Abandonment of the gold standard in August 1971 amounted to a declaration of bankruptcy by the US government.[73]

The transformation in methods of controlling flows of oil and finance was completed in the 1973–74 crisis, to which the following chapter turns. We do not know for certain how far these changes were planned by the oil companies,

---

71   The major oil companies wanted the import quotas rationalised, to remove the hundreds of exemptions that favoured mostly small operators, and steadily increased. Vietor, *Energy Policy in America*: 135–44.

72   Eugene Birnbaum, *Changing the United States Commitment to Gold*, Princeton: Department of Economics, Princeton University, 1967.

73   Fred Block, *The Origins of International Economic Disorder: A Study of United States International Monetary Policy from World War II to the Present*, Berkeley: University of California Press, 1977: 164–202; William Engdahl, *A Century of War: Anglo-American Oil Politics and the New World Order*, 2nd edn, London: Pluto Press, 2004: 127–49. In contrast to Engdahl, Block makes no mention of the oil dimension of the crisis.

and how far the transformation came about through the rivalries between them, their conflict with the producer countries, and the changing agendas of the US government. But there was no doubt that the creation of a crisis made it easier to blame outside forces for the radical alterations that occurred.

CHAPTER 7

The Crisis That Never Happened

The postwar petroleum order and the prosperity it brought seemed to collapse too easily. The events known as the 1973–74 oil crisis brought an era of generally improving conditions of life in many parts of the world to a sudden and prolonged halt. The crisis confirmed the collapse of the post–Second World War system for managing international finance and a transfer in the management of oil pricing to the producer countries, which began to obtain a greatly increased income from its production. In industrialised countries, the powers of labour that had secured more egalitarian and democratic social orders were weakened, and were to be confronted by a new instrument of control: the neoliberal laws of the market. In the global south, governments with oil revenues built militarised states while those without built debts, as Western banks awash with petrodollars recycled them into risky loans to financially weakened governments.

The description of a sequence of events as a 'crisis' simplifies changes in multiple fields, involving various agents, into a unique event, so that a single moment, with a single agent, appears responsible for a collapse of the old order. To understand the setbacks to democratic politics, we must follow changes in the multiple dimensions of the oil order, and the work that was done to simplify what happened into a crisis, for which an outside force – the Arab oil states – could be made culpable.

SIMPLE SUPPLY AND DEMAND

What is known as the 1973–74 oil crisis gave many people in western Europe and North America their most memorable encounter with the laws of the market. Middle-class citizens faced the unfamiliar experience of a shortage of what had always been plentiful, anxiety over the future availability of an essential commodity, mile-long queues in competition with other consumers, and prices that increased almost by the day. On 17 October 1973, eleven days after the outbreak of another Arab–Israeli war, six Arab oil-producing countries announced a 5 per cent cut in the supply of oil. They promised a further 5 per cent reduction every month, until the United States stopped obstructing a settlement of the Israel–Palestine conflict. With each reported cut, the price of fuel rose. The experience offered entire populations in the West an unwelcome object lesson in the principles of neoclassical economics.

The lesson made its way into the lectures and textbooks of economists, to be repeated as a widely familiar illustration of the simple theory of supply and demand. Decades later, the oil crisis was still a favourite tool for reaffirming a straightforward point about markets. The economist Deirdre McCloskey used it in 2002 to respond to a critic who had asked if there was anything in standard economic theory worth keeping. Since the assumptions of microeconomics 'contradict almost everything that we observe around us', the critic complained, 'it is increasingly impossible to discuss real-world economic questions with microeconomists – and with almost all neoclassical theorists. They are trapped in their system, and don't in fact care about the outside world any more.' McCloskey defended economic theory with a single example: when the Arab states cut the supply of oil in 1973, 'didn't the relative price of oil rise, just as a simple supply-and-demand model would suggest?' Good economics textbooks are full of real-world examples like this, McCloskey said, demonstrating that the simplified concepts of economic theory 'can be made as quantitatively serious as you want. They are real scientific ideas.'[1]

Offering the 1973–74 oil crisis as evidence that economists care about the real world is an unfortunate response. The crisis caught most economists by surprise, and the events that led to it brought many of them to abandon their old, Keynesian ways of thinking about the economy. However, the broader criticism that economists are trapped in their system of ideas misses the mark. Like their critics, orthodox economists care about the world. They care about it, however, in a different way. They do not want to alter their ideas to make them like the real world; they want to alter the real world to make it perform according to their ideas.[2] In the 1973–74 oil crisis, the law of supply and demand was not a fiction, but a fabrication. It was a piece of equipment carefully fabricated by certain parties to a dispute. To achieve their goals, those participants tried to organise an event that was assembled and performed in such a way that the laws of economics might operate.

A critic of standard economic theory could raise several problems with the use of the oil crisis to illustrate the model of supply and demand. These can be mentioned briefly, although they are not our main concern. First, it is difficult to know how much of the increase in the price of oil in the winter of 1973–74 was associated with a cut in supply, or even by how much the supply was cut. While Saudi Arabia and Kuwait reduced their exports of oil, other Middle Eastern producers, led by Iran, increased production. In Iraq, the government of Saddam Hussein supported the embargo on oil shipped to the United States but opposed the decision to reduce supplies to Europe and Japan – a decision that helped the

---

1   Bernard Guerrien, 'Is There Anything Worth Keeping in Standard Microeconomics?' *Post-Autistic Economics Review* 12, 15 March 2002; Deirdre McCloskey, 'Yes, There is Something Worth Keeping in Microeconomics', *Post-Autistic Economics Review* 15, 4 September 2002.

2   See Michel Callon, *The Laws of the Markets*, Oxford: Blackwell, 1998; and Donald MacKenzie, Fabian Muniesa and Lucia Siu, eds, *Do Economists Make Markets? On the Performativity of Economics*, Princeton: Princeton University Press, 2007.

United States by limiting its political isolation and spreading the economic hardship. Iraq blamed the wider cutbacks on the governments of Saudi Arabia and Kuwait, 'well known for their links with America and American monopolistic interests', and increased supplies to Europe.[3] By December, Iraq was producing 7 per cent more oil than in the month before the embargo. Libya, Algeria and Abu Dhabi also took advantage of higher prices to raise production after a brief cutback, maintaining their overall level of supply. Since none of these countries provided information on how much oil they were producing, it was impossible to know how far the total world supply was reduced. Even the figures based on the surveillance of tankers leaving the six main oil terminals of the Middle East – the standard method of estimating global oil supply – were disputed, with some reports showing a net increase in shipments. There was equal uncertainty about the price of oil. For fifty years the oil companies had worked to prevent the creation of a 'market price' for crude oil (see Chapter 6). As a result, there was no place, publication or regular mechanism of exchange for determining the going price, so as the crisis unfolded 'no one knew what "the market" was'.[4]

Second, since interruptions in the supply of oil from one source could be made up from another, the embargo against the United States 'never happened'.[5] Other factors contributed to the sharp increase in oil prices. In the US Congress, the leader of the militarist wing of the Democratic Party, opposed to a Middle East peace settlement, introduced emergency legislation requiring the government to prepare mechanisms for fuel rationing and a programme to reduce the country's oil consumption.[6] Commercial users of petroleum products and individual motorists began to panic, unnerved by public discussions of the 'oil weapon' the Arabs had unleashed against the West. Uncertain about future supply, consumers purchased more petroleum than they needed. Governments worsened the problem by mismanaging the crisis, adopting emergency measures that impeded the distribution of oil and made the shortages more severe.[7] Public debate contributed to the sense of threat, linking the oil embargo to a wider 'energy crisis', a problem of 'limits to growth', and the vulnerability of 'the environment' – a word that had previously meant milieu or surroundings, but had recently come to be used with the definite article, like the term 'economy' two decades earlier, to designate an object of widespread political concern.

3   *Middle East Economic Survey* 3, 1973: 14–16.

4   Francisco Parra, *Oil Politics: A Modern History of Petroleum*, London: I. B. Tauris, 2004: 183; Joe Stork, *Middle East Oil and the Energy Crisis*, New York: Monthly Review Press, 1975: 230; Christopher Rand, *Making Democracy Safe for Oil: Oilmen and the Islamic East*, Boston: Little, Brown, 1975: 317–18, 328–30.

5   Morris Adelman, 'The Real Oil Problem', *Regulation* 27: 1, 2004: 16–21.

6   Dan Morgan, 'Legislation Proposed by Jackson to Offset Possible Oil Losses,' *Washington Post*, 18 October 1973: A6.

7   Daniel Yergin, *The Prize: The Epic Quest for Oil, Money, and Power*, New York: Simon & Schuster, 1991: 617.

A further problem with making oil conform to the model of supply and demand reflects a peculiar feature of oil itself. Since most users cannot easily switch to alternative sources of energy, it is said to have a very low elasticity of demand. Even small shortages can lead to large price increases. In many circumstances, however, oil enjoys a *reverse* elasticity of demand: as the price goes up, people buy more of it. Changes in annual world demand for oil are connected to changes in energy infrastructure, in industrial and social structure, in income growth, in excise taxes and in other factors. Demand for oil is usually unlinked to its price. The exception to this pattern is when very large increases in price occur in a very short period. The oil crisis was an example of such an exception. The simple supply and demand model that this event is deployed to illustrate is a model supported by this exceptional event, but contradicted by the more everyday price fluctuations in the market for oil.[8] The economists' model played its own role in the making of this exceptional episode.

In order for these flows of oil, military actions, industry rumours, supply figures, political calculations and consumer reactions to come together as a textbook case of the laws of economics, a new socio-technical world had to be assembled to hold them together. Periods of crisis provide useful occasions for understanding how such worlds are assembled and rearranged. The declaration of a crisis often marks an attempt to introduce new forces or to identify threats against which decisive action must be taken. It also requires defining the object or assemblage under threat. The forces introduced, the threats identified and the assemblages defined may all escape the control of those attempting to mobilise or master them.

Three matters of concern emerged and intersected in the early 1970s: the problem of energy as an interconnected and vulnerable system, especially as seen from the United States; the production and distribution of oil from the Middle East, as a flow of energy that a single set of actors could coordinate, and even turn into an instrument with which to work towards other political goals – in particular the settlement of the Palestine question; and the emergence of 'the environment' to rival 'the economy' as a central object of politics, defined not by the limitless expansion of a country's GDP but by physical limits to growth.

I argued in Chapter 5 that carbon-based industrial democracies were characterised by a new mode of government, emerging in the middle decades of the twentieth century and coinciding with their increasing dependence on oil. The making of the economy, built with the help of cheap and abundant energy, created an object in relation to which claims to a more egalitarian life could be measured and adjusted, and matters of common concern could be removed to the administration of experts. As we saw in Chapter 6, the mechanisms for supplying low-cost energy, along with the means of governing the continuous

---

8   Robert Mabro, 'OPEC and the Price of Oil', *Energy Journal* 13: 2, 1992.

threat to democracy caused by large-scale financial speculation, were coming undone. As a result, it was becoming increasingly difficult to govern populations through their economy. As these modes of managing democratic politics weakened, the crisis of 1973–74 was to pave the way for the elaboration of new modes of government, using the new machinery of 'the market'. Not just the oil crisis, but almost any conflict between rival political claims, according to this new technology of rule, was to be grasped – and governed – as a matter of simple supply and demand.

HOW ENERGY BECAME A SYSTEM

The American magazine *Science Journal* devoted its issue of October 1967 to the new field of technological forecasting. Alongside articles on science, automation, communication and space, it included an essay on energy. Written by the director of the science and technology division of the Institute for Defense Analyses, the article declared that 'energy is so ubiquitous that it is taken for granted'.[9] While noting problems like air pollution caused by motor vehicles and economic blight in the coal fields, there was no suggestion of a system under threat or an impending crisis.

The term 'energy crisis' did not appear in American political debate until three years later, in the summer of 1970.[10] The ensuing events are now remembered as a problem caused by an embargo on the supply of Middle Eastern oil.[11] Yet when the American press first reported the crisis, it described the problem with little reference to the Middle East, or even to oil.

The announcement of the new threat came on 10 August 1970, when the head of the Federal Power Commission, John Nassikas, gave a speech at the National Press Club on 'The National Energy Crisis'. For the second summer in succession, New York and other large US cities were suffering shortages of electrical power. While the problems were partly caused by delays in installing

---

9   Ali Bulent Cambel, 'Energy', *Science Journal* 3: 10, 1967.

10   Over the preceding twenty-five years, since 1945, references to an 'energy crisis' in leading American newspapers are found only in discussions of postwar Europe (where the term 'fuel crisis' is more common), and, for the *New York Times*, on one other occasion – in a 1954 review of Harrison Brown's *The Challenge of Man's Future* (Orville Prescott, 'Books of the Times', *New York Times*, 9 March 1954: 21). In the 1950s and 1960s, the concern with oil and other fuels was usually part of a general issue of 'natural resources', with postwar fears put to rest by the report of the President's Commission on Natural Resource, known as the Paley Commission.

11   In Daniel Yergin's account, for example, although the mobilisation of environmental campaigns, especially following the large oil spill in the Santa Barbara Channel in March 1969, was a factor affecting the production of oil, the main problems were the rapid increase in demand for oil, especially in the United States, the shortage of US supplies as the rate of domestic oil production reached its peak, and the tightening of oil supplies from the Middle East as OPEC first began to push for a higher price, and then in October 1973 reduced supplies in response to the US taking Israel's side in the Arab–Israeli war.

power generation and transmission facilities, the main reason for 'our develop-ing energy crisis', the FPC chairman told the assembled journalists, was a lack of fuel – in particular, shortages of natural gas for industry. Fuel might have to be rationed and manufacturing plants closed. The long-term solution to the energy crisis lay in the development of nuclear power, he suggested; but in the mean-time the remedy was to reduce government regulation, including the relaxation of antitrust laws to allow the power industry to adopt 'economies of large-scale operation'.[12]

There had been earlier crises in the distribution of fuels, access to and mining of raw materials, and the generation of electric power. But this was the first time the problem had been described as an energy crisis. There was a wide variety of industries, materials, transmission systems and forms of energy involved in the production and distribution of power: coal and the miners and mining companies that produced it, the railways that transported it, oil and natural gas fields, pipeline companies, petrol stations, public utilities, electri-cal generating and transmission equipment and its manufacturers, construction firms building nuclear power plants, uranium-mining companies, owners of oil tankers, and small and large oil companies. Each of these facilities, networks or materials faced particular problems at different times: a wave of wildcat strikes in the Appalachian coal industry, technical setbacks in the operation of nuclear power plants, a shortage of oil tankers following the closing of the Suez Canal, delays in the construction of electrical power stations due to the need for low-sulphur fuels, and the development of community organising as a new set of techniques enabling 'realistic radicals', in the words of Saul Alinsky's popular primer *Rules for Radicals*, to challenge the damage done by power companies to communities and environments.[13] In the early 1970s, all these issues were suddenly linked together as aspects of a single 'energy crisis'.

As the OPEC states began to take control of the production of oil, in the ways examined in Chapter 6, the international oil companies wanted to raise the price by as much as 50 per cent, perhaps more. The increased income of the producing countries could then be paid by consumers, rather than by any reduc-tion in the income of the large oil firms. A main obstacle to such an increase was that users of oil might switch to alternative fuels, including natural gas, coal and nuclear power. It was not enough to collaborate in restricting the supply of oil: the oil companies, with the help of the Nixon White House, had to extend

---

12   Richard Halloran, 'FPC's Head Warns Power Shortages Are Possible Next Winter', *New York Times*, 11 August 1970: 20; Richard Harwood, 'Fuel-Short US May Face Plant Closings, Rationing', *Washington Post*, 17 August 1970: A1.

13   Saul Alinsky, *Rules for Radicals: A Practical Primer for Realistic Radicals*, New York: Random House, 1971. See also William Cleaver, 'Wildcats in the Appalachian Coal Fields', in *Midnight Notes Collective, eds, Midnight Notes, Midnight Oil: Work, Energy, War, 1972–1992*, Brooklyn: Autonomedia, 1992: 169–83.

the system of 'sabotage' to other forms of fuel. They were to be linked together, through corporate ownership, government administration, news reporting and scholarship, as a single issue facing a collective predicament: the energy crisis.

The giant oil companies had been importing capital into the US, most of which represented the windfalls acquired from their monopoly of the sale of Middle Eastern oil to Europe and other parts of the world. Much of the imported money was paid as dividends to American shareholders, but hundreds of millions of dollars were set aside every year to buy up rival sources of energy in the United States. The oil companies consolidated their control of natural gas production, so that by the late 1960s two dozen US oil firms produced three-quarters of the country's natural gas. They purchased coal companies, helping to transform the US coal industry from a group of cartelised coal producers into divisions of larger industries that used coal or produced other fuels. They also entered the nuclear power industry, in particular the mining of uranium, and by 1970 controlled 40 per cent of US uranium reserves.[14] In an echo of events from an earlier period in the Middle East, officials in the Department of the Interior accused the oil companies of buying up leases on federal lands for uranium mining, and then sitting on the leases to drive up prices and produce the 'energy crisis'.[15]

To enable oil prices to rise, the oil companies pushed for higher natural gas prices. When the Federal Power Commission rejected their appeal for a rate increase in 1968, the producers suddenly announced a dwindling supply. From then on, the rate of new discoveries began to fall.[16] Appointed to head the Federal Power Commission by President Nixon the following year, John Nassikas, the man who was soon to declare an energy crisis, approved an unprecedented increase in the price of gas, claiming this would encourage the industry to invest in new production.[17] The promised investment never followed, and subsequent Congressional investigations revealed that Nassikas had relied on industry figures about shortages, rather than the much higher estimates produced by the Commission's own staff. He also acknowledged to

---

14   Stork, *Middle East Oil*: 121–5.

15   James Ridgeway, 'Who Owns America?' *New York Times Book Review*, 24 October 1971: 7. See also US Congress, Office of Technology Assessment, 'Assessment of Oil Shale Technologies, Vol. II: A History and Analysis of the Federal Prototype Oil Shale Leasing Program', July 1980, available at www.princeton.edu/~ota. A bill passed by the US Senate in 1975 requiring oil companies to divest themselves of holdings in coal, uranium and photovoltaics was defeated by subsequent oil company lobbying (Andrew S. McFarland, 'Energy Lobbies', *Annual Review of Energy* 9, 1984: 504). In 1966 the government had banned the use of imported uranium in US reactors as a means of supporting higher domestic prices. Gulf Oil and other US oil companies then joined an international uranium cartel, set up by the government of Canada in response to the US import ban, which further increased the price of uranium (William Greider, 'Gulf: Uranium Cartel Raised US Prices', *Washington Post*, 17 June 1977: A1).

16   Stork, *Middle East Oil*: 128.

17   Robert Sherill, 'Nassikas Sets Your Gas Bill', *Nation*, 17 Jan 1972: 73–9.

Congress that he had no evidence that deregulation would lead to increased production.[18]

The oil companies also produced a concern about inadequate supplies of oil, by simultaneously increasing the estimates of future demand and reducing those of recoverable reserves. In 1972 the US National Petroleum Council predicted that the country's primary energy consumption would reach 125 quadrillion Btu, or 125 quads, by 1985. The actual requirement that year was only 74 quads, less than 60 per cent of the estimate. Following the 1973–74 oil embargo, the Federal Energy Administration developed Project Independence, which produced similar overestimates of future demand. The calculations helped frame the National Energy Act of 1978, which banned the use of natural gas in new power plants and industrial boilers and allowed the oil companies to increase its price eight-fold (from 22 cents per million Btu in 1973 to $1.75, for gas from new wells). Portrayed as a means of protecting the nation's reserves as a defence against the Arab oil weapon, the restrictions achieved a 26 per cent decline in natural gas consumption between 1973 and 1986 – helping to protect not the American consumer but the demand for Middle Eastern oil. 'I am now troubled by the fact that . . . I participated in these seemingly self-serving exercises', wrote Henry Linden, following his retirement as director of the Institute of Gas Technology, which helped produce the exaggerated estimates. 'I also accepted many other tenets of what turned out to be a fictitious "energy crisis".'[19]

The transformation of power generation and resource extraction into a single field of 'energy' was encouraged by the White House. The responsibility for different forms of fuel and power was spread across various parts of the US government. In June 1973, after Congress had repeatedly rejected his requests to create a Department of Energy and National Resources, Richard Nixon set up a National Energy Office in the White House.[20] Consolidating the different concerns over fuel and power into a single agency enabled the emergence of a new field of scholarship concerned with energy and energy policy. Before the early 1970s, most research on these topics in history, economics and policy-making focused on a single fuel. After the early 1970s, scholarly interest proliferated in the question of energy as a singular topic of concern.[21]

---

18   Jack Anderson, 'FPC Chief and Natural-Gas Rate Rise', *Washington Post*, 14 June 1971: B11; Jack Anderson, 'FPC Staff Disputed Industry Plan', *Washington Post*, 15 June 1971: B13; 'General Accounting Office, Report to the FPC', in 'Fattening Gas Prices', *Time*, September 1974; Sherill, 'Nassikas Sets Your Gas Bill'; Stork, *Middle East Oil*: 125–31.

19   Henry R. Linden, 'The Evolution of an Energy Contrarian', *Annual Review of Energy and the Environment* 21, 1996: 32, 34, 38.

20   In 1974 the White House Energy Office was transformed into the Federal Energy Administration. The Department of Energy was eventually set up by the Carter Administration in 1977.

21   Richard H. K. Vietor, *Energy Policy in America since 1945: A Study of Business–Government Relations*, Cambridge, UK: CUP, 1984: 1–2.

While the energy crisis in the US was first discussed as a complex interaction of developments involving different natural resources and modes of generating power, there suddenly emerged at its core the question of an 'oil crisis'. The oil crisis was declared by James Akins, the diplomat who a decade before had welcomed the overthrow of Qasim by the Ba'th in Iraq (see Chapter 6) and approved of the execution of the political opposition. He was now director of the Office of Fuels and Energy in the Department of State. In an article in *Foreign Affairs* in April 1973, Akins argued that the repeated warnings by the Arab States of an oil boycott of the US now represented a real threat.[22] OPEC had successfully negotiated higher tax rates, Iraq had nationalised its oil production, and other large producers were threatening the same. Large increases in the price of oil were therefore inevitable, and would result in an unprecedented flow of capital to the oil producers. The task was to arrange for this movement of capital to the Persian Gulf to be recycled into investments in the United States.

'The world "energy crisis" or "energy shortage" is a fiction', argued the oil economist Morris Adelman. 'But belief in the fiction is a fact. It makes people accept higher oil prices as imposed by nature, when they are really fixed by collusion.'[23] He presented evidence that there was a surplus of world oil supply, that demand was rising less quickly than it had been in the 1960s, and that the State Department and the oil companies were indeed colluding with the producer states to benefit jointly from a large increase in the oil price.[24]

THE PALESTINE EQUATION

Let us consider closely how the increase in the price of oil happened. The October 1973 embargo was triggered by the Arab states' announcement that the availability of oil would be linked to progress in settling the Arab–Israeli conflict. The price of oil, therefore, could not be a question simply of demand and supply, for the demand for oil was now joined to another demand: that the United States should end its opposition to a resolution of the Palestine question. The United States had refused to support Egypt's 1971 peace proposal, when President Anwar Sadat had abandoned the principle that Israel should agree to a comprehensive settlement of the question of Palestinian rights, addressing the expulsion and dispossession of 1948, and offered to negotiate instead an interim bilateral arrangement over the Egyptian territory Israel had seized in 1967.

---

22   James E. Akins, 'International Cooperative Efforts in Energy Supply', *Annals of the American Academy of Political and Social Science* 410, 1973: 75–85.

23   Morris Adelman, 'Is the Oil Shortage Real? Oil Companies as OPEC Tax-Collectors', *Foreign Policy* 9, Winter 1972–73: 73.

24   A few years later, V. H. Oppenheim gave a more detailed account in the same journal of how this collusion unfolded: 'Why Oil Prices Go Up: The Past: We Pushed Them', *Foreign Policy* 25, 1976–77.

Egypt's decision in July 1972 to expel Soviet military advisers helping to operate its air defence systems in expectation of improved relations with Washington produced no American response.[25] Henry Kissinger, Nixon's National Security Advisor, put off Sadat's requests that he meet with his Egyptian counterpart, Hafiz Ismail. He finally agreed to talks the following February and May, provided they were kept secret, and then rejected Egypt's proposals for a separate peace with Israel.[26] The Soviet leader, Leonid Brezhnev, met with Nixon in June 1973 and proposed a joint statement on the principles of a peace settlement, which Nixon rejected.[27] Saudi Arabia, placed under increasing pressure as a client state of the United States by its patron's intransigence, requested throughout the spring and summer of that year that Washington support a settlement based on UN Security Council Resolution 242, without success.[28] In July, a Security Council Resolution expressing concern at Israel's 'lack of cooperation' with the UN mediator attempting to implement Resolution 242 was approved by all fourteen members of the Council except the United States, which vetoed it.[29]

The decision by Egypt and Syria to attack the Israeli forces occupying parts of their territory on 6 October 1973 was a response to this impasse. The war was widely expected. More than two years earlier, in August 1971, the United States had learned that Egypt was preparing for a 'strong offensive of limited size' to retake territory across the Suez Canal, with the objective of forcing Israel into negotiations.[30] Repeated warnings followed that

---

25   Richard B. Parker ed., *The October War: A Retrospective*, Gainesville: University Press of Florida, 2001, contains a discussion of this diplomatic history by several of its key participants. While describing Israel's response to Sadat's overtures as 'singularly inflexible, unresponsive, and unimaginative' (p. 58), they fail to note the fact that the US position was effectively the same.

26   Memorandum of Conversation between Muhammad Hafez Ismail and Henry A. Kissinger, 20 May 1973, National Archives, RG 59, Department of State, Records of Henry Kissinger, Box 25, Cat C Arab–Israeli War, available at www.gwu.edu/~nsarchiv. Kissinger explained the US position in a conversation with the shah: White House, 'Memorandum of Conversation', 24 July 1973, at www.gwu.edu/~nsarchiv.

27   The four principles Brezhnev proposed were: '(1) Guarantees for Israel and the other states . . . (2) . . . no confrontation from the occupied territories. (3) Israeli withdrawal from Arab territories. (4) . . . unobstructed passage for all through the straits' (Henry Kissinger, 'Memorandum for the President's Files, President's Meeting with General Secretary Leonid Brezhnev on Saturday, June 23, 1973 at 10:30 p.m. at the Western White House', San Clemente, California, HAKO, Box 75, Brezhnev Visit 18–25 June 1973, Memcons, available at www.gwu.edu/~nsarchiv.

28   On the eve of the October 1973 war, Saudi Arabia called on the United States to require Israel to accept United Nations Security Council Resolution 242 of 1967, which laid out a settlement based on Israel's withdrawal from the West Bank, Gaza Strip, and other territories occupied in the 1967 war (Alexei Vassiliev, *The History of Saudi Arabia*, New York: New York University Press, 2000: 391). See also Donald Neff, 'Nixon Administration Ignores Saudi Warnings, Bringing On Oil Boycott', *Washington Report on Middle East Affairs*, October–November 1997: 70–2.

29   United Nations Security Council, draft resolution S/10974, 24 July 1973, at unispal. un.org.

30   White House, 'Henry Kissinger is provided with a report on the situation in Vietnam and other world developments', memo., 20 August 1971, CK3100551156, Declassified Documents Reference System, Farmington Hills, MI: Gale, 2011.

America's refusal to support a settlement would lead Egypt to take military action.

Ten days after launching the war, as the fighting continued, Sadat repeated his proposal for a separate Egyptian–Israeli peace settlement. The next day four foreign ministers representing eighteen Arab countries met with Nixon and Kissinger and asked the United States to support a settlement of the crisis based on 'Israeli withdrawal to the pre-1967 lines and respect for Palestinian rights, according to UN resolutions, to return to their homes or be compensated'.[31] After refusing to support the proposal, Kissinger told the White House crisis group later the same day that the leader of the delegation, the Saudi foreign minister, had 'come out like a good little boy and sa[id] they had very fruitful talks with us'. A report in the press that Saudi Arabia might embargo the supply of oil to the United States was blamed on State Department officials or the oil companies, who 'have an unparalleled record of being wrong', said Kissinger, assuring the group that 'we don't expect an oil cut-off now'.[32] The following day, the Arab states announced the first cutback in supplies.

To reduce pressure on Israel to negotiate, Nixon had decided to supply Israel with additional aircraft, tanks, artillery and ammunition. The White House wanted to use the war not to address the causes of conflict in the Middle East, but as consolation for its defeat in Vietnam. 'This is bigger than the Middle East', he told his officials. 'We can't allow a Soviet-supported operation to succeed against an American-supported operation.' Discussing the difficulty in forcing Israel to negotiate, he argued perversely that rearming it was the only way 'to bring Israel kicking and screaming to the table'.[33] The supply of weapons was intended to be secret, in order to hide from Europe and the Arab states America's rejection of a negotiated settlement to the Palestine question. To keep it hidden, the new Lockheed C-5A aircraft bringing the weapons from the US were to land in Israel at night. The C-5A could airlift tanks and other heavy equipment normally transported by sea, and had a range that could cover the distance from the eastern seaboard of America to the Middle East nonstop (European states refused to allow the use of their airfields). Due to errors in its wing design, however, the aircraft was unable to carry a full payload the required distance. To reach Israel, the planes had to stop and refuel in the Azores. Strong crosswinds in the Azores, where it was difficult for the new size of aircraft to land, delayed the departure of the planes from the US and postponed their arrival in Israel

31   David Hirst, 'Arabs Acclaim Sadat Peace Plan as a Major Breakthrough', *Guardian*, 18 October 1973; William B. Quandt to Kissinger, 'Memoranda of Conversations with Arab Foreign Ministers', 17 October 1973, *National Security Archive*, 'The October War and US Policy', at www.gwu.edu/~nsarchiv, referred to in following notes as NSA, 'October War'.

32   Edward Cowan, 'A Saudi Threat on Oil Reported', *New York Times*, 16 October 1973: 1; Minutes, 'Washington Special Action Group Meeting', 17 October 1973, NSA, 'October War.'

33   Minutes, 'Washington Special Action Group Meeting', NSA, 'October War.'

until daylight. Secrecy was lost, the airlift became public, and thus also did the US rejection of peace negotiations.[34]

Oil ministers from the Gulf states were then meeting in Kuwait as part of a month-long negotiation between OPEC (whose members included non-Arab states) and the oil companies, to revise the 1971 agreement on tax rates. Based on a nominal 'posted price' 40 per cent above the price at which oil was then trading, the previous agreement had been overtaken in the intervening two years by rising oil prices. Oil company profits had doubled, while the producer states' share of those profits had declined, with their real value further eroded by runaway inflation. After failing to reach a new arrangement, on 16 October the OPEC states announced they would unilaterally raise the posted price (the basis for calculating the tax rate) by 70 per cent, restoring the benchmark to a level 40 per cent above the price at which oil was trading.[35]

Oil ministers from the Arab Gulf states stayed on in Kuwait the next day, and were joined by oil ministers from other Arab countries to discuss the war situation. They agreed to respond to the obduracy of the US by announcing a modest 5 per cent reduction in their production of oil, reducing by a further 5 per cent each month until Israel evacuated the territories it had occupied in the June 1967 war. The producer states allied with the US resisted a demand for more effective measures, informing Washington that the cut in supply was merely a warning that they were serious 'that Israel must give up occupied Arab lands', as the US embassy in Kuwait reported. 'The longer satisfactory settlement with Israel was delayed', the Kuwaiti oil minister, Abdul Rahman al-Atiqi, explained, 'the shorter the oil supply would become for everyone'.[36] Nixon responded by submitting a request to Congress two days later for $2.2 billion in military aid for Israel. 'We have to keep the stuff going into Israel', Kissinger told his staff. 'We have to pour it in until someone quits'.[37] Saudi Arabia then announced an embargo on the shipment of oil to the US, which the other Arab states then joined, connecting the availability of oil to the unwillingness of the United States to support negotiations that would address the question of Palestine.

Western commentators linked the decision taken by the Arab states on 17 October to reduce the supply of oil, and the subsequent embargo on the supplies to the US, with the decision taken by OPEC the previous day to raise their tax on oil production by 70 per cent. In fact they tended to collapse the two decisions and portray them as a single event, much as they are linked by the model of supply and demand. Even today, the two events are misleadingly referred

34   'C-5 History', at www.globalsecurity.org; James Schlesinger, 'The Airlift', in Richard B. Parker, ed., *The October War: A Retrospective*, Gainesville: University Press of Florida, 2001: 153–60.

35   Parra, *Oil Politics*: 177–9.

36   US Embassy Kuwait to State Department, 'Atiqi Comment on OAPEC Meeting', 18 October 1973, NSA, 'October War'.

37   Minutes, 'Washington Special Action Group Meeting', NSA, 'October War'.

to as 'the OPEC embargo'. The frequent reference to increased taxation of oil company profits as 'the OPEC price rise' is equally misleading. For the countries involved the coincidence was accidental, and neither decision was taken in order to raise the price of oil; OPEC, moreover, had no role in the embargo. The first decision was the culmination of a month of negotiations between OPEC and the oil companies over the rate of taxation of oil profits. The reduction in supply announced by a group of Arab states the following day was a response to the decision of the United States to take Israel's side in the October war and block their attempt to force Israel to accept a peace settlement based on relinquishing the occupied territories. The cutbacks 'had nothing to do with wanting to increase the price of oil', according to Ali Attiga. The aim was to draw the attention of the public in the West to the unresolved question of Palestine.[38]

Accounts of the supply cuts and the embargo seldom mention what their purpose was. Daniel Yergin, for example, writes that 'the Arab oil ministers agreed to an embargo, cutting production 5 per cent from the September level, and to keep cutting by 5 per cent in each succeeding month until their objectives were met'.[39] Nowhere does he discuss those objectives. The Arab producer states were trying to create a linkage, to set up an equation between the availability of oil and the policy of the United States towards the Palestine question. Historians of the event sever that linkage. The general public was in the same position, too busy queuing for petrol, thinking only of the laws of the market. Meanwhile, opponents of peace negotiations in the US Congress, led by Henry Jackson, the Democrat from Washington State known as 'the Senator from Boeing' (America's largest military contractor, based in Seattle, Washington), who championed the increasing militarisation of US foreign policy, were organising rationing schemes and other devices that would enable the laws of the market to operate.

Two months after the war the OPEC states met again, to readjust the tax rate. By that point oil was trading at prices sometimes as high as $17 a barrel – more than four times the price at which it was selling when they had met in October. On the eve of the later meeting Kissinger gave a speech, saying, 'We must bear in mind the deeper causes of the energy crisis'. While exacerbated by the October war, the crisis was 'the inevitable consequence of the explosive growth of worldwide demand outrunning the incentives for supply'. If the

---

38   Anthony Sampson, *The Seven Sisters: The Great Oil Companies and the World They Made*, London: Hodder & Stoughton, 1975: 265, quoting an interview with Attiga, secretary general of the Organization of Arab Petroleum Exporting Countries (OAPEC – not, as Sampson writes, of OPEC) held in February 1975. Aimed at the supporters of Israel's refusal to negotiate, the embargo was initially imposed on the US, and then extended to the Netherlands, South Africa and Rhodesia. Portugal was added after it allowed the US to use Portuguese territory – the Azores – for airlifting weapons to Israel (Ian Seymour, *OPEC: Instrument of Change*, New York: St Martin's Press, 1981: 119).

39   Yergin, *The Prize*: 607.

price increase was the result of these long-term market forces, and therefore in Washington's view inescapable, there was no reason for the OPEC states not to adjust by resetting tax rates accordingly. Led by Iran, the closest ally of the US among its members, OPEC raised the posted price to $11.65. This increased the tax rate to $7 a barrel, implying a selling price (allowing for production costs and company profits) of under $9 a barrel, or about half the price at which oil had recently traded.[40]

Having helped to make the higher oil prices stable, Kissinger tried to reap the benefits. Europe and Japan would suffer higher energy costs, easing the pressure on the dollar, and the US would now be able to open up its Alaskan reserves.[41] Even as the war unfolded, Kissinger made plans for Nixon to send a message to Congress 'two weeks after this thing comes to an end', saying that events had 'brought home our vulnerability' and demanding that Congress drop its opposition to an Alaskan oil pipeline. 'The Alaska oil at its peak will equal the total lifting from the Arab countries', an enthusiastic White House energy adviser informed Kissinger's strategy group as the fighting on the Suez Canal intensified. 'We need two pipelines', added his assistant. This forecast of the Alaskan bonanza turned out to be wildly exaggerated.[42]

A FORTUITOUS FIELD TRIAL

The October 1973 war enabled Washington and the oil companies to move to a system of higher energy prices, and also gave a boost to something else that was increasingly associated with the price of oil: militarism. The conflict involved the largest tank battles since the Second World War. The design flaws of the C-5A prevented America from keeping its airlift secret, but the tanks that the aircraft carried to the Middle East secured a victory not only for the Israeli army but for a beleaguered US military.

Earlier that year, having acknowledged its defeat by Vietnam and withdrawn its last forces, the Pentagon embarked on a review of its military strategies in the light of anticipated budget cuts and the loss of a war against a small state. The defeat appeared to demonstrate the futility of relying on large conventional armed forces equipped for heavily armed tank-based battles of the kind fought in the Second World War. The enormous destruction of the 1973 war,

---

40   Parra, *Oil Politics*: 183–4.

41   On Kissinger's support for higher prices, see Tore T. Petersen, *Richard Nixon, Great Britain, and the Anglo-American Alignment in the Persian Gulf and Arabian Peninsula: Making Allies Out of Clients*, Eastbourne: Sussex Academic Press, 2009: 8–14, and Parra, *Oil Politics*: 197–205.

42   Minutes, 'Washington Special Action Group Meeting', NSA, 'October War'. At its peak, in 1988, Alaska produced 2 million barrels of oil per day; production from the Arab states that year exceeded 15 mbpd – www.eia.gov, and DeGolyer & MacNaughton, *Twentieth Century Petroleum Statistics*, Dallas: DeGolyer & MacNaughton, 2009.

in which the Syrian and Egyptian tank losses in an eighteen-day battle were equal to the total number of US tanks deployed at that time in Europe, appeared to reinforce this conclusion. But proponents of re-equipping the US with new tanks and other heavy weaponry used the October war as 'a fortuitous field trial'. After touring the battle sites in occupied Syria and Egypt with their Israeli counterparts, the American generals presented the devastation and the eventual Israeli victory as evidence that, with the right equipment, tactics and training, contrary to the lessons of Vietnam, large conventional armoured battles could be fought and won.

The US armed forces liked to blame the loss of the Vietnam war on democracy. It was not military weakness but popular opposition at home that caused the defeat. The Israeli success in 1973 offered an answer to this problem of democracy. The destructive power of tanks and other heavy weapons made them more suitable for a war fought by a democratic state, it was said, because their destructiveness brought rapid results, before popular opinion or international censure forced the civilian leadership to halt the fighting.[43] These conclusions from the 1973 war, reinforced by frequent return visits to the sites of the field trial and incorporated into training manuals and congressional presentations, enabled the Pentagon to defeat the advocates of smaller, mobile forces and to rebuild a heavily armed military.

In defeating efforts to resolve the Palestine question, the war also helped to maintain the Middle East as a zone of insecurity. The large arms transfers to Israel and Iran, discussed in the previous chapter, were now joined by increasing sales to Saudi Arabia and other Arab Gulf states, and to Egypt. The crisis cemented the new relations between oil-producing countries and the United States, based on the selling of arms.[44] The real value of US arms exports more than doubled between 1967 and 1975, with most of the new market in the Middle East.[45] The flow of weapons, and related opportunities in construction, consulting, military assistance and banking, now depended on new levels of militarism. It also depended on a US policy of prolonging and exacerbating local conflicts in the Middle East, and on an increasingly disjunctive relationship with the Salafist forms of Islam that had helped defend the mid-twentieth-century oil order against nationalist and popular pressures in the region. As we will see in Chapter 8, the tensions between militarism, Salafism and armed conflict would render the prospects for a more democratic politics of oil production even weaker in the post-1974 period.

---

43   Saul Bronfeld, 'Fighting Outnumbered: The Impact of the Yom Kippur War on the US Army', *Journal of Military History* 71: 2, 2007.

44   Jonathan Nitzan and Shimshon Bichler, 'The Weapondollar–Petrodollar Coalition', in *The Global Political Economy of Israel*, London: Pluto Press, 2002: 198–273.

45   SIPRI Arms Transfers Database, available at armstrade.sipri.org.

LIMITS TO GROWTH

Another set of calculations was brought to the price of oil by the 1973–74 crisis. The fourfold increase in prices was probably a larger rise than the oil companies had intended. They now needed extraordinary measures to prevent demand for oil from collapsing, in particular by ensuring that natural gas and nuclear power increased in price. One method of achieving this was for oil companies to champion conservation and the protection of the environment.

Leading oil economists argued that the supply of petroleum, for the practical purposes of economic calculation, was inexhaustible. Although reserves were depleted by extraction, they were replenished by exploration, discovery and new technology. Their exhaustion was so far in the future, they argued, that it could have no impact on the oil price. Oil reserves were less a natural resource being used up, more an inventory being run down and then replenished. 'Minerals are inexhaustible and will never be depleted', argued Morris Adelman in 1972. 'A stream of investment creates additions to proved reserves from a very large in-ground inventory. The reserves are constantly being renewed as they are extracted. How much was in the ground at the start and how much will be left at the end are unknown and irrelevant.'[46]

This cornucopian view of the nature of oil reserves had been criticised by a number of petroleum geologists, who had a different conception of the nature and availability of oil. In 1956, M. King Hubbert, a geologist at Shell Oil, presented a paper at the Annual Meeting of the American Petroleum Institute estimating that US oil production would peak within ten to fifteen years (1966–71), and then enter a period of continuous decline.[47] Hubbert's estimate was based on prevailing industry measures of recoverable reserves, but made use of novel assumptions about the relationship of the rate of production of oil to the rate of its discovery to change the picture of the future.[48]

Before 1971, the US oil industry felt threatened by Hubbert's predictions. Oil companies launched an attack on his methods, and produced rival figures that suddenly doubled or tripled the estimates of recoverable reserves. If oil was soon going to be in short supply, the government quotas and price protection that encouraged production were unjustified.

---

46   Morris Adelman, *The World Petroleum Market*, Baltimore: Johns Hopkins University Press, 1972; Adelman, 'Is the Oil Shortage Real?'.

47   Hubbert had been associated in the 1930s and 1940s with the technocracy movement, an organisation of engineers linked with the work of Thorstein Veblen, mentioned in Chapter 5, on Engineers and the Price System. The movement sought to replace the price system of the economists and the corporate power of big business with the technocratic management of society and its resources by engineers.

48   Gary Bowden, 'The Social Construction of Validity in Estimates of US Crude Oil Reserves', *Social Studies of Science* 15: 2, May 1985: 207–40.

After 1971, with the OPEC producer states now managing the process of maintaining a scarcity of oil and bringing world prices up to the level of US domestic prices, the oil companies no longer needed the system of quotas and price protections. They adjusted their estimates in line with those of Hubbert, and agreed that US oil production was reaching its peak and about to start its decline. In 1971, the chief geologist of BP suggested that the world's currently proven reserves of oil would be exhausted in the 1980s, and that the projected rise in demand meant that in less than thirty years the undiscovered reserves likely to be found would no longer be able to meet rising demand.[49] When the oil crisis passed, however, the oil company geologists reverted to cornucopian positions.

The concerns about the depletion of oil reserves coincided with the emergence of a politics of 'the limits to growth' and the protection of 'the environment' as an alternative project to that of 'the economy'.[50] Curiously, the oil companies themselves helped trigger the production of the environment as a rival object of politics. They did this in part inadvertently, by adopting ways of drilling and transporting oil that led to giant oil spills, around which environmentalists were able to organise. But they also helped produce the environment as a matter of political concern, by the changes in the way they calculated the world's reserves of oil. In 1971 the oil companies abruptly abandoned their cornucopian calculations of oil as an almost limitless resource (calculations that had underpinned postwar theories of the economy as an object capable of limitless growth), and began to forecast the end of oil.[51]

In the early 1970s, geologists' arguments about the future exhaustion of oil reserves gained much wider circulation. In 1973, E. F. Schumacher, the economic advisor to the National Coal Board in Britain and a persistent critic of the postwar switch from coal to oil engineered by the US, published the book *Small is Beautiful*.[52] A few months earlier, the Club of Rome had published *The Limits to Growth*, a report for the Club's project on 'The Predicament of Mankind'. Deploying computer modelling carried out at MIT, the report argued that, if current trends in energy consumption, resource depletion, industrialisation, pollution, food production and population growth continued, 'the limits to growth on this planet will be reached sometime within the next hundred

---

49   As we will see in the Conclusion, these predictions were not far off. James Bamberg, *History of the British Petroleum Company*, vol. 3: *British Petroleum and Global Oil, 1950–1975: The Challenge of Nationalism*, Cambridge, UK: CUP, 2000: 209.

50   See Donella H. Meadows, Dennis L. Meadows, Jorgen Randers and William W. Behrens, *The Limits to Growth: A Report for the Club of Rome's Project on the Predicament of Mankind*, New York: Universe Books, 1972; E. F. Schumacher, *Small is Beautiful: Economics as if People Mattered*, New York: Harper & Row, 1973.

51   Gary Bowden, 'The Social Construction of Validity in Estimates of US Crude Oil Reserves', *Social Studies of Science* 15: 2, 1985: 207–40.

52   Schumacher, *Small is Beautiful*.

years'.[53] Warning also of the accumulation of carbon dioxide in the atmosphere caused by the burning of hydrocarbons and the consequent threat of global warming, the report was a serious challenge to the petroleum industry, and to economists whose models of the market depended on an absence of limits to energy, and appeared to offer no way to address the question of the exhaustion of resources and the limits to growth.

THE OIL COMPANIES FRAME THE ENVIRONMENT

As the State Department struggled to justify its support for higher oil prices, the idea that oil formed part of a larger system of 'energy' became increasingly important. On 10 April 1973, a week before Nixon's energy message to Congress, James Akins had delivered a presentation in Denver, Colorado, before a meeting of the American Petroleum Institute, the collective organisation of the oil industry. He repeated his argument about the inevitability of higher prices, but warned that 'there is one spectre which will always lurk in every producer's mind: the development of new sources of energy which will make oil irrelevant. As improbable as this is in the short run, it is always possible that some dramatic, sudden technological development could render oil superfluous.'[54] He proposed that

> hydrocarbon prices should continue to rise until they reach the cost of producing alternative energy – that is, from coal, shale, tar sands or even garbage conversion. The price of energy from hydrocarbons would then roughly parallel the cost of alternative energy sources until, toward the end of the century, alternative sources would supply the growth in demand. At that time, hydrocarbons could be expected to be devoted to higher uses: plastics, building materials, medicines and even food.

As long as they represented 'a significant portion of the energy mix', he argued, 'it must be assumed that hydrocarbons will be sold for at least the cost of alternative energy'. He added that future generations would probably 'curse us for having burned this irreplaceable commodity'.[55]

The argument that hydrocarbons were a relatively scarce and irreplaceable part of 'the energy mix' indicates an important aspect of the new politics of energy. In making it possible to connect the price of oil to that of other forms of fuel and power, discussions of the energy system could link the price of oil to the new politics of the environment.

---

53   Meadows, Meadows, Randers and Behrens, *The Limits to Growth* 29, 75, 85–6.
54   Akins, 'International Cooperative Efforts': 78.
55   Ibid.: 79.

For the Nixon administration the politics of energy was simultaneously a politics of the environment. Nixon's 1973 State of the Union address, issued as a series of written statements over several weeks rather than as a single oral address, included as its first substantive message a 'State of the Union Message to the Congress on Natural Resources and the Environment'.[56] We have learned, he said, that

> natural resources are fragile and finite, and that many have been seriously damaged or despoiled. When we came to office in 1969, we tackled this problem with all the power at our command. Now there is encouraging evidence that the United States has moved away from the environmental crisis that could have been and toward a new era of restoration and renewal.

In Nixon's speeches these themes were continually linked: energy as the crisis approaching, the environment as the crisis that could have been.

On Tuesday, 28 January 1969, one week after Nixon took office, a blowout in an underwater well that Union Oil was drilling in the sea six miles off the coast of Santa Barbara, California, led to ruptures of the sea floor that allowed 200,000 gallons of oil to escape to the surface, and took eleven days to seal.[57] Caused partly by the use of weak pipe casings, the disaster enabled environmentalists to focus attention on the threat posed by the expansion of oil production into offshore drilling, as well as the proposed development of oil production on the North Slope in Alaska and the construction of a trans-Alaska pipeline. Later that year, David Brower, forced out of his post as executive director of the Sierra Club after his political campaigns lost the club its charitable status, founded Friends of the Earth, 'a global, media-savvy, politically muscular activist group' that created franchises in other parts of the industrialised West, becoming the first international environmental organisation.[58] The pressure that this and similar groups began to exert on issues such as oil drilling, nuclear power, emissions from coal-fired electricity generation, and the Alaska pipeline became a significant challenge to many different parts of the fuel and power industries.

For the oil industry and the White House, the question of an 'energy crisis' became a way to address this challenge. On the one hand, the need to conserve fossil fuels as a scarce and depletable source of energy provided a justification for higher oil prices. On the other hand, the environmental movement could be encouraged to focus on the more serious threat represented by the nuclear

---

56   Nixon, 'Special Message to the Congress on Energy Resources'.
57   Keith C. Clarke and Jeffrey J. Hemphill, 'The Santa Barbara Oil Spill: A Retrospective', in Darrick Danta, ed., *Yearbook of the Association of Pacific Coast Geographers*, vol. 64, Honolulu: University of Hawai'i Press, 2002.
58   Daniel Coyle, 'The High Cost of Being David Brower', *Outside Magazine*, December 1995.

power industry. Most economists saw the development of nuclear power as the solution to the problem of high energy costs and the eventual exhaustion of fossil fuels.[59] This was also a solution to the energy crisis proposed by the Nixon administration. In the 1950s John Von Neumann had famously written that, with the development of nuclear fusion, in 'a few decades hence energy may be free – just like the unmetered air – with coal and oil used mainly as raw materials for organic chemical synthesis, to which, as experience has shown, their properties are best suited'.[60] By the 1970s the cost estimates were less optimistic, but there was still the risk that the vast funds that the government was committing to the development of the new fast-breeder reactors would produce energy at a price that would threaten the high profits now enjoyed by the oil industry. The environmental movement could help reduce this threat to oil. By insisting that nuclear power generation be forced to take account of the risks of accidents and the costs of disposing of spent fuel, environmental campaigns helped make nuclear energy less affordable, and thus less likely to become a lower-priced alternative to fossil fuels.

For the oil companies, the large increase in oil prices had carried a risk. It threatened to make affordable a rival source of energy – nuclear power. However, if the oil companies could force the producers of nuclear power to introduce into the price of the energy they sold a payment to cover its long-term environmental effects – the cost of decontaminating reactors when they went out of service and of storing spent fuel for millennia – it would remain more expensive than oil. To promote such calculations, the oil companies joined the effort to frame the environment as a new object of politics, and to define it and calibrate it in particular ways. Like the economy, the environment was not simply an aspect of external reality, against which the oil industry had to contend. It was a set of forces and calculations that rival groups attempted to mobilise.

The role of oil companies in framing the politics of the environment suggests another dimension of the relationship between oil and democracy that we have not yet considered: compared with the production of coal, oil production has a different way of deploying and distributing expertise. I suggested earlier that the democratic militancy of coal miners could be traced in part to the autonomy that miners exercised at the coalface, especially prior to the large-scale mechanisation of production. The autonomy of those who mined the ore placed a significant amount of expertise in their hands. Oil, in contrast, leaves its workers on the surface and distributes more of the expertise of production into the offices of engineers and managers.

---

59 Robert M. Solow, 'The Economics of Resources or the Resources of Economics', *American Economic Review* 64: 2, 1974: 1–14.

60 John von Neumann, 'John von Neumann on Technological Prospects and Global Limits' (1955), *Population and Development Review* 12: 1, March 1986: 120.

This difference goes further, extending both to the period before the mineral is extracted and to what is done with it afterwards. The coal industry does not invest large funds in exploration, because the geology of accessible coal deposits makes their location readily known, while extracting remote deposits is uneconomic. In the oil industry, exploration is a large, capital-intensive part of the industry, in which companies can realise large profits. Large firms depend on an extensive body of technical, political and economic expertise to support the discovery of new deposits.[61]

Once mined, moreover, coal is ready to use. It may require cleaning and sorting, but it needs no chemical transformation. Oil, on the other hand, comes out of the ground in the unusable form known as crude oil. The crude must be heated in a furnace, separated into its different hydrocarbons by fractional distillation, and further processed into usable and uniform products. Initially, as we saw in Chapter 1, its main use was in the form of kerosene for lighting and, with heavier oils, in the form of fuel oil for steam boilers and mineral oils for lubrication. Gasoline and other lighter by-products of the refining process were treated as waste. To increase their profit margin, oil companies developed large research and development divisions to find uses for these unused by-products, distribution and marketing divisions to promote their use, and political and public relations departments to help build the kinds of societies that would demand them.[62] The major oil companies also collaborated to deny expertise to others, including the coal industry. The cartel formed in 1928 by the major oil companies was actually a broader hydrocarbon cartel, because it consisted of an agreement not just to control the production of oil, but to prevent the use of patents that would allow coal companies to move into the production of synthetic oils.[63]

Compared with coal companies, oil companies developed much larger and more extended networks for the production of expertise, which became increasingly involved in making of the wider world a place where its products could thrive. For this reason, the international oil industry was well equipped to meet the challenge of the 1967–74 crisis. Facing both the demand from producer states for a much larger share of oil revenues and the rise of environmentalist challenges to carbon democracy, the major oil companies could draw upon a wide array of resources in public relations, marketing, planning, energy research, international finance and government relations – all of which could be used to help define the nature of the crisis and promote a particular set of solutions.

61   Gavin Bridge, 'Global Production Networks and the Extractive Sector: Governing Resource-Based Development', *Journal of Economic Geography* 8: 3, 2008: 414.

62   See Bruce Podobnik, *Global Energy Shifts: Fostering Sustainability in a Turbulent Age*, Philadelphia: Temple University Press, 2005.

63   Gregory P. Nowell, *Mercantile States and the World Oil Cartel, 1900–1930*, Ithaca: Cornell University Press, 1994.

THE RESOURCES OF ECONOMICS

Issues of concern were multiplying: the exhaustion of natural resources; destruction of the environment; the warming of the atmosphere caused by burning fossil fuels; the increasing cost of energy; the devaluation of the dollar; the decline of manufacturing and the end of postwar economic growth; a continuing anti-war movement; conflict in the Middle East; and the financial corruption of American politics (including large illegal payments by oil companies), culminating in the Watergate crisis. A prominent political scientist, Samuel Huntington, reflected a common view among the political elite in America when he declared that the country suffered from an 'excess of democracy'.[64]

This excess could no longer be contained by subordinating political claims to the calculations of what was possible according to the principles of 'the economy'. The development of the national economy had been calculated without taking into account the cost of depleting non-renewable resources, the wastefulness of war, alterations to the earth's climate, or the destruction of the environment. Measuring the world at the scale of the nation-state, macro-economics could not address the oil crisis except as an external 'supply shock', or calculate the transnational relations between militarism, the value of the dollar, and the changing control of oil.

For economists opposed to the role of the government in regulating economic life, as an influential number were, the inability to explain the oil crisis was both a challenge and an opportunity. The opportunity was taken up at the eighty-sixth annual meeting of the American Economic Association, in December 1973. Addressing the entire assembly of the profession in the Richard T. Ely Lecture, Robert Solow discussed the sudden political concern to control the depletion of mineral resources. To counter plans for government regulation of energy consumption, he set out to demonstrate that the conservation of mineral resources could be managed by laws of the market.

Solow addressed a profession that was reacting to the wider social and political crisis of the period with profound disagreement and uncertainty. Two years earlier, the Richard T. Ely lecture had been delivered by Joan Robinson, a left-leaning neo-Keynesian (and one of only three women to deliver the lecture in its fifty-year history). Her lecture on 'The Second Crisis in Economic Theory' compared the current disarray of 'an economics profession that builds intricate theories in the air that have no contact with reality' to the state of the profession in the 1930s when, prior to Keynes's *General Theory*, it was unable to explain or provide remedies for the Great Depression. She described 'the evident

---

64   Samuel P. Huntington, 'The United States', in Michel Crozier, Samuel P. Huntington and Joji Watanuki, eds, *The Crisis of Democracy: Report on the Governability of Democracies to the Trilateral Commission*, New York: New York University Press, 1975: 59–118, 113.

bankruptcy of economic theory which for the second time has nothing to say on the questions that, to everyone except economists, appear to be most in need of an answer' – principally the question of explaining the unequal distribution of wealth.[65]

Solow began by confirming 'that economic theorists read the newspapers'. Having read a variety of recent reports about the advancing scarcity of minerals, and 'having, like everyone else, been suckered into reading *The Limits to Growth*', he decided to see what economics might have to say about the problems connected with exhaustible resources. He found that the literature was not very large. While he was drafting his own paper, however, 'just about then it seemed that every time the mail came it contained another paper by another economic theorist on the economics of exhaustible resources. It was a little like trotting down to the sea, minding your own business like any nice independent rat, and then looking around and suddenly discovering that you're a lemming.'[66]

Solow recovered the forgotten work of a prominent economist of an earlier generation, Harold Hotelling. In an article on 'The Economics of Exhaustible Resources', published in 1931, Hotelling had argued that in a competitive market there was an equilibrium price path, in which the price of oil would rise at the prevailing rate of interest for capital invested in projects with a similar degree of risk. Since a resource left in the ground increases in value as its market price rises, owners will in theory extract less of it as the price goes up, preferring to leave it to grow in value as a stored resource while investing their capital elsewhere. The higher price should cause demand to fall and the price of the resource to drop. Once its price falls below the prevailing rate of interest, Hotelling suggested, owners of the resource lose money by storing it for the future and therefore invest in increased production. The laws of the market thus provided a mechanism for regulating the speed of extraction of a natural resource, pushing the rate towards one that produced the exponential price path of the compound rate of interest.

It was no accident that Hotelling's work had been forgotten. He was writing at an earlier time of increased demands for the public regulation of the depletion of natural resources – in particular the cutting of forests and drilling of oil wells – and of wildly erratic swings in the price of petroleum. Like Solow's intervention four decades later, his attempt to prove that market mechanisms could regulate petroleum and other natural resource industries was directed against government intervention. As Hotelling's article went to press, however, prospectors in East Texas drilled what turned out to be the largest oilfield yet

65   Joan Robinson, 'The Second Crisis of Economic Theory', *American Economic Review* 62: 1/2, 1972: 9–10. See also Michael A. Berstein, *A Perilous Progress: Economists and Public Purpose in Twentieth-Century America*, Princeton: Princeton University Press, 2001: 148–84.

66   Solow, 'Economics of Resources': 1–2.

discovered. The oil that gushed from the wells caused the price of petroleum to collapse. Four months later, the governors of Oklahoma and Texas declared martial law and sent the National Guard to occupy the oilfields and shut down the new wells, as a means of increasing the price.[67] Hotelling's argument for market regulation was ignored. The year after he published his paper, the US introduced the system of production quotas and price regulation governed by the Texas Railroad Commission.

Four decades later, with military rule of the oilfields now outsourced to the Middle East and the regulatory authority of the Texas Railroad Commission devolved onto OPEC, Solow recovered Hotelling's work and once again proposed using market laws to regulate the extraction of natural resources. Solow's lecture was followed by a stream of articles and PhD dissertations on the subject, creating a new field of study: resource economics. This work contributed little to explaining the forces that determined the price of oil or governed its production.[68] Solow acknowledged this in the lecture. He had not written it, he claimed, 'with current problems in mind. After all, nothing I have been able to say takes account of the international oil cartel, the political and economic ambitions of Middle Eastern potentates, the speeds of adjustment to surprises in the supply of oil, or the doings of our own friendly oligopolists.'[69] His purpose, rather, was to design calculative devices that could produce a different way of governing prices.

For Solow and many of his fellow economists, market devices were intended as an alternative to democratic methods of governing matters of public concern, by converting them into matters of private regulation by those with the resources to operate as market agents. Even if his market solution produced a steady, unerratic price for oil or other natural resources, Solow acknowledged, the mechanism did not guarantee that prices would take account of the needs of future generations – the major concern of the new debates about the depletion of resources and the protection of the environment. In fact, he admitted, market prices were more likely to discount those interests. However, he argued against any attempt to curb current consumption and take account of future needs by means of democratic government. Politicians look only to the next election, he said, so the political process cannot be 'relied on' to be more future-orientated than energy corporations. Transferring an oil company executive to the government bureaucracy 'does not transform him into a guardian of the far future's interests.'[70] Instead of trusting politicians to take care of the long run,

---

67   Harold Hotelling, 'The Economics of Exhaustible Resources', *Journal of Political Economy* 39: 2, 1931: 137–75; 'Military Rule in Texas May Boost Oil', *Wall Street Journal*, 18 August 1931: 1.

68   Robert Mabro, 'OPEC and the Price of Oil', *Energy Journal* 13: 2, 1992: 1–17.

69   Solow, 'Economics of Resources': 13.

70   Ibid.: 12.

people should trust in technology, which would devise new sources of energy to replace fossil fuels. For the near future, the government should limit its role to improving the use of market calculations. Two specific measures would allow market devices to better regulate the oil industry: the establishing of a futures market, as a means of introducing calculation for the nearer future, and gathering and publishing information on the future trends in technology, oil reserves and energy demand, to make the futures market more efficient.[71]

This technology was developed in relation to oil in two forms. One was the state and intergovernmental coordination of knowledge about oil. The US government established the Department of Energy, within which it created the Energy Information Administration, which centralised in one office the production of statistics and analysis on oil and other energy resources. At the same time the industrialised countries, through the OECD, quickly established the International Energy Agency in Paris, to counter the threat of another oil embargo by organising the stockpiling of oil and publishing data and reports on energy supplies. The other was to organise another technical device for oil – a set of market arrangements to supplement the system of fixed contracts by which oil had previously been traded. In the late 1970s, an oil futures market was established at the New York Mercantile Exchange, where Solow's arguments were developed as a set of tools for predicting the future movement of oil prices.

The success in increasing oil prices undermined the Keynesian management of the economy, easing the way for the development of market-based devices promoted as an alternative to an 'excess' of democracy and the 'failures' of democratic government. A long struggle unfolded through the 1970s and beyond, to today, in which oil companies continually used their political connections to defeat legislation aimed at restricting their influence or at managing natural resources. The market-based solutions offered tools and arguments for derailing alternative efforts at regulation. In the 1980s, neoliberal think tanks began promoting another set of tools: carbon trading.[72] To limit government regulation of the increased burning of fossil fuels, and reduce the costs of such regulation to corporate profits, a variety of schemes were devised whereby reductions in pollution in the West could be traded against much cheaper putative reductions in the global south.

The rapid increase in the price of oil assisted this process in a more direct way. As oil companies prospered in the boom, a handful of families in the United States turned their fortunes from oil into windfall funds for the neoliberal movement. Richard Mellon Scaife, heir to the Gulf Oil fortune of the Mellon family, used these funds to become the country's largest benefactor of

---

71   Ibid.: 13.
72   Larry Lohmann, *Carbon Trading: A Critical Conversation on Climate Change, Privatisation and Power*, Development Dialogue, no. 48, September 2006.

neoliberal free-market political organisations, giving at least $340 million over four decades to such organisations as the Heritage Foundation, the American Enterprise Institute, the Hoover Institution, the Manhattan Institute and the Center for Strategic and International Studies.[73] Charles and David Koch, whose company Koch Industries was the largest privately held oil company in the US, played a similar role, and Charles Koch co-founded the Cato Institute in 1977. These think tanks and policy organisations oversaw the neoliberal movement, with a programme assembled since the late 1930s to remove from the state its role in regulating the economy and replace this public regulation of collective life with its private regulation by the market.[74]

The academic profession that had 'nothing to say on the questions that . . . appear to be most in need of an answer' was to be reinvigorated by the neoliberal movement, in which many of its members came to play a leading role. Closely tied to the movement's think tanks, it would commit itself to the market technologies of neoliberalism and to addressing the problems of an excess of democracy.

The dramatic increase in the price of oil in 1973–74 has been described as a textbook illustration of the law of supply and demand. Rather than rejecting this account as too narrow an explanation of what happened, we have followed the work that had to be done to make such an explanation viable. That work involved bringing together a series of conflicts and transformations in the control of raw materials, the generation of power, the claims of energy workers and social communities, and the regulation of corporate profit, into a single field of political concern and government intervention in the United States, to be known as the 'energy crisis'. It also involved the series of strikes, acts of sabotage, political rivalries and confrontations in the Middle East examined here and in the previous chapter, which made it possible to transform the networks that moved oil supplies from the major producing regions to sites of consumption in western Europe into a political instrument. This instrument was fashioned in its turn to serve a dual purpose – concerned both with redirecting the flow of profits from oil and with the settlement of the Palestine question. The efforts to prevent a settlement of the Palestine question made particular use of market mechanisms, relying on arguments about supply and demand and devices for rationing consumption in an attempt to frame the probable causes and possible solutions to the crisis.

---

73   Robert G. Kaiser and Ira Chinoy, 'How Scaife's Money Powered a Movement', *Washington Post*, 2 May 1999: A1, A25; James Allen Smith, *The Idea Brokers: Think Tanks and the Rise of the New Policy Elite*, New York: Free Press, 1991: 200–1.

74   See David Harvey, *A Brief History of Neoliberalism*, Oxford: OUP, 2005; and Timothy Mitchell, 'The Work of Economics: How a Discipline Makes its World', *European Journal of Sociology* 46: 2, 2005: 297–320.

In several ways, however, the events of 1973–74 overflowed the attempts to contain them within the realm of market forces. The question of supply raised new doubts about the possible limits to reserves of oil; the increasing difficulty of forecasting future demand and prices opened up new ways of mapping the future; and the inability to prevent catastrophic oil spills helped trigger the emergence of new issues of concern – in particular the preservation of the environment. Yet the events of 1973–74 also helped trigger the unravelling of Keynesian economics, attacked by market technologies developed from the mid-1970s in revitalised neoliberal think tanks – many of them funded by the private fortunes of American oil families, swollen by windfall profits from the 1973–74 oil crisis.

CHAPTER 8

McJihad

On 3 February 1997, a delegation of the Taliban government of Afghanistan visited Washington, DC. Ten days earlier, Taliban forces had won control of the countryside around Kabul, and with the south and east of the country already in their hands they were now making preparations to conquer the north. In Washington the Taliban delegation met with State Department officials and discussed the plans of Unocal, a California oil company (later part of Chevron), to build a pipeline from Central Asia through Afghanistan. A senior US diplomat explained his government's thinking: 'The Taliban will probably develop like the Saudis did. There will be Aramco, pipelines, an emir, no parliament and lots of Sharia law. We can live with that.'[1]

US support for the Taliban, who received arms, financial assistance and military recruits from Pakistan and Saudi Arabia with the agreement of Washington, was a policy 'ridden with inner tensions', the American embassy in Islamabad suggested, 'as we simultaneously engage with the Taliban and criticize their abuses.'[2] But the diplomat's reference to Aramco – the American oil company that, sixty years earlier had financed the creation of Saudi Arabia – was a reminder that the United States was accustomed to working with emirs whose power depended upon strict interpretations of Islamic law. The US grew increasingly frustrated with the Islamic Emirate of Afghanistan, as the country was now called, over its refusal to arrest and hand over the Saudi dissident Osama bin Laden following attacks in 1998 on US embassies in East Africa. As late as September 2000, however, while in public describing the actions of the Taliban as 'despicable', the US assured a senior official of the Emirate in private that its policy 'has always been to try to find a way to engage the Taliban.'[3] The 'inner tensions' of building alliances with conservative Islamic regimes were a familiar part of American policy.

In recent decades, the problem of oil and democracy has come to be associated increasingly with the question of Islam. Political scientists point out that

---

1 Ahmed Rashid, *Taliban: Militant Islam, Oil, and Fundamentalism in Central Asia*, New Haven: Yale University Press, 2000: 179.

2 The official presumably meant to write 'riven' with inner tensions. US Embassy (Islamabad), 'Official Informal for SA Assistant Secretary Robin Raphel and SA/PAB', 10 March 1997, in National Security Archive, 'Pakistan: "The Taliban's Godfather"?' at www.gwu.edu/~nsarchiv.

3 US Embassy (Islamabad), 'Searching for the Taliban's Hidden Message', 19 September 2000, National Security Archive, The Taliban File Part IV, at www.gwu.edu/~nsarchiv.

not every country heavily dependent on oil revenues fails to develop more democratic forms of government. For example, three of the largest oil-producing states in the global south – Venezuela, Nigeria and Indonesia – have alternated between periods of military government and more democratic and populist regimes. A variety of explanations and qualifications have been offered to make sense of these patterns.[4]

In earlier chapters we have seen why the Middle East was both the most critical site for international companies or imperial states that wanted to control world oil production and the most difficult. On the one hand, it was the region where oil was most abundant and at the same time cheapest to produce. On the other, so many large oil states were concentrated together that concessions to local demands in one country were liable to upset arrangements in several neighbouring states. There is no reason, therefore, to look to Islam to find reasons for the difficulties encountered by those in the region who fought to advance democratic and egalitarian claims. Since the 1970s, however, forms of political Islam have played an increasingly significant role in the politics of the Middle East, and thus in the political economy of oil.

ON THE PLUS SIDE

As a rule, the most secular regimes in the Middle East have been those most independent of the United States. The more closely a government is allied with Washington, the more Islamic its politics. Egypt under Nasser, republican Iraq, the Palestine national movement, post-independence Algeria, the Republic of South Yemen, Ba'thist Syria – all charted courses independent of the United States. None of them declared themselves an Islamic state, and many of them repressed local Islamic movements. In contrast, those governments dependent on the United States typically claimed an Islamic authority, whether ruled by a monarch who claimed descent from the Prophet, as in Jordan, North Yemen and Morocco, or asserting a special role as protector of the faith, as in the case of Saudi Arabia. When other governments moved closer to the United States

---

4 Fernando Coronil, *The Magical State: Nature, Money and Modernity in Venezuela*, Chicago: University of Chicago Press, 1997; Michael Watts, 'Resource Curse? Governmentality, Oil, and Power in the Niger Delta', *Geopolitics* 9: 1, 2004: 50–80; Thad Dunning, *Crude Democracy: Natural Resource Wealth and Political Regimes*, Cambridge, UK: CUP, 2008; Terry Lynn Karl, *The Paradox of Plenty: Oil Booms and Petro-States*, Berkeley: University of California Press, 1997. The problem of the rentier state was first formulated in Hussein Mahdavy, 'The Patterns and Problems of Economic Development in Rentier States: The Case of Iran', in M. A. Cook, ed., *Studies in the Economic History of the Middle East*, London: OUP, 1970. Subsequent contributions on the Middle East include Hazem Beblawi and Giacomo Luciani, eds, *The Rentier State*, New York: Croom Helm, 1987; Ghassan Salamé, ed., *Democracy Without Democrats: The Renewal of Politics in the Muslim World*, London: I. B. Tauris, 1994; and Isam al-Khafaji, *Tormented Births: Passages to Modernity in Europe and the Middle East*, London: I. B. Tauris, 2004, 309–25.

– Egypt under Anwar Sadat in the 1970s, Pakistan under Zia ul-Haq in the 1980s – their political rhetoric and modes of legitimation became avowedly more Islamic.

Iran might seem an exception to this pattern. Under the pro-American government of the shah it was a secular state; after the 1979 revolution it became an Islamic republic, opposed to America's ambitions. In fact, however, the shah mobilised conservative religious forces in his support, depending on a CIA-funded clerical leadership to overthrow a nationalist government in 1953, and losing power only when the leading clerics in the country turned against him. And many scholars of Iran would argue that the Islamic Republic, the Middle Eastern country most independent of the United States, is one in which appeals to religion are increasingly unable to legitimise the exercise of power. Especially among its youth, the Islamic Republic has created one of the most secular societies in the region.

This pattern, once it has been noticed, lends itself to a straightforward but unsatisfactory explanation. The United States depends on the support of conservative political regimes, it is often pointed out, and these have tended to rely on religion to justify their power. In contrast, many of the populist or nationalist regimes carried out post-independence programmes of land reform, the advancement of women's rights, industrialisation and the provision of free education and healthcare, and achieved whatever legitimacy they gained through these egalitarian social reforms rather than through the authority of religion.

This explanation is unsatisfactory because the conservative political morality offered by certain forms of Islam is not some enduring feature of the religion that rulers adopt at their own convenience. Its usefulness reflects the fact that moral conservatism expresses the views of powerful social and political movements. Political regimes enter into uneasy alliances with these movements, depending on a force they do not directly control. The dominant school of Islam in Saudi Arabia, for example, represents an intellectual tradition founded in the mid-eighteenth century and reborn as a political movement at the start of the twentieth. It has its own legal scholars, teachers, political spokesmen and militants. Wahhabism, as outsiders call it, after its eighteenth-century founder, or the doctrine of *tawhid* (the oneness of God) as its adherents (the *muwahhidun*) prefer to call it, developed in the era of British colonial expansion, and aimed to transform and re-moralise the community. The Deobandi school in India (including the part that became Pakistan) and Afghanistan, in which the Taliban movement had its roots, was another influential social and intellectual force of the colonial period. In Egypt, the intellectual reform movement known as Salafism inspired the Muslim Brotherhood, founded in 1929, which became the country's largest popular force opposing the British military occupation and the corruption of the ruling class.

Governments drew on the support of these movements at different times and with differing success. When Unocal and US government officials decided that, along with the government in Pakistan, they could 'live with' the Taliban, they were proposing to cement an alliance with a movement whose powers of moral authority, social discipline and political violence represented forces that were to be engaged and put to work – to enable the building of a 1,000-mile pipeline. 'On the plus side', the US noted, 'the Taliban have restored security and a rough form of law and order in their area of control'.[5] In Egypt, from the 1970s onwards, the state (and indirectly the US government) relied on a tacit alliance with the Muslim Brotherhood to help suppress both secular progressive and militant Islamic opposition. In Arabia, the *muwahhidun* were not just the ideologues of Saudi rule but a social force that made possible the building of the Saudi state, and hence the operations of the American oil industry. In every case this alliance between ruling powers and Islamic movements was a source of considerable tension.

It follows that such religious movements have played a small but pivotal part in the global political economy of oil. If conservative religious reform movements such as the *muwahhidun* in Saudi Arabia or the Muslim Brotherhood in Egypt have been essential to maintaining the power and authority of those states, and if, as we are often told, the stability of the governments of Egypt and Saudi Arabia, perhaps more than that of any other governments in the global south, are vital to the protection of US interests, in particular the control of oil, it would seem to follow that political Islam plays an unacknowledged role in the making of what we call global capitalism.

It has become increasingly popular today to say that we live in an era of what Benjamin Barber has labelled 'Jihad vs. McWorld'. The globalising powers of capitalism ('McWorld') are confronted with or resisted by the forces that Barber labels 'Jihad' – the variety of tribal particularisms and 'narrowly conceived faiths' opposed to the homogenising force of capital.[6] Even those with a critical view of the growth of American empire and the expansion of what is erroneously termed the global market usually subscribe to this interpretation. In fact it is the critics who often argue that we need a better understanding of these local forms of resistance against the 'universal' force of the market.

The terms of this debate are quite misleading. We live in an age, to adapt Barber's nomenclature, of 'McJihad'. It is an age in which the mechanisms of what we call capitalism appear to operate, in certain critical instances, only by adopting the social force and moral authority of conservative Islamic movements. It

---

5   US Embassy (Islamabad), 'Official Informal for SA Assistant Secretary Robin Raphel'.

6   Benjamin R. Barber, *Jihad vs. McWorld: How Globalism and Tribalism are Reshaping the World*, New York: Ballantine Books, 1995: 4. Barber discusses a 'dialectic' of Jihad and McWorld, but means only that the forces he labels Jihad must be understood as a reaction to modernity, not a relic of the past (p. 157).

may be true that we need a better understanding of the local forces that oppose the globalisation of capital; but, more than this, we need a better understanding of the so-called global forces of capital.

The American government presented the war in Afghanistan that followed the attacks of 11 September 2001 as a fight to eliminate 'forces of evil', whose violence stemmed from an irrational and anti-modern hatred of the West. More sceptical accounts pointed to the role of the United States and its allies, from the mid-1970s to the early 1990s, in sustaining the Islamic forces fighting in Afghanistan – including al-Qaeda, the group led by Osama bin Laden and thought to be responsible for the September 11 attacks – and in facilitating, from 1994, the rise of the Taliban. These accounts attributed the crisis, at least in part, to the incoherence, contradictions and short-sightedness of US policy towards the region. While agreeing with such criticisms, a further point needs to be appreciated: the crisis in Afghanistan reflects the weaknesses of a form of empire, and of powers of capital, that can exist only by drawing on social forces that embody other energies, methods and goals.

THE *MUWAHHIDUN* AND THE MARKET

In 1930, Abd al-Aziz Ibn Saud, the ruler of what was to become Saudi Arabia, was short of funds as the Great Depression reduced the flow of pilgrims to Mecca – a city he had conquered five years earlier. He began negotiations with American oil companies to sell the rights to Arabian oil. The intermediary in these talks was an English businessman, Harry St John Philby. Born in British-ruled Ceylon, the son of a tea planter, Philby was an administrator in Britain's Indian Civil Service in Punjab and Kashmir. He had come to Iraq with the Indian army during the First World War, and went on to Arabia as an agent of Britain's Indian government to supply Ibn Saud with money and arms. He stayed on as a confidant of Ibn Saud, resigned from the Indian service, and set himself up in business in Jiddah, the trading port near Mecca, in 1925, the year it fell under Ibn Saud's control. He became the local agent of the Ford Motor Company, the Franklin Motor Company, and the Singer Manufacturing Company, and helped the Standard Oil Company of California negotiate the rights to Saudi oil. He also converted to Islam, and to the teachings of Ibn Wahhab. Although some doubted his sincerity, he went out of his way to publish articles in English newspapers in London and Cairo explaining his conviction. After discussing the puritanism of Oliver Cromwell as a reason for England's strength, he explained his belief

> that the present Arabian puritan movement harbingers an epoch of future political greatness based on strong moral and spiritual foundations. Also I regard the Islamic ethical system as a real democratic fraternity, and the general conduct of life . . .

resulting in a high standard of national public morality, as definitely superior to
the European ethical code based on Christianity . . . I consider an open declaration
of my sympathy with Arabian religion and political ideals as the best methods of
assisting the development of Arabian greatness.[7]

Philby's conversion may well have been sincere, although he continued to be
marked by convictions of 'agnosticism, atheism, anti-imperialism, socialism
and general progressive revolt against the philosophical and political cannons
in which I was brought up', and was later disillusioned with Ibn Saud's rule.[8]
But the American oil companies, too, were converts to Wahhabism, in the sense
that Standard Oil of California and its partners came to depend on and support
what they called 'unitarian' Islam as the method and the means to operate in
Arabia – and thus to maintain and develop the global oil economy.

Scholars of international political economy have devoted a lot of attention
to the world oil industry, but little to the role played in the economics of oil by
the *muwahhidun*. Four features of the political economy of oil, already familiar
from earlier chapters, can help us understand this role. First, as a main source
of energy for industrialised life, it offers the possibility of enormous rents – it
can be sold at one hundred times the cost of production. Second, contrary to
popular belief, throughout the twentieth century there was almost always too
much of it. Any producer was always at risk of being undercut by another. If all
one wanted was a market in oil to supply those who need it, this would pose no
problem. But the oil industry was concerned with profits, not markets, and large
profits are impossible to sustain under competitive conditions. The potential
rents – or 'premiums on scarcity' as they are called – could be realised only if
mechanisms were put in place to create that scarcity.

The international politics of oil is usually explained in terms of the desire of
the United States to protect the global supply. But that was not the problem. The
real issue, where the *muwahhidun* came in, was to protect the system of scarcity.
John D. Rockefeller solved the difficulty in the 1860s, when the oil industry
first developed, by building a monopoly – not of oil wells, but of refineries and
then transportation, later building Standard Oil into an integrated monopoly
controlling refining, transportation, marketing, and finally the wellheads themselves. In the twentieth century, when the major integrated oil companies began
to produce large quantities of oil outside the United States, they developed a
different system of scarcity: they collaborated to divide the world's resources
between themselves, and to limit production to maintain prices. In 1928, on
reaching the long-delayed agreement to share the development of oil in Iraq,

---

7   H. St. John B. Philby, 'Why I Turned Wahhabi', *Egyptian Gazette*, 26 September 1930,
cited in Elizabeth Monroe, *Philby of Arabia*, Reading: Ithaca Press, 1998 [1973]: 157–8.

8   Monroe, *Philby of Arabia*: 152, 200.

which included an undertaking to limit the development of oil elsewhere in the Middle East – and as efforts to prevent the export of oil by the Soviet Union collapsed – they made a parallel deal to divide the world's markets among themselves, and to limit production to maintain prices. They later agreed to try to maintain those prices at the relatively high price at which oil was produced and sold in Texas.

These arrangements prevented the emergence of market competition, and thus ensured extraordinary profits to those who controlled the cheaply produced oil of the Middle East. After the Second World War the oil companies were producing oil at less than 30 cents a barrel, including the costs of exploration, pumping, storage and depreciation; later that figure fell to 10 cents a barrel, while the companies were selling oil to refineries at $2 a barrel.[9] In the 1960s the producer countries of the south began to play a more independent role, and in the following decade the organisation they had created, the Organization of Petroleum Exporting Countries (OPEC), took over the role of maintaining the scarcity of supply, generally in collaboration with the international oil corporations and major non-OPEC producer countries.

The third salient feature of global oil is that, through these arrangements, one country – Saudi Arabia – came to play a special role. In the 1970s the country developed into one of three very large producers of oil, alongside the United States and Russia. By the 1990s, these three countries each produced two or three times as much oil as any of the other producers among the top dozen (Canada, Norway, the United Kingdom, China, Venezuela, Mexico, Kuwait, the United Arab Emirates and Iran).[10] Saudi Arabia's importance lay not simply in its abundance of supply, however, but in its pivotal role in the system of scarcity. With a population about one-tenth the size of Russia's and one-sixteenth that of the United States, Saudi Arabia at that time still had a relatively low domestic demand for oil and could afford to keep part of its production capacity switched off. By the 1990s, this unused capacity (then estimated at more than 3 million barrels per day) was close to or exceeded the *total* production of any other country except Russia and the US.[11] The excess allowed Saudi Arabia the ability to play the role of 'swing' producer (played in the pre-OPEC period by Iraq, and later by Kuwait, under the control of BP), threatening to switch its surplus on and off to discipline other producers who tried to exceed their production

9   Christopher T. Rand, *Making Democracy Safe for Oil: Oilmen and the Islamic East*, Boston: Little, Brown, 1975, 16–18.

10   For production figures see US Energy Information Administration, at www.eia.doe. gov. With the decline of North Sea production after 2000, Norway and the UK dropped out of the top dozen, to be replaced by Brazil and Iraq.

11   US Energy Information Administration, at www.eia.doe.gov. Surplus capacity is defined as oil production that can be brought on line within thirty days and sustained for at least ninety days.

quotas, thus maintaining the system of scarcity. It did so in collaboration with the United States, on whom it depended for military protection. As a result of these three factors – inelastic demand, overabundance and the Saudi surplus – the possibility of large oil rents anywhere in the world in the second half of the twentieth century depended on the political control of Arabia.

The fourth relevant characteristic of the global economy of oil is the method of creating this political control. In 1930 there was no state of 'Saudi Arabia', and no colonial power alone was strong enough to create one. This reflects the historical moment at which the global oil economy emerged – something the literature on the political economy of oil does not explore. It was not unusual for large corporations to avoid the risks of markets by establishing oligopolies or exclusive territories of operation. In fact, the modern, large-scale commercial corporation was invented precisely for that purpose. Its origins lie in the colonising corporations of the seventeenth to nineteenth centuries – the East India Company, the Hudson's Bay Company, the British South Africa Company, and many others – that were given exclusive rights and sovereign power to monopolise the trade in particular goods for specific territories. However, the major oil companies, which were the first and the largest of the new transnational corporations of the twentieth century, established their global presence at the historical moment when the old system of empire, built up originally through colonising corporations, was finally disintegrating.

The interwar period, when the oil corporations consolidated their global control of oil, coincided with the defeat and collapse of the forms of empire that had shaped world trade for more than three centuries. Four features of this power help to explain the significance of Islamic movements after its collapse. First, sovereign power belonged not only to a handful of European states, but also to the colonising corporations. The collapse of this form of power began much earlier in some places (in America in the revolt of 1776, for example, and in India in the uprising of 1857) than in others – in Africa, for example, European corporate power and the monopolies it created persisted well into the twentieth century. Second, earlier imperial power enjoyed a great advantage in military violence (always available to, and often established by, the colonising corporations), which could be used to defeat, and in many cases annihilate, local opposition to the colonial authority. Third, imperialism made use of the dispossessed agrarian populations of Europe to propagate white settler communities around the globe, which were rarely, if ever, subject to non-Western forms of law or political authority. Fourth, imperialism deployed a widely accepted principle of political, moral and intellectual organisation to create its social order: racism.

By 1945, all four of these elements of imperial power had been eroded. First, the new transnational oil companies had to establish their oligopolies and exclusive territories by secret collusion rather than imperial edict; they had to acquire the rights to particular territories by negotiation with local powers rather than by force. Military support was now available only in exceptional circumstances.

Second, although by 1945 the United States enjoyed preponderant global military power, its use was quite restricted. In the Arab world, the popular uprisings of 1919–20 (see Chapter 4), followed by the more extended Palestinian rebellion of 1936–39, had shown the British the difficulties of maintaining military occupation by force, and the Americans were to learn the same lesson a little later in south-east Asia. Part of the difficulty was that countries of the global south would no longer accept foreign military bases. In 1945 the United States had military bases in occupied Germany and Japan – but almost nowhere else in between. That year, it negotiated and began construction of a military base at Dhahran, the centre of Aramco's oil operations in Saudi Arabia. In the 1950s Dhahran became the largest US military base anywhere between Germany and Japan. Washington managed to retain the base only until 1962, when popular anti-imperialism forced the Saudi government to ask the Americans to leave. Not until three decades later, following Iraq's invasion of Kuwait in August 1990, were the Americans provided with an opportunity to reoccupy the base.

Third, by the 1930s, population growth in most northern European countries had slowed drastically or halted altogether, and there was no longer a large white settler population able to accompany the establishing of overseas corporate operations. Moreover, the smaller groups of white settlers that accompanied corporate expansion abroad, such as the American colony in Dhahran, no longer enjoyed complete immunity from local law.

Finally, the rise of fascism and the Nazi holocaust in Germany had suddenly rendered European racism an embarrassing system of political and social organisation. Corporations like Aramco brought all the methods of American racial segregation of labour to Arabia, with separate residential compounds and standards of living for four separate racial groups (Americans, Italians, Indians and non-Saudi Arabs, and Saudis), and the British imported similar arrangements to Iran and Iraq from India. But corporate racism led to frequent labour protests, making the position of the oil companies increasingly fragile.[12]

This historical context, then, represents the fourth significant feature of the political economy of oil: the major oil companies required a system based on the exclusive control of oil production and limits to the quantity of oil produced – only an anti-market arrangement of this sort could guarantee their profits. But they sought to consolidate such an arrangement, beginning in the 1930s, and again after the Second World War, at precisely the moment when the old

---

12   Robert Vitalis, *America's Kingdom: Mythmaking on the Saudi Oil Frontier*, 2nd edn, London: Verso, 2009.

methods for establishing exclusive control over the production of resources overseas – colonialism – were in the process of collapse. It was these factors that were to give political Islam its special role in the political economy of oil.

A MORAL ALLIANCE

Ibn Saud, the future king of the future Saudi Arabia, grew up in exile in the British protectorate of Kuwait. In 1902 he captured his family's former base, the town of Riyadh in central Arabia, and for the following quarter of a century was one of several warlords competing to control the Arabian peninsula. He depended initially on funds from British India, and subsequently on an alliance with the *muwahhidun*. Although not himself especially devout, he drew his strongest military force from the Ikhwan, or Brotherhood – an egalitarian movement attempting to replace the increasingly threatened life of Arabian tribal nomadism with settlement and agriculture, and the degenerate practices of saint worship and excessive veneration of the Prophet with the strict monotheism of *tawhid*. The Ikhwan revived the classical doctrine of *jihad* (the duty to struggle against unbelievers) and expanded it to justify war even against those fellow Muslims whom they considered to have abandoned the true form of Islam. In place of tribal raiding and the extraction of income from the declining trans-Arabian caravan trade, the Ikhwan joined Ibn Saud in a war against what they saw as the polytheism of the wider Muslim community.

In 1913–14 Ibn Saud took control of eastern Arabia (whose mainly Shi'a population the *muwahiddun* considered heretics). 'Akhwanism is not the entirely bad movement it is made out to be', reported the British agent in Bahrain, following an investigative trip to al-Hasa in 1920. 'It seems to be a genuine religious revival, an attempt on the part of the masses of Central Arabia to improve themselves religiously and mentally.' Ibn Saud, the agent reported, 'thought to make use of the movement to strengthen his position, but in the end found he was forced to spread its doctrines and become its leader lest he should go under himself'. However, both Ibn Saud and his lieutenants 'have the movement well in hand'.[13] After capturing north-western Arabia, in 1925 Ibn Saud seized the kingdom of Hejaz in the west, which contained the holy cities of Mecca and Medina with their powerful merchant families, and provided its ruler with a large annual income from pilgrimages to Mecca. The Ikhwan began to impose their form of purified Islam on the Hejazis, destroying a memorial at the prophet Muhammad's birthplace, and other places of worship they considered improper, and banning the consumption of alcohol and tobacco. To control the Ikhwan's zeal, Ibn Saud set up his own committees on public morality, charged

---

13   H. R. P. Dickson, 'Notes on the "Akhwan" Movement', June 1920, National Archives of the UK: Public Record Office: Cabinet Office Records, PRO CAB 24/107.

with the suppression of vice and, increasingly, policing the spread of 'harmful ideas' and participation in anti-government meetings.[14]

The autocratic rule that Ibn Saud was building relied on British funding and weapons to defeat rival powers in Arabia; the Ikhwan were dedicated to ridding Arabia of personal corruption and immorality, which they associated with the presence and power of colonialism. Inevitably a tension arose between the ruler's need for foreign support and the puritan force that helped him conquer and rule Arabia. Following the conquest of Hejaz, the Ikhwan began pushing to expand their jihad northwards into Jordan, Kuwait and Iraq – British protectorates that Ibn Saud could not afford to challenge. In 1927 the Ikhwan rebelled against Ibn Saud's restraint on their expansion. With British help, he crushed the revolt, and by 1930 had neutralised the Ikhwan movement.

The *muwahhidun* remained a powerful force in Arabian politics, but were unable to prevent Ibn Saud's accommodation with the imperial powers that financed him. In the same year that he defeated the Ikhwan, he began negotiations with the Standard Oil Company of California (now Chevron), mediated by St John Philby, and began to switch from British to American protection. To win acceptance for this foreign support, he made a compromise with the religious establishment. The *muwahhidun* leadership would tolerate the role of the foreign oil company, and in return their programme to convert Arabia to the teachings and discipline of *tawhid* would be funded with the proceeds from oil.

Thus this successful warlord depended on two different forces to construct the new political order in Arabia. The Arabian-American Oil Company (Aramco) provided the funds, as well as technical and material assistance.[15] The company built the country's new towns, road system, railway, telecommunications network, ports and airports, and acted as banker to the ruling family and investor in Saudi enterprise, especially in contracting local companies to serve Aramco's needs in eastern Arabia. Aramco paid the oil royalty not to a national government but to a single household, that of Ibn Saud, who now called himself king and renamed the country, previously the provinces of Hejaz and Nejd, the 'Kingdom of Saudi Arabia', creating the only country in the world to be named after a family. As a consequence of this corporate arrangement, the millions and

---

14   Alexei Vassiliev, *The History of Saudi Arabia*, New York: New York University Press, 2000: 270–1.

15   Standard Oil of California established Aramco in 1933 as the California Arabian Standard Oil Company, adding Texaco as co-owner in 1936. In 1943, Socal persuaded the US government to take over the company's and Great Britain's funding of the Saudi government. The US government then decided to nationalise the company. Socal managed to limit the proposed state ownership to one-third, but then Exxon and Mobil defeated the plan. In response to these threats, in 1944 Socal renamed the company the Arabian American Oil Company (Aramco), and in 1946 agreed to add Exxon and Mobil as co-owners. Irvine H. Anderson, *Aramco, the United States, and Saudi Arabia: A Study of the Dynamics of Foreign Oil Policy*, 1933–1950, Princeton: Princeton University Press, 1981.

later billions of dollars paid for oil each year became the private income of a single kin group – albeit one that reproduced so successfully that within three or four generations Ibn Saud's offspring were said to number some 7,000.[16] This 'privatisation' of oil money was locally unpopular, and required outside help to keep it in place. In 1945 the US government established its military base at Dhahran, and later began to train and arm Ibn Saud's security forces, which imprisoned, threatened, tortured, executed or exiled those who opposed the ruling family. The religious establishment, on the other hand, created the moral and legal order of the new state, imposing the strict social regime that maintained discipline in the subject population and suppressed political dissent.

When Aramco began to expand its operations after the Second World War, opposition emerged among the workforce to the company's system of racial segregation and inequality. In response to a series of strikes in 1945 in protest against the unequal pay and living conditions of different racial groups, Aramco set up an Arabian Affairs division, to gather better intelligence on its workforce and try and root out 'labor agitators'.[17] A further series of protests culminated in a general strike in July 1956. The workers' demands included the introduction of a political constitution; the right to form labour unions, political parties and national organisations; an end to Aramco's interference in the country's affairs; the closure of the US military base; and the release of imprisoned workers. Aramco's security department identified the leaders to the Saudi security forces, including the Ikhwan. The government had re-established Ikhwan militias in the 1950s, renamed the National Guard – although its members were still called *mujahideen* ('those engaged in jihad') – to provide a counterweight to the army, itself the locus of considerable dissent. Hundreds of protesters were arrested, tortured and sentenced to prison terms or deported from the country. During these events, as ever, American oil executives and the forces of jihad worked hand-in-hand to keep the political economy of oil in place.[18]

With internal opposition to this political economy of oil silenced, the main threat came from abroad – from the nationalist governments of Egypt and Iraq, which in the later 1950s began to denounce the corruption of the Saudi monarchy and its misappropriation of what they now referred to as 'Arab oil'. To meet this threat, the government of Saudi Arabia used oil money to enable the religious establishment to promote its programme of moral authority and

---

16   Saïd K. Aburish, *The Rise, Corruption, and Coming Fall of the House of Saud*, 2nd edn, New York: St Martin's Griffin, 1996: 7. Aburish estimates that about 15 per cent of national oil income is taken as the private income of the royal family. Most of this money is deducted from the country's oil income before it is recorded in national accounts, so precise figures are unavailable. This money excludes the family's income from pay-offs on arms purchases and other non-oil trade (pp. 294–5).

17   Vitalis, *America's Kingdom*: 92–8.

18   Vitalis, *America's Kingdom*: 176–83; Vassiliev, *History of Saudi Arabia*: 337.

social conservatism abroad. In particular, they funded the revival of an Islamic political movement in Egypt, which the government of Gamal Abdel Nasser had attempted to suppress in the late 1950s. They supported similar movements in Pakistan and throughout the region.

Aramco's political officers had helped devise this scheme. William Eddy, the CIA agent on Aramco's staff, had called for 'a moral alliance between Christians and Muslims against the common threat of communism'. Informed of 'the coolness of the response' when the idea was relayed to ambassadors of the more secular governments of Lebanon, Jordan and Iraq, he acknowledged 'it was not their dish and it was not meant for them'.[19] By 1956, Eisenhower was being won over to the idea of promoting King Saud, who had succeeded his father Ibn Saud in 1953, as a rival regional leader to Nasser. The US president noted in his diary that 'Arabia is a country that contains the holy places of the Moslem world, and the Saudi Arabians are considered to be the most deeply religious of all the Arab groups. Consequently, the King could be built up, possibly, as a spiritual leader. Once this were accomplished, we might begin to urge his right to political leadership'.[20] King Saud preferred to side with Arab nationalists and reformers, so the Americans shifted their support to his rival, Prince Faisal, who served as his brother's prime mister and then ousted him in 1964. Faisal removed reformists and modernisers from government, including the minister of petroleum, Abdullah Taraki, who had helped establish OPEC, was planning the gradual Saudi takeover of Aramco, and was one of a group of Saudi administrators and intellectuals making plans for a written constitution, an elected parliament and a programme of industrialisation. Championed by the Americans as an enlightened monarch, the reactionary Faisal resumed the campaign against Nasserism and in support of Islamist movements abroad.[21] The Americans, it seems, were ready to help. A former foreign affairs editor of *Newsweek*, Harry Kern, who according to the British embassy in Cairo 'runs an intelligence machinery for the oil companies in the region and cooperates in this with the CIA', was said by local sources to be 'behind the use of "Islam" as a political springboard for King Feisal's role outside his country'.[22]

19   William A. Eddy Papers, letter from Myron B. Smith, 19 December 1950, and reply from Eddy, 29 December 1950, Box 8, General Correspondence, Folder 7, 1948–54, Public Policy Papers, Department of Rare Books and Special Collections, Princeton University Library.

20   'Diary Entry by the President', 28 March 1956, FRUS, 1955–57, XV, cited Matthew F. Jacobs, 'The Perils and Promise of Islam: The United States and the Muslim Middle East in the Early Cold War', *Diplomatic History* 30: 4, 2006: 734. See also Salim Yaqub, *Containing Arab Nationalism: The Eisenhower Doctrine and the Middle East*, Chapel Hill: University of North Carolina Press, 2004: 44.

21   Vitalis, *America's Kingdom*: 188–264; Nathan J. Citino, *From Arab Nationalism to OPEC: Eisenhower, King Sa'ud, and the Making of US-Saudi Relations*, Bloomington: Indiana University Press, 2002: 95–6, 125–33.

22   Canadian Embassy (British Interests Section), Cairo, to Foreign Office, 8 July 1966, National Archives of the UK: PRO, FO 371/185483-0001.

Meanwhile, former Aramco employees now working for the CIA helped hatch plots to kill the presidents of Egypt and Iraq, whose governments had introduced land reform, women's rights, universal education and other populist programmes. Nasser survived, but in 1963 the Iraqi government was overthrown and the president killed in a US-supported military coup that brought to power the Ba'th – the party of Saddam Hussein (see Chapter 6).[23] One other pillar of US Middle East policy was established in the same period, from around 1958: the decision to arm and finance the state of Israel, as another agent, alongside Islamic conservatism, that would help undermine Arab nationalism.[24]

The fact that oil money helped develop the power of the *muwahhidun* in Arabia after 1930 and made possible the resurgence of Islamic political movements in the 1970s has often been noted. But it is equally important to understand that, by the same token, it was an Islamic movement that made possible the profits of the oil industry. The political economy of oil did not happen, in some incidental way, to rely on a government in Saudi Arabia that owed its own power to the force of an Islamic political movement. Given the features of the political economy of oil – the enormous rents available, the difficulty in securing those rents due to the overabundance of supply, the pivotal role of Saudi Arabia in maintaining scarcity, the collapse of older colonial methods of imposing anti-market corporate control of the Saudi oilfields – oil profits depended on working with those forces that could guarantee the political control of Arabia: the House of Saud in alliance with the *muwahhidun*. The latter were not incidental, but became an internal element in the political economy of oil. 'Jihad' was not simply a local force antithetical to the development of 'McWorld'; McWorld, it turns out, was really McJihad, a necessary combination of a variety of social logics and forces.

The idea of McJihad requires a distinctive understanding not so much of the historical role of particular Islamic movements, but of the nature of what we call global capitalism. Even among its critics, capitalism is usually talked about in terms of its logic and its power. 'Jihad', in this view, stands for a localised and external resistance to capitalism's homoficient historical logic.[25] The history of McJihad, in contrast, is a history of a certain incoherence and weakness, of a

---

23   On the possible role of the CIA in the plot to kill Nasser, see Aburish, *House of Saud*: 128. On the CIA's failed attempt to murder President Qasim of Iraq in February 1960, see Thomas Powers, 'Inside the Department of Dirty Tricks: Part One, An Isolated Man', *Atlantic Monthly*, August 1979. On CIA support for the 1963 coup see PBS/Frontline, 'The Survival of Saddam: An Interview with James Akins', at www.pbs.org.

24   The consequences of this alliance with Israel were explored in our discussion of the 1973–74 oil crisis.

25   The 'homoficience' of capital refers to the view that, regardless of local variation, at some level capitalism always does the same thing, or has the same effect. See Timothy Mitchell, *Rule of Experts: Egypt, Techno-Politics, Modernity*, Berkeley: University of California Press, 2002: 245.

politics 'ridden with inner tensions'. It is a concept that directs attention to the impossibility of securing the enormous profits of oil except through arrangements that relied on quite dynamic but seemingly uncapitalist social forces. But in what sense were these forces 'uncapitalist'? They were not some pre-capitalist, 'cultural' element resisting capitalism from the outside. Whatever their historical roots, they were dynamic forces of the twentieth century, whose role developed with the development of oil. Yet their role in the economy of oil was a disjunctive one. While it was essential to the making of oil profits, political Islam was not itself orientated towards that goal. The *muwahhidun* and other Islamic movements had their own agendas – sometimes stemming from injustices and inequalities that people suffered, or from threats to local ways of living a moral life or to local arrangements of hierarchy and respect, including male prerogatives in family and gender relations. Seen as a process of McJihad, oil-based industrial capitalism no longer appears self-sufficient. Its success depends on other forces, which are both essential to and disjunctive with the process we call capitalist development.

MAINTENANCE WORK

In 1967–74, as we saw in the previous two chapters, relations between producer states, the major oil companies and the United States were transformed. Following that transformation, militarism, crisis and war played an increasing role in managing the tensions of McJihad. The greatly increased oil revenues after 1973 were recycled into the US and other Western economies – partly through Saudi purchases of US Treasury bonds and other investments in the West, but also through extensive purchases of American and European military equipment, which accelerated after the oil boom. Arms manufacturers joined oil companies in the increasing dependence of their profits on political arrangements in the Middle East. Meanwhile, Western banks, awash in the flood of petrodollars, embarked on a disastrous series of loans to governments in the global south. When the loans failed, the banks helped devise the programme known as structural adjustment, which made the people of those countries rather than their governments or the bankers pay for the failure. In Egypt, for example, where the banks made especially bad loans, structural adjustment reduced spending on schools, medicines, factories and farming, but left lucrative state construction projects and large military budgets intact.[26] The United States found it increasingly difficult to keep in power the autocratic governments on which this political economy of oil depended, and the essential role played within it by political Islam became increasingly disjunctive.

---

26   Ibid.: 209–303.

The series of crises is well known. From 1975, opposition to the shah's dictatorship in Iran gathered strength, and critical sections of the religious establishment began to turn against the regime, whose resort to violence and repression stimulated a revolutionary movement in 1978–79 that overthrew the state. In Egypt, the government encouraged the Islamist movement in the 1970s as a means of weakening secular political opposition, but faced increasing popular protest and dissent, culminating in the January 1977 food riots, when crowds protesting against the government's doubling of the price of bread occupied Tahrir Square in Cairo. After the security forces killed dozens, and possibly hundreds, of protesters, the demonstrations spread across the country. The government was able to re-establish control only when it rescinded the price increases.[27] In October 1981, the members of a militant Islamist cell seeking to take advantage of this popular outrage assassinated President Sadat and attempted an armed uprising, which the military regime quickly suppressed.

Over the following decade Washington increased its involvement in maintaining or prolonging a series of wars and political conflicts, through the arming of protagonists and the blocking of diplomatic solutions. Other outside powers – principally Britain, France and the Soviet Union – also supplied weapons, and several local states resorted to military violence, in some cases using it continuously as a means of repression. But what distinguished the United States was the breadth of its involvement in the use of violence across the region, its increasing reliance on wars of attrition as a normal instrument of politics, and its efforts to prevent the resolution of conflicts. There were three major instances of this policy – Iran/Iraq, Afghanistan, and Israel/Palestine.

The Iranian Revolution had left the United States without an ally in either of the two major powers in the Gulf, Iran and Iraq. In September 1980 Iraq invaded Iran, with no objection from Washington, and possibly with its encouragement.[28] The United States then seized the opportunity to weaken both countries by working to prevent a resolution to the war. Washington gave Iraq enough financial and military support to avoid defeat, but left it unable to extricate itself from the conflict. At the same time US weapons were supplied to Iran, mostly by Israel,

---

27   Yahya M. Sadowski, *Political Vegetables? Businessman and Bureaucrat in the Development of Egyptian Agriculture*, Washington, DC: Brookings Institution, 1991: 156.

28   Iraq planned a short war modelled on Israel's Six-Day War of 1967, to seize the Shatt al-Arab waterway and a section of adjoining territory. Achieving this on the fifth day of the war, 28 September, Iraq halted its advance and announced it was willing to cease fighting and negotiate a settlement. The United States delayed action at the Security Council until this point, then passed a resolution that called for a ceasefire but made no mention of Iraq's aggression or a return of forces to the international border. Efraim Karsh, 'Military Power and Foreign Policy Goals: The Iran–Iraq War Revisited', *International Affairs* 64: 1, Winter 1987–88: 92; Saïd K. Aburish, *Saddam Hussein: The Politics of Revenge*, New York: Bloomsbury, 1999: 186–9, gives evidence of closer US–Iraqi ties on the eve of the war.

while Washington rejected Soviet attempts to organise peace talks.[29] In 1983–84, Iraq attempted to end the war by escalating it to new levels – first by using chemical weapons against Iran, then by attacking oil facilities and shipping in the Gulf. When the US envoy Donald Rumsfeld discussed this escalation with Saddam Hussein in December 1983, the Iraqi president explained that 'what was needed was to stop the war, or put the Gulf in a balanced situation for both belligerents'. The United States chose the latter course, increasing its support for Iraq.[30] Washington also worked to prevent any UN resolution that would penalise Iraq for launching the war or make it liable for reparations – the conditions Iran demanded for ending the fighting. The US helped to keep the war going for eight years, at a cost of more than a million people killed and wounded in the two countries.

After the war the United States hoped to turn Iraq's wartime dependence on its support into a long-term economic and political relationship. But Saddam Hussein's invasion of Kuwait in August 1990, intended to solve the financial crisis the earlier war had caused, put an end to that possibility. Instead it provided Washington with a further opportunity to weaken Iraq through a protracted conflict. After driving the Iraqi forces from Kuwait, the United States and Britain established the UN sanctions regime, officially to disarm Iraq, but in practice used to keep the country financially crippled and prevent its economic recovery. Washington justified this policy by claiming that Iraq had failed to disarm, although it produced no evidence for the claim. The available evidence indicated that Iraq was known to have eliminated its proscribed weapons and weapons programmes by 1995. The United States and Britain kept this knowledge secret in order to delay the removal of the sanctions.[31] In March 1997, Washington

---

29   M. S. El Azhary, 'The Attitudes of the Superpowers Towards the Gulf War', *International Affairs* 59: 4, Autumn 1983: 614, 616.

30   Rumsfeld had been warned by US diplomats before the talks that, 'Given its desperation to end the war, Iraq may again use lethal or incapacitating CW [chemical weapons]'. Rumsfeld told Saddam Hussein that 'it was not in interest of region or the West for conflict to create instability or for outcome to be one which weakened Iraq's role or enhanced interests and ambitions of Iran'. US Department of State, Office of the Assistant Secretary for Near Eastern and South Asian Affairs, Action Memorandum from Jonathan T. Howe to Lawrence S. Eagleburger, 'Iraqi Use of Chemical Weapons', 21 November 1983; and United States Embassy in United Kingdom Cable from Charles H. Price II to the Department of State, 'Rumsfeld Mission: December 20 Meeting with Iraqi President Saddam Hussein', 21 December 1983, both documents available at National Security Archive, 'Shaking Hands with Saddam Hussein', www.gwu.edu/~nsarchiv.

31   The evidence available before the 2003 war, and confirmed after it, indicated that Iraq's nuclear weapons programme and its chemical weapons stocks and production facilities were destroyed under UN supervision soon after the 1991 war. Iraq also destroyed its biological weapons stocks then, but without informing the UN. The existence of the pre-1991 biological weapons programme was not revealed until 1995, when two senior Iraqi officials defected; the biological weapons facility was destroyed by UNSCOM in 1996. The defectors also revealed that the programme had been disbanded, but this part of their information was kept secret by Washington, as it would remove the argument for retaining sanctions. The US and Britain also claimed that it was technically feasible for Iraq to have produced more chemical weapons in the 1980s than the quantities it declared and destroyed after 1991. They had no evidence to support this hypothesis,

declared that sanctions would remain in place indefinitely, even if Iraq were found to have complied with its obligations regarding proscribed weapons, and eighteen months later passed a law allocating to 'democratic' groups attempting to overthrow the Iraqi government funds of $99 million, of which $97 million was for military assistance.[32] A bombing campaign to enforce no-fly zones, which had no UN authorisation, was escalated periodically to further harass the Iraqi regime, and information gathered in the UN weapons inspections was used in a series of unsuccessful American efforts to assassinate the Iraqi leadership.

By 1998, Washington's policy of protracted violence in the Gulf had been in place for two decades; but it was proving difficult to sustain. Grassroots campaigns against the sanctions publicised the fact that they had contributed to as many as half a million infant deaths in Iraq, and that the United States was continuing to use them to block the supply of medicines, water-purification equipment and food-processing machinery. France and Russia, to whom Iraq owed billions of dollars, wanted to pursue economic opportunities in the country. In response, in December 1998 Washington withdrew the UN inspectors and escalated the bombing. By halting the inspections the United States delayed the risk of their completion and thus of an end to the sanctions, buying more time for its efforts to bring down the Iraqi regime.

On Iran's other flank, in Afghanistan, Washington helped exacerbate a second conflict and transform it into a protracted war. US involvement in Afghanistan is usually seen as a response to the Soviet military intervention of 1979. In fact it began earlier, and its goal may have been to provoke the invasion by Soviet troops and prevent their withdrawal. In 1973, army officers had overthrown the Afghan monarchy and, in alliance with the left, promised a programme of land reform and social transformation. The shah's Iran, encouraged by the United States, initiated a scheme of aid and intervention to weaken

---

despite exhaustive UN inspections. The effectiveness of the hypothesis as an argument for sanctions (and later war) lay not in any supporting evidence, but in the fact that there was no way Iraq could disprove it. This inability to disprove allegations was presented by the US government and media as a sign of Iraq's duplicity. 'We said Saddam Hussein was a master of denial and deception', a senior US member of the UN inspection team later said. 'Then when we couldn't find anything, we said that proved it, instead of questioning our own assumptions.' Quoted in Bob Drogin, 'US Suspects It Received False Iraq Arms Tips', *Los Angeles Times*, 28 August 2003. See Sarah Graham-Brown, *Sanctioning Saddam: The Politics of Intervention in Iraq*, London: I. B. Tauris in association with MERIP, 1999; and Glen Rangwala, 'Claims and Evaluations of Iraq's Proscribed Weapons', 18 March 2003, available at www.grassrootspeace.org/iraqweapons.html. On the failure of a CIA mission to find any evidence of proscribed weapons or weapons programmes after the 2003 war, see 'Statement on the Interim Progress Report on the Activities of the Iraq Survey Group', 2 October 2003, available at www.cia.gov/news-information/speeches-testimony/2003/david_kay_10022003.html.

32   Secretary of State Madeleine Albright explained: 'We do not agree with the nations who argue that if Iraq complies with its obligations concerning weapons of mass destruction, sanctions should be lifted.' Speech at George Washington University, 26 March 1997, available at www. globalsecurity.org/wmd/library/news/iraq/1997/bmd970327b.htm. The text of the Iraq Liberation Act is available at thomas.loc.gov/home/bills_res.html.

the leftist elements in Kabul and draw the country away from its longstanding reliance on Soviet support into the orbit of US–Iranian power. Like other US-backed interventions, this one ended in failure. In April 1978, the Afghan left seized power, introduced a radical programme of land reform in an attempt to overthrow the old social order by force, and turned to the Soviet Union for increased support. As political unrest spread across the country, the United States began to underwrite Pakistan's efforts to destabilise the government, and in March 1979 started discussing plans for what a Pentagon strategist called 'sucking the Soviets into a Vietnamese quagmire' in Afghanistan.

Informed by its Soviet specialist that 'a substantial US covert aid programme could raise the stakes and induce the Soviets to intervene more directly', in April the National Security Council approved a secret programme of support for counter-revolutionary forces attempting to overthrow the Afghan government.[33] In July Washington began to arm the Pakistan-supported Islamic political parties known as the *mujahideen*. The jihad was to be funded jointly by the United States and Saudi Arabia, equipped with Soviet-style weapons from Egypt, China and Israel, and supplied with additional recruits from the Islamic movements of Egypt, Saudi Arabia, Yemen and other countries.[34] US support for the Islamic forces based in Pakistan began almost six months before the Soviet invasion, and its aim was not to oppose that invasion but, if anything, to provoke it. As US national security advisor Zbigniew Brzezinski later confirmed, the US hoped to cause a war that would embroil the Soviet Union in 'its own Vietnam'.[35] The Soviet attempt to negotiate a withdrawal beginning in 1983 was rejected by Washington in favour of prolonging the war. The pro-war party within the US government, led by Richard Perle, arranged to more than double the supply of arms to the *mujahideen* in a successful effort to delay the Soviet departure.[36]

The third major conflict that the United States helped maintain was that between Israel and the Palestinians. Like the other two, it is a conflict in which

---

33   Robert Michael Gates, *From the Shadows: The Ultimate Insider's Story of Five Presidents and How They Won the Cold War*, New York: Touchstone, 1997: 145–6. On the political unrest that spread in response to the attempt to break the old social order through land reform, see Barnett R. Rubin, *The Fragmentation of Afghanistan: State Formation and Collapse in the International System*, 2nd edn, New Haven: Yale University Press, 2002: 111–21.

34   John K. Cooley, *Unholy Wars: Afghanistan, America and International Terrorism*, 2nd edn, London: Pluto Press, 2000; Rubin, *Fragmentation of Afghanistan*: 197.

35   'How Jimmy Carter and I Started the Mujahideen: Interview with Zbigniew Brzezinski', *Le Nouvel Observateur*, 15–21 January 1998: 76. The interview was not included in the abridged edition of the magazine sold in the United States.

36   Diego Cordovez and Selig S. Harrison, *Out of Afghanistan: The Inside Story of the Soviet Withdrawal*, London: OUP, 1995: 102–5, details the Reagan administration's efforts to prevent a Soviet withdrawal. Cordovez, the United Nations undersecretary-general for special political affairs, negotiated the Geneva Accords of 1988 that provided a framework for the Soviet withdrawal, completed in 1989. US aid to the *mujahideen* increased from $120 million in fiscal year 1984 to $250 million in 1985, and almost doubled again in the later 1980s, when combined US and Saudi aid reached $1 billion per year (Rubin, *Fragmentation of Afghanistan*: 180–1).

the US role is widely misunderstood. Following the June 1967 war, the Israeli government adopted the Allon plan, a programme for the gradual colonisation of the newly occupied Palestinian lands and their incorporation into Israel, while reserving pockets of territory for the occupied population, to be administered by Jordan or a quisling Palestinian authority. In opposition to this scheme, the United Nations, the European Union and the Arab states presented a series of proposals to resolve the conflict, based on an end to the occupation and the creation of a Palestinian state alongside Israel.[37] These proposals were ignored or rejected by the United States, which vetoed all calls for an international peace conference.[38] Instead, Washington helped Israel implement the Allon plan. As an alternative to an internationally imposed settlement, which would require an immediate end to the Israeli occupation, Washington promoted a series of agreements – the 1979 Camp David accords, the 1993 Oslo accords, and the 2003 Road Map – all of which left the occupation in place.[39] In April 2011, when President Barack Obama called on the Palestinians to negotiate with Israel for the creation of a state 'based on the 1967 lines with mutually agreed swaps', he was continuing this strategy.[40] The policy of forcing an occupied people to negotiate the terms of its subjugation

---

37   The United States refused to support the 1971 Sadat peace proposal, the UN Security Council proposal of January 1976, the PLO proposals of 1977, the 1980 Venice Declaration, the 1981 Fahd peace plan, the 1982 Rabat initiative, the 1983 UN peace conference proposal, and numerous subsequent efforts to end the occupation on the basis of a two-state solution, including the Arab Peace Initiative announced in 2002 and reissued on multiple occasions.

38   See Chapter 7. The partial exceptions to this US veto were the Geneva talks planned for 1977 and the Madrid talks of 1991–93, although at Israel's request the US prevented the participation of the Palestinian leadership in both cases. When the talks still threatened to put pressure on Israel to end the occupation, Israel undermined them by opening secret talks outside the conference, offering a concession to a single party – with the Egyptians in 1977, offering them the return of the Sinai, and with the PLO in 1993, offering them a role in administering Palestinian enclaves in the occupied territories and future talks about their status.

39   On 24 June 2002, the United States appeared to end its policy of refusing to support the creation of a Palestinian state, when President George W. Bush mentioned that 'My vision is two states, living side by side in peace and security'. Unopposed by Washington, however, Israel had by then started constructing a wall around and within the West Bank (the Gaza Strip had been fenced in a decade earlier) separating Palestinian neighbourhoods of Jerusalem and its environs from the rest of the West Bank and further dividing the latter into enclaves cut up by Zionist settlements and Jewish-only roads, making it clear that the Palestinian 'state' was to be a series of Israeli-controlled enclosures, as envisioned in the Allon plan, rather than a sovereign political territory. Maps of US and Israeli boundary proposals since the Oslo accords show how closely they follow the Allon plan (available at www.passia.org).

40   Obama retained the US position that any Palestinian state could be established only by mutual agreement with Israel, and that in the interim, whose duration was unspecified and also subject to Israel's agreement, Palestinians had to demonstrate the 'effectiveness of security arrangements' – exactly the conditions that enabled Israel to use the Oslo accords as a delaying mechanism to consolidate its colonisation of large areas of greater Jerusalem and other parts of the occupied territories. The White House, Office of the Press Secretary, 'Remarks by the President on the Middle East', at www.whitehouse.gov/briefing-room.

with the occupying power, for which there was no precedent in any other modern conflict, enabled Israel to proceed with the colonisation, accelerating its seizure of land and the planting of Zionist settlements with each successive 'peace plan', while the US gave Israel the financial and military support necessary to maintain the occupation and suppress Palestinian resistance to it.

None of the three conflicts discussed here was initiated by the United States. In each case there was an existing conflict or international dispute in which local parties were willing to resort to force. Other outside powers were involved, either indirectly through the supply of arms to the protagonists, or directly, for example in the Soviet intervention in Afghanistan. Most governments in the region used military or police violence as a normal instrument of politics, either against specific groups (Turkey against its Kurdish population; the Sudanese government against its rural populations; Israel against the Palestinians), or as a general instrument of repression. The role of the United States, however, was different. It was distinguished by the breadth of its involvement in the use of violence across the Middle East, the scale of its financial commitment to providing the means for carrying it out, and its increasing reliance on long-running conflict as a normal instrument of politics. These policies contributed to making the last quarter of the twentieth century perhaps the most violent period in the region's recorded history.

The perpetuation of conflict was a symptom of the relative weakness of the United States, given its imperial ambitions. Unable to establish its hegemony over many parts of the region, or even to control it by force, it fell back upon protracted warfare as the next best means of weakening those local powers that refused to accept its authority.

EXPORT FIGURES

In Saudi Arabia, meanwhile, the increasing levels of opposition to the corruption of the ruling dynasty and the repression of political activity found its outlet in the religious schools and mosque preachers of the *muwahhidun* – the only form of political expression the regime could not suppress. The discontent was briefly visible in November 1979, when armed rebels seized control of significant territory around the holy cities of Mecca and Medina. The following month, one thousand militants seized the Grand Mosque in Mecca, calling for the liberation of the country from the rule of the Saud dynasty. They denounced the hypocrisy of the government for paying outward respect to religion while engaging in 'oppression, corruption, and bribery'. They criticised the Saud family for seizing people's land and squandering the state's money while living 'a dissolute life in luxurious palaces'. Government troops took a week to regain control of the mosque, killing hundreds of the rebels. Their leader and sixty-three other survivors were later executed.[41]

---

41   Vassiliev, *History of Saudi Arabia*.

Political discontent increased in the 1980s, especially after the collapse of the price of oil in 1984–85, which precipitated a fiscal crisis, a sharp fall in national income and high levels of unemployment. The Saudi government saw in Afghanistan a solution to these growing domestic difficulties. It exported as many as 12,000 young religious activists, increasingly critical of the corruption of the ruling family, to fight the crusade against the Soviet Union in Afghanistan.[42] Osama bin Laden emerged as the coordinator of the anti-communist crusade, benefiting from both his family's close connections to the Saudi regime and his standing outside the country's system of powerful kin groups, as the son of an immigrant from Yemen, enabling him to appeal to followers across boundaries of kinship. In the 1990s, as the *mujahideen* returned from Afghanistan, the country's economic difficulties worsened. The 1990–91 war against Iraq galvanised a much broader opposition. Despite the billions of dollars squandered on arms purchases in preceding years, the regime suddenly appeared helpless, hastily agreeing to the arrival of American forces to save it from the Iraqi threat. The combination of factors keeping the regime in power – the military resources of the West and the local authority of the *muwahhidun* – was becoming increasingly difficult to hold together. Returning from Afghanistan, and gaining new recruits, the jihadists launched campaigns to drive the foreign troops out of the Arabian peninsula, as they had done in Afghanistan, while others launched a campaign to destabilise the American-supported government in Egypt. They also turned their attention to direct attacks against the United States, culminating in the September 11 attacks on New York and Washington in 2001.

BACK TO IRAQ

In the decade that followed the September 11 attacks, two events transformed the politics of the Middle East. The first was the American-led invasion of Iraq in 2003; the second was the wave of revolutionary uprisings that moved across the region in 2011.

The Iraq war was an attempt to overcome the weaknesses of McJihad, but ended by generating greater difficulties and an increased dependence on disjunctive local forces. The US decision to invade Iraq was a response to the impasse reached by the end of the 1990s, after two decades of war, sanctions and covert operations had failed to bring about the collapse of either the Islamic Republic in Iran or the Ba'thist state in Iraq. The sanctions against Iraq had in fact strengthened the state and the ruling party, by making the general population more dependent on the regime for food rations and other necessities. In addition, as a British intelligence report explained, 'Regionally, Saddam has won

---

42   Gwenn Okruhlik, 'Networks of Dissent: Islamism and Reform in Saudi Arabia', *Current History* 101: 651, January 2002: 22–8.

the Street, posing a threat to pro-Western states and clients.'[43] As the report's author later explained, Iraq, the only Arab country apart from Egypt 'with depth, human resources, enough water, [and] with a good bureaucratic tradition', had re-emerged as a major regional power and was becoming 'a real threat' to the Anglo-American relationship with Saudi Arabia and other oil states. He had remarked at the time, that 'the lack of our response to the re-emergence of Iraq as a serious regional power was like having tea with some very proper people in the drawing room and noticing that there was a python getting out of a box in one corner'.[44]

Two factors added to the weakness of America's position. First, Russia, China and France were pursuing commercial relations with Iraq, the European Union had begun political initiatives, and even Britain was proposing an end to the Iraq sanctions.[45] Unable to develop ties with the two states that Republican Party strategists had designated, along with Syria, as 'the new axis', later renamed 'the axis of evil', the US had become increasingly isolated.[46] Second, there was growing evidence of an approaching global shortage of oil, as international oil companies were no longer able to replace all of the oil they produced through the discovery of new supplies. With Iran and Iraq possessing the world's largest known reserves of oil after Saudi Arabia, the US policy of trying to prevent the development of both countries' oil industries was only adding to its own weakness.

The difficulty of Washington's position was exploited by a group of American militarists whose influence in American politics reached back to the era of the 1968–74 policy transformation, when Richard Perle and others had served under Senator Henry Jackson, assisting his efforts to militarise American relations with the Middle East and block a peaceful settlement of the Palestine question. After helping to escalate and prolong the conflict in Afghanistan in the 1980s, they had advocated further American intervention following the 1990–91 Gulf War, to overthrow the government of Iraq. When out of office they were

---

43   'Letter from Richard Dearlove's Private Secretary to Sir David Manning', 3 December 2001, at www.iraqinquiry.org.uk/transcripts/declassified-documents.aspx; Toby Dodge, 'What Accounts for the Evolution of International Policy Towards Iraq 1990–2003?' at www.iraqinquiry. org.uk/articles.aspx.

44   'SIS4' – anonymous witness, the head of the Middle East section at MI6, Transcript Part 1, at www.iraqinquiry.org.uk/transcripts/private-witnesses.aspx.

45   Alan Goulty to Tom McKane, 'Letter and attachment, "Iraq Future Strategy"', 20 October 2000, and 'Letter . . . to Sir David Manning', at www.iraqinquiry.org.uk/transcripts/declassified-documents.aspx.

46   The term 'the new axis' was introduced in 1992 by Yossef Bodansky, the Israeli-American director of the Congressional Republican Party's Task Force on Terrorism and Unconventional Warfare. See Yossef Bodansky and Vaughn S. Forrest, 'Tehran, Baghdad and Damascus: The New Axis Pact', Task Force on Terrorism and Unconventional Warfare, House Republican Research Committee, US House Of Representatives, available at www.fas.org/irp/congress/1992_rpt/index. html.

housed in the think tanks of the neoliberal/neoconservative movement, which, as we saw, had been built with the help of the windfalls reaped by American oil billionaires from the 1973–74 rise in oil prices.[47] Returned to office under President George W. Bush in the November 2000 election, they began planning immediately for a war against Iraq, and seized on the September 11 attacks, which were unrelated to Iraq, to win support for the invasion of March 2003.

There was no shortage of reasons for the war. A senior MI6 officer in London, asked in December 2001 to provide the prime minister's office at short notice with a set of reasons to justify the overthrow of the Iraqi regime, came up with the following list: 'The removal of Saddam remains a prize because it could give new security to oil supplies; engage a powerful and secular state in the fight against Sunni extremist terror, open political horizons in the GCC states, remove a threat to Jordan/Israel, [and] undermine the regional logic on WMD.'[48] To win public support for the war, the United States and Britain focused on threats of terrorism and fears of weapons of mass destruction. 'Bush wanted to remove Saddam, through military action', the head of the British secret intelligence service reported after meetings in the US in July 2002, 'justified by the conjunction of terrorism and WMD.' Since the decision to invade had already been taken, 'the intelligence and facts were being fixed around the policy'.[49]

Alan Greenspan, chairman of the Federal Reserve, noted after ending his term in 2006 that 'it is politically inconvenient to acknowledge what everyone knows: the Iraq war is largely about oil'.[50] By that point, however, such arguments were no longer inconvenient. The idea that America's inept and mismanaged invasion and occupation of Iraq, launched in March 2003, was driven by a grand geostrategic plan, or even by a simple intention to take control of the Middle Eastern 'oil spigot', seemed improbable.[51] If there was a commercial imperative involved in the war, it lay in the interests of military contractors, security firms and arms suppliers, for whom the 'strategic' importance of oil continued to supply a rationale and location for the expansion of business opportunities,

---

47   See Philip Mirowski and Dieter Plehwe, eds, *The Road from Mont Pèlerin: The Making of the Neoliberal Thought Collective*, Cambridge, MA: Harvard University Press, 2009, and Chapter 7, above. The terms 'neoliberal' and 'neoconservative' were interchangeable, the first reflecting the movement's origins in right-wing European liberalism (and used more in relation to its economic programme), the second its place in American politics (and used more in relation to foreign policy).

48   'Letter . . .to Sir David Manning'.

49   Mathew Rycroft to David Manning, 'Iraq, Prime Minister's meeting, 23 July', 23 July 2002, published in the *Sunday Times*, 1 May 2005, at www.timesonline.co.uk. The war's proponents were careful not to portray the invasion as a war for oil, but used the 'stability' of the Gulf as a way to refer to oil interests.

50   Alan Greenspan, *The Age of Turbulence: Adventures in a New World*, London: Penguin, 2007: 463.

51   David Harvey offers a more eloquent outline of the 'oil spigot' argument in *The New Imperialism*, Oxford: OUP, 2008: 1–25.

rather than with oil companies, which were well aware that imperial powers and international firms could no longer 'control' the supply of oil. In any case, the impasse and isolation in which the US was caught following the failures of McJihad, combined with the supportive public mood in the wake of September 11, provided reasons enough for the war.

The protagonists of the Iraq war also presented the country's invasion as an opportunity to bring democracy to the Middle East. The brutality of America's enormous military power was an unlikely instrument of democratisation, especially as Washington combined it with another form of ruthlessness: a neoliberal scheme to impose on the country a deregulated, market-driven economic and political order, much of it to be built by the US private-sector contractors to whom the occupying power subcontracted the work of reconstruction, and even many of the processes of armed occupation.[52] The destruction, death and political disarray brought by the war quickly aroused opposition to the occupation, not only among those who had prospered under the old regime or feared a wider social revolution, but, as casualties and chaos ensued, even among many who would have been glad to see the old order fall. Hardliners in Washington blocked a plan to transfer power quickly to an Iraqi administration, in favour of a more extended US occupation, installing a US civilian authority whose neoliberal programme to dismantle much of the Iraqi state and its entire armed forces, to close down its state-run industries, to remove all restrictions on foreign control of business and the export of profits, and to privatise its oil industry caused economic suffering and widened the opposition to the occupation. Neoliberal policies have always been intended to weaken democratic and egalitarian politics by moving control from public representatives to the private forces of the market.

The US preferred to rule through an unelected governing council, whose members were appointed to 'represent the diversity of Iraq' – meaning Shi'a Arabs, Sunni Arabs, Kurds, Turkmen and Assyrian Christians. Thus the actual diversity of Iraq, with its multiple, overlapping, frequently secular forms of political affiliation, and its modes of engagement that might be concerned with well-being, equality, or personal or national aspirations, rather than some form of sectarian identity, whether ethnic or confessional, was to be replaced with a simple American-devised identitarian politics of religion and ethnicity.[53] Unpopularity forced the occupation authorities to put an interim Iraqi government in power, but the Americans remained in control of construction contracts, the armed forces and many of the ministries.

---

52   Naomi Klein, *The Shock Doctrine: The Rise of Disaster Capitalism*, London: Allen Lane, 2007: 323–82.

53   Greg Muttit, *Fuel on the Fire: Oil and Politics in Occupied Iraq*, London: Bodley Head, 2011: 95.

The plans for the immediate privatisation of the petroleum industry were derailed by the large international oil companies, who preferred to negotiate arrangements with a single state authority than face a disorderly competition with an emergent local oil oligarchy, as they had faced in post-Soviet Russia, and were able to use the delay to cultivate ties within the new Iraqi Oil Ministry.[54]

Workers in the country's main oilfields and refineries, and in other industries, tried to organise independent unions. But the US occupation authority had retained the former government's Law 150, outlawing independent labour unions in the public sector, and the new Iraqi government that took office in 2006 refused to remove the ban. The oil workers carried out strikes and protests over the payment of wages, the placing of contract workers on full-time salaries, the employment of foreign workers, and other issues. In 2010–11, the scale of protests increased, but the Oil Ministry was able to identify the union leaders and disperse them to other locations. In June 2010, dockworkers demonstrated against the ban on unions, and again the leaders were transferred to jobs in other parts of the country. In July 2010, the Electrical Utility Workers Union – the first independent national union led by a woman, Hashmiya Muhsin – organised demonstrations in Basra in protest against the misuse of $13 billion allocated for rebuilding electricity supplies, which were still subject to frequent blackouts. The Ministry responded by ordering the union to be shut down and expelled from its offices.[55]

Unfortunately for the oil workers and others hoping for a more democratic future for Iraq, the United Nations Security Council failed to stand up to the Americans. At the time of the US invasion, all revenues from the production of oil in Iraq were under the control of the UN. Under the sanctions regime imposed on the country following its invasion of Kuwait in 1990, modified by the oil-for-food programme of 1995, income from the sale of Iraq's oil was paid into a UN-controlled account, to be used only for the purchase of food and medicines. Introduced in response to pressure from international groups concerned about the impact of sanctions on ordinary Iraqis, the programme was reminiscent of the plan for the League of Nations advocated during the First World War by the labour movement in Britain, which wanted the exploitation of raw materials to be governed by the League to ensure that its proceeds were used for the benefit of ordinary people rather than the enrichment of investors and local rulers (see Chapter 3).

Two months after launching its attack on Iraq, the UN Security Council handed over control of Iraq's oil revenues to the US, giving away the opportunity to require America, from the start, to follow a democratic process in the

54   Greg Palast, 'OPEC on the March', *Harper's Magazine*, April 2005: 74–6; Greg Muttit, *Fuel on the Fire*: 70–6, 107–10.

55   David Bacon, 'Unionbusting, Iraqi-Style', *Nation*, 25 October 2010: 25–6.

control of oil. Democratic government, as we know, depends on the power to interrupt critical flows, whether of energy or of revenue. The difficulty for the citizens of oil states is how to build that power when the state's revenue comes not from the productive life of the general population, but almost entirely from a single source: the revenues from the export of oil. Washington won control of the oil revenues from the UN with only very limited conditions, and handed over a large proportion of them to the US contractors it hired, at the expense of Iraqi engineers and oil workers, to begin rebuilding the infrastructure of the oil industry.[56]

The US awarded contracts for the reconstruction of Iraq, and even for contractors to run its increasingly privatised military occupation, to American firms, and attempted to do the same with oil. There was no strengthening of labour rights in the oil industry. Other opportunities to democratise the oil industry – for example by requiring that firms bidding for oil had democratic structures of ownership – were ignored. (Such procedures are common in the US, where public contracts are often structured to benefit or require bids from minority and women-owned businesses, for example.) The outcome of a long political struggle over the Iraqi oil law was that international oil firms were invited back in to develop new oilfields in the country, on what at first appeared very tough financial terms. But the terms were full of loopholes and exceptions – for example, if Iraq were to reduce its oil output to meet OPEC quotas, it had to compensate oil companies for lost oil production.[57]

Meanwhile, the American occupation of Iraq, like the British occupation nine decades earlier, turned to the conservative forces of 'tribal' leaders and Islamist parties to help it keep control, and began looking for a method to withdraw the bulk of the army of occupation at minimum cost. The end result was another form of McJihad, a hybrid compound of American military power, international oil companies, and conservative and Islamic domestic politics. As the diplomat had remarked of the effort a decade earlier to engage with the Talban, 'we can live with that'.

LIBERATION SQUARE

Among opponents of the American invasion of Iraq, many had argued that it would cause an explosion of popular anger in the streets of the Arab world, which would threaten to bring down US-supported governments in Egypt and other countries. For those thinking that this might be one of the more positive consequences of an attack on Iraq, the reaction in Cairo and other Arab capitals was not immediately encouraging. The popular response was delayed by almost

---

56   Muttit, *Fuel on the Fire*.
57   Ibid.

eight years. In January 2011, mass protests brought down the government of President Ben Ali in Tunisia, followed on 11 February by the fall of President Mubarak in Egypt and by revolutionary uprisings in Yemen, Bahrain, Libya, Syria and other parts of the Arab world. The wave of revolts had multiple causes. Rather than attribute them to events in Iraq, one could plausibly argue that the war delayed the fall of these autocratic governments.

On 15 February 2003, opponents of the impending US invasion of Iraq had organised anti-war marches in large cities around the world, including one in Cairo. More than 1 million people marched in London and Rome, hundreds of thousands in New York and Berlin, and thousands more in Tokyo, Seoul and Jakarta. In Cairo, the number of demonstrators was 600.[58] Gathering in the centre of Cairo, the protesters planned to form a human chain around the US embassy, which occupied a triangular block several acres in size just off the city's main square, Midan al-Tahrir. Government security forces overwhelmed and broke up the demonstration and arrested its leaders, who joined the thousands of political prisoners held, mostly without trial under emergency laws, in the country's prisons. Two weeks later another demonstration was organised. This was held in the Cairo International Stadium, located in an outlying section of the city several miles from the centre, well away from the US embassy. At least 120,000 protesters filled the stadium, and thousands more were turned away at the gates.[59] The rally was organised by the Muslim Brotherhood, with the consent of the regime, as a means of accommodating and containing popular opposition to the war in a manner that did not draw attention to the regime's relationship with the United States.

The two demonstrations illustrated the dynamics of oppositional politics in Egypt. The largely secular left opposition was allowed almost no room to organise, and its criticisms of neoliberal economic policy, US imperialism and the corruption of the state that accommodated these agendas was given no space. The Muslim Brotherhood also opposed the government, but with a far milder critique in defence of moral and cultural conservatism. Its moral conservatism often took the form of popular anti-Americanism, which operated as a means to circumscribe and weaken the left. It offered no real threat to the regime.[60]

---

58 'People Power Takes to the World's Streets', *Observer*, 16 February 2003; Amira Howeidy, 'Where Did All the Anger Go?' *Al-Ahram Weekly*, 20–26 February 2003, at weekly. ahram.org.eg.

59 Gihan Shahine, 'A Harmonious Protest', *Al-Ahram Weekly*, 6–12 March 2003, at weekly. ahram.org.eg.

60 On 20 and 21 March 2003, as the US invasion of Iraq began, the left organised further demonstrations in the centre of Cairo. From 10,000 to 20,000 protestors gathered, some of whom attempted to break through a police cordon and march on the US and British embassies. Further government repression of political opponents followed these events. Paul Schemm, 'Egypt Struggles to Control Anti-War Protests', *Middle East Report Online*, 31 March 2003, at www.merip.org.

Eight years later, another protest in Tahrir Square led to the overthrow of the Mubarak regime. There had been increasing opposition even before the Iraq war, provoking a brief move towards political reform as the old guard in the main apparatus of civilian rule, the National Democratic Party, tried to adjust to its weakening grip on power and to a challenge from a younger, technocratic faction within the ruling elite. New opposition parties formed, but the main challenge came in the mobilisation of industrial workers, who launched a wave of strikes, beginning in the early 2000s and gathering pace after 2004, in protest against the government's privatising of public-sector enterprises. The neoliberal campaign to reverse the post-independence programmes of agrarian land reform, rent and price controls, and state-led industrialisation had been underway for more than two decades; but in 2004 Mubarak appointed a new administration that accelerated the pace of privatisation, and began to target the textile industry and other large employers that had been passed over in earlier rounds. The fight against declining real wages – and against the threat of wider unemployment, still lower wages, and the loss of labour rights that came with privatisation – led to more than 1,900 strikes and other protests involving over 1.7 million workers between 2004 and 2008, representing the most sustained social protest movement since the postwar unrest that led to the overthrow of the monarchy in 1952. These included strikes in December 2006 and September 2007 at one of the country's largest industrial enterprises, the Misr Spinning and Weaving Company at Mahalla al-Kubra in the Egyptian Delta, and another two years later at the newly privatised Tanta Linen Company.[61]

In the past, the government had been able to diffuse social unrest, offering price subsidies, small pay bonuses and other modest concessions in cases of economic protest, backed up by the continuous repression of any effective political organising. By the late 2000s, this policy was becoming more difficult to implement. On the one hand, with the programme of economic restructuring now targeting large industry, the regime was more vulnerable to industrial action. On the other, a main source of revenues used for concessions to weaken economic protest had disappeared. In 2010, for the first time since recovering its Red Sea oilfields from Israel in 1975, Egypt became a net importer of oil. In the mid-1990s Egypt had been able to export almost half of its production of more than 900,000 barrels per day, providing the country's main source of export earnings and of government revenue. But production from its oilfields began to decline after 1996, while domestic consumption, encouraged by a boom in private car ownership among the better off, began a rapid growth.[62]

61   Joel Beinin, *Justice for All: The Struggle for Worker Rights in Egypt*, Washington, DC: Solidarity Center, 2010; and 'Egyptian Workers Rise Up', *Nation*, 7–14 March 2011, at www.nation. com.

62   Figures from www.eia.gov and the Energy Export Data Browser at mazamascience. com.

Accounts of the protests that brought down the Mubarak government stressed the role of new internet-based social media, which helped organisers and supporters plan the protests. The critical event in toppling the regime, however, was the initial seizure of Tahrir Square on 25 January – a development in which the social media functioned partly as a decoy. Knowing that the security forces would use violence to break up any attempt to occupy the square, the organisers used social media to plan protests at twenty sites in working-class districts of the city, hoping to strain the security forces by dispersing them to multiple locations, while drawing large crowds that would increase the chance of breaking through security cordons and linking up at Tahrir Square. They planned one additional gathering, in Bulaq al-Daqrur, a working-class neighbourhood close to the centre of the city, with an industrial workforce employed in a nearby cigarette factory and in railway yards. They avoided announcing this gathering over the internet, allowing a crowd of several hundred to gather without the presence of security forces. This was the group that marched to Tahrir, swelling to several thousand along the way, and seized the square, by which time the protest was too large for the armed police force to crush.[63]

The Muslim Brotherhood refused to support the initial protest, and stayed out for the first week.[64] At the same time the Brotherhood began negotiating with the regime, where power was removed from the hands of Mubarak and his family and taken over by his minister of defence. A hastily organised constitutional reform committee proposed minor changes to the constitution, in ways that would benefit the ruling party and the Muslim Brotherhood. The struggle continued.

It is often said that the politics of the Middle East have been shaped by the power of the international oil industry. It would be better to say that they have been shaped by its weakness. Extraordinary rents could be earned from controlling the production and distribution of oil. The multinational oil corporations sought to secure and enlarge these rents, in a rivalrous collaboration with the governments that controlled the oilfields. Large rents could also be made from controlling the production and distribution of weapons, for which the same governments had become the largest overseas customers. The oil and arms industries appear as two of the most powerful forces shaping what is called the capitalist world economy. Yet their power existed to overcome a weakness, a deficiency that always threatened the enormous potential for profit.

---

63 Charles Levinson and Margaret Coker, 'The Secret Rally that Sparked an Uprising', *Wall Street Journal*, 11 February 2011, at online.wsj.com.

64 Documents retrieved from the offices of the Egyptian state security following the fall of the Mubarak regime offered evidence of the ties between the security forces and right-wing Salafist groups. See, for example, 'Wathiqa Musriba min Amn al-Dawla', *Al-Masry al-Yawm*, 7 March 2011, available at www.almasryalyoum.com/node/342155.

On the one hand, throughout the twentieth century there was the over-abundance of oil, creating the permanent risk that the high rents earned by the oil industry might collapse. The industry had to constantly manufacture a scarcity of oil, to keep this threat at bay. On the other hand, political structures came into being to help achieve this end. Since the oil industry was never strong enough to create a political order on its own, it was obliged to collaborate with other political forces, social energies, forms of violence and powers of attachment. Across the Middle East, there were various forces available. But each of these allies had its own purposes, which were never guaranteed to coincide with the need to secure the scarcity of oil. At the heart of the problem of securing scarcity, for reasons we have seen, was the political control of Arabia. The geophysics of the earth's oil reserves determined that the rents on the world's most profitable commodity could be earned only by engaging the energies of a powerful religious movement.

'McJihad' is a term that describes this deficiency of capitalism. The word refers not to a contradiction between the logic of capitalism and the other forces and ideas it encounters, but rather to the absence of such a logic. The political violence that the United States, not alone but more than any other actor, has promoted, funded and prolonged across so many parts of the Middle East over recent decades is the persistent symptom of this absence.

Conclusion: No More Counting On Oil

We are entering the declining decades of the fossil-fuel era, that brief episode of human time when coal miners and oil workers moved an extraordinary quantity of energy, buried underground in coal seams and hydrocarbon traps, up to the earth's surface, where engines, boilers, blast furnaces and turbines burned it at an ever-increasing rate, providing the mechanical force that made possible modern industrial life, the megalopolis and the suburb, industrialised agriculture, the chemically transformed world of synthetic materials, electrical power and communication, global trade, military-run empires, and the opportunity for more democratic forms of politics. Yet, even as the passing of this strange episode comes into view, we seem unable to abandon the unusual practice to which it gave rise: ways of living and thinking that treat nature as an infinite resource.

Fossil fuels are not about to run out, but two predicaments make the world they engineered unexpectedly fragile. First, after 150 years of continuously increasing supply, the era of abundant oil appears to have ended. The world is using up stores of petroleum faster than those who develop them can discover new supplies. Just 110 giant oilfields, out of around 70,000 oilfields worldwide, produce half the world's petroleum. A majority of these giant fields were discovered more than half a century ago, between the 1930s and early 1960s. Many of them, including at least sixteen of the twenty largest, are in decline, producing less oil each year.[1]

By 2008, the amount of oil that flowed from fields already in production was declining by more than 4 per cent each year. Producers had to find additional fields supplying over 3 million barrels of oil per day, every year, merely to offset this collapse in supply from existing sources.[2] Optimists pointed to the discovery of large fields such as those found in 2006 and 2007 off the coast of Brazil, heralded as potentially a new Saudi Arabia – albeit an Arabia lying 250 kilometres out to sea in water three kilometres deep, with the oil buried another five

---

1   Fredrik Robelius, 'Giant Oil Fields – The Highway to Oil: Giant Oil Fields and Their Importance for Future Oil Production', PhD thesis, Teknisk-naturvetenskapliga vetenskapsområdet, Department of Nuclear and Particle Physics, Uppsala University, March 2007, available at publications.uu.se.

2   Steve Sorrell et al., *Global Oil Depletion: An Assessment of the Evidence for a Near-Term Peak in Oil Production*, UK Energy Research Centre, 2009: 44–46, 66, at www.ukerc.ac.uk; International Energy Agency, *World Energy Outlook 2008*: 221–48; Euan Mearns, Samuel Foucher and Rembrandt Koppelaar, 'The 2008 IEA WEO: Production Decline Rates', 17 November 2008, at http://europe.theoildrum.com.

to seven kilometres beneath the seabed. The Brazilian discoveries were among the largest in decades, but were only a fraction of the size of the Saudi fields. Yet, to make up for the decline in existing production, the world has to bring online the equivalent of a new Saudi Arabia every four years. And since the rate of decline is geometric, compounding from one year to the next, and newer fields are exploited more quickly and therefore tend to go into decline sooner and more rapidly than older fields, producers need to find new Saudi Arabias at an increasing frequency if they are to maintain even the current level of supply.

There has been little evidence in recent years that new sources of oil can be found at a rate that keeps pace with the decline of existing fields. During the decade from 1995 to 2005, only about 40 per cent of the oil the world consumed was replaced by additional discoveries. In the five years that followed, the world had to get by with no increase in supplies.[3] The production of oil from conventional sources appeared to have reached, if not its peak, at least the long, uneven plateau from which it would be increasingly difficult to maintain levels of production.

Some argue that the plateau is temporary, caused by political factors over the preceding decade such as the sanctions and war against Iraq, which made it difficult to develop new fields. They point to estimates that the world's ultimately recoverable resources total 3 trillion or even 4 trillion barrels of oil, rather than the 2.5 trillion implied by those who argue that global production has already reached its peak. But these higher estimates make little difference in the longer term. They postpone the predicted date of peak production by only six years, to 2016 (for 3 trillion barrels), or by less than two decades, to 2028 (for 4 trillion), and imply a faster rate of decline and thus a more difficult adjustment to energy shortages after the peak.[4]

For many countries, moreover, the supply of oil may be already passing from a plateau to a declining slope. This is due to changes in who is consuming the oil. Several of the largest oil exporters, including Saudi Arabia and Iran, are using an increasing share of their oil at home, leaving a smaller proportion available for export.[5] At the same time, the share of those available exports consumed by China and India is increasing – it grew from 11 per cent to 19 per cent between 2005 and 2010. The volume of global net oil exports not consumed by those two countries in that period fell from 41 to 35 million barrels per day.[6]

---

3   Rembrandt Koppelaar, 'USGS WPA 2000', 30 November 2006, at europe.theoildrum. com. World production of crude oil (including lease condensate) increased from 53.97 million barrels per day (mbd) in 1985 to 62.38 mbd in 1995 and 73.71 in 2005. Production failed to increase over the following five years, standing at 73.68 mbd in 2010. Data from www.eia.doe.gov.

4   Sorrell et al., Global Oil Depletion: 134–8.

5   Energy export data browser, at mazamascience.com/OilExport.

6   Jeffrey J. Brown and Samuel Foucher, 'Peak Oil Versus Peak Net Exports', ASPO-USA Oil & Energy Conference, 2010, at www.aspousa.org.

Many countries were already experiencing a period in which the supply of oil, for the first time in its 150-year history, could no longer continuously increase.

The second predicament is that burning these supplies of oil has taken carbon that was once stored underground and dispersed it in the atmosphere, at an ever increasing rate. More than half the oil consumed in the century-and-a-half between the founding of the modern petroleum industry in the 1860s and 2010 was burned in the three decades after 1980. The carbon dioxide produced in its combustion has contributed to the warming of the earth's atmosphere and oceans that now threatens to cause catastrophic climate change.

Nature is unable to speak for itself. The ecosystem appears to be approaching two limits simultaneously: an end to the easy availability of fossil fuel, whose abundance allowed the development of modern, mechanised life; and the loss of its ability to regulate global temperatures within the range that allowed human sociality itself to develop. Yet these linked predicaments do not enter political debate on their own. The facts of nature speak only with the help of measuring devices and tools of calculation. Meteorologists, geologists, petroleum engineers, investment advisers and economists assemble the equipment and the methods used to measure the past, record the present and predict the future. Much as coal miners and railway workers once used the equipment built for moving coal in order to manufacture an effective political voice, the ability to organise a political response to the current predicament depends on the control of equipment – and on the forces of nature on whose behalf one can then speak.

The problems of peak oil and climate breakdown are connected, as both arise from and threaten the modes of social life created using fossil fuels, including the forms of democratic politics that carbon energy made possible. Yet a surprising difference separates the two problems. Uncertainty over the future of the earth's climate and the ecological balance of its biosphere, widely discussed among climate scientists since the 1960s and brought to global attention at the Rio Earth Summit of 1992, became over the following two decades the object of a great deal of scientific investigation, political debate, media discussion and grassroots democratic organising. Uncertainty over the possible peak and decline in oil production did not. Concerns about the future control of oil may have motivated the US government to respond to the failure of its policy of isolating Iraq by invading the country to remove Saddam Hussein from power. The shortage of oil from 2005 to 2008, due in part to the continued inability to rebuild production in Iraq, caused a six-fold increase in its price – a financial shock about three times the size of the 1974 and 1979 oil shocks. The surge in oil prices triggered the global financial crisis of 2008–09, whose damage was felt more widely than any of the disasters so far ascribed to climate breakdown. The scale of the military violence and economic hardship already attributable to the growing threat of oil shortages makes even more surprising the difference between the political mobilisation around climate change and the relatively muted debate about oil.

Global oil resources, as the disagreements about peak oil suggest, cannot easily be counted, but until recently they could be counted *on*, for there were always reserves available. Occasional shortages arose from political upheavals, such as the Russian and Mexican revolutions during the First World War and the struggles in the Middle East in the 1970s. Oil companies often used those interruptions to raise fears about a more prolonged threat to supplies, using the public alarm to obtain increased government subsidies and tax exemptions, or to justify higher prices. Throughout the twentieth century, however, there was generally an abundance of supply, allowing the industrialised world to count on the future availability of oil.

For these reasons, oil could be counted on in a further sense. Its ready availability, in ever-increasing quantities, and mostly at relatively low and stable prices, meant that oil could be counted on *not to count*. It could be consumed as if there were no need to take account of the fact that its supply was not replenishable. In turn, not having to count the cost of humankind using up (largely within the space of two or three centuries) most of the earth's limited stores of fossil fuel made another kind of counting possible – new kinds of economic calculation. The economy came into being as an object of calculation and a means of governing populations not with the political economy of the late eighteenth century or the new academic economics of the late nineteenth century, but only in the mid-twentieth century (see Chapter 5). Its appearance was made possible by oil, for the availability of abundant, low-cost energy allowed economists to abandon earlier concerns with the exhaustion of natural resources and represent material life instead as a system of monetary circulation – a circulation that could expand indefinitely without any problem of physical limits. Economics became a science of money; its object was not the material forces and resources of nature and human labour, but a new space that was opened up between nature on one side and human society and culture on the other – the not-quite-natural, not-quite-social space that had come to be called 'the economy'.

Before the mid-twentieth century, this assumption that political life could be organised on the principle of limitless growth would have been an unlikely idea. In the earlier part of the century the limits of nature were everywhere. In Britain, the warning of William Jevons about the peak in British coal supplies had proved accurate, and production from the country's mines had begun an irreversible decline. In the United States, as the ecological destruction brought by the westward expansion of European settlement reached its limits, conservationists were battling to save the last great forests and mountains of the far west from logging companies and coal mining interests. But by the end of the 1920s, American oil drillers in East Texas and British drillers in northern Iraq had struck oil that gushed into the sky in quantities never seen before. The sudden abundance of oil helped the emergence of a science of the allocation of resources – economics – that treated them as infinite. The discoveries of oil were so large that there was no practical method or need to take account of their depletion. The world's most valuable non-renewable resource could be consumed without calculating the cost of its replacement. The oil industry gave birth in turn to the manufacture of plastics and other synthetic materials, and to the use of synthetic chemicals as fertilisers and pesticides in farming. Both organic and inorganic materials could now be produced in unprecedented quantities, using supplies of fossil fuel that appeared almost limitless. The government of resources no longer appeared as a problem of nature and its material limits. The birth of the economy, based upon oil, made possible a form of politics that was dematerialised and de-natured.

The difference between peak oil and climate change is found not only in different histories and politics of calculation. These differences appear to correspond to different degrees of political debate and action. The threat of climate collapse is now the object of international treaties and protocols, sustained government action (however inadequate the actual measures taken), and publications, protests and political pressure coordinated by large national and international organisations.

In contrast, during the decade of sharply rising oil prices starting around 2000, there were no major international pressure groups or activist organisations mobilised around the question of the limits to the supply of fossil fuels. In the United States, the issue of oil supply was taken up by the right, which sought the relaxation of environmental controls to allow increased domestic production – a campaign supported by the populist, anti-Arab claim, unsupported by any evidence, that this would reduce America's dependence on 'Arab oil'. (In 2009, Arab countries supplied the United States with less than 9 per cent of its oil consumption, most of which came from Saudi Arabia under a special arrangement set up as part of a favour to Washington to support the value of the US dollar.)[7] In Britain, oil supply was also an issue for the right. The only political party to make the problem of peak oil a pillar of its platform was the neo-fascist British National Party.[8] In the wake of the September 2000 fuel protests, when truck drivers and farmers across western Europe closed down major roadways and blockaded oil refineries, and a briefer round of protest in 2005, the BNP, a party sympathetic to those who denied the evidence of human-induced climate change, calculated that its programme of white supremacy

7   US Energy Information Agency, *Petroleum Supply Annual, 2009*, July 2010, at www.eia. gov. US dependence on imported oil is self-inflicted, attributable to the failure to introduce more efficient vehicle engines and other transportation technologies already widely available. Vaclav Smil, 'America's Oil Imports: A Self-Inflicted Burden', *Annals of the Association of American Geographers*, 104: 4, 2011: 712–6.

8   'The Archive for Peak Oil', British National Party, 2008, at bnp.org.uk/category/peak-oil.

and anti-Muslim xenophobia would be enhanced by the coming crisis of peak oil. The fuel protests had shown that energy issues offered an opening for the right, as discontent focused on government taxation, foreign oil states and multinational companies had found a way to paralyse the country. The strikes of January 2009 at the Lindsey Oil Refinery, in protest against jobs going to Portuguese and Italian workers housed in barges in nearby docks, shut down Britain's third-largest oil refinery and spread to refineries across the country. These anti-immigrant protests suggested further opportunities to transform the politics of fuel supply into a field for recruitment to movements on the right.[9] Even mainstream political parties, however, took up the xenophobic potential of energy politics, denouncing dependence on 'foreign oil', referring to the dangers of relying on oil produced in Arab and Muslim-majority countries.

Do rising fuel prices and future shortages of oil produce a new kind of politics – a politics of refinery strikes, truck driver protests, the blockading of fuel depots and shutting down of pipelines, fuelling a new xenophobic nationalism? This question has a history (see Chapter 1). A century ago, the widespread use of coal gave workers a new power. The movement of unprecedented quantities of fuel along the fixed, narrow channels that led from the coal mine, along railway tracks and canals, to factories and power stations created vulnerable points of passage where a labour strike could paralyse an entire energy system. Weakened by this novel power, governments in the West conceded demands to give votes to all citizens, impose new taxes on the rich, and provide healthcare, insurance against industrial injury and unemployment, retirement pensions, and other basic improvements to human welfare. Democratic claims for a more egalitarian collective life were advanced through the flow and interruption of supplies of coal.

In the second half of the twentieth century, governments sought to weaken this unusual power that workers had acquired by an equally simple engineering project: switching from using coal to using oil and gas. As early as the 1940s, the architects of the Marshall Plan in Washington argued for subsidising the cost of importing oil to western Europe from the Middle East, in order to weaken the coal miners and defeat the left. In Britain, this attack on the energy system that had empowered the left culminated several decades later in the attempt by the Conservative government to destroy most of what remained of British coal mining in order to eliminate what the prime minister, Margaret Thatcher, termed 'the Enemy Within' – the country's most powerful labour union.[10] The

---

9   Robert Booth, 'Mediators Called in as Wildcat Strikes Spread Across UK', *Guardian*, 31 January 2009. The employment of workers from southern Europe followed a ruling in the European Court of Justice in 2008 that employers need to pay workers from other countries of the EU only the lower wage they would receive in their home country, rather than the national minimum wage in the host country. The BNP sent a group to support the strikers.

10   Seumas Milne, *The Enemy Within: The Secret War Against the Miners*, 3rd edn, London: Verso, 2004.

National Union of Mineworkers had led the battle that developed between organised labour and the state following the 1967 financial crisis, when the blocking of oil supplies had triggered the collapse of the pound, and in 1974 had defeated an attempt to use another crisis in energy supplies to weaken its power, bringing down the Conservative government. A decade later, the development of nuclear power stations and the oil and natural gas fields of the North Sea provided government planners with the means to end the country's dependence on coal for generating electrical power. The Conservatives were able to reopen the war against the miners in 1984 with a new round of pit closures. The strike that followed was the longest in British history, and the most intense labour conflict since the general strike of 1926. The government failed to destroy the NUM, but six years later the domestic security agency, MI5, with help from American intelligence agencies, leaked to the press false allegations that the NUM leadership had misappropriated funds from Libyan leader Muammar al-Gaddafi.[11] (Created in 1916 in response to a panic over German spies, MI5 had quickly turned its attention to those organising the wartime labour strikes mentioned in Chapter 3, and to the intellectuals on the left attempting to establish the 'democratic control' of empire.)[12] The Libya allegation was an effective weapon with which to weaken the NUM by destroying its popular support, allowing the government to carry through its programme of putting an end to British coal mining – an industry that had employed over 2 million workers in 1982–83. By 2009, just five long-wall coal mines were left in operation.

As Europe switched from coal to oil, the earlier successes of its miners and railway workers proved much harder to replicate for the oil workers of Dhahran, Abadan and Kirkuk, or at the pipeline terminals and refineries on the coasts of Palestine and Lebanon. As we have seen, oil moved by pipeline rather than rail, was light enough to carry across oceans, followed more flexible networks, and created a great separation between the places where energy was produced and those where it was used. The demands of oil workers for labour rights and political freedoms could be translated into programmes of nationalisation, while production cartels could restrict supply so that gluts of oil throughout most of the twentieth century could be transformed into a vulnerable 'strategic resource' that needed imperial armies and vassal states to protect it. These and many other socio-technical features of the oil industry made it increasingly difficult to build mechanisms of more democratic politics out of the production of oil.

What kind of politics might follow from the declining flow of oil and other fossil fuels? Many attempts to answer this question fall into some kind of energy

11   Ibid.
12   Christopher Andrew, *The Defence of the Realm: The Authorized History of MI5*, London: Penguin, 2010: 94–109.

determinism, as though each form of energy produces a corresponding politics. Greenpeace proposes building a decentralised energy system, dispensing
with the electrical grid and turning every building into a generator of heat and
power. By reducing the influence of large power and energy firms, the organisation argues, 'decentralising energy would also democratise energy'. Desertec, a
project backed by Deutsche Bank and other European investors to build giant
solar thermal power stations in the Sahara, disagrees, arguing that the circum-
Mediterranean network it proposes to build is an effective market device, allowing price competition and the increased use of renewable sources, creating a
path to 'the democratization of energy'.[13] These projects and the arguments that
support them indicate not that forms of energy determine modes of politics,
but that energy is a field of technical uncertainty rather than determinism, and
that the building of solutions to future energy needs is also the building of new
forms of collective life.

Arguments about the future politics of oil, on the other hand, often fall into
a dispute between two opposing camps: the Malthusians and the technologists.
For the Malthusians, politics will be determined by the limits of nature, which
the demands of increasing human consumption will inevitably exceed. For the
technologists, the progress of science will continue to find ways to overcome
those limits, using methods that, due to the nature of technical innovation, can
never be predicted in advance. Both arguments offer to eliminate the uncertainty of the present – the Malthusian one by uncovering the fixed thresholds
of nature, the technological one by trusting in the limitless potential of science.

An alternative to both positions is to acknowledge that, rather than politics being determined by natural forces, or, conversely, being freed from natural constraints by the continued progress of science and technology, we find
ourselves in the midst of increasing numbers of socio-technical controversies.
Technical change does not remove uncertainties, as the conventional view of
science proposes – it causes them to proliferate.[14] This happens in any field
of technical innovation, from containing new human–animal strains of the
influenza virus, building markets to trade carbon emissions, planting geneti-
cally modified crops and isolating and patenting human genes, to constructing third-generation pressurised water reactors, reorganising schooling around
standardised testing, harvesting embryonic stem cells for medical research, and

---

13   Greenpeace, *Decentralising Power: An Energy Reserve for the 21st Century*, 2005, at
www.greenpeace.org.uk/MultimediaFiles/Live/FullReport/7154.pdf; Desertec-UK, 'Electricity
Transmission Grids', 2010, at www.trec-uk.org.uk/elec_eng/grid.htm; Anni Podimata, 'Energy
from the Desert', Desertec Industry Initiative Annual Conference 2010, at www.dii-eumena.com.
14   The following argument draws on Michel Callon, Pierre Lascoumes, and Yannick
Barthe, *Acting in an Uncertain World: An Essay on Technical Democracy*, Cambridge, MA: MIT
Press, 2009. See also Andrew Barry, *Political Machines: Governing a Technological Society*, London:
Athlone Press, 2001.

innumerable others. Such technical controversies are always socio-technical controversies. They are disputes about the kind of technologies we want to live with, but also about the forms of social life, of socio-technical life, we would like to live.

Modern secular and democratic society is often described as a stage of history shaped by the development of modern science. Scientific modes of understanding enabled us to distinguish clearly for the first time between nature and society, it is said, and to organise collective life so that the world of nature stood on one side and the human world of passions, beliefs, social forces and political power on the other.

If that is the meaning of modernity, Bruno Latour suggests, then we should acknowledge that 'we have never been modern'.[15] We have always inhabited a mixed world, made up of imbroglios of the technical, the natural and the human. As the kinds of controversies we face clearly show, our world is an entanglement of technical, natural and human elements. Any technical apparatus or social process combines different kinds of materials and forces, involving various combinations of human cognition, mechanical power, chance, stored memory, self-acting mechanisms, organic matter and more. In introducing technical innovations, or using energy in novel ways, or developing alternative sources of power, we are not subjecting 'society' to some new external influence, or conversely using social forces to alter an external reality called 'nature'. We are reorganising socio-technical worlds, in which what we call social, natural and technical processes are present at every point.

These entanglements, however, are not recognised in our theories of collective life, which continue to divide the world according to the conventional divisions between fields of specialist knowledge. There is a natural world studied by the various branches of natural science, and a social world analysed by the social sciences. Debates about human-induced climate change, the depletion of non-renewable resources, or any other question, create political uncertainty not so much because they reach the limits of technical and scientific knowledge, but because of the way they breach this conventional distinction between society and nature. They cannot be settled by experts alone, because they involve questions not only about the nature of the world – the arena traditionally monopolised by scientific and technical expertise – but also about the nature of the collective.[16] With what forces, human and non-human, do we want to form alliances? To what powers do we want to be subject ourselves?

15   Bruno Latour, *We Have Never Been Modern*, Cambridge, MA: Harvard University Press, 1993.

16   Bruno Latour, *Politics of Nature: How to Bring the Sciences into Democracy*, Cambridge, MA: Harvard University Press, 2004; Michel Callon, 'Some Elements of a Sociology of Translation: Domestication of the Scallops and the Fishermen of St Brieuc Bay', in John Law, ed., *Power, Action and Belief: A New Sociology of Knowledge?*, London: Routledge, 1986: 196–223.

Socio-technical controversies also challenge a second distinction, founded on the first: the separation between experts and laypersons. In an increasing number of ways, the construction of technical expertise involves the participation of ordinary citizens.[17] New drugs have to be tested on participants in clinical trials, who report on their symptoms and their experience of side effects, and in some cases organise patient groups that fund and set priorities for further research. New market technologies require the participation of consumers whose choices shape the outcome of the economic experiment. Military hardware is tested on the battlefield where, as in the aftermath of the 1973 Arab–Israeli war (see Chapter 6), the remains of manned fighting vehicles become objects for demonstrating the continued feasibility of conventional war. Algorithms used to determine how much credit to extend to the user of a credit card are adjusted in response to spending habits.[18] Innovations in standardised testing must be implemented by schoolteachers, and performed by those they teach. The users of Blu-ray disc players become unofficial beta-testers, and thus developers and re-enforcers of the complex data-protection methods with which media conglomerates hope to overcome the problem of the pirating of DVDs. Carbon offset programmes, devised by economists as a solution to global warming, turn the lives of those in tropical rainforests into an experiment for sustaining our own ways of consuming energy.

In these situations, political subjects become not just objects of socio-technical experiments but participants in them. Many such procedures appear at first as a threat to the rights of citizens, consumers, or human subjects in general, and are sometimes subject to protocols that attempt to protect those rights. In response to threats as widespread as peak oil or climate collapse, however, rival technical solutions become experiments in the composition of the collective world. Even in response to more mundane issues, expert knowledge employs human subjects in devising new forms of socio-technical life. These situations offer occasions not simply to defend existing democratic rights or extend them to others, but to re-democratise the forms of democracy.

Democratic politics, as we know, came into being after ordinary people came to form critical, collective components in the new machineries of industrial life. The modes of mass democracy that emerged in response to these popular pressures were organised by separating professional politicians, authorised and regulated through political parties, from ordinary citizens, who were asked to delegate their role in decision-making to the governing party. From the mid-twentieth century, democratic politics was further regulated through

17   Callon et al., *Acting in an Uncertain World*.
18   Martha Poon, 'Scorecards as Devices for Consumer Credit', *Sociological Review* 55, supplement S2, 2007: 284–306.

a distinction between techno-scientific experts and laypersons. Specialists in the fields of science, technology, warfare, industrial management, public health, accounting, law, and above all economic planning, acquired responsibility for deciding issues of public concern.

In unsettling two divides – between society and nature, and between experts and ordinary citizens – technical controversies can provide the opportunities to rebuild more 'technical' forms of democracy.[19] The need to reassemble socio-technical worlds can open up new points of vulnerability, where experts and professional politicians might become liable, once again, to the claims of those through whose lives new arrangements must be built. There is no inevitability to this. But in order to take advantages of opportunities that may arise, we must bring these questions of nature, technology and expertise into view as the place where opportunities for democratisation occur.

Can we draw on these ways of thinking to think about the politics of oil? Does the uncertainty over the future of fossil fuels create a set of questions that cannot be answered if we insist on a clear distinction between nature and society; between the resources of nature on the one hand, and the kind of social order that can be sustained on the other? Or between the expertise that speaks about facts of nature and the non-experts who are asked to accept the word of experts, and to delegate to professional politicians the decisions to be made on the basis of those facts? If controversies overflow this distinction, do they create a new kind of political space, a forum in which the composition of the collective is at stake in questions over possible states of the world?

For much of the twentieth century, the boundary between nature and society was established not as a vulnerable line created by the rise of the natural sciences, which established nature as their object, set apart from politics, but as a broad space – the territory we call 'the economy'. The separation of nature from politics was maintained not so much by the authority of large-scale science and engineering, which monopolised statements about nature, but by the work of economists who laid out the large no-man's land between the two. The production of energy – especially oil – has provided a fertile field for establishing the divide between nature and society, or what oil companies call 'below ground' and 'above ground'. For this reason, it is in the uncertain future of the world's energy system that one finds some of the latest and most vigorous efforts today to defend this 'economisation' that separates nature from society.

One of the differences between the politics of climate change and the politics of peak oil lies in the forms of measurement that have made it possible to construct

---

19   Callon et al., *Acting in an Uncertain World.*

a body of knowledge about the earth's climate. There is a science of climate change, but not of peak oil. This difference can be seen in the different ways that the supply of oil and the composition of the atmosphere are measured. It lies not in the amount of measuring done, but in the degree of deliberate imprecision. The measuring of oil is organised in a way that creates an important margin of uncertainty. Despite efforts to produce a similar uncertainty in the measurement of the atmosphere, the production of accuracy has been harder to dismantle.

The level of greenhouse gases in the atmosphere was at first no easier to calculate than the quantity of oil reserves. Before the 1960s, chemical measurements of the air had indicated that the amount of carbon dioxide it contained was highly variable. The first efforts to organise the measuring of CO_2 levels around the world, in the late 1950s, were intended not to monitor changes in the climate but to provide a means to track the global movement of air masses, since meteorologists thought that each body of air would contain a different proportion of the gas. However, Charles Keeling, an atmospheric chemist, had built a device to measure concentrations of CO_2 mechanically, rather than by chemical analysis. The 'man with the machine', as the meteorologists called him, used his equipment to show that the level of CO_2 was constant around the world, at about 312 parts per million. More importantly, he could use his mechanical apparatus to calibrate other machines, enabling his collaborators to operate measuring devices continuously at different locations around the world and compare the results over time. By 1961 Keeling's team was able to demonstrate that the concentration of CO_2 in the free atmosphere was increasing, and that the rate of increase was so rapid that its only plausible cause appeared to be the combustion of fossil fuels.[20]

Keeling's measurement of the atmosphere survived several attempts to dismantle the measuring equipment or render it less accurate. Most of the attacks came from the US Congress or government agencies. In 1963 Congress cut the budget of the Weather Bureau, which had funded Keeling's programme, restricting the Bureau's work to weather forecasting. Keeling kept his measurements going with support from the National Science Foundation, and in 1970 helped launch a worldwide monitoring programme under the auspices of the World Meteorological Organization. After Keeling's work gained public attention, he was invited to address the American Philosophical Society, where he expressed concern about the effect of returning to the atmosphere the carbon slowly extracted from the air by plants and buried as sediment during 500

---

20   Charles D. Keeling, 'Rewards and Penalties of Monitoring the Earth', *Annual Review of Energy and the Environment* 23, 1988: 32–42. Keeling's team later realised that the rate of increase in CO_2 levels speeded up and slowed down, a variation attributable to the periodic change in air pressure across the equatorial Pacific Ocean known as the southern oscillation.

million years of the earth's history. The NSF then informed him that his measuring equipment was being used for 'routine monitoring' rather than 'basic science' – a new distinction – and in 1971 halted its support. Following the 1973–74 oil shock, the monitoring programme was revived with support from Oak Ridge National Laboratory, part of the US nuclear energy establishment, which wanted to show those objecting to the risks of nuclear energy that fossil fuels were more dangerous.

The 'coordinated plan' to put an end to Keeling's measuring of atmospheric CO_2 resumed in the 1990s. The Department of Energy would fund only research measuring the favourable consequences of the increased burning of fossil fuels, such as whether it stimulated higher rates of growth of vegetation. Eventually the battle was fought over the glass flasks of gas that Keeling kept at the Scripps Institution for Oceanography in Southern California for calibrating the carbon dioxide–measuring devices. After failing in an attempt to take control of them, the Department of Energy declared their calibration standards 'unsatisfactory' and ordered the National Bureau of Standards to issue new, less accurate standards, which it tried to force the World Meteorological Organization to accept. The flasks survived these attacks, allowing the accurate measurement of rising CO_2 levels to continue, and to demonstrate the increasing effect of fossil fuels on the atmosphere.[21]

With petroleum, imprecision and uncertainty were easier to produce. The measuring devices and calculative infrastructures for measuring oil are older and more extensive than the equipment for measuring climate change. Exploration and production companies gather geophysical data (prospect maps and seismic sections) and geochemical data (types of source rocks, burial history, maturation history); they collect information on the oil reservoir, measuring the porosity, temperature, pressure and water saturation of the source rock, from which in turn they estimate the proportion of the oil in the rock formation that is likely to be recovered; and they accumulate data on the wells drilled, recording their location and depths, core analysis, stem tests, mechanical logs, and the history and location of dry wells.[22]

There are three important differences between measuring climate change and measuring the size of oil supplies. First, measurements attempting to predict the future supply of oil sample the lithosphere. They are sampling a space that is fractured and inaccessible, an irregular mixture of solid, liquid and gas, of the viscous and non-viscous, of the porous and semi-porous, the permeable and the impermeable. All of these elements interact in a dynamic, pressurised system of seepages, flows, fracturing, folding and flooding. The knowledge that results

21   Keeling, 'Rewards and Penalties': 45–63.
22   P. J. Lee, *Statistical Methods for Estimating Petroleum Resources*, Oxford: OUP, 2008: 140.

is partial, particular to a given location, probabilistic rather than certain, and difficult to aggregate.[23]

Second, the measurements oil companies make in this way, unlike meteorological measurements, are almost never made public. This difference is related to the first one. An oil reservoir is a carbon energy machine – an apparatus of heat, pressure, fluid migration and seismic movement that generates rare and potent stores of buried solar energy. The geological processes that make measurement so uncertain are the source of the extraordinary profits that oil producers can earn. As oil becomes more difficult and more expensive to find, the geological complexity of its location requires ever greater amounts of capital investment. The potential for profit and the increasing size and vulnerability of investments make oil companies unwilling to publicise those measurements. In the past the companies exerted extraordinary efforts to keep secret even the methods used to make the measurements.[24]

To these two differences we can add a third, related to the first two. A reserve of oil refers not to the entire geological deposit but to the part that can be brought to the surface. It cannot be measured directly, not only because it lies underground but because reserves are estimates of future production, whose calculation requires assumptions about future costs and levels of demand, and estimates of the technical feasibility of projects to extract the resource. It is an estimate of geological, petrochemical, economic and political factors. The fractured and increasingly inaccessible geological formations in which oil is found make the size of reserves increasingly dependent on unmeasurable estimates of the likelihood that equipment can be devised to discover and extract them. The size of reserves further depends on the fact that the carbon released from these underground stores ends up in the atmosphere, so precautions taken to prevent climate catastrophe by reducing carbon emissions will increasingly affect the cost and thus the rate at which oil can be extracted.

As a result, no apparatus has been put in place comparable with those of the World Meteorological Organization or the Intergovernmental Panel on Climate Change to create a science of peak oil based on global petroleum estimates. Following the 1973–74 oil crisis, the US government created the Energy Information Administration (EIA), which draws on the work of the US Geological Survey (USGS), and the OECD in Paris set up the International Energy Agency. These agencies do not have direct access to company information, and do not install, operate or coordinate measuring devices. Instead, they have to come up with other ways of estimating how much oil is left.

---

23   G. C. Bowker, *Science on the Run: Information Management and Industrial Geophysics at Schlumberger, 1920–1940*, Cambridge, MA: MIT Press, 1994.

24   Ibid.

A Cold War research project produced the method later used to construct the first systematic estimate of the quantity of the world's oil reserves, known and unknown: the Delphi method. Developed at the Rand Corporation as a procedure for estimating the probability and strength of an attack on the United States by the Soviet Union, and named after the Greek oracle, it was a technique for planning how to fight a war when one had no reliable data on the size of enemy forces or the performance and firepower of their weapons. The method makes up for the absence of dependable measurements by asking a panel of experts to estimate the likelihood of different outcomes, and to explain their reasons. It then presents each expert with the estimates and reasoning of other members of the panel, and asks them to revise their estimates, repeating this process over several rounds. The procedure leads to the gradual development of a consensus around a narrow range of estimates.

When the USGS began to publish estimates of world petroleum reserves in the 1990s, it used a version of this method. With no reliable access to enemy data – the knowledge systems of the oil companies – the experts based their estimates on 'the principles of petroleum geology, published literature, and (where they could get their hands on it – mostly from one particular oil industry consulting firm) unpublished information from the petroleum industry'.[25] In 2000, the USGS replaced this with a new method, still with no access to well data or seismic coverage, based on a new object – a 'hydrocarbon fluid system'. The 2000 assessment report remains the basis for all official estimates of world oil reserves, including the annual World Energy Outlook of the International Energy Agency (IEA) and the International Energy Outlook of the United States EIA.

Petroleum engineers, geologists and others working within the oil industry have assembled a set of measuring and calculative devices that may be more numerous and complex than those assembled for the measuring and monitoring of the global climate. But the knowledge of oilfields has not become a political field, or even a unified science, in the way that the study of climate change has managed to do. The measurements are conducted privately and held separately, field by field, by rival companies, or by oil services firms contracted to private or national oil-production companies. It is common to blame the lack of reliable data on OPEC, whose very large reserve estimates reflect the fact that OPEC quotas are based on the reported size of reserves, and no contemporary historical data are given on rates of production from individual fields. But in fact, apart from the British and Norwegian zones of the North Sea, there is no production region in the world for which field-by-field production data are publicly available.

25   L. B. Magoon and J. W. Schmoker, 'The Total Petroleum System: The Natural Fluid Network that Constrains the Assessment Unit', *US Geological Survey Digital Data Series 60*, 2000, at energy.cr.usgs.gov.

The fractured and privatised nature of oilfield data makes possible the circulation of the only alternative official data – the very high estimates of the USGS assessment of 2000, on which in turn the IEA and EIA base their annual outlooks.

'Nature', Latour suggests, is a term we should abandon, for it is a way of assembling the common world 'without due process'.[26] The appeal to nature short-cuts political debate and contestation. Nature is understood as a realm of facts, separate from values, from the messy, subjective world of politics. Only experts are fully equipped to explore the world of nature, reporting their findings back to the political world in incontestable form. Although in many areas we have abandoned this naïve conception of the natural world, in the case of oil the nature–society divide continues to be maintained. The government of technical uncertainty about the future of oil is performed by maintaining the calculative space of economics.

How do the economists keep control of their territory? They create and take advantage of the extraordinary gap between 'proven' reserves, compiled largely from company data, and estimates of undiscovered reserves of oil, based on USGS estimates of 'total petroleum systems' and similar forms of uncertainty.

If the oil being produced is only a small part of the total of still-to-be-discovered reserves, the economists tell us, then the problem of the future supply is not a question of geology but one of economic and political calculation. We are dealing not with the facts of nature, which remains a potentially infinite resource, but with the representation of nature in the form of proven reserves. The economists are the specialists in questions of representation. Proven reserves, like all representations, they tell us, are partial, incomplete, and can vary according to the way they are measured, the standards of reporting and the development of new techniques. Economists acquire their strength from their command of these representations. They do not deal with the material world, which is objective but too large to represent; nor do they deal with culture and society, which appear subjective and insubstantial. They master the system of representations that they have erected to govern relations between the two.

As a question of representation, the problem of oil supplies belongs, as the oil economists say, 'above ground, not below ground'. In other words, it is a question of human choice and technical ingenuity, not of the objective facts of nature. The obstacles to producing more oil lie in the cost of drilling, the level of demand, and thus the price, which needs to rise to make it feasible to search for and produce oil in more inaccessible places; the restrictions placed on drilling by environmental campaigns that prevent the exploitation of coastal regions

---

26   Latour, *Politics of Nature*: 54.

of the US; and local political arrangements or US sanctions in the Middle East that limit the access of multinational oil companies to new sources of reserves.

None of this is necessarily untrue. Oil companies historically developed large political, intelligence and economic forecasting departments. In the era of relatively plentiful oil, investment planning was typically far more dependent on these 'above ground' calculations than on geological or petrochemical calculation.

But the distinction between 'above ground' and 'below' – between economic or political calculation, and geology – is not a straightforward one. As in other cases, there is no simple distinction between politics and nature, but the oil industry works hard to maintain one – to maintain a space of uncertainty, of economic possibility, that intervenes between nature and politics. For example, while the price of oil partly determines which reserves it is feasible to produce, it is equally the case that geological estimates of reserves of oil affect its price. When the IEA, or Shell, or Saudi Aramco report the availability of plentiful reserves of oil, they encourage large investments in future production and dissuade users of petroleum from switching to alternatives – especially to radically different alternatives that require large initial investments, such as renewable energy or nuclear power.

The control of individual measurement and data by corporations and their consulting firms, and the publication of very high estimates of undiscovered oil by international agencies compelled to operate at a level of generality by this lack of access to measuring devices and field-level data, provide the mechanisms for managing a separation between above-ground and below-ground, between society and nature. It is through this practical work of calculation that economics governs and maintains the difference between society and nature.

How might the economists' mastery of these methods of representation be challenged? The main efforts today are unsuccessful, because they are aimed at developing rival representations of nature. As we will see, the more effective challenge arises differently. We saw in Chapter 5 that the birth of the economy – a dematerialised conception of economic flows – was enabled by the arrival of oil, an energy source so cheap and so plentiful, from the 1930s, that a system of general economic calculation could be devised that made no reference to questions of the exhaustion of non-renewable resources or the cost of energy. This made possible the idea of growth without limits.

In the US, a rival school to neoclassical economics and the 'price system' – the school of American institutional economics that developed from the work of economists like Richard Ely and Thorstein Veblen – had been defeated. However, their ideas survived in the hands of a group in New York, the Technocracy movement, a collection of heterodox economists and engineers who argued that wealth depended not on the circulation of money, as neoclassical economics was now able to argue, but on the flow of energy and its transformation in materials and services. In the 1920s, while Irving Fisher was compiling his 'price index' on the precursor of the Rolodex, the group undertook an 'Energy Survey of North America', which gathered data on natural resource extraction, manufacturing and energy usage. In conjunction with the Department of Industrial Engineering at Columbia University, they then carried out a rival project to Fisher's measurement of the national economy, which was based on the movement of money: an analysis of production and employment in North America measured in energy units.

One of the leaders of the movement in the 1930s, M. King Hubbert, is known today for his studies of the depletion of oil reserves, and his prediction in 1956 that the production of oil in the US would reach a peak by 1970 and then decline. As a lecturer at Columbia University, Hubbert had studied the flow of fluids underground. After going on to work for the Shell Oil Company, he applied this thinking to the flow of oil; borrowing methods of analysis developed in the study of the exhaustion of coal reserves, which was already a major concern, he had shifted his object of study. Estimating the future supply of petroleum was no longer a question of the total size of an oil reservoir, or the quantity of reserves still in the ground. The issue, instead, was the rate at which oil could be made to flow to the surface. The rate of flow, he argued, has a history, and this history follows a typical pattern, shaped by methods of exploration, rates of discovery, technologies of extraction, and the properties of different source rocks and oils. From these it is possible to predict the probable future flow of oil. If for the economists oil deposits were a fact of nature, and were unknowably immense, for the petroleum geologist the flow of oil was a measurable socio-technical process.[27]

In the 1990s a heterodox community of oil specialists, composed of retired oil company geologists, investment bankers, independent oil drillers, academics and concerned laypersons, revived and extended Hubbert's work. Using his methods, and several variations on them, they developed predictions of the point at which production of oil will peak and begin a permanent decline. The answers varied, but most predicted a peak in the period 2005–10.[28]

Confronted by these increasingly ingenious efforts to show that the future flow of oil can be predicted and represented, the economists face a difficult task in

---

27   Gary Bowden, 'The Social Construction of Validity in Estimates of US Crude Oil Reserves', *Social Studies of Science* 15: 2, May 1985: 207–40; Michael Aaron Dennis, 'Drilling for Dollars: The Making of US Petroleum Reserve Estimates, 1921–25', *Social Studies of Science* 15: 2, May 1985: 241–65.

28   M. King Hubbert, *Nuclear Energy and the Fossil Fuels*, Houston: Shell Development Company, Publication 95, June 1956; Kenneth S. Deffeyes, *Hubbert's Peak: The Impending World Oil Shortage*, Princeton: Princeton University Press, 2001; Colin J. Campbell and Jean H. Laherrère, 'The End of Cheap Oil', *Scientific American* 278: 3, March 1998; Kjell Aleklett and Colin J. Campbell, 'The Peak and Decline of World Oil and Gas Production', *Minerals and Energy* 18: 1, 2003: 5–20.

maintaining its incalculability – in maintaining nature as an infinite resource, by preserving a distinction between the representations of oil (which the economists assure us are partial, unreliable and political) and of reality (which is said to be infinite, unknowable, and thus apolitical). As long as this is fought as a battle over rival representations of nature, the economists have the upper hand. However, as we know from the making of 'the economy', building representations of the world always involves building a world that can be represented. This is where the economists are vulnerable.

There have been two responses from those we can call the cornucopians to the growing evidence of peak oil (meaning not the exhaustion of oil, but a rate of flow that can no longer continually increase): first, to redefine nature, or at least oil; and second, to redefine the problem of oil supplies as merely a question of political arrangements.

Almost all oil produced so far has now been renamed 'conventional oil'. This reflects the fact that the only large discoveries of new oil occur deep offshore, at depths of thousands of meters. Everyone agrees that the supply of conventional oil will start declining soon, if it has not already started to do so. But we are to be saved from the political uncertainties and reorientations that this presents by defining other kinds of things as oil – so-called 'unconventional oil', to which we can now add unconventional reserves of natural gas.

Unconventional oil refers to two kinds of minerals. The first and largest is a mineral formation called oil shale. The rock is an organic marlstone and contains not oil but kerogen, an organic material that has not undergone the full geological process, over tens or hundreds of thousands of years, of conversion by pressure and heat into oil. With the assistance of human technology, however, this geological process can be carried out artificially. The rock is converted into synthetic oil by a process known as cracking or pyrolysis (a general term for the process of carbonising organic matter by heating, similar to making charcoal out of wood or coke out of coal). With conventional oil, the heavy crude brought out of the ground is broken down into lighter hydrocarbons such as gasoline by cracking in refineries – applying heat to crack long-chain hydrocarbon molecules into shorter chains. With shales, the rock itself has to be converted into synthetic oil by pyrolysis. However, excavating the rock and processing it above ground has proved prohibitively expensive and energy-intensive. Pilot programmes have experimented with synthesising oil from rock 'in situ' by turning the subterranean deposit site into a vast retort, heating the rock over a period of months to about 350°C and then pumping up the liquidised kerogen. This also involves freezing the perimeter of the production zone to construct 'ice walls' to stop the flow of ground water.[29]

29   Anthony Andrews, 'Oil Shale: History, Incentives, and Policy', CRS Report for Congress, Washington, DC: Library of Congress, Congressional Research Service, 2006; Andrew Gulliford, *Boomtown Blues: Colorado Oil Shale, 1885–1985*, Niwot: University Press of Colorado, 1989.

In other words, to be economically feasible, the pyrolytic process moves underground, leaving the mineral in place and carrying out the chemical transformation by turning the earth into a cracking machine. The industry must first replace a geological process of oil formation carried out over millennia with a human and mechanical one; then it must transform the lithosphere itself from nature into machine by moving the site of the synthetic process underground. Despite decades of government funding in the United States, none of this has yet proved feasible.

The other form of unconventional oil is the resource known as 'oil sands', especially the Athabasca oil sands in Alberta and the Orinoco Basin sands in Venezuela. This too is not oil, as conventionally known. It is bitumen, the heaviest and most viscous fraction of oil, traditionally used for road-surfacing. The Athabasca tar sands have been mined commercially since 1967, but were reclassified as part of Canada's 'oil reserves' only in 2002, causing those reserves to jump from 5 to 180 billion barrels (becoming the second-highest in the world after Saudi Arabia).[30] The Canadian oil is produced by strip mining the sands on the surface.

As with shale oil, the bitumen must be artificially transformed into synthetic crude oil. Processing it uses large amounts of water to remove the sand – about 120 gallons of water for every barrel of oil produced. But the sand contains other materials, including toxic elements such as nickel, vanadium, lead, chromium, mercury and arsenic. These are collected in storage ponds, with no easy means of disposal. If the walls of the storage ponds are not strong enough, environmentalists warn, there is a risk of overflows. Since the overflows threaten both the rivers and wildlife, nature is brought back into politics. This happens not simply because the environmental movement is strong, or strip mining controversial (as the coal industry discovered), but because energy itself no longer lies conveniently underground, sealed beneath a flat earth, in the almost ready-to-use form of 'nature.'

There is a similar story today with production of unconventional natural gas. Conventional oil and natural gas flow to the wellhead by migrating through pores and fissures in the source rock. Natural gas also exists in large quantities in shales, which are not porous or permeable enough to produce a commercially viable flow of gas. However, by setting off controlled explosions in the well shaft and then pumping down the well under high pressure a mixture of fluid and sand, natural gas producers can mechanically fracture the rock to make it

---

30   Bengt Söderbergh, 'Canada's Oil Sands Resources and Its Future Impact on Global Oil Supply', Uppsala Hydrocarbon Depletion Study Group, MSc degree project, Systems Engineering, Uppsala University, 2005, available at www.fysast.uu.se/ges/sv. Söderbergh argues that its dependence on natural gas makes the Canadian bitumen industry unsustainable, and incompatible with Canada's carbon-reduction obligations as a signatory of the Kyoto protocols.

fissured and porous. By analogy with the high-pressure breakdown of hydro-carbons in conventional oil production known as cracking, this high-pressure fracturing of the shale beds is known as fracking. As with shale oil, the manu-facturing process has to be moved underground, sending into the earth chemi-cal agents ('propants') which, like millions of miniature coal miners, open up spaces in the rock to extract its energy.

Like coal miners, the propants are difficult to control. The millions of gallons of water used in the hydraulic fracking fluid include acids and toxic chemicals, whose use in the US is not subject to standard environmental regu-lation. Found at depths from 250 to 8,000 feet, shale reservoirs can lie close to water sources used by humans, allowing the chemicals used to contaminate supplies of drinking water. In Europe, where the underground fracturing has caused small earthquakes, these concerns have led to the suspension of shale gas drilling and legislation to ban it.[31] Whereas oil is now discovered mainly deep offshore, adding to the cost and difficulty of extracting it but helping to reinforce the separation of nature and politics, shale gas often lies close to large popula-tion centres, reducing the cost of delivering energy to its users. But this means it is found close to large drinking-water supplies. When the propant makes its way from the gas seam into drinking water, it remixes nature and politics.

Twentieth-century politics was constructed around a new object: the econ-omy. The politics of the economy was a de-natured politics. Nature was excluded from politics by practices of calculation. There were two ways in which this was achieved: first, in the mid-twentieth century, by means of constructing the economy as an intervening space, formed out of the dematerialised circulation of money, made possible partly by not having to count the cost of using energy, or of using it up; second, since the 1990s, by the use of cornucopian techniques for representing the size of the world's energy reserves. These techniques rest on the peculiar arrangement by which two entirely separate calculative agen-cies carry out the counting of oil, using different methods of calculation. The oil companies count individual wells and reservoirs, with the use of elaborate measuring devices. The international agencies count global reserves, relying on the abstractions and models of geological theory. The two methods produce very different totals – for the known and unknown oil, for the represented and the real. This gap between the declining quantity of known oil and the expand-ing quantity of unknown, yet-to-be-discovered oil creates a (new) space: a space to be governed by *economic* calculation. For it is economists who claim to have mastered the methods of representation.

---

31   Joseph H. Frantz Jr. and Valerie Jochen, 'Shale Gas White Paper', Schlumberger, 2005, at www.slb.com; Lisa Sumi, *Our Drinking Water at Risk: What EPA and the Oil and Gas Industry Don't Want us to Know About Hydraulic Fracturing*, Washington, DC: Oil and Gas Accountability Project, 2005, available at www.earthworksaction.org; Sylvia Pfeifer and Elizabeth Rigby, 'Earthquake Fears Halt Shale Gas Fracking', *Financial Times*, 1 June 2011.

However, challenged by the evidence of peak oil – that the rate at which oil can flow from these sources has reached a plateau – the economists' account can only survive by opening up anew the politics of nature. To transform kerogen-impregnated rock formations and bitumen-filled sands into oilfields is to acknowledge that what we call nature is a machinated, artificial territory in which all kinds of novel claims and political agencies can form.

The other response of the cornucopians to the evidence of peak oil is to argue that the availability of conventional oil is largely a political question. Most of the additional supplies in the future will come from OPEC states, in particular from the three large Gulf states – Saudi Arabia, Iran and Iraq – each of which is reported to have large reserves whose development has been set back by war, sanctions and the policies of OPEC. Additional supplies will also come from Africa, from countries in which civil wars and political corruption are often said to inhibit investment in oil. There are three things to note about this recourse to 'political' explanations for the shortage of oil: first, there are reasons to suspect that the reserves of most OPEC countries are overstated, for OPEC production quotas are based on the size of reserves. Reserve estimates, therefore, operate not as a partial representation of reality but as part of the mechanism governing rates of extraction. Second, the 'political' obstacle is also a geotechnical problem – below ground as well as above – because the sanctions regimes and wars that have inhibited production in Iran and Iraq have forced them to resort to low-tech means of maintaining pressure in oil reservoirs. These methods may have permanently reduced the amount of oil that is recoverable. Third, if oil supply is a political matter, involving questions of war, human rights and collective futures, this is precisely the argument for a new kind of politics of nature to replace the old, in which the relationship of politics to nature was governed only by economic calculation.

Acknowledging that the size of the main source of conventional reserves – in the Persian Gulf – is an uncertain techno-political question, not an economic one, and not one simply of 'natural resources', places the economic management of political uncertainty in question. It is upon this kind of possibility, rather than any form of energy determinism, that the future politics of energy, and the course of carbon democracy, will unfold.

This book does not offer a general theory of democracy. General theories of democracy, of which there are many, have no place for oil, except as an exception. Rather, the goal has been to follow closely a set of connections that were engineered over the course of a century or more between carbon fuels and certain kinds of democratic and undemocratic politics.

The forms of democracy that emerged in leading industrialised countries by the middle decades of the twentieth century were enabled and shaped by the extraordinary concentrations of energy obtained from the world's limited stores of hydrocarbons, and by the socio-technical arrangements required for extracting and distributing the energy they contained. When the production of energy shifted to oil from the Middle East, however, the transformation provided opportunities to weaken rather than extend, both in the West and the Middle East, the forms of carbon-based political mobilisation on which the emergence of industrial democracy had depended. Exploring the properties of oil, the networks along which it flowed, and the connections established between flows of energy, finance and other objects provides a way to understand how the relations between these various elements and forces were constructed. The relations connected energy and politics, materials and ideas, humans and nonhumans, calculations and the objects of calculation, representations and forms of violence, the present and the future.

Democratic politics developed, thanks to oil, with a peculiar orientation towards the future: the future was a limitless horizon of growth. This horizon was not some natural reflection of a time of plenty. It was the result of a particular way of organising expert knowledge and its objects, in terms of a novel world called 'the economy.' Innovations in methods of calculation, the use of money, the measurement of transactions, and the compiling of national statistics made it possible to imagine the central object of politics as an object that could expand without any form of ultimate material constraint. In the 1967–74 crisis, the relations between these disparate elements were all transformed, and they are being transformed again in the present.

Understanding the contemporary politics of oil involves the difficult task of bringing together the violence that has been repeatedly deployed to secure arrangements for the production of oil and the forms of spectacle and representation that seem somehow an equally indispensable aspect of the undemocratic politics of oil – not least the representation of the most recent rounds of US militarism as a project to bring democracy to the Middle East.[32]

We can better understand the relationship between spectacle and violence, and between other apparently disparate or discordant features of the politics of oil, by following closely the oil itself; not because the material properties or strategic necessity of oil determine everything else (on the contrary, as we have seen, a lot of hard work went into producing America's 'strategic dependence' on its control of Middle Eastern oil), but because, in tracing the connections that were made between pipelines and pumping stations, refineries and shipping routes, road systems and automobile cultures, dollar flows and economic knowledge, weapons experts and militarism, one discovers how a peculiar set of relations was engineered between oil, violence, finance, expertise and democracy.

---

32 Retort (Iain Boal, T. J. Clark, Joseph Matthews and Michael Watts), *Afflicted Powers: Capital and Spectacle in a New Age of War*, London: Verso, 2005.

These relations are quite different from those of the coal age. If the emergence of the mass politics of the early twentieth century, out of which certain sites and episodes of welfare democracy were achieved, should be understood in relation to coal, the limits of contemporary democratic politics can be traced in relation to oil. The possibility of more democratic futures, in turn, depends on the political tools with which we address the passing of the era of fossil fuel.

Bibliography

Besides the articles and books listed below, my research has drawn on a number of archives and databases. Historical statistics on oil production are taken from *Twentieth Century Petroleum Statistics*, Dallas: DeGolyer & MacNaughton, 2009. Current oil and coal statistics are from the US Energy Information Administration, available at www.eia.gov; the International Energy Agency, available at www.iea.org; and the Energy Export Data Browser, available at mazamascience.com. Data on the international arms trade are from the Arms Transfers Database, Stockholm International Peace Research Institute, available at www.sipri.org. UK government documents are from the National Archives of the UK, Public Record Office – in some cases from the online collections available at www.nationalarchives.gov.uk, but in most cases from the collections held at Kew. UK parliamentary debates and reports are from Hansard, available at hansard.millbanksystems.com. United States Government documents are from *Papers Relating to the Foreign Relations of the United States*, available at digital.library.wisc.edu for volumes up to 1960, and for more recent volumes at history.state.gov; and from the invaluable collections at the National Security Archive, available at www.gwu.edu/~nsarchiv. Among the private papers consulted are the James V. Forrestal Papers, the Harry Dexter White Papers and the William A. Eddy Papers, all from the Department of Rare Books and Special Collections, Princeton University Library.

Abisaab, Malek, '"Unruly" Factory Women in Lebanon: Contesting French Colonialism and the National State, 1940–1946', *Journal of Women's History* 16: 3, 2004: 58–82.
Abrahamian, Ervand, *Iran Between Two Revolutions*, Princeton: Princeton University Press, 1982.
────── 'The 1953 Coup in Iran', *Science and Society* 65: 2, 2001: 185–215.
Aburish, Saïd K., *The Rise, Corruption, and Coming Fall of the House of Saud*, New York: St Martin's Griffin, 1996.
Adelman, M. A., 'Is the Oil Shortage Real? Oil Companies as Opec Tax Collectors', *Foreign Policy* 9, 1972–73: 69–107.
────── *The World Petroleum Market*, Baltimore: Johns Hopkins University Press, 1972.
────── *The Genie Out of the Bottle: World Oil Since 1970*, Cambridge, MA: MIT Press, 1995.
──────'My Education in Mineral (Especially Oil) Economics', *Annual Review of Energy and the Environment* 22, 1997: 13–46
────── 'The Real Oil Problem', *Regulation* 27: 1, 2004: 16–21.
Afary, Janet, 'Social Democracy and the Iranian Constitutional Revolution of 1906–11', in John Foran, ed., *A Century of Revolution*, Minneapolis: University of Minnesota Press, 1994.
Akins, James E, 'International Cooperative Efforts in Energy Supply', *Annals of the American Academy of Political and Social Science* 410, 1973: 75–85.

Aldrich, Mark, 'Capital Theory and Racism: From Laissez-Faire to the Eugenics Movement in the Career of Irving Fisher', *Review of Radical Political Economics* 7: 3, October 1975: 33–42.

Alinsky, Saul, *Rules for Radicals: A Practical Primer for Realistic Radicals*, New York: Random House, 1971.

Altvater, Elmer, 'The Social and Natural Environment of Fossil Capitalism', *Socialist Register* 43, 2007: 37–59.

Amman, Daniel, *The King of Oil: The Secret Lives of Marc Rich*, New York: St Martin's Press, 2009.

Anderson, Irvine H., *Aramco, the United States, and Saudi Arabia: A Study of the Dynamics of Foreign Oil Policy, 1933–1950*, Princeton: Princeton University Press, 1981.

Andrew, Christopher, *The Defence of the Realm: The Authorized History of MI5*, London: Penguin, 2010.

Anghie, Antony, 'Colonialism and the Birth of International Institutions: Sovereignty, Economy, and the Mandate System of the League of Nations', *New York University Journal of International Law and Politics* 34: 3, 2002: 513–633.

—— 'Finding the Peripheries: Sovereignty and Colonialism in Nineteenth-Century International Law', *Harvard International Law Journal* 40: 1, 1999: 1–71.

Antonius, George, 'Syria and the French Mandate', *International Affairs* 13: 4, July–August 1934: 523–39.

Ardagh, Colonel John, 'The Red Sea Petroleum Deposits', *Proceedings of the Royal Geographical Society and Monthly Record of Geography* 8: 8, August 1886: 502–7.

Arrighi, Giovanni, *Adam Smith in Beijing: Lineages of the Twenty-First Century*, London: Verso, 2007.

Arrow, Kenneth J., and Gerard Debreu, 'Existence of an Equilibrium for a Competitive Economy', *Econometrica* 22: 3, 1954: 265–90.

Ayres, Robert U., and Benjamin Warr, 'Accounting for Growth: The Role of Physical Work', *Structural Change and Economic Dynamics* 16: 2, 2005: 181–209.

Bamberg, James, *History of the British Petroleum Company*, vol. 3: *British Petroleum and Global Oil, 1950–1975: The Challenge of Nationalism*, Cambridge, UK: CUP, 2000.

Barber, Benjamin R., *Jihad vs McWorld: How Globalism and Tribalism Are Reshaping the World*, New York: Ballantine Books, 1995.

Barber, William J., 'Irving Fisher of Yale', *American Journal of Economics and Sociology* 64: 1, 2005: 43–55.

Barry, Andrew, *Political Machines: Governing a Technological Society*, London: Athlone Press, 2001.

—— 'Technological Zones', *European Journal of Social Theory* 9: 2, 2006: 239–53.

Batatu, Hanna, *The Old Social Classes and the Revolutionary Movements of Iraq: A Study of Iraq's Old Landed and Commercial Classes and of Its Communists, Ba'thists, and Free Officers*, London: Saqi Books, 2004.

Beblawi, Hazem, and Giacomo Luciani, eds, *The Rentier State*, New York: Croom Helm, 1987.

Beeby-Thompson, Arthur, *The Oil Fields of Russia*, London: Crosby Lockwood & Son, 1904.

Beer, George Louis, 'The Future of Mesopotamia', in *African Questions at the Paris Peace Conference: With Papers on Egypt, Mesopotamia, and the Colonial Settlement*, ed. Louis Herbert Gray, New York: Macmillan, 1923.

Beinin, Joel, *Justice for All: The Struggle for Worker Rights in Egypt*, Washington, DC: Solidarity Center, 2010.

Beinin, Joel, and Zachary Lockman, *Workers on the Nile: Nationalism, Communism, Islam, and the Egyptian Working Class, 1882–1954*, Princeton: Princeton University Press, 1987.

Bell, Daniel, *The Coming of Post-Industrial Society: A Venture in Social Forecasting*, New York: Basic Books, 1976.

Bernstein, Michael A., *A Perilous Progress: Economics and Public Purpose in Twentieth-Century America*, Princeton: Princeton University Press, 2001.

Bialer, Uri, 'Fuel Bridge Across the Middle East: Israel, Iran, and the Eilat–Ashkelon Oil Pipeline', *Israel Studies* 12: 3, 2007: 29–67.

Bill, James A., *The Eagle and the Lion: The Tragedy of American-Iranian Relations*, New Haven: Yale University Press, 1988.

Birnbaum, Eugene A., *Changing the United States Commitment to Gold*, Princeton: International Finance Section, Dept. of Economics, Princeton University, 1967.

Blair, John Malcolm, *The Control of Oil*, New York: Pantheon Books, 1976.

Blewett, Neal, 'The Franchise in the United Kingdom 1885–1918', *Past and Present* 32, December 1965: 27–56.

Block, Fred, *The Origins of International Economic Disorder: A Study of United States International Monetary Policy from World War II to the Present*, Berkeley: University of California Press, 1977.

Bowden, Gary, 'The Social Construction of Validity in Estimates of US Crude Oil Reserves', *Social Studies of Science* 15: 2, 1985: 207–40.

Brailsford, Henry Noel, *After the Peace*, London: L. Parsons, 1920.

—— *The War of Steel and Gold: A Study of the Armed Peace*, 10th edn, London: G. Bell & Sons, 1918.

Brand, Carl F., *British Labour's Rise to Power*, Stanford: Stanford University Press, 1941.

—— 'The Attitude of British Labor toward President Wilson During the Peace Conference', *American Historical Review* 42: 2, 1937: 244–55.

Brandt, Adam, 'Technical Report 6: Methods of Forecasting Future Oil Supply', *UKERC Review of Evidence for Global Oil Depletion*, London: UK Energy Research Centre, 2009, available at www.ukerc.ac.uk.

Bridge, Gavin, 'Global Production Networks and the Extractive Sector: Governing Resource-Based Development', *Journal of Economic Geography* 8: 3, 2008: 389–419.

'British Labor's War Aims: Text of a Statement Adopted at the Special National Labor Conference at Central Hall, Westminster, on December 28, 1917', *International Conciliation* 4: 123, 1918: 45–56.

Bromley, Simon, *American Hegemony and World Oil*, University Park: Pennsylvania State University Press, 1991.

—— 'The United States and the Control of World Oil', *Government and Opposition* 40: 2, 2005: 225–55.

Brown, Geoff, *Sabotage: A Study in Industrial Conflict*, Nottingham: Bertrand Russell Peace Foundation for Spokesman Books, 1977.

Brown, Nathan, *Peasant Politics in Modern Egypt: The Struggle Against the State*, New Haven: Yale University Press, 1990.

Burke, Edmund, *Prelude to Protectorate in Morocco: Precolonial Protest and Resistance, 1860–1912*, Chicago: University of Chicago Press, 1976.

Busch, Briton Cooper, *Britain and the Persian Gulf, 1894–1914*, Berkeley: University of California Press, 1967.

Butler, Judith, *Precarious Life: The Powers of Mourning and Violence*, New York: Verso, 2004.

Cain, P. J., *Hobson and Imperialism: Radicalism, New Liberalism, and Finance 1887–1938*, Oxford: OUP, 2002.

Callon, Michel, *The Laws of the Markets*, Oxford: Blackwell Publishers/Sociological Review, 1998.

—— 'Some Elements of a Sociology of Translation: Domestication of the Scallops and the Fishermen of St Brieuc Bay', in John Law, ed., *Power, Action and Belief: A New Sociology of Knowledge?*, London: Routledge, 1986.

Callon, Michel, Pierre Lascoumes and Yannick Barthe, *Acting in an Uncertain World: An Essay on Technical Democracy*, Cambridge, MA: MIT Press, 2009.

Cambel, Ali Bulent, 'Energy', *Science Journal* 3: 10, 1967: 57–62.

Campbell, Colin J., and Jean H. Laherrère, 'The End of Cheap Oil', *Scientific American* 278: 3, March 1998: 78–83.

Canning, Kathleen, *Languages of Labor and Gender: Female Factory Work in Germany, 1850–1914*, Ithaca: Cornell University Press, 1996.

Carew, Anthony, *Labour Under the Marshall Plan: The Politics of Productivity and the Marketing of Management Science*, Detroit: Wayne State University Press, 1987.

de Cecco, Marcello, *The International Gold Standard: Money and Empire*, 2nd edn, New York: St Martin's Press, 1984.

Church, Roy A., Quentin Outram and David N. Smith, 'The Militancy of British Miners, 1893–1986: Interdisciplinary Problems and Perspectives', *Journal of Interdisciplinary History* 22: 1, Summer 1991: 49–66.

Churchill, Randolph S., *Winston S. Churchill: Young Statesman 1901–1914*, London: Heinemann, 1967.

Churchill, Winston, *The World Crisis, 1911–1918*, abridged and revised edn, London: Penguin, 2007.

Citino, Nathan J., 'Defending the "Postwar Petroleum Order": The US, Britain and the 1954 Saudi–Onassis Tanker Deal', *Diplomacy & Statecraft* 11: 2, 2000: 137–60.

—— *From Arab Nationalism to OPEC: Eisenhower, King Sa'ud, and the Making of US–Saudi Relations*, Bloomington: Indiana University Press, 2002.

Clarke, Keith C., and Jeffrey J. Hemphill, 'The Santa Barbara Oil Spill: A Retrospective', in Darrick Danta, ed., *Yearbook of the Association of Pacific Coast Geographers*, Honolulu: University of Hawai'i Press, 2002.

Cleaver, William, 'Wildcats in the Appalachian Coal Fields', in Midnight Notes Collective, eds, *Midnight Notes, Midnight Oil: Work, Energy, War, 1972–1992*, Brooklyn: Autonomedia, 1992.

Coatsworth, John H., 'Welfare', *American Historical Review* 101: 1, February 1996: 1–12.

Cocks, Frederick Seymour, *E. D. Morel: The Man and His Work*, London: G. Allen & Unwin, 1920.

Cohen, Lizabeth, *Making a New Deal: Industrial Workers in Chicago, 1919–1939*, Cambridge, UK: CUP, 1990.

Cohen, Stuart A., *British Policy in Mesopotamia, 1903–1914*, Reading: Ithaca Press, 2008.

Committee on the Royal Mint, Great Britain, *Report from the Select Committee on the Royal Mint*, London: HMSO, 1849.

Cooley, John K., *Unholy Wars: Afghanistan, America and International Terrorism*, 2nd edn, London: Pluto Press, 2000.

Corbin, David, *Life, Work, and Rebellion in the Coal Fields: The Southern West Virginia Miners, 1880–1922*, Champaign: University of Illinois Press, 1981.

Cordovez, Diego, and Selig S. Harrison, *Out of Afghanistan: The Inside Story of the Soviet Withdrawal*, London: OUP, 1995.

Coronil, Fernando, *The Magical State: Nature, Money and Modernity in Venezuela*, Chicago: University of Chicago Press, 1997.

Crummey, D., *Banditry, Rebellion, and Social Protest in Africa*, Oxford: J. Currey, 1986.

Curtis, Lionel, *The Problem of the Commonwealth*, London: Macmillan, 1915.

Daly, Herman E., *Steady-State Economics: The Economics of Biophysical Equilibrium and Moral Growth*, San Francisco: W. H. Freeman, 1977.

Daoudi, M. S., and M. S. Dajani, 'The 1967 Oil Embargo Revisited', *Journal of Palestine Studies* 13: 2, 1984: 65–90.

Dasgupta, Partha, and Geoffrey Heal, *Economic Theory and Exhaustible Resources*, Cambridge, UK: CUP, 1979.

Davis, Mike, *Late Victorian Holocausts: El Niño Famines and the Making of the Third World*, London: Verso, 2001.

Davis, Simon, *Contested Space: Anglo-American Relations in the Persian Gulf, 1939–1947*, Leiden: Martinus Nijhoff, 2009.

Deffeyes, Kenneth S., *Hubbert's Peak: The Impending World Oil Shortage*, Princeton: Princeton University Press, 2001.

De Geer, Hans, 'Trading Companies in Twentieth-Century Sweden', in Geoffrey Jones, ed., *The Multinational Traders*, New York: Routledge, 1998.

De Grazia, Victoria, *Irresistible Empire: America's Advance through Twentieth-Century Europe*, Cambridge, MA: Harvard University Press, 2005.

Dennis, Michael Aaron, 'Drilling for Dollars: The Making of US Petroleum Reserve Estimates, 1921–25', *Social Studies of Science* 15: 2, May 1985: 241–65.

DeNovo, John A., 'A Railroad for Turkey: The Chester Project, 1908–1913', *The Business History Review* 33: 3, 1959: 300–29.

——— *American Interests and Policies in the Middle East, 1900–1939*, Minneapolis: University of Minnesota Press, 1963.

Desrosières, Alain, 'Managing the Economy: The State, the Market, and Statistics', in T. Porter and D. Ross, eds, *The Cambridge History of Science, vol. 7: The Modern Social Sciences*, Cambridge, UK: CUP, 2003: 553–64.

Dirks, Nicholas, *The Hollow Crown: Ethnohistory of an Indian Kingdom*, 2nd edn, Ann Arbor: University of Michigan Press, 1993.

Disch, Lisa, 'Representation as "Spokespersonship": Bruno Latour's Political Theory', *Parallax* 14: 3, August 2008: 88–100.

Dix, Keith, *What's a Coal Miner to Do? The Mechanization of Coal Mining*, Pittsburgh: University of Pittsburgh Press, 1988.

Dodge, Toby, *Inventing Iraq: The Failure of Nation-Building and a History Denied*, New York: Columbia University Press, 2003.

——— 'What Accounts for the Evolution of International Policy Towards Iraq 1990–2003?' Iraq Inquiry, 5 November 2009, available at www.iraqinquiry.org.uk.

Dunning, Thad, *Crude Democracy: Natural Resource Wealth and Political Regimes*, Cambridge, UK: CUP, 2008.

Earle, Edward Mead, 'The Turkish Petroleum Company: A Study in Oleaginous Diplomacy', *Political Science Quarterly* 39: 2, 1924: 269–75.

——— *Turkey, the Great Powers, and the Bagdad Railway: A Study in Imperialism*, New York: Macmillan, 1923.

Edwards, P. K., *Strikes in the United States, 1881–1974*, New York: St Martin's Press, 1981.

Eichengreen, Barry, 'The British Economy Between the Wars', in Rodrick Floud and Paul Johnson, eds, *The Cambridge Economic History of Modern Britain*, Cambridge, UK: CUP, 2004: 314–43.

——— *Global Imbalances and the Lessons of Bretton Woods*, Cambridge, MA: MIT Press, 2007.

Eichholtz, Dietrich, *Die Bagdadbahn, Mesopotamien Und Die Deutsche Ölpolitik Bis 1918: Aufhaltsamer Übergang Ins Erdölzeitalter: Mit Dokumenten*, Leipzig: Leipziger, Universitätsverlag, 2007.

El Azhary, M. S., 'The Attitudes of the Superpowers Towards the Gulf War', *International Affairs* 59: 4, Autumn 1983: 609–20.

Eley, Geoff, *Forging Democracy: The History of the Left in Europe, 1850–2000*, Oxford: OUP, 2002.

Engdahl, William, *A Century of War: Anglo-American Oil Politics and the New World Order*, 2nd edn, London: Pluto Press, 2004.

Engels, Friedrich, 'The Bakunists at Work', in Karl Marx and Friedrich Engels, eds, *Revolution in Spain*, London: Lawrence & Wishart, 1939 (first published in *Der Volksstaat*, 31 October, 2 and 5 November, 1873).

Fagge, Roger, *Power, Culture, and Conflict in the Coalfields: West Virginia and South Wales, 1900–1922*, Manchester: Manchester University Press, 1996.

Farouk-Sluglett, Marion, and Peter Sluglett, *Iraq Since 1958: From Revolution to Dictatorship*, 3rd edn, London: I. B. Tauris, 2001.

Feis, Herbert, 'The Anglo-American Oil Agreement', *Yale Law Journal* 55: 5, 1946: 1,174–90.

Ferrier, Ronald W., *The History of the British Petroleum Company, vol. 1: The Developing Years: 1901–1932*, Cambridge, UK: CUP, 1982.

Forrestal, James, *The Forrestal Diaries*, ed. Walter Millis and E. S. Duffield, New York: Viking Press, 1951.

Foucault, Michel, *Security, Territory, Population: Lectures at the Collège de France 1977–1978*, London: Palgrave Macmillan, 2007.

Frank, Alison Fleig, *Oil Empire: Visions of Prosperity in Austrian Galicia*, Cambridge, MA: Harvard University Press, 2007.

Frankel, P. H., *Mattei: Oil and Power Politics*, London: Faber & Faber, 1966.

Frantz, Joseph H., and Valerie Jochen, 'Shale Gas White Paper', Schlumberger, 2005, available at www.slb.com.

Fremdling, Rainer, 'Anglo-German Rivalry in Coal Markets in France, the Netherlands and Germany 1850–1913', *Journal of European Economic History* 25: 3, 1996: 599–646.

Fursenko, A. A., *The Battle for Oil: The Economics and Politics of International Corporate Conflict over Petroleum, 1860–1930*, Greenwich: Jai Press, 1990.

Galpern, Steven G., *Money, Oil, and Empire in the Middle East: Sterling and Postwar Imperialism, 1944–1971*, Cambridge, UK: CUP, 2009.

Gates, Robert Michael, *From the Shadows: The Ultimate Insider's Story of Five Presidents and How They Won the Cold War*, New York: Touchstone, 1997.

Gavin, Francis J., *Gold, Dollars, and Power: The Politics of International Monetary Relations, 1958–1971*, Chapel Hill: University of North Carolina Press, 2004.

Gelvin, James L., *Divided Loyalties: Nationalism and Mass Politics in Syria at the Close of Empire*, Berkeley: University of California Press, 1998.

Gendzier, Irene, *Notes from the Minefield: United States Intervention in Lebanon, 1945–1958*, New York: Columbia University Press, 2nd edn, 2006.

Gerretson, Frederik Carel, *The History of the Royal Dutch*, Leiden: E. J. Brill, 1953–1957.

Gilmour, David, *Curzon: Imperial Statesman*, 1st US edn, New York: Farrar, Straus & Giroux, 2003.

Goldberg, Ellis, 'Peasants in Revolt – Egypt 1919', *International Journal of Middle East Studies* 24: 2, 1992: 261–80.

Goldberg, Ellis, Erik Wibbels and Eric Mvukiyehe, 'Lessons from Strange Cases: Democracy, Development, and the Resource Curse in the US States', *Comparative Political Studies* 41: 4–5, 2008: 477–514.

Goldman, Marshall I., 'The Soviet Union', in Raymond Vernon, ed., *The Oil Crisis*, New York: Norton, 1976.

Goodrich, Carter, *The Miner's Freedom: A Study of the Working Life in a Changing Industry*, Boston: Marshall Jones Co., 1925.

Graham, Benjamin, *Storage and Stability: A Modern Ever-Normal Granary*, New York: McGraw-Hill Book Company, Inc., 1937.

Graham-Brown, Sarah, *Sanctioning Saddam: The Politics of Intervention in Iraq*, London: I. B. Tauris/MERIP, 1999.

Greenpeace, *Decentralising Power: An Energy Reserve for the 21st Century*, 2005, available at www.greenpeace.org.uk.

Greenspan, Alan, *The Age of Turbulence: Adventures in a New World*, London: Penguin, 2007.

Grieb, Kenneth J., 'Standard Oil and the Financing of the Mexican Revolution', *California Historical Quarterly* 50: 1, 1971: 59–71.

Grovogui, Siba N., *Sovereigns, Quasi Sovereigns, and Africans: Race and Self-Determination in International Law*, Minneapolis: University of Minnesota Press, 1996.

Guerrien, Bernard, 'Is There Anything Worth Keeping in Standard Microeconomics?' *Post-Autistic Economics Review* 12, 2002: Article 1.

Gulliford, Andrew, *Boomtown Blues: Colorado Oil Shale, 1885–1985*, Niwot: University Press of Colorado, 1989.

Haberl, Helmut, 'The Global Socioeconomic Energetic Metabolism as a Sustainability Problem', *Energy* 31: 1, 2006: 87–99.

Hakimian, Hassan, 'Wage Labor and Migration: Persian Workers in Southern Russia, 1880–1914', *International Journal of Middle East Studies* 17: 4, 1985: 443–62.

Halliday, Fred, 'Trade Unions and the Working Class Opposition', *MERIP Reports* 71, October 1978: 7–13.

Hanak, H., 'The Union of Democratic Control During the First World War', *Historical Research* 36: 94, 1963: 168–80.

Hansen, James, Makiko Sato, Pushker Kharecha, Gary Russell, David W. Lea and Mark Siddall, 'Climate Change and Trace Gases', *Philosophical Transactions of the Royal Society A* 365, 2007: 1,925–54.

Harrison, Royden, ed., *Independent Collier: The Coal Miner as Archetypal Proletarian Reconsidered*, New York: St Martin's, 1978.

Harvey, David, *A Brief History of Neoliberalism*, Oxford: OUP, 2005.

—— *The New Imperialism*, Oxford: OUP, 2003.

—— *Spaces of Capital: Towards a Critical Geography*, Edinburgh: Edinburgh University Press, 2001.

Hayek, F. A., 'A Commodity Reserve Currency', *Economic Journal* 53: 210/211, June–September 1943: 176–84.

Hazlitt, Henry, *Will Dollars Save the World?*, New York: Appleton-Century, 1947.

Hecht, Gabrielle, *The Radiance of France: Nuclear Power and National Identity After World War II*, Cambridge, MA: MIT Press, 1998.

Henry, James Dodds, *Baku: An Eventful History*, New York: Arno Press, 1977 [1905].

Hewins, Ralph, *Mr Five Per Cent: The Story of Calouste Gulbenkian*, New York: Rinehart & Company, 1958.

Hicks, John, *Value and Capital*, Oxford: OUP, 1939.

Hobsbawm, Eric, *The Age of Empire, 1875–1914*, New York: Vintage, 1989.

Hobson, J. A., *Imperialism: A Study*, London: James Nisbet & Co., 1902.

—— *The War in South Africa: Its Causes and Effects*, London: James Nisbet & Co., 1900.

—— *Towards International Government*, New York: Macmillan, 1915.

Hoch, Myron L., 'The Oil Strike of 1945', *Southern Economic Journal* 15: 2, 1948: 117–33.

Holter, Darryl, *The Battle for Coal: Miners and the Politics of Nationalization in France, 1940–1950*, DeKalb: Northern Illinois University Press, 1992.

Hotelling, Harold, 'The Economics of Exhaustible Resources', *Journal of Political Economy* 39: 2, 1931: 137–75.

Houtsma, M. Th., A. J. Wensinck and T. W. Arnold, eds, *The Encyclopaedia of Islam: A Dictionary of the Geography, Ethnography and Biography of the Muhammadan Peoples*, Leiden: E. J. Brill, 1913–1936.

Hubbert, M. King, *Nuclear Energy and the Fossil Fuels*, Houston: Shell Development Company (Publication 95), 1956.

Hull, Edward, *The Coal-Fields of Great Britain: Their History, Structure, and Duration, With Notices of the Coal-Fields of Other Parts of the World*, London: Edward Stanford, 1861.

Huntington, Samuel P., 'The United States', in *The Crisis of Democracy: Report on the Governability of Democracies to the Trilateral Commission*, ed. Michel Crozier, Samuel P. Huntington and Joji Wantanuki, New York: New York University Press, 1975.

Hyslop, Jonathan, 'Martial Law and Military Power in the Construction of the South African State: Jan Smuts and the "Solid Guarantee of Force", 1899–1924', *Journal of Historical Sociology* 22: 2, 2009: 234–68.

Intergovernmental Panel on Climate Change, *Fourth Assessment Report*, 2007, available at www.ipcc.ch.

International Energy Agency, *World Energy Outlook 2008*, New Milford: Turpin Distribution, 2008.

'International Notes', *Journal of International Relations* 11: 1, 1920: 120–54.

Jack (Kent), Marian, 'The Purchase of the British Government's Shares in the British Petroleum Company 1912–1914', *Past and Present* 39: 1, April 1968: 139–68.

Jacobs, Mathew, 'The Perils and Promise of Islam: The United States and the Muslim Middle East in the Early Cold War', *Diplomatic History* 30: 4, 2006: 705–39.

Jaggers, Keith, and Ted Robert Gurr, 'Tracking Democracy's Third Wave with the Polity III Data', *Journal of Peace Research* 32: 4, 1995: 469–82.

Jevons, H. Stanley, *The British Coal Trade*, London: E. P. Dutton, 1915.

Jevons, William Stanley, *The Coal Question: An Inquiry Concerning the Progress of the Nation and the Probable Exhaustion of Our Coal-Mines*, London: Macmillan, 1865.

Jones, Charles O., and Randall Strahan, 'The Effect of Energy Politics on Congressional and Executive Organization in the 1970s', *Legislative Studies Quarterly* 10: 2, 1985: 151–79.

Jones, Geoffrey, *The State and the Emergence of the British Oil Industry*, London: Macmillan, 1981.

Jorgenson, Dale W., ed., *The Economics of Productivity*, Cheltenham: Edward Elgar, 2009.

Kanafani, Ghassan, *The 1936–39 Revolt in Palestine*, New York: Committee for a Democratic Palestine, 1972.

Kandiyoti, Rafael, *Pipelines: Flowing Oil and Crude Politics*, London: I. B. Tauris, 2008.

Kane, N. Stephen, 'Corporate Power and Foreign Policy: Efforts of American Oil Companies to Influence United States Relations with Mexico, 1921–1928', *Diplomatic History* 1: 2, 1977: 170–98.

Kanefsky, John W., 'Motive Power in British Industry and the Accuracy of the 1870 Factory Return', *Economic History Review* 32: 3, 1979: 360–75.

Karl, Terry Lynn, *The Paradox of Plenty: Oil Booms and Petro-States*, Berkeley: University of California Press, 1997.

Karsh, Efraim, 'Military Power and Foreign Policy Goals: The Iran–Iraq War Revisited', *International Affairs* 64: 1, Winter 1987–88: 83–95.

Keeling, Charles D., 'Rewards and Penalties of Monitoring the Earth', *Annual Review of Energy and the Environment* 23, 1988: 25–82.

Kent, Marian, 'Agent of Empire? The National Bank of Turkey and British Foreign Policy', *Historical Journal* 18: 2, 1975: 367–89.

——— *Moguls and Mandarins: Oil, Imperialism, and the Middle East in British Foreign Policy*, London: Frank Cass, 1993.

——— *Oil and Empire: British Policy and Mesopotamian Oil, 1900–1920*, London: Macmillan, 1976.

Kerr, Clark, and Abraham Siegel, 'The Interindustry Propensity to Strike: An International Comparison', in Arthur Kornhauser, Robert Dubin and Arthur M. Ross, eds, *Industrial Conflict*, New York: McGraw-Hill, 1934: 189–212.

Keynes, John Maynard, *Indian Currency and Finance*, London: Macmillan, 1913.

——— *The Collected Writings of John Maynard Keynes*, ed. Donald Moggridge, London: Macmillan, 1971–1989.

——— *The General Theory of Employment, Interest and Money*, London: Macmillan, 1936.

——— 'William Stanley Jevons, 1835–1882: A Centenary Allocation on His Life and Work as Economist and Statistician', *Journal of the Royal Statistical Society* 99: 3, 1936: 516–55.

al-Khafaji, Isam, *Tormented Births: Passages to Modernity in Europe and the Middle East*, London: I. B. Tauris, 2004.

Khalidi, Rashid, *Resurrecting Empire: Western Footprints and America's Perilous Path in the Middle East*, Boston: Beacon Press, 2004.

——— *The Iron Cage: The Story of the Palestinian Struggle for Statehood*, Boston: Beacon Press, 2006.

Khalidi, Walid, ed., *From Haven to Conquest: Readings in Zionism and the Palestine Problem Until 1948*, Washington, DC: Institute for Palestine Studies, 1971.

Kimball, Jeffrey, 'The Nixon Doctrine: A Saga of Misunderstanding', *Presidential Studies Quarterly* 36: 1, 2006: 59–74.

Klare, Michael, *Resource Wars: The New Landscape of Global Conflict*, New York: Henry Holt, 2001.

——— *Rising Powers, Shrinking Planet: The New Geopolitics of Energy*, New York: Metrolpolitan Books, 2008.

Klein, Naomi, *The Shock Doctrine: The Rise of Disaster Capitalism*, London: Allen Lane, 2007.

Knaack, Marcelle Size, *Encyclopedia of US Air Force Aircraft and Missile Systems*, vol. 1, Washington, DC: Office of Air Force History, 1978.

Knights, Mark, *Representation and Misrepresentation in Later Stuart Britain: Partisanship and Political Culture*, Oxford: OUP, 2006.

Knock, Thomas J., *To End All Wars: Woodrow Wilson and the Quest for a New World Order*, New York: OUP, 1992.

Kuznets, Simon, Lillian Epstein and Elizabeth Jenks, *National Income and Its Composition, 1919–1938*, New York: National Bureau of Economic Research, 1941.

Ladjevardi, Habib, *Labor Unions and Autocracy in Iran*, Syracuse: Syracuse University Press, 1985.

Laslett, John H. M., *Colliers Across the Sea: A Comparative Study of Class Formation in Scotland and the American Midwest, 1830–1924*, Champaign: University of Illinois Press, 2000.

—— 'State Policy Towards Labour and Labour Organizations, 1830–1939: Anglo-American Union Movements', in Peter Mathias and Sidney Pollard, eds, *The Cambridge Economic History of Europe*, vol. 8: *The Industrial Economies: The Development of Economic and Social Policies*, Cambridge, UK: CUP, 1989: 495–548.

Latour, Bruno, *Politics of Nature: How to Bring the Sciences into Democracy*, Cambridge, MA: Harvard University Press, 2004.

—— *We Have Never Been Modern*, Cambridge, MA: Harvard University Press, 1993.

Lee, P. J., *Statistical Methods for Estimating Petroleum Resources*, Oxford: OUP, 2008.

Leith-Ross, Frederick, 'Financial and Economic Developments in Egypt', *International Affairs* 28: 1, 1952: 29–37.

Lenin, V. I., *Collected Works*, Moscow: Progress Publishing, 1960.

Levinson, Marc, *The Box: How the Shipping Container Made the World Smaller and the World Economy Bigger*, Princeton: Princeton University Press, 2006.

Linden, H. R., 'The Evolution of an Energy Contrarian', *Annual Review of Energy and the Environment* 21, 1996: 31–67.

Lippmann, Walter, *The Cold War: A Study in US Foreign Policy*, New York: Harper, 1947.

List, Friedrich, *National System of Political Economy*, transl. G. A. Matile, Philadelphia: J. P. Lippincott, 1856 [1841].

Little, Douglas, 'Cold War and Covert Action: The United States and Syria, 1945–1958', *Middle East Journal* 44: 1, 1990: 51–75.

—— 'Mission Impossible: The CIA and the Cult of Covert Action in the Middle East', *Diplomatic History* 28: 5, 2004: 663–701.

—— 'The United States and the Kurds: A Cold War Story', *Journal of Cold War Studies* 12: 4, 2010: 63–98.

Lockman, Zachary, *Comrades and Enemies: Arab and Jewish Workers in Palestine, 1906–1948*, Berkeley: University of California Press, 1996.

Lohmann, Larry, *Carbon Trading: A Critical Conversation on Climate Change, Privatisation and Power*, Development Dialogue no. 48, September 2006.

Long, David, *Towards a New Liberal Internationalism: The International Theory of J. A. Hobson*, Cambridge, UK: CUP, 1996.

Longrigg, Stephen Hemsley, *Oil in the Middle East: Its Discovery and Development*, London: OUP, 1968.

Louis, William Roger, *Ends of British Imperialism: The Scramble for Empire, Suez and Decolonization: Collected Essays*, London: I. B. Tauris, 2006.

Lowi, Theodore J., 'The State in Political Science: How We Become What We Study', *American Political Science Review* 86: 1, 1992: 1–7.

Lugard, Frederick, *The Dual Mandate in British Tropical Africa*, 5th edn, Hamden, CT: Archon Books, 1965.

Luxemburg, Rosa, *The Mass Strike, the Political Party, and the Trade Unions* (a translation of *Massenstreik, Partei und Gewerkschaften*, 1906), Detroit: Marxist Educational Society, 1925.

Mabro, Robert, 'OPEC and the Price of Oil', *Energy Journal* 13: 2, 1992: 1–17.

MacKenzie, Donald, *An Engine, Not a Camera: How Financial Models Shape Markets*, Cambridge, MA: MIT Press, 2006.

—— *Statistics in Britain, 1865–1930: The Social Construction of Scientific Knowledge*, Edinburgh: Edinburgh University Press, 1981.

MacKenzie, Donald, Fabian Muniesa and Lucy Siu, eds, *Do Economists Make Markets? On the Performativity of Economics*, Princeton: Princeton University Press, 2007.

Mackenzie King, William Lyon, *Industry and Humanity: A Study in the Principles Underlying Industrial Reconstruction*, Boston: Houghton Mifflin, 1918.

Madureira, N. L., 'Oil in the Age of Steam', *Journal of Global History* 5: 1, 2010: 75–94.

Magoon, L. B., and J. W. Schmoker, 'The Total Petroleum System – the Natural Fluid Network that Constrains the Assessment Unit', in *US Geological Survey Digital Data Series 60*, 2000.

Mahaim, Ernest, and Harald Westergaard, 'The General Strike in Belgium, April 1902', *Economic Journal* 12: 47, 1902: 421–30.

Mahdavy, Hussein, 'The Patterns and Problems of Economic Development in Rentier States: The Case of Iran', in M. A. Cook, ed., *Studies in the Economic History of the Middle East*, London: OUP, 1970.

Mallet, Serge, *Essays on the New Working Class*, St Louis: Telos Press, 1975.

—— *The New Working Class*, Nottingham: Bertrand Russell Peace Foundation for Spokesman Books, 1975.

Mamdani, Mahmood, *Citizen and Subject: Contemporary Africa and the Legacy of Late Colonialism*, Princeton: Princeton University Press, 1996.

Manela, Erez, *The Wilsonian Moment: Self-Determination and the International Origins of Anticolonial Nationalism*, Oxford: OUP, 2007.

Mantena, Karuna, *Alibis of Empire: Henry Maine and the Ends of Liberal Imperialism*, Princeton: Princeton University Press, 2010.

Marks, Shula, and Stanley Trapido, 'Lord Milner and the South African State', *History Workshop* 8, 1979: 50–80.

Marshall, Alfred, *Principles of Economics*, 8th edn, London: Macmillan, 1920.

Maunsell, F. R., 'The Mesopotamian Petroleum Field', *Geographical Journal* 9: 5, 1897: 528–32.

Mayer, Arno J., *Wilson vs Lenin: Political Origins of the New Diplomacy, 1917–1918*, Cleveland: World Publishing Company, 1969.

McCarthy, Tom, *Auto Mania: Cars, Consumers, and the Environment*, New Haven: Yale University Press, 2007.

McCloskey, Deirdre, 'Yes, There Is Something Worth Keeping in Microeconomics', *Post-Autistic Economics Review* 15: 4, 2002.

McFarland, Andrew S., 'Energy Lobbies', *Annual Review of Energy* 9, 1984: 501–27.

Meadows, Donella H., Dennis L. Meadows, Jorgen Randers and William W. Behrens, *The Limits to Growth: A Report for the Club of Rome's Project on the Predicament of Mankind*, New York: Universe Books, 1972.

Mehrling, Perry, 'Retrospectives: Economists and the Fed: Beginnings', *Journal of Economic Perspectives* 16: 4, 2002: 207–18.

Meredith, Martin, *Diamonds, Gold, and War: The British, the Boers, and the Making of South Africa*, New York: Public Affairs, 2008.

Miller, Geoffrey, *Straits: British Policy Towards the Ottoman Empire and the Origins of the Dardanelles Campaign*, Hull: University of Hull Press, 1997.

Milne, Seumas, *The Enemy Within: The Secret War Against the Miners*, 3rd edn, London: Verso, 2004.

Milner, Alfred, *England in Egypt*, 11th edn, London: Edward Arnold, 1904.

Mirowski, Philip, *Machine Dreams: Economics Becomes a Cyborg Science*, Cambridge, UK: CUP, 2002.

Mirowski, Philip, and Dieter Plehwe, eds, *The Road from Mont Pèlerin: The Making of the Neoliberal Thought Collective*, Cambridge, MA: Harvard University Press, 2009.

Mitchell, Timothy, 'Economists and the Economy in the Twentieth Century', in George Steinmetz, ed., *The Politics of Method in the Human Sciences: Positivism and Its Epistemological Others*, Durham: Duke University Press, 2005.

—— *Rule of Experts: Egypt, Techno-Politics, Modernity*, Berkeley: University of California Press, 2002.

—— 'The Work of Economics: How a Discipline Makes Its World', *European Journal of Sociology* 46: 2, 2005: 297–320.

Monroe, Elizabeth, *Philby of Arabia*, Reading: Ithaca Press, 1998.

Morel, E. D., *King Leopold's Rule in Africa*, London: Heinemann, 1904.

—— *Morocco in Diplomacy*, London: Smith, Elder & Co., 1912.

—— *Red Rubber: The Story of the Rubber Slave Trade Flourishing on the Congo in the Year of Grace 1906*, London: T. Fisher Unwin, 1906.

Morgan, Mary S., *The History of Econometric Ideas*, Cambridge, UK: CUP, 1990.

Mortimer, Joanne Stafford, 'Commercial Interests and German Diplomacy in the Agadir Crisis', *Historical Journal* 10: 4, 1967: 440–56.

Mosley, Leonard, *Gideon Goes to War*, London: Arthur Baker, 1955.

Mumford, Lewis, *Technics and Civilization*, New York: Harcourt, Brace, 1934.

Muttit, Greg, *Fuel on the Fire: Oil and Politics in Occupied Iraq*, London: Bodley Head, 2011.

Nalbantian, Tsolin, 'Fashioning Armenians in Lebanon, 1946–1958', PhD thesis, Department of Middle Eastern, South Asian, and African Studies, Columbia University, 2010.

Neatby, H. Blair, 'William Lyon Mackenzie King', in *Dictionary of Canadian Biography Online*, at www.biographi.ca.

von Neumann, John, 'John von Neumann on Technological Prospects and Global Limits', *Population and Development Review* 12: 1, March 1986 [1955]: 117–26.

Neville, Robert G., 'The Courrières Colliery Disaster, 1906', *Journal of Contemporary History* 13: 1, 1978: 33–52.

Nitzan, Jonathan, and Shimshon Bichler, *The Global Political Economy of Israel*, London: Pluto Press, 2002.

Nowell, Gregory, *Mercantile States and the World Oil Cartel, 1900–1939*, Ithaca: Cornell University Press, 1994.

Nuvolari, Alessandro, 'Collective Invention During the British Industrial Revolution: The Case of the Cornish Pumping Engine', *Cambridge Journal of Economics* 28: 3, 2004: 347–63.

Nuvolari, Alessandro, and Bart Verspagen, 'Technical Choice, Innovation and British Steam Engineering, 1800–1850', *Economic History Review* 62, 2009: 685–710.

Nuvolari, Alessandro, Bart Verspagen and Nick von Tunzelmann, 'The Early Diffusion of the Steam Engine in Britain, 1700–1800: A Reappraisal', *Cliometrica*, 2011: 1–31.

Nye, David E., *Consuming Power: A Social History of American Energies*, Cambridge, MA: MIT Press, 1999.

Odell, Peter R., *Oil and World Power*, 5th edn, Harmondsworth: Penguin, 1979.

Okruhlik, Gwenn, 'Networks of Dissent: Islamism and Reform in Saudi Arabia', *Current History* 101: 651, 2002: 22–8.

Olusoga, David, and Casper W. Erichsen, *The Kaiser's Holocaust: Germany's Forgotten Genocide and the Colonial Roots of Nazism*, London: Faber & Faber, 2010.

Oppenheim, Lassa, *A Treatise on International Law*, ed. Ronald F. Roxburgh, London: Longmans, Green, 1920.

Orwell, George, 'You and the Atomic Bomb' (1945), in Sonia Orwell and Ian Angus, eds, *The Collected Essays, Journalism and Letters of George Orwell*, vol. 4: *In Front of Your Nose, 1945–1950*, New York: Harcourt, Brace & World, 1968: 6–10.

Painter, David S., 'Oil and the Marshall Plan', *Business History Review* 58: 3, 1984: 359–83.

——— *Oil and the American Century: The Political Economy of US Foreign Oil Policy, 1941–1954*, Baltimore: Johns Hopkins University Press, 1986.

——— 'The Marshall Plan and Oil', *Cold War History* 9: 2, 2009: 159–75.

Parker, Richard B., ed., *The October War: A Retrospective*, Gainesville: University Press of Florida, 2001.

Parra, Francisco, *Oil Politics: A Modern History of Petroleum*, London: I. B. Tauris, 2004.

Peart, Sandra J., '"Facts Carefully Marshalled" in the Empirical Studies of William Stanley Jevons', *History of Political Economy* 33, 2001 (annual supplement): 252–76.

Pedersen, Susan, 'The Failure of Feminism in the Making of the British Welfare State', *Radical History Review* 43, 1989: 86–110.

Penrose, Edith, and E. F. Penrose, *Iraq: International Relations and National Development*, London: Ernest Benn, 1978.

Petersen, Tore T., *Richard Nixon, Great Britain and the Anglo-American Alignment in the Persian Gulf: Making Allies out of Clients*, Brighton: Sussex Academic Press, 2009.

Podeh, Elie, 'Making a Short Story Long: The Construction of the Suez–Mediterranean Oil Pipeline in Egypt, 1967–77', *Business History Review* 78: 1, 2004: 61–88.

Podobnik, Bruce, *Global Energy Shifts: Fostering Sustainability in a Turbulent Age*, Philadelphia: Temple University Press, 2006.

Polanyi, Karl, *The Great Transformation: The Political and Economic Origins of Our Time*, New York: Farrar & Rinehart, 1944.

Polanyi, Karl, Conrad M. Arensberg and Harry W. Pearson, *Trade and Market in the Early Empires: Economies in History and Theory*, Glencoe: Free Press, 1957.

Polasky, Janet L., 'A Revolution for Socialist Reforms: The Belgian General Strike for Universal Suffrage', *Journal of Contemporary History* 27: 3, 1992: 449–66.

Pollard, Sidney, *Peaceful Conquest: The Industrialization of Europe, 1760–1970*, Oxford: OUP, 1981.

Pomeranz, Kenneth, *The Great Divergence: China, Europe, and the Making of the Modern World Economy*, Princeton: Princeton University Press, 2000.

Porter, Theodore, 'Locating the Domain of Calculation', *Journal of Cultural Economy* 1: 1, 2008: 39–50.

——— *The Rise of Statistical Thinking, 1820–1900*, Princeton: Princeton University Press, 1986.

Potter, Pitman B., 'Origin of the System of Mandates Under the League of Nations', *American Political Science Review* 16: 4, November 1922: 563–83.

Pouget, Émile, *Le Sabotage*, Paris: M. Rivière, 1911 [1909], English translation: *Sabotage*, Chicago: C. H. Kerr & Co., 1913.

Qaimmaqami, Linda Wills, 'The Catalyst of Nationalization: Max Thornburg and the Failure of Private Sector Developmentalism in Iran, 1947–51', *Diplomatic History* 19: 1, 1995: 1–31.

Quam-Wickham, Nancy Lynn, 'Petroleocrats and Proletarians: Work, Class and Politics in the California Oil Industry, 1917–1925', PhD thesis, Department of History, University of California, Berkeley, 1994.

Quataert, Donald, *Miners and the State in the Ottoman Empire: The Zonguldak Coalfield, 1822–1920*, New York: Berghahn Books, 2006.

——— *Workers, Peasants and Economic Change in the Ottoman Empire: 1730–1914*, Istanbul: Isis Press, 1993.

Radice, Hugo, 'The National Economy: A Keynesian Myth?' *Capital and Class* 8: 1, 1984: 111–140.

al-Rafi'i, Abd al-Rahman, *Thawrat sanat 1919: Tarikh misr al-qawmi min sanat 1914 ila sanat 1921*, 2 vols: Cairo: Maktabat al-Nahda al-Misriya, 1955.

Rancière, Jacques, *Hatred of Democracy*, London: Verso, 2005.

Rand, Christopher T., *Making Democracy Safe for Oil: Oilmen and the Islamic East*, Boston: Little, Brown, 1975.

Randall, Stephen J., *United States Foreign Oil Policy, 1919–1948: For Profits and Security*, Montreal and Kingston: McGill–Queen's University Press, 1985.

Rashid, Ahmed, *Taliban: Militant Islam, Oil, and Fundamentalism in Central Asia*, New Haven: Yale University Press, 2000.

Redish, Angela, 'The Evolution of the Gold Standard in England', *Journal of Economic History* 50: 4, December 1990, 789–805.

Rees, Jonathan, *Representation and Rebellion: The Rockefeller Plan at the Colorado Fuel and Iron Company, 1914–1942*, Boulder, CO: University Press of Colorado, 2010.

Reifer, Thomas E., 'Labor, Race and Empire: Transport Workers and Transnational Empires of Trade, Production, and Finance', in Gilbert G. Gonzalez, Raul Fernandez, Vivian Price, David Smith and Linda Tinh Vo, eds, *Labor Versus Empire: Race, Gender, and Migration*, London: Routledge, 2004: 17–36.

Retort (Iain Boal, T. J. Clark, Joseph Matthews and Michael Watts), *Afflicted Powers: Capital and Spectacle in a New Age of War*, New York: Verso, 2005.

Revelle, R., W. Broecker, H. Craig, C.D. Keeling and J. Smagorinsky, 'Atmospheric Carbon Dioxide', in *Restoring the Quality of our Environment: Report of the Environmental Pollution Panel*, Washington: White House, President's Science Advisory Committtee, November 1965: 111–33.

Rimlinger, G. V., 'Labour and the State on the Continent, 1800–1939', in Peter Mathias and Sidney Pollard, eds, *The Cambridge Economic History of Europe*, vol. 8: *The Industrial Economies: The Development of Economic and Social Policies*, Cambridge, UK: CUP, 1989.

Rippy, Merrill, *Oil and the Mexican Revolution*, Leiden: Brill, 1972.

Robelius, Fredrik, 'Giant Oil Fields – The Highway to Oil: Giant Oil Fields and Their Importance for Future Oil Production', PhD thesis, Department of Nuclear and Particle Physics, Uppsala University, March 2007, available at publications.uu.se.

Ross, Michael L., 'Does Oil Hinder Democracy?' *World Politics* 53: 3, April 2001: 325–61.

Rosser, Andrew, 'Escaping the Resource Curse: The Case of Indonesia', *Journal of Contemporary Asia* 37: 1, 2007: 38–58.

Rubin, Barnett R., *The Fragmentation of Afghanistan: State Formation and Collapse in the International System*, 2nd edn, New Haven: Yale University Press, 2002.

Ruotsila, Markku, 'The Great Charter for the Liberty of the Workingman: Labour, Liberals, and the Creation of the ILO', *Labour History Review* 67: 1, 2002: 29–47.

Rutledge, David, 'Estimating Long Term World Coal Production with Logit and Probit Transforms', *International Journal of Coal Geology* 85: 1, 2011: 23–33.

Sabin, Paul, *Crude Politics: The California Oil Market, 1900–1940*, Berkeley: University of California Press, 2005.

Sachs, Jeffrey D., and Andrew M. Warner, 'Natural Resource Abundance and Economic Growth', Development Discussion Paper no. 517a, Cambridge, MA: Harvard Institute for International Development, 1995.

Sadowski, Yahya M., *Political Vegetables? Businessman and Bureaucrat in the Development of Egyptian Agriculture*, Washington, DC: Brookings Institution, 1991.

Salamé, Ghassan, ed., *Democracy Without Democrats: The Renewal of Politics in the Muslim World*, London: I. B. Tauris, 1994.

Sampson, Anthony, *The Arms Bazaar*, London: Hodder & Stoughton, 1977.

—— *The Seven Sisters: The Great Oil Companies and the World They Made*, London: Hodder & Stoughton, 1975.

Samuelson, Paul A., *Foundations of Economic Analysis*, Cambridge, MA: Harvard University Press, 1947.

Sartre, Jean-Paul, *Critique of Dialectical Reason*, vol. 1: *Theory of Practical Ensembles*, London: Verso 1977.

Satia, Priya, 'Developing Iraq: Britain, India and the Redemption of Empire and Technology in the First World War', *Past and Present* 197: 1, 2007: 211–55.

Saul, Samir, 'Masterly Inactivity as Brinkmanship: The Iraq Petroleum Company's Route to Nationalization, 1958–1972', *International History Review* 29: 4, 2007: 746–92.

Schabas, Margaret, 'The "Worldly Philosophy" Of William Stanley Jevons', *Victorian Studies* 28: 1, 1984: 129–47.

Schlesinger, James, 'The Airlift', in Richard B. Parker, ed., *The October War: A Retrospective*, Gainesville: University Press of Florida, 2001.

Schorske, Carl E., *German Social Democracy, 1905–1917: The Development of the Great Schism*, Cambridge, MA: Harvard University Press, 1983.

Schulze, Reinhard, *Die Rebellion Der Ägyptischen Fallahin 1919*, Bonn: Ballbek Verlag, 1981.

Schumacher, E. F., *Small Is Beautiful: Economics as if People Mattered*, New York: Harper & Row, 1973.

Schumpeter, Joseph, 'The Common Sense of Econometrics', *Econometrica* 1: 1, January 1933: 5–12.

Schwarz, Solomon M., *The Russian Revolution of 1905: The Workers' Movement and the Formation of Bolshevism and Menshevism*, transl. Gertrude Vakar, Chicago: University of Chicago Press, 1967.

Searle, G. R., *A New England? Peace and War, 1886–1918*, Oxford: Clarendon Press, 2004.

Serres, Michel, *The Parasite*, Minneapolis: University of Minnesota Press, 2007.

Service, Robert, *Stalin: A Biography*, Cambridge, MA: Belknap Press of Harvard University Press, 2005.

Seymour, Ian, *OPEC: Instrument of Change*, New York: St Martin's Press, 1981.

Shafiee, Katayoun, 'Cracking Petroleum with Politics: Anglo-Persian Oil and the Socio-Technical Transformation of Iran, 1901–54', PhD thesis, Department of Middle Eastern and Islamic Studies, New York University, 2010.

Sheail, John, 'Torrey Canyon: The Political Dimension', *Journal of Contemporary History* 42: 3, 2007: 485–504.

Shields, Sarah, *Mosul Before Iraq: Like Bees Making a Five-Sided Cell*, Albany: State University of New York Press, 2000.

Shubert, Adrian, *The Road to Revolution in Spain: The Coal Miners of Asturias, 1860–1934*, Urbana: University of Illinois Press, 1987.

Sieferle, Rolf Peter, *The Subterranean Forest: Energy Systems and the Industrial Revolution*, Cambridge, UK: White Horse Press, 2001.

—— 'Why Did Industrialization Start in Europe (and Not in China)?' Rolf Peter Sieferle and Helga Breuninger, eds, *Agriculture, Population, and Economic Development in China and Europe*, Stuttgart: Breuninger Stiftung, 2003: 7–89.

Silver, Beverly J., *Forces of Labor: Workers' Movements and Globalization Since 1870*, Cambridge, UK: CUP, 2003.

Skidelsky, Robert, *John Maynard Keynes*, vol. 2: *The Economist as Saviour, 1920–1937*, London: Macmillan, 1992.

Sluglett, Peter, *Britain in Iraq: Contriving King and Country, 1914–1932*, New York: Columbia University Press, 2007.

Smil, Vaclav, *Energy in Nature and Society: General Energetics of Complex Systems*, Cambridge, MA: MIT Press, 2008.

—— 'America's Oil Imports: A Self-Inflicted Burden', *Annals of the Association of American Geographers*, 104: 4, 2011: 712–16.

Smith, Adam, *An Inquiry into the Nature and Causes of the Wealth of Nations*, London: Methuen, 1950 [1776].

Smith, James Allen, *The Idea Brokers: Think Tanks and the Rise of the New Policy Elite*, New York: Free Press, 1991.

Smuts, Jan Christiaan, 'The League of Nations: A Practical Suggestion', in John Dugard, ed., *The South West Africa/Namibia Dispute; Documents and Scholarly Writings on the Controversy Between South Africa and the United Nations*, Berkeley: University of California Press, 1973.

—— *Selections from the Smuts Papers*, 7 vols, W. K. Hancock and Jean Van Der Poel, eds, Cambridge, UK: CUP, 2007.

Söderbergh, Bengt, 'Canada's Oil Sands Resources and Its Future Impact on Global Oil Supply', MSc degree project, Systems Engineering, Uppsala University, 2005.

Solow, Robert M., 'The Economics of Resources or the Resources of Economics', *American Economic Review* 64: 2, 1974: 1–14.

Soltau, Irene C., 'Social Responsibility in the Lebanon', *International Affairs* 25: 3, 1949: 307–17.

Sorel, Georges, *Reflections on Violence*, transl. Thomas Ernest Hulme, New York: B. W. Huebsch, 1914.

Sorrell, Steve, *Global Oil Depletion: An Assessment of the Evidence for a Near-Term Peak in Oil Production*, UK Energy Research Centre, 2009, available at www.ukerc.ac.uk.

Spring, D. W., 'The Trans-Persian Railway Project and Anglo-Russian Relations, 1909–14', *Slavonic and East European Review* 54: 1, 1976: 60–82.

Stabile, Donald R., 'Veblen and the Political Economy of the Engineer: The Radical Thinker and Engineering Leaders Came to Technocratic Ideas at the Same Time', *American Journal of Economics and Sociology* 45: 1, 1986: 41–52.

Stead, W. T., *Methods of Barbarism: The Case for Intervention*, London: Mowbray House, 1901.

Steinhouse, Adam, *Workers' Participation in Post-Liberation France*, Lanham: Lexington Books, 2001.

Stevens, Paul, 'Pipelines or Pipe Dreams? Lessons from the History of Arab Transit Pipelines', *Middle East Journal* 54: 2, 2000: 224–41.

Stewart, Rory, *Occupational Hazards: My Time Governing in Iraq*, London: Picador, 2006.

Stivers, William, *Supremacy and Oil: Iraq, Turkey, and the Anglo-American World Order, 1918–1930*, Ithaca, Cornell University Press, 1982.

Stocking, George W., *Middle East Oil: A Study in Political and Economic Controversy*, Nashville: Vanderbilt University Press, 1970.

Stoff, Michael B., 'The Anglo-American Oil Agreement and the Wartime Search for Foreign Oil Policy', *Business History Review* 55: 1, 1981: 59–74.

Stokes, Raymond G., *Opting for Oil: The Political Economy of Technical Change in the West German Industry, 1945–1961*, Cambridge: CUP, 1994.

Stork, Joe, *Middle East Oil and the Energy Crisis*, New York: Monthly Review Press, 1975.

——— 'Oil and the Penetration of Capitalism in Iraq', in Petter Nore and Terisa Turner, eds, *Oil and Class Struggle*, London: Zed Press, 1980.

Strunk, William, 'The Reign of Shaykh Khaz'al Ibn Jabir and the Suppression of the Principality of Arabistan', PhD thesis, Department of History, Indiana University, 1977.

Sumi, Lisa, *Our Drinking Water at Risk: What EPA and the Oil and Gas Industry Don't Want Us to Know About Hydraulic Fracturing*, Washington, DC: Oil and Gas Accountability Project, April, 2005, available at www.earthworksaction.org.

Suny, Ronald Grigor, 'A Journeyman for the Revolution: Stalin and the Labour Movement in Baku, June 1907–May 1908', *Soviet Studies* 23: 3, 1972: 373–94.

——— *The Making of the Georgian Nation*, 2nd edn, Bloomington: Indiana University Press, 1994.

Tessler, Mark, and Amaney Jamal, 'Political Attitude Research in the Arab World: Emerging Opportunities', *PS: Political Science and Politics* 39: 3, 2006: 433–7.

Thomas, Paul, *Karl Marx and the Anarchists*, London: Routledge & Kegan Paul, 1980.

Thompson, E. P., *The Making of the English Working Class*, New York: Pantheon Books, 1964.

Thompson, Elizabeth, *Colonial Citizens: Republican Rights, Paternal Privilege, and Gender in French Syria and Lebanon*, New York: Columbia University Press, 2000.

Throntveit, Trygve, 'The Fable of the Fourteen Points: Woodrow Wilson and National Self-Determination', *Diplomatic History* 35: 3, June 2011: 445–81.

Tilly, Chris, and Charles Tilly, *Work Under Capitalism*, Boulder, CO: Westview Press, 1998.

Tobin, James, 'Irving Fisher (1867–1947)', in John Eatwell, Murray Milgate and Peter Newman, eds, *The New Palgrave: A Dictionary of Economics*, London: Macmillan, 1987.

Tolf, Robert W., *The Russian Rockefellers: The Saga of the Nobel Family and the Russian Oil Industry*, Stanford: Hoover Institution Press, Stanford University, 1976.

Tooze, J. Adam, 'Imagining National Economies: National and International Economic Statistics 1900–1950', in Geoffrey Cubitt, ed., *Imagining Nations*, Manchester: Manchester University Press, 1998.

——— *Statistics and the German State, 1900–1945: The Making of Modern Economic Knowledge*, Cambridge, UK: CUP, 2001.

Tribe, Keith, *Land, Labour, and Economic Discourse*, London: Routledge & Kegan Paul, 1978.

——— *Strategies of Economic Order: German Economic Discourse, 1750–1950*, Cambridge, UK: CUP, 1995.

Tvedt, T., 'Why England and Not China and India? Water Systems and the History of the Industrial Revolution', *Journal of Global History* 5: 1, 2010: 29–50.

United Nations Conference on Trade and Development (UNCTAD), *Review of Maritime Transport 2007*, Geneva: United Nations Conference on Trade and Development, 2007.

Vassiliev, Alexei, *The History of Saudi Arabia*, New York: New York University Press, 2000.

Veblen, Thorstein, *The Theory of the Leisure Class: An Economic Study of Institutions*, New York: Macmillan, 1899.

——— 'On the Nature of Capital', *Quarterly Journal of Economics* 23: 1, 1908: 104–36.

——— *Imperial Germany and the Industrial Revolution*, New York: Macmillan, 1915.

——— *An Inquiry into the Nature of Peace and the Terms of Its Perpetuation*, New York: MacMillan, 1917.

——— *On the Nature and Uses of Sabotage*, New York: Oriole Chapbooks, 1919.

——— *The Industrial System and the Captains of Industry*, New York: Oriole Chapbooks, 1919.

——— *The Engineers and the Price System*, New York: B. W. Huebsch, 1921.

Vietor, Richard H. K., *Energy Policy in America since 1945: A Study of Business Government Relations*, Cambridge, UK: CUP, 1984.

Visser, Reidar, *Basra, the Failed Gulf State: Separatism and Nationalism in Southern Iraq*, Münster: Lit Verlag, 2005.

Vitalis, Robert, *America's Kingdom: Mythmaking on the Saudi Oil Frontier*, 2nd edn, London: Verso, 2009.

al-Wardi, Ali, *Lamahat ijtima'iya min tarikh al-'iraq al-hadith*, 6 vols, vol. 5: *Hawla thawrat al-'ishrin*, 2nd edn, London: Kufan, 1991.

Watts, Michael, 'Resource Curse? Governmentality, Oil and Power in the Niger Delta, Nigeria', *Geopolitics* 9: 1, 2004: 50–80.

Werth, Alexander, *France, 1940–1955*, New York: Henry Holt, 1956.

Williams, Beryl, '1905: The View from the Provinces', in Jonathan Smele and Anthony Haywood, eds, *The Russian Revolution of 1905*, London: Routledge, 2005.

Williamson, Harold F., *The American Petroleum Industry*, 2 vols, Evanston: Northwestern University Press, 1959.

Wilson, Arnold Talbot, *SW. Persia: A Political Officer's Diary, 1907–1914*, London: OUP, 1941.

Winkler, Henry J., 'British Labor and the Origins of the Idea of Colonial Trusteeship, 1914–1919', *Historian* 13: 2, 1951: 154–72.

Woodward, David R., 'The Origins and Intent of David Lloyd George's War Aims Speech', *Historian* 34: 1, November 1971, 22–39.

Wright, John, *Libya: A Modern History*, Baltimore: Johns Hopkins University Press, 1982.

Wright, Quincy, 'The Mosul Dispute', *American Journal of International Law* 20: 3, July 1926: 453–64.

Wrigley, E. A., *Poverty, Progress, and Population*, Cambridge, UK: CUP, 2004.

Wriston, Henry M., 'Institute of Politics', *American Political Science Review* 20: 4, 1926: 852–60.

Yaqub, Salim, *Containing Arab Nationalism: The Eisenhower Doctrine and the Middle East*, Chapel Hill: University of North Carolina Press, 2004.

Yates, Douglas A., *The Rentier State in Africa: Oil Rent Dependency and Neocolonialism in the Republic of Gabon*, Trenton: Africa World Press, 1996.

Yergin, Daniel, *The Prize: The Epic Quest for Oil, Money, and Power*, New York: Simon & Schuster, 1991.

Zelizer, Viviana A., *The Social Meaning of Money: Pin Money, Paychecks, Poor Relief and Other Currencies*, Princeton: Princeton University Press, 1997.

Zittel, Werner, and Jörg Schindler, 'Coal: Resources and Future Production', EWG Paper no. 1/01, 10 July 2007, at www.energywatchgroup.org.

Zupnick, Elliot, 'The Sterling Area's Central Pooling System Re-Examined', *Quarterly Journal of Economics* 69: 1, 1955: 71–84.

Index

Abadan, 54, 91, 107, 144, 237
Abu Dhabi, 175
Aburish, Saïd K., 211n16, 213n23
Adelman, Morris, 168, 181, 188
Admiralty. *See* Royal Navy
Afary, Janet, 64n48
Afghanistan, 200, 201, 204, 215, 217–21
African National Congress, 73
Agriculture,
    and industrialisation, 16, 140–1
    See also land reform
Akins, James, 150, 181, 190
Alaska, 170, 186, 191
Albright, Madeleine, 217n32
Algeciras Conference (1906), 74–5, 83–4
Algeria, 144, 151, 165n58, 166, 175, 201
Alinsky, Saul, 178
Allon plan, 219
Altvater, Elmer, 7n15
American Bankers Association, 171
American Economics Association, 132
American Petroleum Institute, 188, 190
American Philosophical Society, 242
anarchism, 24
Anatolian Railway. *See* Baghdad Railway
Andrews, Thomas, 25n38
Anglo-American Petroleum Agreement (1944),
    118, 123, 142
Anglo-Iranian Oil Company, 142, 144–6
    See also Anglo-Persian Oil Company; BP
Anglo-Persian Oil Company, 50–68, 89, 94, 107
    See also BP
Arab Barometer project, 3–4
Arab Revolt (1936–39), 104
Arab uprisings of 2011, 1, 11, 221, 226–9
Aramco (Arabian-American Oil Company), 104,
    114–5, 164n53, 169, 208, 210–3, 247
    and racial division of labour, 106, 211
Armenia, 80
arms trade, 155–62, 183, 187, 214
    and dollar recycling, 155–62
Arrow-Debreu model, 140
Asiatic Petroleum Company, 53
Aswan Dam, 49
al-Atiqi, Abdul Rahman, 184
Attiga, Ali, 185, 185n38
Austria-Hungary, 18
Ayres, Robert U., 140n67
Azores, 183, 185n38

Baghdad Railway, 54–8, 74, 103
Bahrain, 164, 227
Baku oil industry, 33–6, 46–54, 64, 69, 88
Bakunin, Mikhail, 24n33
Bambatha rebellion (1906), 72
Barber, Benjamin, 203
Basra, 58, 87, 91, 103, 147–8, 151, 225
Batumi, 33, 36, 50
Beer, George, 83
Belgium, 19
    general strike in, 24
Ben Ali, Zine el Abidine, 227
Berlin Act of 1885, 73, 77
Bichler, Shimshon, 156n32
Bin Laden, Osama, 200, 204, 221
Birnbaum, Eugene, 171
Bismarck, Otto von, 21
Black Hundreds, 35
Block, Fred, 171n73
BMW, 42
Boer republics. *See* South Africa and Afrikaner
    republics
Boer Wars. *See* South African war (1899–1902)
Bolivia, 113
Bolshevism, 33–4, 68–9
BP (British Petroleum), 5, 43–4, 146–51, 189, 206
Brailsford, Henry Noel, 73–6, 83–4
Brazil, 231–2
Bretton Woods, 109–12, 123, 155, 171
Brezhnev, Leonid, 182, 182n28
Bridge, Gavin, 7n16
British National Party, 235–6
British Petroleum. *See* BP
Bromley, Simon, 41n79
Brower, David, 191
Brown, Harrison, 177n10
Brzezinski, Zbigniew, 218
Burma, 46
Burmah Oil, 46–59
Bush, George W., 219–20, 223

California, 27, 31, 70
California-Arabian Oil Company. *See* Aramco
Callon, Michel, 7n16, 238n14
CalTex oil refinery, 152
Cambodia, 160
Canada, 206
capitalists, 41n79, 49, 70–1, 101
carbon democracy, 1, 4–6, 9–11, 17–8, 123, 143, 156,
    193, 253–4

and Islam, 200
carbon energy. *See* energy
carbon trading, 197
cartels. *See* oil firms and monopoly power
Cassel, Ernest, 49, 57–8, 75
Cecil, Edward, 49
Chartist movement, 23
Chase Manhattan Bank, 171
Chester, Colby M., 56–7
Chester Concession, 56–7, 96n34
Chiah Surkh, 50
China, 12, 16, 83–4, 146, 206, 218, 222, 232
Churchill, Winston, 23, 44, 60–5, 76, 93, 96, 115
CIA (Central Intelligence Agency), 149, 212–3, 217n31
 Iranian coup, 107–8
 Syrian coup, 105
Citroën, 41
climate change, 6–7, 140, 190, 194, 233
 calculation of, 241–6
Club of Rome, 189
coal, 7–43
 and autonomy of miners, 20–1
 and calculation, 6, 127–30
 comparisons to oil, 37, 39–42
 consumption of, 37n74
 and depletion of reserves, 124, 128–30
 and imperialism, 84
 as mechanical power, 13
 mining of, 19, 19n14, 36–39
 and population growth, 14–15
 transition to oil from, 12–5, 31–6
 transportation of, 37, 37n72, 37n73
coal industry, 193
Cold War, 10, 115, 122–3, 158–68, 245
colonialism. *See* imperialism
Columbia University, 248
Compagnie Française des Pétroles (Total), 95n30, 97n36, 147
consent of the governed, 9, 79–80, 92–4, 98–100
Constitutional Revolution of 1905–11 (Iran), 64
containerisation, 154–5
Cordovez, Diego, 218n36
Cornwall, 13, 38, 72
Coronil, Fernando, 2n2
corporation, history of, 207. *See also* oil firm
Courrières colliery disaster, 23
Cox, Sir Percy, 88–9, 92, 96
cracking (pyrolysis), 249–51
Cromwell, Oliver, 204
Curaçao, 5
Curzon, Lord, 52–3, 89, 95

D'Arcy, William Knox, 50–9
Darwin, Charles, 130
Dawes Committee, 136
democracy,
 as assembled machinery, 9, 109

and collective life, 241
and crisis, 173, 177
and expertise, 192, 240–1
and the general strike, 8, 12–4, 23–7, 42, 254
as idea, 1–2, 21, 85
and imperialism, 15–8, 101
and militarism, 187, 220–6, 253
and oil, 4–5, 43, 66, 109, 142–3
as struggle for material resources, 73–6
translation into 'self-determination', 67–72, 84–5
See also democratisation
Democratic Party, 175
democratisation, 3–4, 224, 241
 and labour after the First World War, 76–85
 and neoliberalism, 224–8
 resistance to, 4
 and vulnerability, 146
Deobandi school, 202
Department of Energy, 197, 243
Department of the Interior, 179
Desertec, 238
Deutsche Bank, 32, 46–59, 94
development, 86, 100–1, 114–5, 122, 125
 as separate development, 82–5, 120–1
Dhahran, 208, 211, 237
Díaz, Porfirio, 64
Dinshaway, 73, 73n17
Dumbarton Oaks, 112

Eastern and African Concessions Syndicate, 49
economics, 134, 138, 247–8
 calculation, 234–5, 246–54
 and eugenics, 130–33
 and market, 11, 173–7, 184–6
 and natural resources, 131–3, 194–9, 234–5, 248–54
 and oil, 246–54
economy, the, 109, 123–7, 132–6, 144, 175–7, 189, 192, 194, 234, 249–51, 253
 and circulation of money, 134–9, 247–8
 emergence of, 9, 123–7, 132–9
 and energy, 139–43
 as machinery of government, 109
 and nature–society divide, 241
 as object of development, 101
Eddy, William, 120, 212
Egypt, 17, 119, 151, 158, 164–5, 181–3, 187, 201–3, 211–5, 218, 221, 226–9
 as British protectorate, 91, 94
 declaration of independence, 88, 99
 oil fields of, 48–9, 60
 strikes in, 87–8
Eisenhower, Dwight D., 167–8, 212
electrical power, 32, 177–8
Eley, Geoff, 18n12
Ely, Richard T., 132, 247
energy, 1–15, 176–81, 190, 194
 alternatives to hydrocarbons, 190, 247
 compression of space and time, 15

decentralisation of, 238
and democracy, 4–5, 14, 43, 66, 109, 142–3, 254
and determinism, 237–9
and 'the economy', 109–43
exhaustion of, 6
and the 'great divergence', 15–6
and imperialism, 15–8
networks of, 7–8, 18–42, 65, 66, 103, 144, 236–7
transition from coal to oil, 12–5, 31–6
energy crisis, 170–2, 175–81, 194
Energy Information Administration, 197, 244, 246
Engdahl, William, 171n73
Engels, Friedrich, 23–4
ENI, 165
environment, 38, 38n75, 175, 188–9
as object of politics, 176, 189–93
and oil spills, 189, 191
eugenics, 82, 131–3
European Coal and Steel Community, 29
European Cooperation Administration, 30n50
European Petroleum Union, 47, 56
European Recovery Program (ERP). See Marshall Plan
expertise, 192–3, 238–41, 246
Exxon, 95n30, 166, 171

Faisal, Emir, 93, 96, 212
fascism, 109, 208
Featherstone massacre of 1893, 62
Federal Energy Administration, 180
Federal Power Commission, 177–8
Federal Reserve, 223
Feis, Herbert, 115
First World War, 8, 23, 54–5, 58, 61, 66–9, 74, 86, 91,
    141, 204, 225, 234
labour protest during, 24–5, 78–9
Fisher, Irving, 131–5, 248
Ford Motor Company, 204
Forrestal, James, 41
fossil fuels. See energy; oil; coal; natural gas
Foundation for Economic Education, 142
fracking, 249–51
France, 18, 22–3, 25, 28–9, 39, 56, 58, 64, 69, 74, 80,
    83, 86, 87, 90, 94, 100, 157, 161, 166, 215, 217, 222
Franco, Francisco, 165
Franklin Motor Company, 204
Frisch, Ragnar, 135

Galicia (Eastern Europe), 32, 46
Galton, Francis, 130–1
Gandhi, Mohandas, 73
General Dynamics, 157
George, Lloyd, 79–80
Germany, 18, 21–2, 25–8, 32, 39, 45, 56, 58, 63, 66, 70,
    74, 79, 81, 128, 136, 156, 164, 208
Glasgow, 22
Global Barometer, 4. See also Arab Barometer
    project
global capitalism, 3, 203, 213, 229–30
and political Islam. See McJihad

global financial crisis 2008–09, 233
gold standard, 109–11, 155, 170–1
and coal, 127
and currency speculation, 110
gold-mining, 70
Gómez, Juan Vicente, 5
Goodrich, Carter, 20
Graham, Benjamin, 112
Great Britain, 13–5, 110, 149, 161, 206, 215,
    depletion of coal reserves in, 124
    and occupation of Middle East, 87
    revolts against rule of, 93–4
    and sterling area, 118–9, 142
    and strikes, 22–3
Great Coalfield War of 1913–14, 25
Great Depression, 194, 204
Great Game, 52, 163
Great Syrian Revolt (1925–27), 87
Great Unrest (1910–14), 62–3
Greece, 18
Greenpeace, 238
Greenspan, Alan, 223
gross national product, 136–40
growth, limits to, 175–6, 188–90, 234–5, 247–8, 253
Guam Doctrine. See Nixon Doctrine
Gulbenkian, Calouste, 48, 97, 147
Gulf Oil, 179n15, 197
Gulf War, 221–2

Hansen, James, 7n14
Hardinge, Arthur, 59
Harvey, David, 223n51
Hayek, Friedrich, 112, 141
Hazlitt, Henry, 142
Hecht, Gabreille, 28n47
Hirtzel, Arthur, 92
Hobson, J.A., 69–72, 76, 82–4
Hochschild, Adam, 74n20
Hoffman, Paul, 30n50
Honolulu Oil Corporation, 142
Hotelling, Harold, 195–6
House, Colonel (Edward M.), 83–4
Hubbert, M. King, 188, 248
Hull, Edward, 128–9
Huntington, Samuel, 194
Hussein, Saddam, 174, 213, 216, 221–3, 233

Ibn Saud, Abd al-Aziz, 30, 41, 92, 120, 204–5,
    209–12
Ibn Wahhab, Muhammad, 204
    See also Wahhabism
IEA (International Energy Agency), 197, 244–7
Ikhwan (Saudi Arabia), 209–11. See also Muslim
    Brotherhood
imperialism, 68–81, 89
    financial burden of, 93–4
    and air power, 93
    and democracy, 101
    and political Islam, 202

strategic interests, 158–62, 227
  and racism, 207–8
Inchcape, Lord, 58
Index Visible. See Rolodex
India, 12, 17, 49–65, 89, 94, 202, 232
Indian Railways, 59–60
Indonesia, 201
industrial democracy, 26–8
Institute for Defense Analyses, 177
Institute of Economic Affairs, 142
Institute of Gas Technology, 180
Intergovernmental Panel on Climate Change, 244
International Bank for Reconstruction and
  Development. See World Bank
International Labour Office, 78, 130
International Monetary Fund (IMF), 77, 110, 138
International Petroleum Commission, 118
International Petroleum Council, 112–3
Iran, 144–7, 149, 157–61, 167–71, 174–5, 186, 202, 206,
  215, 221, 232, 252
  labour unrest in, 107
  1953 coup, 107–8, 144–5, 202
  oil dispute in, 121
Iran–Iraq War, 215–6
Iraq, 5, 10, 67, 81–3, 86, 88, 144–51, 158–9, 167, 174–5,
  201, 205, 208, 211–7, 221–7, 234–5, 252. See also
  Mesopotamia
  and arms trade, 10, 155–62, 170–1
  Ba'th Party, 151, 181, 213, 221
  Communist Party of, 145, 149–51
  control of oil industry, 47–8, 96–8, 102–5, 225–6
  'native rule' in, 92–3
  Oil Ministry, 151, 225
  sabotage in, 94, 103
  US invasion of, 1–2, 84, 227
Iraq National Oil Company, 151
Iraq Petroleum Company (IPC), 96–7, 102, 105,
  147–51, 155, 169–70
Iraq War (2003), 216–7, 217n21, 221–7, 232
Ireland, 94
iron industry, 13–14
Irwin, John, 169
Ismail, Hafiz, 182
Israel–Palestine Conflict, 161–2, 176, 187, 215,
  218–20, 222
  1967 War, 151, 157–8, 164, 182n28, 215n28, 219
  October 1973 War, 173, 181–7, 240
Israel, 151, 158–62, 168, 181–6, 213, 215, 228
  as oil conduit, 164–6
Italy, 18, 150n19, 161

Jackson, Henry, 185, 222
Japan, 156, 169, 174, 186
Jennings, Brewster, 41
Jevons, H. Stanley, 124n28
Jevons, William Stanley, 124, 126–30, 132, 141, 234
jihad, 203, 209, 213, 218
Jones, Tom, 159
Jordan, 201, 212, 219

Jumblatt, Kamal, 106

Kasr-i Shirin, 50
Keeling, Charles, 242–3
Kennan, George, 121–2
Kern, Harry, 212
kerosene, 31–2, 34, 46–7, 58
Kerr, Philip, 79
Keynes, John Maynard, 111–3, 123, 134–6, 140
Keynesianism, 174, 194, 197
Khanaqin, 50
Kindleberger, Charles, 37n73
Kipling, Rudyard, 52
Kirkuk, 102, 237
Kissinger, Henry, 160–1, 182–6
Kitchener, Lord, 52
Klare, Michael, 41n79
Koch, Charles and David, 198
Korean War, 157
Kurds, 161–2, 220
Kuwait, 145–6, 149–50, 162, 167, 174–5, 184, 206,
  208–9, 216
Kuznets, Simon, 136–7

Labour Party, 76–9, 84, 92, 94, 98–101
labour, 5, 19–39, 60–5, 70, 130, 225
  and automation, 152–3
  and coal, 19–31, 66, 106–8, 232
  and democratisation after the First World War,
  76–85
  and energy networks, 27
  and oil, 31–9, 44–6, 151–5, 225–6, 228
  racial segregation of, 70, 82–3
  unions, 8, 18, 26–7
  and welfare, 77
land reform, 64, 145–6, 202, 213, 217–8, 228
Lansing, Robert, 81n36
Laos, 160
Latour, Bruno, 239, 246
Laughlin, J. Laurence, 135
Lawrence, T. E., 101n47
League of Nations, 8, 75–86, 92, 97–8, 138, 225
Lebanon, 106, 119, 212
Lend Lease aid, 114, 120
Lenin, Vladimir Ilyich, 69
'liberal internationalism', 94
Libya, 144, 151, 162, 164–5, 168, 175, 227
Liebig, Justus von, 127
Linden, Henry, 180
Lindsey Oil Refinery, 236
Lippmann, Walter, 122, 141
List, Friedrich, 126, 128
Lockheed C-5A, 183, 186
Ludlow Massacre, 25
Lugard, Frederick, 86n1, 99–101
Luxemburg, Rosa, 24, 33
Lynch Brothers, 50n14, 58

Mackay, James (Lord Inchcape), 58

Mackenzie King, William Lyon, 26
Macready, Nevil, 62
al-Maghribi, Mahmud Sulaiman, 165
Mallet, Serge, 152–3
Mamdani, Mahmood, 80n34, 160n43
Mandates Commission, 86, 98, 101
mandates, 75, 77–86, 94, 122
    and civilisation, 86
    and development, 100–1
    'dual mandate', 86
    as mechanism of consent, 98–9
Manin, Bernard, 18n11
market,
    as mode of governing democracy, 196–8
    in oil, 167–70
    and political Islam, 203–4
Marshall, Alfred, 135–6
Marshall, George, 29
Marshall Plan, 29–31, 37n73, 122, 142, 152, 236
Marx, Karl, 24n33
Masjid-i-Suleiman, 43, 44, 50n14, 54, 89
Malthusians, 238
Mattei, Albert, 142
Mattei, Enrico, 165
Mazower, Mark, 72n15
McCloskey, Deirdre, 174
McJihad, 11, 200–30
Mellon Family, 46, 197
Memorandum on War Aims, 76–8
Mendès-France, Pierre, 29
Merriman, J.X., 82
Mesopotamia, 47–68, 72–5, 80–4, 86
    map of, 51
    See also Iraq
Mexican Eagle, 64
Mexico, 64, 67, 113–4, 167n65, 206
MI5, 237
Michigan, 27
Middle East,
    and democracy, 1–4
    and early oil exploration, 43–65
    oil production in, 86, 97, 102–3, 113–4, 110
    and security, 187
Mikunis, Samuel, 105
Milner, Lord Alfred, 71, 79n32, 86, 98–9
Mobil, 95n30
Mombauer, Monnika, 74n22
Morel, E.D., 73–6, 96
Morgenthau, Henry, 110
Moroccan Crisis of 1911, 60
Morocco, 63, 72–5, 83–4, 201
Morris Motor Company, 41
Mossadegh, Muhammad, 107–8, 144–5, 159
Mosul, 47–8, 58, 84, 87n3, 91, 94–8
Mubarak, Hosni, 227–9
Mufti, Malik, 149n14
mujahideen, 211, 218, 221
Mumford, Lewis, 37
Mun, Thomas, 126

Muslim Brotherhood, 202–3, 227–9
muwahhidun. See Wahhabism; Saudi Arabia

Nasser, Gamal Abdel, 201, 212–3
Nassikas, John, 177, 179
National Bank of Egypt, 49, 80
National Bank of Turkey, 57
National Bureau of Economic Research, 136
National Coal Board, 189
national economy, 132, 134–9, 248
National Energy Act, 180
National Science Foundation, 242
National Security Act, 41
National Security Council, 218
National Union of Dock Labourers, 22
National Union of Mineworkers, 236–7
nationalisation, 28, 49, 67, 107, 114, 137–9, 144–51,
    169, 237
nationalism, 144
native rule, 86,
    in Iraq, 92–3, 226
    protectorates as, 90–1
    See also self-determination
NATO, 163
natural gas, 178–80, 188, 237, 249
natural resources, 177, 191
    and market, 194–9
nature,
    and collective life, 239
    and expertise, 238–41, 246
    limits of, 231, 238
    politics of, 233, 252–4
neoliberalism, 112, 141–2, 173, 197–9, 223–8
Neumann, John von, 192
New Deal, 124, 134, 141
Nigeria, 201
Nitzan, Jonathan, 156n32
Nixon Doctrine, 158–62
Nixon, Richard, 160, 178–86, 190–2, 194
Nobel Brothers, 46–50
Northrop Corporation, 159
Norway, 206
nuclear power, 28n47, 178, 188, 191–2, 237, 243, 247
Nye, David E., 41n81

Obama, Barack, 219
Occidental Petroleum, 166
OECD (Organisation for Economic Co-operation
    and Development), 244
Office of Fuels and Energy, 181
oil,
    comparisons to coal, 37, 39–42
    and conception of economy, 139–43
    currency linked to flow of, 109–13, 119–23
    and democracy, 43, 146n4, 156–62, 192, 252–4
    depletion of reserves, 167, 188–90, 222, 231–46,
        252. See also peak oil
    as kerosene, 31–2
    'market price', 167–70, 175

as mechanical power, 32–3
and militarism, 155–62, 186–7, 214, 223–4
and nature-society divide, 245
networks, 5–6, 36–9, 163, 176
and politics, 47, 235–41, 253
price of, 30, 139–41, 154–5, 173–6, 190, 206, 233
problem of abundance, 39–42, 43, 140, 163, 206
production of, 1, 32–3, 144n1, 191, 232
Royal Navy and, 44, 57–65, 94
sands, 250–1
shale, 249–51
as strategic resource, 237
taxation of, 162, 166–70, 184–6
volume of trade in, 111
oil crisis of 1973–74, 10–1, 171–99, 223, 243–44
and 'oil weapon', 175, 180
'oil curse', 1–2, 5–6, 7n16
oil firms, 46–65, 104n60, 115
alternative energy, 178–9
as apparatus of control, 44–5
and calculation, 243–7
control of Middle East oil by, 86
and crisis, 149–51, 170–2, 178–81, 193
and environment, 188–93
and 'imperial' interests, 45, 57–61
and imperialism, 207, 229–30
and monopoly power, 39, 60–1, 66–7, 97, 147, 163–7, 193, 205–7, 237
and oil price, 166–72
and production of scarcity, 40–5, 54–9, 86, 96–7, 146–7, 180–1, 205–7, 234
and 'strategic' interests, 121–2
and tax rate, 184–6
oil industry, 193
and automobile manufacturers, 41–2, 42n82
competition in, 39
development of, 45–9
and weakening the workforce, 35
oil pipelines, 147–9, 150–1, 163–4, 186, 200, 203
from Baku to Persian Gulf (trans-Persian), 49–50
invention of, 36
from Kirkuk to Haifa, 102–5
from Kirkuk to Tripoli (Lebanon), 102–6
and Zionism, 104–5
Oil Policy Committee, 167
oil states, 6–11, 173, 201, 226
oil tankers, 33n56, 37–9, 46, 154, 163, 175, 178
oligopoly. See oil firms and monopoly power
OPEC (Organization of Petroleum Exporting Countries), 10, 167–9, 178, 181, 184–6, 189, 196, 206, 212, 226, 245, 252
'open door', 80
Oppenheim, Lassa, 90
Orinoco Basin, 250
Orwell, George, 122
Ottoman-American Development Company, 56–7, 96n34

Ottoman Empire, 15, 18, 21, 49, 55–8, 66–9, 75–6, 83–95
Ottoman Public Debt Administration, 57, 75n23
Owen, Edgar Wesley, 57n31

Pakistan, 106, 200–3, 218
Palestine, 80, 87, 91, 94, 99–100, 104–5, 237
partition of, 119
Palestine question. See Israel–Palestine Conflict
Paley Commission, 177n10
Panama, 38
parasitism, 45
peak oil, 231–46, 252
calculation, 6, 6n12, 241–6
See also oil, depletion of reserves
Pearson, Karl, 131
Pennsylvania, 36, 46
Pentagon, 186, 218
Perle, Richard, 218, 222
Persia, 43–65
Persian Bank Mining Rights Corporation, 52
Persian Gulf, 30, 47–58, 90, 119, 158, 170, 181, 252
petrodollars, 156, 173, 214
petroknowledge, 139
petroleum. See oil; energy
Petroleum Industry War Council, 142
Petroleum Reserves Corporation, 114
Petty, William, 126
Philby, Harry St John, 92, 204–5, 210
Pigou, Arthur Cecil, 135
Polanyi, Karl, 21n20, 110, 125
political economy, 125
and calculation, 127–8
objects of, 126
of oil, 201, 205–9, 211–4
political Islam, 11, 200–26
and global capitalism. See McJihad
Port Said, 21
Pouget, Émile, 22, 39
protectorates, 84, 88, 90, 99, 209–10
pyrolysis, 249–51

Qaddafi, Muammar, 165–6
al-Qaeda, 204
Qaimmaqami, Linda Wills, 120
Qasim, Abd al-Karim, 145, 147–51, 181

race development. See eugenics
railways, 14, 19–38, 46–77, 82–3, 96, 103–5, 128, 152–8, 233, 236–7
Rancière, Jacques, 9n17, 18n11
Reagan, Ronald, 218n36
recalcitrance. See sabotage
Red Line Agreement of 1928, 97
rentier state, 1–2, 2n2, 201n4
Revolution of 1905 (Russia), 36, 64, 67, 234
and Baku labour unrest, 33–4
Revolution of 1910–20 (Mexico), 64, 75, 234
Revolution of 1919 (Egypt), 87, 98–9

Revolution of 1920 (Iraq), 88
Revolution of 1979 (Iran), 11, 162, 202, 215
Reza Khan, 64
Ricardo, David, 125, 141
Río de la Plata, 37n72
Rio Earth Summit, 233
Robinson, Joan, 194, 195n65
Rockefeller (family), 25–6, 95, 171
Rockefeller, John D., 205
Rockefeller Plan, 26
Rolodex, 132–3, 248
Romania, 46, 165
Roosevelt, Franklin D., 115, 120, 136
Roosevelt, Kim, 159
Roosevelt, Theodore, 133
Röpke, Wilhelm, 142n73
Ross, Michael L., 146n4
Rothschild, 46–57
Royal Dutch/Shell, 5, 33n56, 46–9, 94, 113
Royal Navy, 44
  transition from coal to oil, 57–65
Rumaila oil field, 148–51, 158
Rumsfeld, Donald, 216, 216n30
Russia, 18, 31, 206, 217, 222
  use of oil in, 34

Sabin, Paul, 41n81
sabotage, 43, 47, 87 103–8, 144–72, 235–6
  and coal, 21–7
  new form of, 152–3
  by oil firms, 39–42
  origins of word, 22, 22n26
  organized by the state, 145, 151, 162–6, 178–9
  and transportation, 153
  See also strikes
Sadat, Anwar, 181–3, 202, 215
al-Sa'id, Nuri, 102
Salafism, 187, 202
Samuelson, Paul A., 140
San Remo agreements, 94–6, 95n29
Santa Barbara, 191
Sartre, Jean-Paul, 6
Saudi Arabia, 14, 30, 92, 104–7, 114–5, 144, 146, 152,
  162, 164–6, 169–70, 174–5, 182, 184, 200–14,
  218–20, 231–2, 250, 252
  revolts in, 220–1
  strikes in, 106–7
  US military bases in, 121
Scaife, Richard Mellon, 197–8
Schumacher, E.F., 189
Schumpeter, Joseph, 138–9
Science Advisory Committee, 6
Scripps Institution for Oceanography in Southern
  California, 243
Second World War, 10, 40, 77, 102, 107, 110, 121, 125,
  137, 141, 165, 167, 173, 186, 206, 208, 211
security, 41, 41n79, 158–63, 223n49
  and insecurity, 158, 187
self-government, 26, 71–2

self-determination, 35, 68, 80n35, 90, 98
  as ideal, 68–9, 72, 84–5
  as mechanism of consent, 79–80
  as method of control, 68
  and 'minorities,' 99–100
  as solution for imperialism, 90
September 11 attacks, 204, 221, 223–4
Serbia, 18
shah of Iran, 107–8, 159–60, 202, 215, 217–8
Shatt al-Arab, 91, 215n28
Shell Oil (Shell Transportation Company), 46–60,
  148, 188, 247–8. See also Royal Dutch/Shell
Sierra Club, 191
Six-Day War. See Israel–Palestine conflict, 1967 War
Smil, Vaclav, 6
Smith, Adam, 126
Smuts, Jan, 72–3, 79–83
Söderbergh, Bengt, 250n30
solar energy, 12
Solow, Robert, 194–7
South Africa, 69–73, 81–3
  and Afrikaner republics, 70–2
  general strike in, 72
South African Native Affairs Commission, 82
South African Native National Congress, 73
South African war (1899–1902), 25, 69–70
Soviet Union, 97, 121–2, 151, 155, 157, 163–8, 206, 215–8
Spain, 18, 165
Stalin, Joseph, 33, 115
Standard Oil Company of California (Chevron),
  204–5, 210
Standard Oil of New Jersey. See Exxon
Standard Oil, 27, 32, 40, 46–64, 68, 75, 80–1,
  96–7, 205
  dissolution of, 95n30
  support of unrest by, 32, 95–6
State Department (US), 57, 102, 106, 113–8, 142,
  159–61, 169, 181–4, 190, 200
steam power, 13–14
statistics,
  and coal, 128–30
  emergence of, 130
strikes, 18–42, 61–4, 87, 103–7, 211, 225, 228, 235–7
  general strike, 23–7, 72, 79, 107, 152–3, 211
  and oil, 162–5, 198, 211
  and work stoppages, 153
  See also sabotage
structure, 61–5, 74–5
Sudan, 88, 220
Suez Canal, 37n72, 88, 158, 163–5, 168, 182, 186
Sumatra, 46
Sumner, William Graham, 133
Sweden, 163n51
Sykes-Picot agreement, 87n3
Syria, 80–1, 92, 119, 144, 150–1, 158, 164–6, 187, 201,
  222, 227
  CIA-organized coup in, 105
  independence of, 87
Syrian General Congress, 87

Taft, William, 75
Tahrir Square, 215, 227–9
Talib, Sayyid, 92
Taliban, 200, 202–4
Tapline, 152, 164–6
Taqizadeh, Sayyid Hasan, 64
Tbilisi, 33
Technocracy movement, 247–8
technological zones, 40
technologists, 238
technology and controversy, 238–9
Texas, 27, 195–6, 234
Texas Railroad Commission, 166–7
Thatcher, Margaret, 236
Thawrat al-Ishrin. *See* Revolution of 1920 (Iraq)
think tanks, 158, 197–8, 223
    American Enterprise Institute, 198
    Cato Institute, 198
    Center for International and Strategic Studies, 158, 198
    Heritage Foundation, 198
    Hoover Institution, 198
    Manhattan Institute, 198
    Rand Corporation, 245
Thompson, E.P., 21n20
Tinbergen, Jan, 134
Torrey Canyon, 38, 38n75
Trans-Arabian Oil Company, 105
Trans-Arabian Pipeline Company, 104, 119
Trans-Asiatic Oil Ltd, 164–5
Treaty of Versailles, 78n30
Triple Alliance, 23
Tripoli (Lebanon), 102
Truman, Harry, 120
trusteeship, 113–5, 118, 121–2
Tudeh Party, 107
Tunisia, 227
Turkey, 95, 220
Turkish Petroleum Company, 57–9, 67–8, 94–7

UN (United Nations), 164, 182, 225–6
    sanctions regime (Iraq), 216–7, 221–2, 225, 232
uncertainty, 233, 238
    production of, 241–7
Union of Democratic Control, 76
Union Oil, 191
United Arab Emirates, 206
United Nations, 77, 138
United States, 110, 138, 149–1
    and gold reserves, 111
    oil embargo of, 164–6, 170–99

Unocal (Chevron), 200, 203
uranium, 179, 179n15
US Congress, 175, 179n15, 242
US Department of Commerce, 136
US Federal Reserve, 135
US National Petroleum Council, 180
US Petroleum Administration for War, 114
uselessness, 154–8
USGS (US Geological Survey), 244–6

Veblen, Thorstein, 22n26, 39–40, 132, 156n33, 188n47, 247
Venezuela, 5, 114, 167, 201, 206
Vietnam War, 154, 157, 160, 183, 186, 218
Viner, Jacob, 131
Vitalis, Robert, 2n2, 41n79, 106n69
Volkswagen Beetle, 41

Wahhabism, 202–14, 218–21
Wales, coal-mining strikes in, 22, 37n72, 61–2
Warr, Benjamin, 140n67
Watts, Michael, 2n2
Weather Bureau, 242
White, Harry Dexter, 111, 112n7
Wilhelm II, Kaiser, 21
Wilson, Arnold, 89
Wilson, Woodrow, 8, 68, 75, 80–5
    and Fourteen Points, 80–1
Witwatersrand gold fields, 69–70, 110
Wolfe-Hunnicutt, Brandon, 149–51, 162
women's movement, 27
World Bank, 77, 110, 138
World Meteorological Organization, 242–4
World War I. *See* First World War
World War II. *See* Second World War
Worthington, John, 56

Yalta, 120–1
Yapp, M.E., 52n17
Yemen, 201, 218, 221, 227
Yergin, Daniel, 44, 68, 185
Young Turk Revolution, 55n27, 56, 75

Zapata, Emiliano, 64
Zia ul-Haq, Muhammad, 202
Zionism, 119, 120, 219n39
    and oil pipelines, 104–5
    and settlement in Palestine, 87, 99–100
Zonguldak coalfield, 21